John Chiu
35 ST WERBURGH'S ROAD
CHORLTON
MANCHESTER
M21 0TL

**To Randy,
the late-night maverick and fountain of inspiration.**

CONTENTS

Acknowledgments .... *xvii*
Introduction .... *xix*

1 Network Concepts 1
    LAN History 2
        The Emergence of Novell 4
        The Origin of NetWare Lite 4
    LAN Design Philosophy: Client-Server
        Versus Peer-To-Peer 5
        Client-Server Design 5
        Peer-to-Peer Design 7
    LAN Components 8
        Hardware Components 8
        Software Components 12
    The LAN Administrator 13
    Other Connectivity Methods 14
        Print Buffers 14
        Serial and Parallel Port Connectors 15
        Multiuser Operating Systems 16
        Low-Tech Solutions: Sneakernet and
            Frisbeenet 16

2 Overview of NetWare Lite 19
- Required Hardware and Software 20
  - Clarifying Some Terminology 20
  - Hardware Overview 21
  - Workstations Versus Engineering Workstations 22
  - Software Overview 23
  - Summary of Hardware and Software Requirements 23
- The Primary Uses of NetWare Lite 23
  - Shared Printers 26
  - Shared Data Space 26
  - Shared Database Applications 28
  - Shared Software 31
  - Shared CD-ROM Disk Drive 33
  - Shared Modem 35
- Profiles of Some Real-World NetWare Lite Users 36
  - A Small Professional Office 36
  - A Telemarketing Workgroup 36
  - A Two-Person Home Office 36
  - A LAN with Floppy-Based Workstations 37
  - A Medium-Sized LAN 37
  - A Modem-Intensive LAN 37

3 Planning a NetWare Lite LAN 39
- Why Bother Planning? 40
- Analyze Your Needs 41
  - Situations Appropriate for NetWare Lite Starter Kits 42
  - Situations Inappropriate for NetWare Lite 44
  - Workgroup Characteristics: Needs and Wants 45
  - Number and Types of Shared Peripherals 50
- Understanding Hardware Alternatives 52
  - Physical LAN Topologies: Bus, Star, and Ring 53
  - LAN Bus Versus Computer Data Bus 53

   LAN Signalling Methods: Ethernet, Token
     Ring, and ARCnet 58
  Formulating the Hardware Plan 62
   Locations of Computers and Printers 63
   The Floor Plan 65
   Thin Ethernet Cable Planning 66
   10BASE-T Cable and Hub Planning 67
   Office Environment 68
   Sources of LAN Equipment 69
   Important Software Applications 70
   Your Available Budget 71
  Planning Checklists 71

4 ■■■ Installing the LAN Hardware 73

  Ethernet LAN Products 74
   The Difference Between Installing and
    Starting the Network 75
   Ethernet LAN Adapter Cards 75
   Ethernet Starter Kits 76
  Purchasing Hardware 77
  Installation Overview 78
  Installation Details 79
   Verify Card Settings 79
   Default Settings and Default Values 80
   Power Off and Remove Cover 83
   Choose Slot and Remove Cover Plate 84
   Install the LAN Card 85
   Attach BNC T-Connector 86
   Reinstall the Computer Cover 87
   Attach Cables 87
   Route and Protect Cables 89
   Attach Terminators 89
   Reattach Power Cords 90
   Turn On the Computers 90
  Installation of Independent Hardware 90
  Verifying the Hardware Drivers 91

5 ▬ Installing the NetWare Lite Software 95

Prerequisites for Software Installation 96
    The LAN Card 96
    The IRQ and I/O Base Address 97
    Choosing a Server, a Client, or Both 98
Installation Overview 98
Installation Details 99
    Verify that You Have the Appropriate
      Installation Disks 100
    Back Up the Installation Disks 100
    Insert the Installation Disk 101
    Review README.TXT 101
    Start INSTALL 102
    Upgrading to Version 1.1 103
    Make the Node a Client, Server, or Both 104
    Step 1 for a Server—Specifying the Server
      Name 105
    Step 1 for a Client—Choosing the NetWare
      Lite Directory 107
    Step 2—Specifying Modifications to DOS
      System Files 108
    Understanding FILES and BUFFERS 115
    Step 3—Specifying the Network Adapter
      Card and Driver 115
    Step 4—Installing NetWare Lite 118
    Ending Installation 119
    Removing and Labeling the Floppy Disk 119
Initializing NetWare Lite 120
    Troubleshooting 121
Testing NetWare Lite 122
    Verifying the Network Connections 123
    Ending the Verification Test 124
Reconfiguring an Individual Node 125
Special Installation Situations 125
Installing NetWare Lite on a PC Without a Hard
    Disk 125

Loading SERVER.EXE and CLIENT.EXE into
   Upper Memory 126

6 Working with NetWare Lite: Basic Principles 129

Understanding the NetWare Lite Directory 130
Initializing NetWare Lite 131
   Running STARTNET.BAT 132
   Running Applications Outside the Network 133
Introducing the NET Command 133
   Running the Network Reduces Available
      RAM 134
   Logging in to the Network 135
   Starting the NET Menus 136
Using the Menu System 136
   Overview of the Main Menu 137
   Trying Out the Menu System 137
   Using Function Keys and Other Special
      Keys 140
   Exiting the Menu System 140
Introduction to Resource Sharing 141
   Log in to the Second Computer 141
   Map a Drive Letter 141
   Testing the Drive Mapping 142
   Verifying the Mapping 145
   Terminating the Mapping 145
Using NET from the DOS Prompt 146
Using the NET Help System 148
   Getting Help from the Menu System 148
   Getting Help from the DOS Prompt 149
Shutting Down the Network 149
   Shutting Off a Network Computer 149

7 Sharing Disks and Directories 153

Files and Directories in DOS 154
Overview of Disk Sharing 156
Network Directories 157

A Sample LAN Configuration 158
The Scope of a Network Directory 159
Creating a Network Directory 160
Mapping a Drive Letter to a Network Directory 165
Creating a Mapping 166
Using a Mapped Directory 166
Canceling NetWork Directories and Mapped
Drive Letters 169
Canceling an Existing Mapping 169
Deleting a Network Directory 171
Logging Out of the Network 172
Shutting Down a Server 172
Issuing Commands at the DOS Prompt 172
Displaying a List of Network Directories 173
Displaying a List of Current Mappings 173
Mapping a Drive Letter 174
Canceling an Existing Mapping 174
Saving a Record of Existing Mappings 174

8 Sharing Printers 177

Overview of Printer Sharing 178
Prerequisites to Creating a Network Printer 178
Printer Ports: A Brief Tutorial 179
A Typical LAN Configuration with a Shared
Printer 180
Creating a Network Printer 180
Deleting or Renaming a Network Printer 184
Capturing a Printer Port 185
Capturing Ports on Workstations with Local
Printers 185
How To Capture a Printer Port 186
Testing the Network Printer 188
Printer Access from a Server 189
Canceling Printer Redirection from the NET
Menu 190
Modifying the Capture Port Settings 190
The Print Queue 193

   Viewing the Print Queue 194
   Deleting a Print Job 195
  Error Warnings and Status Messages 196
  Issuing Printer Commands from the DOS
   Prompt 196
   Displaying a List of Network Printers 197
   Capturing a Port 197
   Printing a File on a Network Printer 197
   Modifying the Capture Settings 198
  Using Postscript Printers 199
  Shared Printer Products 199
   Hewlett-Packard Laser Printers 199
   Other Laser Printers 201
   Laser Printer Font Cartridges 201

9 Sharing Other Resources 205

  Individual User Accounts 206
   Creating a User Account 206
   Logging into the Network with an Account
    Name 208
  Communicating with Text Messages 210
   Sending a Message 211
   Selecting Users To Receive Messages 213
   Sending a Message from the DOS Prompt 214
   Receiving a Message 215
   Turning Message Reception On and Off 216
  Sharing CD-ROM Disk Drives 217
   Data Capacity of CD-ROM Disks 218
   CD-ROM Indexes 219
   CD-ROM Costs 220
   Drawbacks to CD-ROM 221
  Installing a CD-ROM Disk Drive 222
   CD-ROM Hardware Installation 223
   CD-ROM Software Installation 225
  Sharing Modems and Other Two-Way Serial
   Devices 230
   Introducing ArtiCom 231

Installing ArtiCom	232
Running ArtiCom	235
Other Modem-Sharing Products	240
Using a Tape Backup System	240
Using Tape Systems with NetWare Lite	241
Tape Backup Suppliers	242
Attaching Portable Computers	244

10 USING APPLICATION SOFTWARE   247

Various Application Software Designs	248
Incompatible	249
Compatible Without LAN Support	251
Compatible with LAN Support	255
LAN Dependent	257
Major Application Software Products	258
Word Processing	258
Spreadsheets	259
Databases	261
Graphics Software	263
Groupware and Electronic Mail	264
Other Application Software	267

11 THE ROLE OF THE LAN ADMINISTRATOR   271

Selecting the LAN Administrator	272
The Primary LAN Administrator	272
The Secondary LAN Administrator	273
Duties of the LAN Administrator	273
Data Integrity	274
Data Backup	275
Backup Strategies	278
Computer Viruses	281
LAN Security	286
User Support	286
Communicating with Users	287
Hardware Maintenance and Checking	288
Routine Hardware Maintenance	288
Server Disk Space	289

Configuration Management 290
Budgeting 291
LAN Optimization 291

12 Securing the LAN 295
Physical Security 296
Controlling Who Can Log in to the Network 297
   Creating Passwords 298
   Logging in to the Network with a Password 302
   Changing Your Password from the DOS
     Prompt 304
   Removing Passwords from an Account 304
   Changing a Password on Another User's
     Account 305
   Creating and Changing the Password on the
     SUPERVISOR Account 305
   Setting Password Attributes 306
   Disabling a User Account 307
   Denying Supervisor Privileges 309
   Determining the Status of a User Account 311
Controlling Access Rights 311
   Network Directory Rights 311
   Network Printer Rights 315
Limiting the Scope of a Network Directory 316
   Replacing CDRIVE with Your Network
     Directories 316
Using Audit Logs and Error Logs 317
   Audit Logs 317
   Error Logs 320
Saving and Restoring a Server's System Files 320

13 Troubleshooting 323
Start with the Obvious 324
   Check for Human Error 325
   Look First for the Most Obvious 325
   Examine Recent Changes 326
   Look Up Error Messages 328

Run INSTALL's Network Connection Verification	329
Isolate the Problem	329
Isolating Hardware Problems	330
Isolating Software Problems	331
Specific Problems	333
Single Computer Lockup	333
Communication Breakdowns	337
Corrupt Disk Files	339
Other Problems	341
UPS Systems	342

14   Optimizing LAN Performance   347

Determining What To Optimize	348
Optimization Methodology	348
Benchmark Tests	349
Optimization by Any Other Name	349
Possible Benchmarks	350
Benchmark Tips	352
Optimizing for Speed	353
Disk Cache	354
Different Types of Memory	355
Preparing To Run NLCACHE	358
Using NLCINST To Install the Disk Cache	359
Using NLCACHE	360
How NLCACHE Disk Caching Works	361
Other Disk Caches	362
Tips on Using Disk Caches	363
Disk Cache Benchmark Results	364
Disk Cache versus a Processor Cache	364
The DEDICATE Program	365
DEDICATE Benchmark Results	366
DOS Parameters	367
Disk Buffers	367
FASTOPEN	368
RAM Disks	368
Other DOS Tips	369

Server Parameters 370
    Receive Buffer Size and IO Buffer Size
        Multiplier 372
    Number of Receive Buffers and Number of
        IO Buffers 372
    Print Buffer Size 372
    Benchmark Results 373
    Adjusting Printer Wait Time 374
Other Speed Tips 375
    Check Your Interleave Factor 375
    Fix Disk Fragmentation 376
    Have Plenty of Server Disk Space Available 377
    Upgrade Your NetWare Lite Software 377
    Upgrade Your Hardware 377
    Eliminate Cable and LAN Card Problems 378
    Separate Your Workload 379
    Don't Use Windows 379
Optimizing the Use of RAM 379
    NetWare Lite Parameters and DOS
        Parameters 380
    Using Upper Memory 382
Optimizing the Use of Disk Space 382
Highlights 383

15   Running on Various Software Platforms 387

Using Windows 388
    Single-User Windows Configuration 389
    Upgrade to Windows Version 3.1 390
    Running Windows as a Shared Application 395
Using SHARE 396
Using NetBIOS 397
Running Regular NetWare 398
    NetWare and NetWare Lite Compatibility 398
    Upgrading NetWare Lite to NetWare 399
Synchronizing Time on Servers and Clients 400
    Synchronizing the Times On Network
        Servers 400

Synchronizing the Time on a Workstation
with the Network Servers 401

A NetWare Lite Status Reports (Error Messages) 405
Status Reports 406

B Checklists for Planning a LAN 417
Inappropriate Situations for NetWare Lite 418
Clarify Objectives 418
Determine Workgroup Needs and Wants 419

C Sample Batch Files 423
Batch Files 424
    AUTOEXEC.BAT 425
    STARTNET.BAT 426
CONFIG.SYS 426
Editing Batch Files and CONFIG.SYS 427
Adding NET Commands to Batch Files 429
Starting NetWare Lite When You Turn On Your
Computer 430
Files for a "Typical" Configuration 431
Troubleshooting Configuration 433
High-Performance LAN Server Configuration 434
Minimum RAM Configuration 435
DOS 5 Extended Memory Configuration 436

D Support From the Authors 439
NetWare Lite Software from the Authors 440

Index 441

ACKNOWLEDGMENTS

This book represents a collaborative effort. Many people made significant contributions. Our thanks go to:

Everyone at Novell, the developers of NetWare Lite. We particularly thank Rose Kearseley of Novell Press, who provided information and software updates quickly and cooperatively.

Everyone at Osborne/McGraw-Hill, the publishers of this book, for their support and assistance. A top-notch staff makes for a top-notch book. Special thanks to Allen Wyatt, Frances Stack, Jill Pisoni, and Cindy Brown.

Gail Burlakoff, for making us sound good.

Robert Scarola, for a thorough and conscientious technical review.

Nick Anis for networking ideas.

And finally, to our families who—when everything is said and done—make it all worthwhile.

INTRODUCTION

The era of peer-to-peer networking is here. For less than $300 per PC, you can buy all the hardware and software you need to connect together a few computers. Once connected, the PCs can share disk files, printers, and other resources. At a modest cost, peer-to-peer networks bring the benefits of local area networks (LANs) to small companies and workgroups.

LANs are a hot topic in today's computer world. Hundreds of thousands of small LANs have been installed in the past two years. Many people are confused about just what a LAN is and what it can do. Before you go any farther in this book, here's a one-paragraph explanation of what a LAN is and why you might want one.

A LAN consists of assorted hardware and software components that connect together your workgroup's PCs. When your PCs are connected with a LAN, everyone can share the same laser printer; you can copy files to and from a shared hard disk, thereby eliminating the need to carry floppy disks from one computer to another; you can all access the same database files (name and address lists, inventory files, or whatever); you can coordinate your appointment calendars; and you can send messages to each other, among other things.

Until the last few years, before peer-to-peer networks, a LAN was made up of two types of machines: *servers* (PCs dedicated to supplying files, printer, and other network resources) and *clients* (PCs that used the resources offered by the servers). With peer-to-peer LANs, such as NetWare Lite, individual PCs can function both as servers and as clients. What's more, connected PCs can still run the stand-alone applications they did before the network was installed.

The basic hardware for a NetWare Lite LAN consists of a LAN card you install in each IBM-compatible PC, plus cables to connect the LAN cards together. The software is the NetWare Lite network operating system, which consists of several programs that run on your PC as an extension to DOS. These programs enable DOS to interact with the other connected PCs and to know how to provide the resource-sharing and other features of the network. You can purchase the hardware in either of two ways—bundled with the software from companies licensed by Novell (the creators of the NetWare Lite software), or from independent manufacturers that sell compatible equipment.

Compared with other LANs, NetWare Lite has the following many advantages:

- ◆ NetWare Lite's cost is low. Less than $300 per computer for the software and hardware is easily achievable, and less than $200 is possible.

- ◆ NetWare Lite is easy to install and use, ideal for first-time networkers. Yet NetWare Lite has all the features needed to provide access to shared data and peripheral devices.

- ◆ NetWare Lite runs on the IBM PCs and compatible machines you already have. You do not need to purchase any additional computers. With the network installed, you can run stand-alone applications as you did before the network, or use the networking features.

- ◆ NetWare Lite is compact and efficient. It requires very little RAM (PC memory) and moves data between PCs fast enough for the needs of almost any group.

- ◆ NetWare Lite is reliable and backed by Novell, the market leader in software for local area networks.

The result of these facts is that increasing numbers of NetWare Lite LANs are being installed every day. Most of these LANs are being used in small offices, connecting from two to six computers. Most NetWare

Introduction

Lite LANs are installed by ordinary PC users who do not have extensive technical experience.

This book's purpose is to explain in simple terms what a LAN is, what you can do with a NetWare Lite LAN, and how to plan for, buy, install, and use a NetWare Lite LAN.

About This Book

This book assumes that you know nothing about LANs and not necessarily much about personal computers. As the title indicates, the goal of this book is to explain NetWare Lite so that it is "made easy" for you. The explanations are no more technical than necessary. The approach is practical—the explanations are aimed at the pragmatic reader who wants to get to the bottom line: How do I do this and what good can it do me? If you are looking for detailed explanations of a LAN's electronic circuitry and software design algorithms, look for another book. Rather, this book explains in straightforward terms the practical aspects of planning, installing, and using a NetWare Lite LAN in a small workgroup.

The typical reader of this book is a PC user, not a computer expert. If you can run a word processor or a spreadsheet program to create simple documents, you have all the background you need. A little understanding of DOS is helpful.

The three categories of readers for this book are

People considering a LAN   If you think that your office or workgroup might benefit from connecting together its PCs, this book explains how to decide. In particular, the first three chapters take you through the basics of how LANs work, what you can do with a LAN, and the alternatives to a LAN. Later chapters show you how to plan and install a NetWare Lite LAN, and how to use the LAN after it is installed. You can read any or all of these chapters to see how a NetWare Lite LAN would fit your office.

People who have just purchased NetWare Lite   Perhaps you have purchased NetWare Lite and are ready to get up and running. This book provides detailed planning and installation instructions for both the hardware and software. Later chapters explain everything you can do with your LAN, including how to share devices and use the special features of NetWare Lite. You also learn many productivity tips.

People already using a LAN If you already use NetWare Lite, this book explains capabilities you may not know about, with step-by-step instructions. You can share CD-ROM disk drives and modems, exchange voice messages, use tape backup systems, and run with Windows, for example. What's more, if you are running a LAN other than NetWare Lite, this book shows what you might gain by switching to Lite. NetWare Lite can run on almost any hardware you have installed (3Com, Western Digital, Artisoft, and others). You may be surprised to learn that, because of the complexity of NetWare 2.x and 3.x, many small offices have switched from those LANs to NetWare Lite.

This book provides you with answers to the following questions:

◆ What is a LAN? What are the different types of LANs? In general terms, how do they work?

◆ What can I do with a NetWare Lite LAN? What are the practical benefits to my workgroup? How does the LAN change what I already do with my PCs?

◆ How should I plan for and buy a NetWare Lite LAN?

◆ How do I install and test a Netware Lite LAN?

◆ How do I share disk space, files, and printers? What other devices can I share, and why might I want to?

◆ How do I send messages across the LAN to other users?

◆ What do I do if something goes wrong? Can I troubleshoot problems myself or should I solicit expert advice? Who can I call?

◆ How do I implement LAN security if I don't want everyone connected to the LAN to have access to all the disk files and other network resources?

◆ What kind of day-to-day administration does the LAN need?

◆ How can I run my LAN in conjunction with Windows?

◆ What steps can I take to optimize the performance of my LAN?

How This Book Is Organized

This book has three sections. The first section—consisting of Chapters 1 through 3—explains LAN background and planning. Chapter 1 explains what a LAN is and briefly describes how a LAN works. Chapter 2 explains what you can do with a NetWare Lite LAN. A good subtitle might be "What's in it for me?" or "Why should I care about NetWare Lite or any LAN?" Finally, Chapter 3 explains how to plan for NetWare Lite, including the decision of whether NetWare Lite is right for you. The various hardware alternatives are presented. The chapter enables you to figure out all the necessary preparations you must make in your workgroup's environment.

The second section, which covers NetWare Lite installation, consists of Chapters 4 and 5. These chapters describe in detail the hardware and software installation process and show you how to verify that your installation is successful.

The book's third section—consisting of Chapters 6 through 15—explains how to use Netware Lite. Chapter 6 introduces the basic principles of resource sharing. Chapter 7 explains how to share files and hard disk space. Chapter 8 focuses on a common use of NetWare Lite: printer sharing. Chapter 9 discusses the sharing of hardware devices other than printers: CD-ROM drives, tape backup systems, modems, and the attachment of portable computers; the NetWare Lite messaging system also is explained. Chapter 10 discusses how you can share and use software applications—including word processors, spreadsheets, databases, and groupware products—with NetWare Lite. Chapters 11 and 12 go into the duties of the LAN administrator. Chapter 11 concentrates on the administrative actions required to ensure a productive LAN. Chapter 12 covers how the LAN administrator can implement passwords and other security measures to prevent outsiders (or insiders) from gaining access to private data. Occasionally, things may go wrong; Chapter 13 shows you how to troubleshoot problems. Chapter 14 is filled with many techniques and tips for optimizing your NetWare Lite LAN (generally, how to make your LAN run faster or how to conserve memory). Chapter 15 shows you how to run NetWare Lite in various software environments, particularly with Microsoft Windows.

The book also has four appendixes. Appendix A lists the NetWare Lite Status Reports, which include the error messages. This appendix contains suggestions for what to do when you get a particular message. Appendix B provides step-by-step checklists to help you plan a LAN from scratch. Appendix C contains typical batch files designed to customize the way your PCs work with NetWare Lite, as well as instructions for modifying these files. Finally, Appendix D explains how to contact the authors.

A Word From the Authors

This is an independent book. We don't work for Novell (which makes NetWare Lite), and we don't resell Novell products. We don't get any of your money when you buy NetWare Lite or associated hardware. As a result, our explanations and recommendations are not influenced by financial gain. Our goal is to make this book understandable and clear, so that you can make the right decisions not only about whether a NetWare Lite LAN is right for you, but also about how to plan, buy, install, and use NetWare Lite.

Of course we have some biases, but they're not biases that line our pockets if we convince you to buy a particular product. One of our biases is simple: We like NetWare Lite. We have worked with other LANs and know how complicated, confusing, and expensive they can be. If you are looking for a simple, effective way to connect together a few PCs, give NetWare Lite a good look.

If anything in this book is not clear or if you disagree with our advice, please let us know. You can reach us either through the publisher, Osborne/McGraw-Hill, or directly at the address shown in Appendix D.

Conventions Used in This Book

The simple conventions used in this book are similar to those you may have seen in other books and manuals.

- ◆ **Boldface** text indicates commands you type from the keyboard; for example, "Type **net** and press [Enter] to activate the menu system." Commands that you enter are shown in lowercase letters, but you can type them using uppercase letters if you like.

- ◆ *Italics* are used to define a term being used for the first time. In command descriptions, *italics* are used to represent a parameter for which you must substitute a value; for example "net capture del *port*."

Introduction

- In generic references to a command name—as opposed to instructions to type a specific command—the command name is shown in uppercase letters, as in the following example: "You can use the NET SEND command to send a message to another user."
- The names of special keyboard keys are enclosed in lozenge-like symbols, as in [Enter], [Esc], [Ins], [Del], and [F1].
- Keystroke combinations, in which you press two or three keys simultaneously, are connected by hyphens. If you are told to press [Ctrl]-[Alt]-[Del], for example, briefly (and simultaneously) hold down the [Ctrl], [Alt], and [Del] keys. For the [Alt]-[F10] combination, hold down [Alt] and then press [F10].

CHAPTER

1 NETWORK CONCEPTS

The underlying theme of all networks is connectivity. *By connecting two computers together, the resources available on each computer can be shared with the other. These resources may include hard disk space, data files, software, printers, and modems.*

Connectivity implies communication. *When your computer is part of a network, you can send and receive messages with other users of the network. Software running on one machine can communicate with software* running on another machine. In one sense, a network creates a *megacomputer*, a whole greater than the sum of its parts. Two concepts emerge:

- A network permits the sharing of resources (such as disk drives and printers) among the connected computers.
- A network makes distant resources (located on other computers) seem local (on your computer).

NetWare Lite is part of the spectrum of local area network products. To understand whether NetWare Lite will help you, and to fully utilize NetWare Lite after you install it, you need some background in LAN history, terminology, and concepts. This chapter gives you that background. Don't worry—you won't feel as though you're in history class; you will get just enough perspective to understand why LANs of *any* kind exist.

The discussion focuses on concepts common to all LANs. The treatment is rather broad based, as technical details are minimized. The following key topics are presented:

- Historical perspective of LANs
- Comparison of client/server and peer-to-peer LANs
- Hardware and software components of a LAN
- Role of the LAN administrator
- Non-LAN connectivity methods

If you are already confident in your LAN background, and impatient to get going with NetWare Lite, you can skip ahead to Chapter 4, "Installing the LAN Hardware." The first three chapters, however, have much to offer anyone who isn't completely comfortable with LAN concepts, the uses of a LAN, and planning a LAN installation.

LAN History

In the early 1980s, personal computers began to emerge as vital office tools. For an investment of $2,000 to $5,000, you could buy your own computer. By the mid-1980's, millions of IBM PCs (and IBM-compatible models from companies such as Compaq) were installed and running word processors, spreadsheets, database managers, and presentation graphics programs.

The word *personal* in personal computer is particularly appropriate for this type of computing. You—the PC user—have your own personal data on your own personal computer. Your PC, and those of your associates, are all separate entities. Such computers are often called *stand-alone* computers because, for the most part, the other PCs do not interact with your PC. Of course, a colleague can give you computer information by copying data files or programs onto floppy disks and carrying or mailing the disks to you, but that is about the extent of interconnectivity between stand-alone PCs.

Some bright, forward-looking companies saw the need to connect all these stand-alone computers. They saw that PC users would soon want to do the following:

✦ Quickly and simply make data files (such as word-processed documents or spreadsheet files) available to all the PCs in a work group, without the bother and delay of passing around floppy disks.

✦ Allow the many PCs in a workgroup to use the same database files simultaneously so that everyone would have access to the identical, up-to-date information.

✦ Give everyone access to a small number of expensive peripheral devices such as laser printers, color printers, plotters, and high-speed modems, without the need to buy one of these devices for every PC.

To address these needs, these companies designed *local area networks* (LANs). Early PC LANs used *proprietary designs*, which meant that you had to buy all your hardware and software from the LAN manufacturer. As time passed, customers demanded products conforming to standardized designs before they would buy a LAN. As a result, more companies offered products that worked on a variety of LANs, and prices for most of the hardware and software components dropped.

The Emergence of Novell

One of the companies that foresaw the future of PC networking was Novell, Inc. of Provo, Utah. Founded by Ray Noorda, Judith Clark, and Craig Burton, the company introduced the NetWare line of LAN operating system software in 1983. The original NetWare ran on PC XTs which, at the time, represented the state of the art in IBM personal computing.

NetWare was a pioneering product that fostered several innovations, both technical and strategic. Perhaps most significant was that NetWare established that networks consisting entirely of PC-class machines were feasible and productive. Before NetWare, multiuser computing required large mainframe computers, minicomputer machines, or a dedicated staff of system programmers.

NetWare provided a multiuser operating system to supplant DOS for networked computers. By itself, DOS could support only stand-alone PCs, not networked PCs. NetWare offered true file sharing among networked computers (as opposed to simply offering users the capability of writing private files on a shared hard disk).

NetWare is an open system—it works with computer equipment from many different vendors.

Another breakthrough was that NetWare worked with network hardware supplied by several different vendors. Novell—primarily a software company, albeit one that occasionally has sold hardware—understood that by fostering competition in the hardware arena, the price of network hardware would fall and quality would improve. A competitive marketplace creates the most attractive conditions for potential network buyers.

NetWare was an enormous success. As the PC market matured, the NetWare product line evolved as well. By late 1991, Novell's higher end versions of NetWare (versions 2.X and 3.X) commanded more than two-thirds of the entire PC network operating-system market.

The Origin of NetWare Lite

As PC networking moves into the 1990s, a new class of potential customers is emerging—small businesses and workgroups interested in connecting a few personal computers. This new customer wants a network solution that offers the following:

♦ **Simplicity**. Most customers are first-time network users.

Network Concepts

- **Functionality**. Basic network features such as printer and file sharing are paramount.

- **Flexibility**. The network is to be established across the company's existing PCs. The connected PCs must function both as individual workstations and as partners in the network.

- **Affordability**. Perhaps most important, customers are cost conscious. The price of the network hardware and software must be a fraction of the cost of the PCs.

In late 1991, Novell addressed this market with the release of NetWare Lite. Designed to be straightforward and inexpensive, NetWare Lite provides basic network capabilities for 2 to 25 connected users.

LAN Design Philosophy: Client-Server Versus Peer-To-Peer

One difference between NetWare Lite and the traditional high-end network products is in their respective design philosophies. The high-end products (such as "regular" NetWare) typically use a *client-server* design, in which the different nodes in the network have different roles. By contrast, the new emerging network products (typified by NetWare Lite) use a *peer-to-peer* design, in which each node in the network is equal. A *node* is simply any PC connected to a network.

Client-Server Design

A *client-server* network works on the principle that a network consists of one or more servers which provide resources for the other nodes, called clients.

A *server* PC is where the action is. The server acts as the nucleus of the network, storing on its large hard disk all the shared data files and applications software. Network printers are attached to the server. Typically, the server PC is the largest, fastest computer on the network. (There are exceptions. On LANS with workstations running intensive graphics applications—such as computer-aided design, for example—the workstations may be faster machines than the server.) Of all the network nodes, the server usually has the largest hard disk and the fastest central processor.

In most installations, the server PC is totally devoted to the task of being the network server. Such a server, called a *dedicated server*, is not available for use as a stand-alone PC. While running the network software, the server is not available as a DOS-based computing machine. (In fact, for some client-server networks, such as NetWare 3.11, the server does not even run DOS. Rather, the server's hard disk is reformatted to run the proprietary network operating system exclusively. NetWare 3.11 workstations are still DOS-based PCs, however.) Because servers are not available to run applications, seldom is anyone physically at a server while the network is running.

In larger networks, individual servers have specialized functions.

Many client-server networks have a single server that provides all the network resources for the LAN. Other client-server networks may have more than one server. In such cases, individual servers may have specialized functions—a *file server* provides only hard disk space, for example, whereas a *print server* provides only network printers.

A *client* PC requests information or hardware resources from a server. The client PC is where productive work takes place; people do their jobs there. When a client requests something from the server, the server's job is to provide the resource. A client may request, for example, that the contents of a file residing on the client PC be printed on the laser printer connected to the server.

Client PCs connected to the network can function as stand-alone PCs. A client PC runs network software as an extension to DOS. A worker at a client PC may one minute be running a stand-alone application, such as a word processor, and the next minute, when a network resource is required, the worker can issue a network request quickly.

The client-server design is most appropriate for large networks anticipating heavy loads. In such environments, the server PC must be large and fast enough to accommodate the demands of the network. The network software must be powerful enough to handle several client PCs making simultaneous requests. The high-end networking products (including "regular" NetWare) are examples of client-server networks. Although most NetWare LANs have fewer than 50 nodes, some

Network Concepts

client-server networks have upwards of 100 nodes. For many networks, nothing short of a 486/33MHz computer with a 300MB hard disk will do for a server.

Peer-to-Peer Design

In a *peer-to-peer* design, each node in the network can act as a client, a server, or both. In other words, every PC on the network can share resources with all the other PCs on the network. If, for example, you make each node a client and server simultaneously, any network PC can offer to any other network PC access to a data file stored on its hard disk. The result is true connectivity, because each node of the network enjoys equal status.

Network software is loaded on a PC as an extension of DOS.

Furthermore, each PC can function as a stand-alone PC while connected to the network. The network software runs on each PC as a *terminate-and-stay-resident* (TSR) program which, in effect, provides an extension to DOS. Even if you are using your PC as a stand-alone computer, the network software runs "behind the scenes" in the same sense that DOS is always running in the background. That means, for example, that you might be working on a spreadsheet while another user requests access to a file located on your machine's hard disk. Both processes can execute simultaneously. You continue to work on your spreadsheet while the network software reads the file on your hard disk to accommodate the other request.

Peer-to-peer networking is the answer to the needs of the small business network market. As you've seen, this market demands a simple, inexpensive networking solution that can run on existing PCs. NetWare Lite is a peer-to-peer LAN. Peer-to-peer LANs often consist of only two to four nodes. By simply hooking together their only two PCs, many businesses can increase productivity and save money. Chapter 2 elaborates on these benefits.

Table 1-1 summarizes in a general way the tradeoffs between a client-server LAN and a peer-to-peer LAN. The prices shown reflect approximate retail costs for NetWare Lite and NetWare 3.11 (Novell's high-end LAN product).

Attribute	Peer-To-Peer LAN	Client/Server LAN
Sample Product	NetWare Lite	NetWare 3.11
Relative Cost	Inexpensive (Hardware:$200 per node, Software:$100 per node)	Expensive (Hardware:$200 per node, Software:$3000 for up to 20 nodes)
Typical Size	2-5 nodes	10-50 nodes
Ease of use	Simple	Complex
Target audience	Small business	Medium/large workgroups
Flexibility	Uses existing PCs	Requires dedicated servers

Comparison of Peer-to-Peer and Client-Server LANs
Table 1-1.

LAN Components

Just what is a LAN? In one sense a LAN is the required hardware—primarily network cards attached to each PC, and the cables that physically connect the cards together. These components are described shortly.

In another sense, a LAN is software. This software includes not only the network-specific software that manages the resource sharing and communication system, but also LAN versions of major applications software which may be used on the network.

The truth is, of course, that a LAN is really a mixture of hardware and software. Table 1-2 lists the major components of LANs.

Hardware Components

The first steps in installing a LAN are purchasing and configuring the hardware. Here is a short look at the hardware components. For more about the hardware, see Chapters 2 through 4.

LAN Card

The LAN card—the PC add-on card you install in an available PC card slot—connects the PC to the LAN. Some LAN cards use 8-bit data paths, which means that, at one time, 8 bits of data (one byte) move between

Network Concepts

Components of Most LANs
Table 1-2.

Hardware Components	Software Components
LAN cards	Network operating system
LAN cables	Applications
Connectors	LAN utilities
Terminators	

the LAN card and the computer's processor. Other cards use 16-bit data paths and therefore move twice as much data at once. A LAN card can be referred to by various names: *LAN adapter card*, *network interface card (NIC)*, *network board*, or *network interface unit (NIU)*. The simplest name—LAN card—is what this book uses.

Figure 1-1 shows a photograph of a typical NetWare Lite LAN card, the NE2000 Ethernet adapter from a company called Eagle Technology. Ethernet is one *protocol* (communication scheme) LAN cards use to send signals to other LAN cards. Different LAN cards have different signalling methods; the most common methods are Ethernet, token ring, and ARCnet, all of which are explained in Chapters 2 through 4.

The Eagle NE2000 Ethernet LAN card.
Figure 1-1.

LAN Cable

LAN cables connect the LAN cards together; because the LAN cards are installed in PCs, the cables connect the PCs. Many types of cable are used. The most prevalent types are *thin coaxial cable* (called *thin coax, thin Ethernet, cheapernet,* or *thin net*), which is similar to the cable used for cable TV, and *unshielded twisted pair* (*UTP*, or just *twisted pair*), which is used in some parts of telephone-wiring networks.

The specific type of thin coaxial cable is designated RG-58. The unshielded twisted-pair cable is actually two twisted pairs, and therefore often called *dual twisted-pair (DTP)*. Standard types are AT&T 104, 205, or 315, or Belden 1227A. None of the twisted-pair cables is the same as flat telephone extension cable, often called *silver satin*. Figure 1-2 shows what thin coax and twisted-pair cabling look like.

A new development called the *wireless LAN* communicates between LAN cards without cables. Instead, either radio or infrared signals carry information between the computers.

Connectors

At the end of each cable is some type of connector that must plug into a matching socket on (or attached to) the LAN card. The standard connector for thin coax cable is the *BNC connector*.

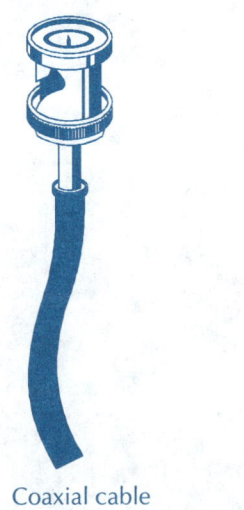

Thin coaxial cable and unshielded twisted-pair cable
Figure 1-2.

Coaxial cable

Twisted pair

Network Concepts

Figure 1-3 shows a T-connector, which permits two different BNC connectors (each on separate cables) to attach to the same device. The stem of the T-connector attaches to the end of the LAN card, causing the top of the *T* to stick out from behind the computer. This T arrangement allows the LAN cards to be *daisy chained* (linked sequentially) together, from one PC to the next. (PC #1 connects to one side of PC #2's T-connector; the other side of PC #2's T connects to PC #3, which connects to #4, and so on.) On some LAN cards, the T-connector comes already attached; on others, you must attach the T-connector yourself.

Instead of T-connectors, twisted-pair cabling uses *RJ-45 modular plugs* and jacks, which look like oversize telephone modular plugs. Most people buy twisted-pair cables in preconfigured lengths with connectors already attached. You can, however, buy bulk cable, cut the cable to your specified lengths, and install the connectors yourself.

Terminators

Some LAN designs (notably those that use thin coaxial cable) require a special attachment at each end of the daisy chain of cables so that the electrical signals don't misbehave when they reach the end. Consider the T-connector on the PC at one boundary of the daisy chain. A terminator is connected to one end of the T, and a cable that leads to the next computer is connected to the other end of the T. Think of a terminator as a dead-end plug that marks the physical end of the LAN.

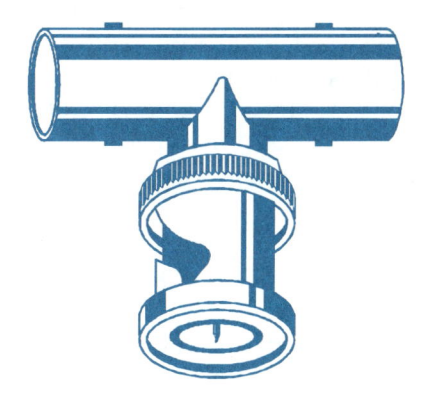

T-Type BNC connector
Figure 1-3.

Software Components

With the hardware in place, the network software can be installed. The following discussion touches briefly on the software that makes up a LAN. Details of NetWare Lite software are covered later in the book, starting with Chapter 5.

The Network Operating System (NOS)

Sometimes called the *LAN operating system* or the *network software*, the NOS is the software your PC runs to interact with other PCs on the LAN. Your DOS software does not have all the capabilities needed to communicate with another PC on a LAN; the NOS has this added intelligence. Novell's peer-to-peer network operating system is called NetWare Lite. (In the client-server arena, Microsoft's NOS is called LAN Manager, Novell's NOS is called NetWare, and Banyan Systems' NOS is called VINES.)

The network operating system controls how your computer interacts with other computers on the network.

In a peer-to-peer network, the NOS software is loaded into each PC and runs as a terminate-and-stay-resident program "on top of" DOS. (The LAN software must coexist with any other software, such as a word processor or spreadsheet program, that may be running simultaneously.)

Application Software

Many application software products, such as word processors, spreadsheets, or database managers, work just fine on a LAN. You can use the software to access shared disk files on the LAN just as you would access disk files on your own hard disk. Some application products need special LAN versions to work properly, or to fully utilize the LAN environment, or to satisfy a manufacturer's licensing restrictions. One new category of application software, called *groupware*, was designed specifically to work on a LAN to make a group of people more productive. Chapter 2, "Overview of NetWare Lite," and Chapter 8, "Using Application Software on the LAN," to explore application software in more depth.

LAN Utility Software

Just as special utilities can help you do your job in a non-LAN environment, other special utility programs can help you do your job in a LAN environment. These programs help you make backup copies

Network Concepts

of shared disk drives, monitor LAN activity, optimize LAN performance, administer user names and passwords, and help with many other functions. Sometimes these utilities come with the network operating system and sometimes you have to buy them separately.

The LAN Administrator

Because a LAN is a shared resource, someone must be in charge of LAN administration. Specific responsibilities are often distributed among two or more individuals. In a large company running a sophisticated client-server LAN, the job of LAN administrator might be a full-time position.

In most peer-to-peer LAN installations, however, the task of LAN administration typically falls upon someone already wearing many other hats. This person may be the boss, a partner in a two-person company, the colleague down the hall, or the only one around who claims to know anything about computers.

Because you're reading this book, it's a good bet that you are the administrator of your LAN. If the title "LAN Administrator" seems too imposing, just think of yourself as the LAN manager, LAN guru, ombudsperson, or maybe head of the complaint department.

Chapter 11, "The Role of the LAN Administrator," covers in detail the responsibilities of managing a NetWare Lite LAN. For now, the following is a brief introduction to administrative issues common to all LANs:

- ✦ **Planning**. Before installing any LAN, you must have a good idea of what hardware and software will be purchased and where and how they will be set up. Once the LAN is established, you must consider future expansion.

- ✦ **Maintenance**. Someone must ensure that shared resources are maintained. For example, is there enough paper in the shared laser printer? Is the shared hard disk reaching capacity? Are critical shared data files being backed up? Are shared software applications upgraded to current versions? Are there regular checks for the intrusion of insidious computer viruses? Much of the maintenance job involves establishing procedures to be performed at regular intervals.

- **Budgeting**. Expenses are always important.
- **Security**. On some LANs, certain users are not permitted access to sensitive data. Each user can have a separate account with a private password. The administrator must compile these accounts and monitor the use of the LAN.
- **Troubleshooting**. As with all hardware and software, problems can occur. The real trick here is to anticipate potential problems as much as possible.

Other Connectivity Methods

The focus of this chapter has been on LANs in general. The specific discussion of NetWare Lite begins in the next chapter. If you are still pondering whether a LAN is what you need, you should consider the alternatives for connecting PCs and sharing resources *without* using a LAN. The following connectivity methods have more limitations than do LANs, but some of the methods are a little less expensive or a little simpler, or both.

Print Buffers

In many offices, the first critical resource that users suddenly want to share is a high-cost printer, usually a laser printer. The budget doesn't permit a separate laser printer on every PC, but everyone occasionally needs laser printing.

The cheap, but annoying, solution is to attach the laser printer to one PC only. Then, anyone who needs laser-quality printing takes a floppy disk over to the laser printer PC and prints from there. This frustrates everyone. The person who does the printing would rather print directly from his or her own PC than have to walk over to another PC and ask to borrow someone else's system for a few minutes. The person who normally uses the laser-printer PC would rather not be interrupted so often by other people who need to borrow the PC.

The more expensive, but less annoying, solution is to buy a print buffer that allows connection of more than one PC to the printer. A *print buffer* is an external hardware device to which a printer and various PCs can be connected with appropriate cables. A typical model has connections for up to five PCs and one printer. Each PC is cabled to the

Network Concepts

print buffer, and the print buffer connects to the shared printer. The print buffer has its own memory—anywhere from 64K (64 kilobytes, approximately 64,000 bytes) to 2MB (two megabytes, approximately 2,000,000 bytes) is common. All five users can simultaneously send printed output to the printer. The buffer stores everyone's print data, and sends each PC's printed output in turn to the printer.

A print buffer is appropriate for an office that needs to share a printer but does not need the many other advantages of a LAN. Prices vary, but most print buffers cost $90 to $150 per PC to connect to a single printer, not counting the cost of the printer. A low cost LAN such as NetWare Lite isn't much more expensive than a good-quality print buffer, but has *much* more capability. (See Chapter 2 for a thorough discussion of the advantages of a NetWare Lite LAN.)

Serial and Parallel Port Connectors

A number of products connect two or more computers with cables that attach to the computers' serial or parallel ports. Some of these products were created to allow data exchange between two PCs that do not have the same type of floppy disk drives. These products enable you, for example, to exchange data between a desktop system with only 5 1/4-inch drives and a laptop system with only 3 1/2-inch drives.

Most products of this type use what is called a *null modem cable* to connect the two serial ports (and/or a special cable to connect the two parallel ports), and software that runs on both PCs. The software displays a menu on each PC, and you select which files you want copied to the other PC. Data is transferred through the serial ports at up to 115,200 bits per second, which usually means about 10,000 bytes per second or less. The parallel ports can move data faster than their serial counterparts—perhaps two to three times faster. Two leading null modem products are LapLink, from Traveling Software, and Brooklyn Bridge, from Fifth Generation Systems.

Other vendors sell what is sometimes called a *zero-slot LAN*. A zero-slot LAN also connects serial or parallel ports, but instead of running special file-transfer software on each PC, you run software that is similar or identical to a full-fledged network operating system. Some vendors have products that can connect as many as 16 PCs. Because data is transferred much more slowly through serial or parallel ports than is possible using a LAN card, these "LANs" are not satisfactory for many uses, especially for more than two PCs. Zero-slot LANS, however, are inexpensive and simple to operate. Two zero-slot LAN products are Printer LAN Plus from Grapevine LAN Products and LANtastic Z from Artisoft.

Multiuser Operating Systems

Another approach to connecting PCs without buying a LAN is to make one of your PCs act as a little mainframe computer, and connect your other PCs to it. If you run a multiuser operating system on a PC, that's essentially what you are doing.

A multiuser operating system, unlike DOS, is designed to communicate simultaneously with many different users. Examples of this type of system are UNIX, Xenix, Citrix Multiuser, and DRMultiuser DOS. Install one of these on your most powerful PC and connect your other PCs to it. Needless to say, this approach is much more complicated than the comparatively simple DOS world, and is beyond the scope of this book.

Low-Tech Solutions: Sneakernet and Frisbeenet

Get ready. You're about to undergo a rite of passage. You cannot claim to be LAN-literate unless you know the Sneakernet and Frisbeenet jokes.

Think about how you share data without a LAN. How do you get data files and programs to nearby PC users? You simply copy files to floppy disks, put on your sneakers, and run around passing out floppy disks to the other users. This low-tech approach has been dubbed *Sneakernet*.

Well, what do you do when your sneakers are at home? With a flick of the wrist, some people can fling a floppy disk as adroitly as they can toss a Frisbee. Some say that by throwing a floppy at just the right angle, with just the right velocity, you can make the floppy fly around obstacles (such as co-workers stationed between you and your target). *Frisbeenet* works best with 5 1/4-inch floppies; 3 1/2-inch disks cause too many painful accidents. Be sure that your liability insurance is paid up before using Frisbeenet.

Some people (who think they're clever) like to joke that a company without a LAN distributes data with a Sneakernet or Frisbeenet network. Many of these part-time comedians sell LANs for a living; some of them use these jokes continually, until no one can stand hearing them.

Now you know the Sneakernet and Frisbeenet jokes. Welcome to the group!

CHAPTER

2 OVERVIEW OF NETWARE LITE

Broad statements about resource sharing among computers are fine, but they don't explain exactly what NetWare Lite offers. This chapter gives you specific information about the following topics:

✦ *Hardware and software required to run NetWare Lite*

✦ *Primary uses of a NetWare Lite LAN*

✦ *Profiles of some actual NetWare Lite installations*

Required Hardware and Software

A NetWare Lite network consists of two or more PCs physically connected with special hardware. NetWare Lite is a software product that runs in conjunction with DOS on each connected PC. Before presenting an overview of the hardware and software required to get NetWare Lite up and running, some explanation of terms is in order.

Clarifying Some Terminology

As you may recall, the term *node* refers to any PC connected to a network. A node that makes its resources (hard disk, printer, or other devices) available to other nodes is called a *server*. A *client* is a PC that uses the resources of a server.

In a client-server network, each machine is either a dedicated server or a client (also known as a *workstation*). Someone sits at a workstation and uses the keyboard to do work—word processing, spreadsheet calculations, or whatever. On the other hand, a server PC can be unattended while its hard disk remains available to workstation users. A client-server LAN with four computers, for example, might be configured as one server and three workstations, for a total of four nodes.

With the emergence of peer-to-peer networks, such as NetWare Lite, several terms that originated with client-server networking now take on expanded meanings. With peer-to-peer, for example, the term "server" refers to any node that performs a serving function, but not necessarily a node that *only* serves. The terms client and workstation refer to any machine that, at least occasionally, uses resources from a server.

The key point is that NetWare Lite's peer-to-peer design enables a single PC to act as *both* a server and a workstation. As you saw in Chapter 1, such a server is called a nondedicated server. You can sit at a nondedicated server PC, using the workstation portion of it to perform your word processing while other network workstations access the server portion's hard disk and printer. (This capability of NetWare Lite to use one PC as both a server and workstation translates into cost savings—you don't have to buy a separate server computer.) A four-computer network can have one server and *four* workstations,

Overview of NetWare Lite

because one computer serves the dual functions of server and workstation.

In peer-to-peer, terms such as *print server* and *file server* refer to any machine that offers, respectively, printers and disk resources. In a client-server network, a print server is devoted exclusively to offering one or more printers to its clients. In peer-to-peer, any PC which offers a printer might be deemed a print server, even though that PC may also offer other resources, may sometimes act as a client, and, at times, may even be used as a stand-alone PC as well.

Hardware Overview

A NetWare Lite network connects as few as 2 and as many as 25 computers. Each computer must be an IBM PC, XT, AT, PS/2, or an IBM-compatible computer. At least one of the networked computers must have a hard disk drive; frequently, every computer has a hard disk. Each PC configured as a server must have a hard disk; workstations may have only floppy drives.

A LAN is physically created by installing network cards in PCs, then connecting them with cables.

As the previous chapter mentioned, you create the physical network by installing a LAN card in an empty slot of each network PC. The edge of each LAN card is accessible at the rear of the computer; a connector attaches to each PC's card. Finally, you physically connect two PCs with a cable. At each end of the cable is a matching connector that attaches to the connector on the back of a LAN card. NetWare Lite supports several different types of LAN cards, connectors, and cables. For a detailed discussion of the supported cards and cables, see Chapter 4, "Installing the LAN Hardware." Figure 2-1 schematically depicts the general hardware connection.

Note that in a NetWare Lite network, every node, whether a server, a client, or both is just a "regular" PC. The NetWare Lite software makes each PC *act* a server or workstation (or both). Some people expect a server or a workstation to be a special kind of computer. Chapter 3 explains why a server PC often needs to have a faster processor or a larger, faster disk drive than other PCs. In many cases, however, a 286-based PC (or even an 8088-based PC) with a small hard disk and MS-DOS can be perfectly adequate as a server or a workstation.

NetWare Lite Made Easy

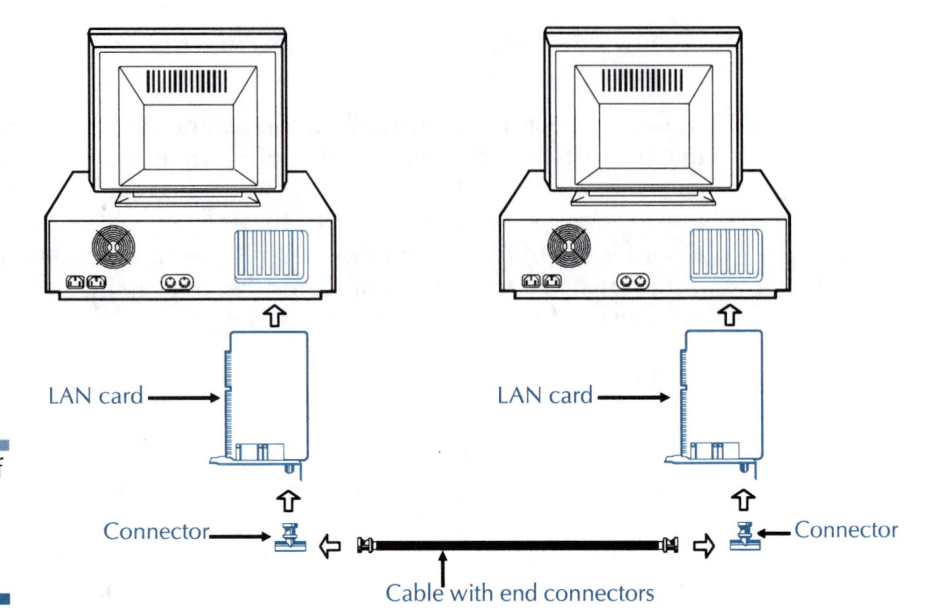

A schematic of the LAN hardware
Figure 2-1.

LAN card
LAN card
Connector
Connector
Cable with end connectors

Workstations Versus Engineering Workstations

A LAN workstation is just a normal personal computer with a LAN card, cables, and LAN software added. Confusion about the term "workstation" is common, due to a special type of computer called an engineering workstation. An *engineering workstation* is a high-speed desktop computer, typically with sophisticated graphics capabilities, used by engineers to design circuits and other products. Major brand names are Sun and Apollo. In engineering contexts and advertisements, an engineering workstation sometimes is simply called a workstation. Don't be confused. A typical LAN workstation is *not* the same thing. A LAN workstation is simply a regular PC connected to a LAN.

Software Overview

The NetWare Lite operating system software must be installed on each PC attached to the network. You must purchase a separate copy of NetWare Lite for each node of the network.

Each PC must be running DOS 3.1 or higher (PC DOS 3.X, 4.X, or MS-DOS 3.X, 4.X, 5.0) or DR DOS 6.0. NetWare Lite runs as a TSR program that provides an extension to DOS.

As explained fully in Chapter 5, "Installing the NetWare Lite Software," you configure each node to be a server, a client, or both and then install the appropriate TSR programs from the NetWare Lite package. Because NetWare Lite runs as a TSR, each node must give up some of its available low RAM memory (the memory below 640K) to run the network software. Fortunately, only a modest amount of memory is required (approximately 25K for a workstation and 50K for a server). In some cases, as Chapter 5 explains, you can load NetWare Lite into high memory (the RAM area above 640K).

Summary of Hardware and Software Requirements

To summarize, NetWare Lite requires the following hardware and software:

- IBM PC, XT, AT, PS/2, or IBM-compatible computers (as few as 2, as many as 25)
- One LAN card per PC
- Connectors and cables, as appropriate
- DOS 3.X, 4.X, 5.0, or DR DOS 6.0
- 50K RAM available for each server PC
- 25K RAM available for each workstation PC

The Primary Uses of NetWare Lite

As you have seen, resource sharing is the most compelling reason to purchase NetWare Lite. This resource sharing takes several forms.

Although many LANs provide sharing capabilities similar to those of NetWare Lite, NetWare Lite offers the following advantages:

- Low cost
- Minimal RAM requirements
- Full set of features
- Simple, reliable installation and use
- Upward compatibility with "regular" Novell NetWare

These benefits make NetWare Lite an attractive choice for small workgroups with IBM-compatible PCs. *Workgroup* is a loose term for a group of people who work together. The group might be two people in a small office, a dozen people in one department of a large company, or an entire company of 25 people. Usually all members of a workgroup are located close to each another.

The resources commonly shared on a NetWare Lite LAN are printers, CD-ROM drives, modems, and disk space.

For many workgroups, the idea of getting NetWare Lite comes right on the heels of the purchase of a laser printer. Everyone wants to use the laser printer. With NetWare Lite installed, a worker at any node can enter simple commands to redirect their printer output over the LAN to the shared printer. The result? You need to buy only one expensive printer. Everyone in the workgroup can use and think of the printer as his or her own, without undue inconvenience to the person using the PC to which the laser printer is physically attached.

A *CD-ROM* (compact disk, read-only memory) disk drive is a special disk drive which looks and acts much like an audio CD player, except that computer data, not music, is stored on the individual CDs. A wide range of reference material (such as encyclopedias, newspaper archives, dictionaries, telephone directories, and specialized databases) recently has become available on CD-ROMs. Using NetWare Lite, you can share a single CD-ROM drive and everyone can access the reference data.

A *modem* is a hardware device that translates electronic computer signals into analog signals sent over telephone lines. With a modem, one computer can communicate with another by telephone. Rather than install a separate modem and telephone line for each PC in your workgroup, you can install one high-speed modem to be shared across the network. Modem sharing is not a standard feature of NetWare Lite, but you can share modems by buying add-on software from third-party vendors.

Probably the most important reason to use NetWare Lite, or any LAN, is to share hard disk space. With NetWare Lite, you can make all or some of a server's disk space available to the other LAN nodes (or to selected users only). You can share disk space in three general ways—as shared data space, as a shared database application, and as shared software—as follows:

✦ **Shared data space**. Simply think of shared data space as a community disk drive that everyone can use. Because each client can copy files to and from a server's shared disk, the files are available to everyone. An example of a shared file is a document that several people are editing with word processors at individual workstations.

✦ **Shared database applications**. A *database* is an organized collection of information for some particular purpose (examples are a mailing list and a parts inventory). With such popular database software as dBASE, Paradox, FoxBASE, PC File, and Q&A, you can manage a database by adding, changing, and deleting data, searching through the data, sorting the data, and printing reports. If you use a LAN, you can put a database on the shared disk drive and everyone can access the same information simultaneously. Other specialized software products (electronic mail, group appointment calendars, conference room schedulers, and specialized accounting software, for example) manage specialized databases for you.

✦ **Shared software**. Without a LAN, you have to install software applications (word processors, spreadsheets, and so on) on each separate PC. With NetWare Lite, you can still run software applications independently of the LAN. Many software products, however, provide the option of installation on a server (instead of at every workstation). Then each workstation user can run the software from the shared disk. As explained later in this chapter, sharing a server copy of a software application usually does *not* mean that you can save a great deal of money by buying only one copy of the software application. With a central server copy, however, you realize tangible advantages: you don't have to install separate copies on every PC, you can be sure that everyone uses the same software version, and upgrading to a new version is simple.

The following discussion provides more detailed explanations of the benefits of each of the resources commonly shared on NetWare Lite LANs.

Shared Printers

Many NetWare Lite customers start by looking for a way to share a printer between two or three PCs. They learn that the cost of sharing printers by using NetWare Lite is similar to that of a good print buffer (which also can provide printer sharing). When they find out that NetWare Lite offers an abundance of additional capabilities, they think, "Why not? If we do decide to use NetWare Lite's other features, we come out ahead. Even if we don't use those other features, we can do the printer sharing at roughly the same cost." For a detailed discussion of printer sharing with NetWare Lite, see Chapter 8.

Printer sharing can decrease individual cost while increasing output quality.

With a LAN installed, the expense of a high-cost laser or color printer is mitigated because the cost is spread over all users. An $1,800 printer used by six people costs the same as six $300 printers. You can create beautiful printed text and graphics at high speed with your shared part of the $1,800 printer. Forever after, you will be dissatisfied with the print quality and speed of any $300 printer (or even a $600 printer). Note that with a shared laser printer on the network, workstation users can still use individual printers attached to their PCs, just as they did before the network. When (and whether) to use the shared printer is up to each user, but once most users learn how easily they can use the shared laser printer with NetWare Lite, the individual dot-matrix printers begin gathering dust.

Shared Data Space

A server's shared data space can quickly increase workgroup productivity. Here's a short explanation of how disk sharing works. (For a detailed description, see Chapter 7. At the DOS prompt, a workstation user types the NetWare Lite command **NET** to bring up NetWare Lite's

Overview of NetWare Lite

Main menu. The user selects `Map drive letters` from this menu and follows a series of menus to select a directory from the server's hard disk. This selected directory then becomes a *virtual disk drive* on the user's workstation. As the name implies, a virtual disk drive is not an actual hard disk (or disk partition) on the workstation computer. Rather, the LAN software fools DOS into acting as though a new disk drive is available.

For example, if the workstation has a hard disk designated as drive C, you assign a higher letter, say L, to the virtual disk drive. From then on, the workstation user can access the L drive just like any other disk drive on the workstation. From the user's perspective, drive L seems to be located on the workstation. Actually, the L drive is equivalent to the directory selected from the server's hard disk. This process of assigning a drive letter to a server's network directory is called *mapping* a drive letter.

Network mapping allows non-local disk drives or directories to be easily accessed.

After the mapping is established, accessing the shared directory is straightforward. You simply use the mapped drive letter in various DOS commands and in application programs. The following DOS command, for example, copies a file named MYFILE.DOC from a workstation's drive C to the shared drive L.

    COPY C:MYFILE.DOC L:

After you issue this command, MYFILE.DOC is saved in the network directory located on the server. The workstation user "sees" this directory as the local drive L. From the L prompt, a DIR command would now show MYFILE.DOC as a saved file.

To load and save files, you can use application programs as well as DOS commands. With WordPerfect, Microsoft Word, Lotus 1-2-3, or nearly any other application, you can load your file from the L drive instead of the C drive, do your work as usual, and then save your updated file back out to the L drive. The application program acts as though you really have an L drive because the NetWare Lite software and DOS work together to create that appearance to the application software. Because NetWare Lite knows that you mapped the L drive to the server's hard disk, the network software redirects the input and output operations across the LAN to the server's disk. This ingenious approach is simple; it permits almost all application software to work with NetWare Lite.

The server can restrict the amount of disk space shared on the network. In some situations, the server offers its entire hard disk for mapping to all users. Most of the time, selected subdirectories are available. With NetWare Lite, you can permit only some users to have access to particular subdirectories. You can even restrict particular users from updating files in individual shared subdirectories. The degree of restriction is up to you.

Shared Database Applications

For most workgroups, printer sharing and data-space sharing are enough to justify the cost of installing a NetWare Lite network. Shared database applications are somewhat more complicated, but even more beneficial for many workgroups.

Shared data access can increase productivity and lower costs.

Most workgroups deal with some kind of information that, if it were instantly available to all, would provide the means for increased productivity. The database may contain customer or supplier names and addresses, the status of orders in process, summaries of recently published research information, or almost anything else. Some workgroup members need to update the information in a database—adding, changing, or deleting portions when new information becomes available. Other people may need to search (or query) the database occasionally to find current information. The main advantage of a shared database on a LAN is that everyone with a need can have access to the same, up-to-date information.

Several options exist for the implementation of databases in a LAN environment, depending on your needs, abilities, and budget. You can use any of these options, except the second, even if you don't have a LAN:

- ✦ Buy a specialized database application product, if one exists to satisfy your particular requirements

- ✦ Buy a groupware software product that solves a particular need

- ✦ Buy a general-purpose database management system (DBMS) and design your own database

- ✦ Hire a consultant to create a customized database application

With a LAN, the difference is that everyone can access the data simultaneously. With no LAN, the data is on a single PC and is available to other workgroup members only after a time delay, either to copy the data to floppy disks (and distribute to others), to print reports that others can read, or simply to wait for one user to finish on a PC and the next user to begin. And without a LAN, only one person can update the data; otherwise, an awkward coordination process is needed to merge everyone's updates.

The following discussion examines each of these four options to see how you can implement shared databases in a NetWare Lite environment.

Option 1: Specialized Database Application

A specialized database product is targeted at a particular group of users. Sometimes these products are categorized as *vertical market software*. This means that the products are designed not to appeal to a broad, horizontal market that includes many categories of users, but rather to users with specialized needs. Examples of such users are accountants, salespeople, attorneys, physicians, and video-rental store owners.

If your needs match one of the products available, buy that product. Chapter 10, "Using Application Software on the LAN," lists many specialized database products (along with other types of products). Of course, you need to verify that the product is compatible with NetWare Lite. Fortunately, most database products that work with any LAN work also with NetWare Lite.

Some examples of the needs served by specialized database application products are accounting, contact management (keeps track of phone and mail contacts), business-form design, retail store management, time and billing, and real estate management.

Option 2: Groupware

Sometimes called *network productivity software*, the term *groupware* refers to software designed to make an entire workgroup more productive. Compared to specialized database products, a groupware product benefits a broader range of workgroups. This software must run on a

LAN to give all group members access to the shared information. Before LANs, groupware didn't exist.

The following categories of groupware are popular today. (Some of the products combine capabilities of more than one category.)

◆ **Electronic mail**. Often called *e-mail*, electronic mail sends messages back and forth between group members. The messages can be stored on a shared disk; software on each workstation permits each user to write, edit, send, receive, and save messages. NetWare Lite includes a very simple e-mail capability. Groupware products such as cc:Mail, WordPerfect Office, and Microsoft Mail offer additional e-mail features. Features vary—some products enable you to send messages to distribution lists, to attach files to messages, or to get notification as soon as the receiver reads your message. An extremely small group in a single room may see no need for e-mail. The larger the group and the more geographically spread apart, the greater the benefits.

◆ **Group calendaring**. For many workgroups, the biggest weekly challenge is finding times when everyone can attend meetings. A group-calendaring product keeps track of everyone's schedule and can display a choice of meeting times acceptable to all. Clearly, for this to work, everyone has to enter all appointments, trips, and vacation time into the calendar.

◆ **Resource scheduling**. Some groupware products allow you to schedule the use of *any* shared resource (not just the computers). Examples include conference rooms, overhead projectors, and company cars. Anyone who wants to use the shared resource enters the date and time it is needed. Anyone else who subsequently looks at the schedule can see the dates and times available.

Option 3: General-Purpose DBMS

A general-purpose *database management system* (DBMS) is the first thing most people think of when they hear the phrase "database software." Because keeping track of organized data lists is such a good use of computers, these database products let you keep track of anything you choose.

Overview of NetWare Lite

If no specialized database application exists to accomplish what your workgroup needs, and no groupware product seems to do the job, you might consider designing your own database applications using a general-purpose DBMS. Be warned that designing a DBMS-based application is not simple. Just look at the intimidating stack of thick manuals that accompany most full-featured DBMS software.

Dozens of general-purpose DBMS products are on the market. Most of them can work on shared databases using NetWare Lite. Some of the leading products that support disk-sharing or have a special LAN version are dBASE III and IV, FoxBASE, Paradox, and Q&A. See Chapter 10, "Using Application Software on the LAN," for more information.

Option 4: DBMS Application from a Consultant

If you ever pick up one of the 1,000-page dBASE books in a bookstore, you may decide that learning how to design database applications with the major DBMS products is a formidable task. Some products are simpler than others, but any DBMS has to be somewhat complex in order to give you all the capabilities you may need.

Custom database programming is time consuming and can be quite expensive.

If you don't want to become a database expert, you can hire one. Free-lance consultants work for from $20 to $100 per hour. A consultant might tell you that, rather than a DBMS application, you need a custom program written in C, Pascal, BASIC, or some other computer language.

The best way to find a consultant is by word of mouth from satisfied clients. Failing that, you can check with your local computer store for the names of database consultants. You can also look in computer publications, business publications, and local newspaper advertisements. A local computer club might also be a source of references.

Shared Software

In a workgroup with no LAN, you install software such as a word processor or spreadsheet on each PC separately. To stay legal, you need to buy a separate copy for each PC.

When you have a LAN in the workgroup, nothing needs to change. You can still install software on each individual PC. To use the LAN, you can copy data files to the shared drive, as explained previously.

Some software products, however, are available in a special LAN edition (or network edition or server edition—names vary). To use one of these products, you install the LAN-server edition on a server. Then other users can run the software by accessing the server copy instead of a copy on their own hard disks. For some software products, you need to install a separate workstation (or node) edition of the product on each workstation that will use the product on the server.

LAN versions of software typically limit, in some way, the number of concurrent users.

Different software manufacturers use different design philosophies for their LAN versions. One method is for the server copy to keep track of the number of users simultaneously running the program. If the number of simultaneous users reaches five (or whatever number the manufacturer picks), no additional users can join in. To permit six users at once, you have to buy another "five-user pack" and install it on the server. Then you can have up to ten simultaneous users.

Another method limits the number of users through a "workstation edition" approach. Again, you install the main software on the server. Then you buy a workstation edition of the software to install on each workstation that will *ever* use the product (not necessarily simultaneously with other workstation users). Any number of users can use the server edition simultaneously, as long as each one has installed a workstation edition.

Many major software applications are not available in special LAN editions. For some products, the software can be installed on a server, but legal restrictions call for each user to buy a copy. The software does not restrict the number of users; rather, the manufacturer relies on your honesty to buy a separate copy for each workstation that will run the product. Frequently, the main motivation for users to buy all these copies—other than honesty, morality, and fear of prosecution—is to provide each user with reference manuals and telephone support in case of a problem.

Other non-LAN software products, if used illegally on a LAN, falter during file sharing. That is, if you and Gina (your co-worker) both try to run a copy of the same software from a server, the software fails because it was designed to run on a single PC with a hard disk no other user can access. For example, the software may create a temporary file (TEMP.RAM) in its disk directory to store data that will not fit in RAM at the moment. If you and Gina both run the program from the server, the program will try to create two copies of TEMP.RAM in the same directory on the server. Either the program will fail because of the duplicate file names, or you and Gina will find your data corrupted because your files overlaid each other. This is just one example. Many other things can go wrong.

In any event, the lesson is simple: follow the legal restrictions and use software the way the publisher intended. If you don't, you may destroy data or your company may be raided for software piracy.

Fortunately, many software manufacturers price LAN versions of their software attractively. If a stand-alone version of a word processor costs $300, the vendor might sell a LAN server edition for $500, plus $100 for each workstation edition. Simple arithmetic shows that you break even for two users, coming out increasingly ahead for each additional user. Another approach might be to sell for $900 a server edition that supports up to three simultaneous users. In this case, you break even for three users. If you have five users, but no more than three ever use the word processor at the same time, you come out ahead because you have to pay for only three, not five.

Keep in mind that not all software manufacturers have the same LAN policies and that they design their software differently. Pricing options and licensing restrictions vary widely and change frequently. Check with the manufacturer to be sure of the current state of affairs.

Shared CD-ROM Disk Drive

CD-ROMs are not yet in widespread use on NetWare Lite networks, but every day more users discover the amazing capabilities offered by these new disk drives. A CD-ROM disk looks exactly like an audio CD disk, the kind that put vinyl record albums on the endangered species list.

One of these CD-ROM disks can hold more than 600 million bytes of information. (To give you an idea of the amount of data on a CD-ROM—the average computer book contains approximately 1 million bytes of information.) The data on CD-ROM is available for reading only. You cannot write new data on a CD-ROM disk—only the manufacturer of the CD-ROM disk can. In large quantities, CD-ROM disks can be manufactured for a few dollars each. (You pay much more for them because the manufacturer has to go through a great deal of work and expense to acquire the data to distribute on the disks.) The price of the disk drives that read CD-ROM disks has dropped; they are now available for less than $400. Thus, a manufacturer can send you a disk containing a huge amount of data much more economically than by using floppy disks, and to read the data you can buy a CD-ROM drive for a reasonable price. If several people can share use of the CD-ROM data and disk drive over a LAN, the price per user drops even lower.

One of the big benefits of reference material on CD-ROM disks is that the disks are designed to permit many different kinds of information searches. In a CD-ROM encyclopedia, for example, you are not limited to looking up entries by the main heading, such as "Frogs." You can enter a command to search the encyclopedia for any article that even *mentions* frogs. Similarly, an archive of newspaper articles allows you to search for virtually any word in any article, not just the headlines or main topics. These capabilities permit research that would be impractical with only printed reference material.

The list of available data on CD-ROM is long and rapidly expanding. Here are a few examples:

- **Microsoft Bookshelf Reference Library.** Contains many reference books you can search in ways you cannot search conventional books. Includes a dictionary, an almanac, a ZIP-code directory, a thesaurus, a book of quotations, sample forms and letters, and other reference material.

- **Newspaper archives.** Major newspapers such as the *Los Angeles Times* and *Washington Post* are available. Six months or a year of articles are on one CD-ROM disk.

- **Telephone lists.** Two CD-ROM disks contain 90 million names, addresses, ZIP codes, and phone numbers. Other products contain specialized lists.

- **Business databases.** A long list includes business databases with information about trademarks, corporate affiliations, small business administration, Standard & Poor's information, and business associations.

- **Medical databases.** Dozens of medical-database CD-ROMs are available, including ones specializing in such areas as biotechnology, cancer research, family practice, internal medicine, nursing, nutritional analysis, and pharmaceuticals. Collections of medical journals also are available on CD-ROM.

- **Government databases.** Census data, agricultural statistics, county and city statistics, the Federal Register, meteorological data, the CIA World Factbook, and many other collections are offered.

- **Computer Select.** This database contains details about almost all computer hardware and software products offered for sale, plus abstracts or complete articles from dozens of last year's computer publications.

- **Justis Weekly Law Reports.** Reports on important Supreme Court decisions and other significant legal developments.

Each CD-ROM disk has its own search software. Most of these programs are compatible with NetWare Lite in such a way that any workstation can access the CD-ROM data on a server. Check with Novell or the CD-ROM manufacturer to be sure. Some manufacturers do not yet offer LAN versions or have not established LAN prices. Also, be aware that CD-ROM drives are much slower than hard disks. If many users try to access the same CD-ROM drive simultaneously, everyone gets extremely slow response.

Shared Modem

Software products from third-party vendors make it possible for any NetWare Lite workstation to access a modem on any other workstation. Chapter 3, "Planning a NetWare Lite LAN," briefly discusses the economic trade-offs involved in modem sharing. Because 2400-bit-per-second (bps) modems are inexpensive (some cost about $50), the demand for modem sharing is not very strong. The cost of installing a 2400-bps modem in every computer is not high.

Higher speed modems, such as 9600-bps models, might be worth sharing in some cases, but their prices have dropped greatly also. The main economy in modem sharing comes if the number of associated phone lines can be reduced also, or if every user in a workgroup only occasionally has an urgent need to use a modem—and then, not everyone at the same time.

Profiles of Some Real-World NetWare Lite Users

This section briefly describes an assortment of workgroups and companies that use NetWare Lite in their everyday work. The list is a fairly wide cross section, to give you an idea of NetWare Lite's diverse capabilities.

A Small Professional Office

A law office has two attorneys and one secretary, each of whom has a 386/33 PC connected on a NetWare Lite network. Each of the three PCs is configured as both a server and a client, so that everyone has access to every hard disk. The office has a shared laser printer, located next to the secretary's desk. Running Microsoft Word for Windows, the lawyers write documents, the secretary retrieves the document files and then edits and prints the documents.

A Telemarketing Workgroup

The sales department of an exercise equipment manufacturer has an assortment of eight PCs, ranging from 386SX/16 models up to 386/25 models. One PC is configured as a server, the other seven as workstations. The main application is the Action Plus contact management program, with which telemarketers monitor sales leads and send out form letters. Two HP LaserJet printers are shared on the LAN—a model III with letterhead stationary and a model IIP with plain paper.

A Two-Person Home Office

A husband and wife writing team work in their home office developing scripts. Each uses a PC AT-compatible 286 computer, connected with NetWare Lite. A laser printer is attached to one of the computers, configured as a server, for access by both. The main application is WordPerfect. Both users save all document files on the server's hard disk.

A LAN with Floppy-Based Workstations

A food-processing company uses NetWare Lite to connect six computers. The server is a 386/25 PC with a 200MB IDE disk drive. The other five computers are 286-based models that have no hard disks and act as workstations. Each workstation boots from a floppy disk and then accesses the server's hard disk via the LAN. The server is dedicated entirely to server functions. The LAN is used primarily to run a Paradox database application that enables people at all workstations to keep track of inventory and work in process.

A Medium-Sized LAN

A courier-dispatching company uses NetWare Lite to connect five computers. A 386SX computer with an 80MB hard disk is configured as a nondedicated server for sharing disk files. A 286 computer, to which three printers are connected, acts as a nondedicated printer server. One printer is a Hewlett-Packard LaserJet; the other two are dot-matrix printers which print invoices that require an impact printer to produce carbons. The other three computers are 286 models. The main application schedules couriers, using Lotus 1-2-3 spreadsheets that someone in the company developed.

A Modem-Intensive LAN

A retail computer business runs a computer bulletin board system (BBS). Six computers are linked, using NetWare Lite. Three of the computers are nondedicated servers, three are workstations. Each computer has its own US Robotics modem. As many as six people can dial into the BBS simultaneously to access all of the publicly available server files. One server has a NEC CDR-72 CD-ROM drive, which holds a CD-ROM disk with more than 500MB of shareware software.

CHAPTER

3 PLANNING A NETWARE LITE LAN

Before plunging into any LAN commitment, you should do some planning. In this chapter, you learn how to analyze your specific needs and determine how NetWare Lite addresses those needs.

While planning your LAN, keep in mind the overriding question you should continually be asking yourself: "What do I want the LAN to do?" By now, you should have a good idea of what you want your LAN to do. If you are not yet clear on your objectives, try to crystallize them while you read this chapter. Your goal is to use NetWare Lite to help you reach your objectives as simply, conveniently, and inexpensively as possible.

Once you decide on NetWare Lite, one of your first concerns is the acquisition of hardware: LAN cards, cables, and connectors. Remember that NetWare Lite is a software product that can run on LANs configured with many different types of LAN cards and cables. This chapter reviews the variety of available hardware components so that you can select the appropriate hardware.

Why Bother Planning?

Suppose that you are responsible for recommending or approving a LAN decision in your workgroup. (Your workgroup might consist of a two-person office, a 10-person group in a large company, or an entire small to medium-sized company.) Ideally, you should perform a detailed, objective analysis of exactly what you need before you buy anything.

Your plan should analyze your current workload and equipment as well as immediate expectations and plans for the next year or more. How many people perform various kinds of work right now and what equipment do they use? How will their work change in the near and far term, and what equipment will they need then? How many new people will be added? How will their work tie in with what others are doing now and will do in the future? What kinds of communications take place between group members, as well as between the group and the outside world?

If you are like the planners for most workgroups, long-range planning is what happens when you occasionally take a few minutes over coffee to think about the next month or two. Ideally the planning should take much more time and effort and be directed toward next year and the years after.

For something like a new local area network for your workgroup, even a little rough planning is much better than no planning at all. You need a LAN that matches *your* needs.

You also need a plan that fits your office situation. If you have a small office with simple computing and communication needs, a simple plan

Planning a NetWare Lite LAN

is fine. If you have a larger office, or an office that needs to link to other offices, or ambitious intentions for "computerizing the office," you need to pay more attention to planning. Of course, you can always bypass planning and later pay the price when things don't work out the way you expected.

> **NOTE:** As a rule, each hour you spend planning will reduce by 10 or even 100 hours the time you will spend later fixing problems you could have avoided. A good plan is good business.

Analyze Your Needs

The most straightforward and productive planning strategy is to analyze your needs and then consider the available solutions that can satisfy those needs. If you find solutions that fit your needs, both now and in the future, you can simply plan to acquire and implement those solutions.

As a starting point for network planning, workgroups considering a NetWare Lite LAN can be classified into four general categories. For each category, the complexity of the plan and the number of possible hardware solutions differs. If one of the following four categories matches your situation, follow the suggested recommendations. If your workgroup is on the fuzzy edge between two categories, take both recommendations into account.

✦ *You have a few PCs located close together (within 20 feet of each other).* Novell licenses several hardware vendors to produce NetWare Lite starter kits. Each kit has all you need (hardware and software) to connect two computers. Add-on kits let you add additional computers to the network. For you, these kits offer a straightforward solution to your LAN hardware requirements. You can skim most of this chapter, but pay close attention to the sections that discuss starter kits. If you have a particular layout problem, such as needing to route a cable between offices, read the section on "Formulating the Hardware Plan."

- *You have approximately five or six PCs, which may be in adjacent offices.* Your situation is on the borderline between a bus LAN and a hub-based LAN. As you will learn later in this chapter, a *bus* LAN connects computers with a cable routed from one node to the next. (The starter kits create a bus LAN.) A hub-based LAN connects each computer to a central unit called a *hub*. You may be able to use starter and add-on kits, but you may also choose an entirely different hardware solution. Read this chapter thoroughly to understand the tradeoffs. Hire a consultant if you are in doubt.

- *Your LAN requires a complex physical layout.* A complex layout may occur in a number of situations. You may need to connect more than six PCs, for example, or you may need to connect computers located down the hall or on different floors—perhaps your computers must be physically relocated with some regularity. Read this chapter to get pertinent planning ideas, but a LAN consultant is recommended to ensure a safe, reliable LAN setup.

- *You already have the LAN hardware installed.* Perhaps you have inherited hardware from a LAN that is no longer in use. Or maybe you or someone else already purchased hardware for your LAN. If you already have the hardware, you just need to buy the NetWare Lite software. Remember—you need a separate copy of the software for each node on your network. If you are confident that the hardware is appropriate for your situation, you can skim the rest of this chapter. If the hardware is already installed, you can skip ahead to Chapter 5, "Installing the NetWare Lite Software." Be sure that you know the type of LAN cards you have. If your hardware is not yet installed, you can skip to Chapter 4, "Installing the LAN Hardware."

Of course, your situation may not exactly match any of these categories. If that is the case, read this chapter to explore your alternatives and formulate a plan.

Situations Appropriate for NetWare Lite Starter Kits

If you have not yet purchased any LAN hardware or the NetWare Lite software, a NetWare Lite starter kit is likely to be the straightforward

Planning a NetWare Lite LAN

answer to your planning and purchase decisions. See whether the following statements apply to your situation:

- ◆ Your workgroup uses a handful (say two to six) DOS-based (or DR DOS-based) computers.
- ◆ Each computer has a 286, 386, or 486 processor.
- ◆ The different computers are located relatively close together (each computer is within 20 feet of at least one other computer).
- ◆ You can afford $275 per PC to buy the LAN hardware and software.

If these conditions apply to you, here is a quick answer to your planning needs. Buy a NetWare Lite starter kit for the first two PCs and an add-on kit for each additional PC. These kits contain all the hardware and software you need to set up a NetWare Lite thin Ethernet network. (The term *Ethernet* refers to the most common type of LAN cable and signalling scheme. Ethernet is explained later in this chapter.)

NetWare Lite starter kits and add-on kits are available from a number of vendors licensed by Novell to market hardware appropriate for NetWare Lite LANs. Each kit contains LAN cards, cables, connectors, and copies of the NetWare Lite software. You can buy the kits from a local Novell dealer or from a company that sells computer equipment by mail order.

The type of NetWare Lite kit you purchase will depend on your type of computer.

Two versions of the kits are available: one with LAN cards for computers that use the ISA internal data bus, and one with LAN cards for the MCA bus. Be sure to buy kits with the appropriate LAN cards for your computers. ISA (Industry Standard Architecture) refers to the data bus design of the IBM PC, XT, and AT. IBM-compatible computers based on 8088, 286, 386, and 486 processor chips use the ISA bus. MCA (Micro Channel Architecture) refers to the internal data bus of most IBM PS/2 computers (PS/2 models 50, 60, 70, 80, and 90). Starter kits are described more fully later in this chapter.

But if you want to connect more than a handful of PCs, or your PCs are not all close together, or you don't want to shell out money before making careful plans, you must consider network solutions other than those offered by a starter kit. The planning process outlined in this chapter will build your confidence that the LAN hardware you choose will fit your needs.

Situations Inappropriate for NetWare Lite

NetWare Lite may not be right for you. If your answer to any of the following simple questions is "yes," NetWare Lite is not recommended for your situation:

✦ *Is your workgroup currently using computers other than DOS-based IBM-PC compatibles?* NetWare Lite currently is not offered for the Apple Macintosh computer. (Because options exist to connect NetWare Lite between PC compatibles and Macs, don't rule out NetWare Lite if a few Macs are mixed into your workgroup. See the discussion of MACLAN Connect in this chapter's "Macintosh Connection" section.) Also, NetWare Lite is not currently available for the OS/2 or UNIX operating systems. NetWare Lite was designed to connect PC-compatible computers that run MS-DOS (or its twin, IBM's PC DOS), DR DOS, or MS-DOS with Microsoft Windows.

✦ *Is a particular hardware or software product you now use incompatible with NetWare Lite?* Most products you run on a stand-alone PC will work with NetWare Lite, but some may not. Later chapters in this book discuss many popular products and their compatibility with NetWare Lite. Chapter 10, "Using Application Software on the LAN," discusses the compatibility of most major software applications. If you are in doubt about a product's compatibility with NetWare Lite, check with the product's manufacturer.

✦ *Do you need to connect many PCs?* NetWare Lite is best suited for small to medium-sized LANs. Although the maximum number of connected PCs is 25, NetWare Lite LANs with more than 15 PCs become complicated and difficult to administer; performance often suffers. The typical NetWare Lite LAN connects 2 to 10 PCs. If you need to connect more than 15 PCs, you should consider carefully whether NetWare Lite is your best choice; read this chapter to understand the issues and then contact a LAN consultant to discuss alternatives.

✦ *In the foreseeable future, will you answer "yes" to any of the preceding questions?* Don't buy a NetWare Lite LAN today if in six months you will run into one of these problems. If you buy now anyway, have your conversion plans in place.

Workgroup Characteristics: Needs and Wants

Every workgroup is different. When you analyze your workgroup needs, some characteristics of your particular workgroup are critical to the decision of how to implement a LAN. This section lists these critical characteristics, along with some comments about how to use NetWare Lite to address each characteristic.

Make a list of all computers you want to connect using NetWare Lite. Include in the list the name of the person who uses each computer, the PC attributes, and any peripheral devices you might share over the LAN. For a small office, your list might look like Table 3-1.

The following sections examine the different elements that make up such a list, explaining what information to put in each column and why.

User

Show who uses each computer. Most computers are used exclusively (or primarily) by one person. Show the principal user first. If other people sometimes use the computer, include their names. Notice that in this sample office, every user conveniently has a unique name. In many offices, more than one person have the same first name. If so, use last initials, last names, nicknames, or something else to uniquely identify each person and computer. Also, if a computer is dedicated to a certain function and is shared by many users, you may want to list that function (such as "Graphics" or "Remote Access") rather than someone's

Table 3-1. A PC Attribute List for LAN Planning

	User	PC Type	Hard Disk	RAM	Peripherals
1.	Juan	XT	10MB	640K	Epson FX-80
2.	Jane	AT	30MB	640K	Epson 286, 1200 bps modem
3.	Ed, Al	386SX	40MB	1MB	HP LaserJet II, 2400 bps modem
4.	Yee	386/33	80MB	2MB	No printer, 2400 bps modem

name. The point here is to identify each computer unambiguously. If nothing else seems right, assign a number or name to each computer and identify each computer that way during planning.

PC Type

In the "PC Type" column, show the most important identifying aspect of each PC type. You may want to be more specific than the example, indicating the exact processor and clock speed, such as "8088 (4.77 MHz)", "80286 (8 MHz)", and so on. If any computers are PS/2 models that use the Micro Channel Architecture (MCA) bus, note that fact. If you are unsure about what type of processor a machine has, many utility programs such as PC Tools and Norton Utilities have options to display the processor type. As you will learn later in this chapter, the processor types and speeds can influence your NetWare Lite adapter card decision.

Hard Disk and RAM

The size of each computer's hard disk and the installed RAM in each machine provide a good starting point for planning which computers will act as servers on the LAN. Again, if you don't know the hard disk or RAM size for your computers, utility programs such as PC Tools and Norton Utilities can provide the information. (The DOS CHKDSK command also shows the hard disk's size. Consult your DOS documentation for CHKDSK.)

A small LAN usually has only one server—typically the fastest computer with the largest hard disk and the most RAM.

NetWare Lite gives you the option of setting up each PC as a dedicated server—a PC that does nothing other than make its resources available to the other LAN computers—or as a nondedicated server, which you can use both as a server and, at the same time, as a workstation. Most NetWare Lite users prefer to set up nondedicated servers, choosing to have a server PC available also as a workstation. The main advantage to setting up a dedicated server is the speed with which it can perform server duties. Workstations that transfer data to and from a dedicated server get faster response.

Typically, a small LAN uses only one computer as a server. Depending on your planned use for the LAN, you may decide to set up more than one PC as a server. You might want two servers, so that one can take over for the other in case of failure. You may want all PCs to act as servers, at least some of the time, so that a tape backup unit on one

Planning a NetWare Lite LAN

workstation can make backup copies of everybody's hard disks. One advantage of a peer-to-peer LAN, such as NetWare Lite, is that any PC can be turned into a server (even just once in a while).

In some cases, you will not want to design a single-server LAN with the fastest computer as the server. If the fastest computer doesn't have the largest or fastest hard disk, the computer with the biggest or fastest hard disk might be a better server. Or if someone needs the fastest computer to run a critical resource-hungry application (perhaps a computer-aided design or desktop-publishing program), you may not want to further burden that computer with the server workload. In these cases, use the next-to-fastest computer as a server. If you don't expect the people on your LAN to move a great deal of data back and forth on the server's hard disk, even the slowest PC could be the best server. In some LANs that just share one or more printers, for example, the slowest PC with the smallest hard disk is set up as a print server.

Your choice of which computers will be servers and which will be workstations can be changed as your needs change.

To make these decisions accurately, you need to know exactly how you will use the LAN. Before you install the LAN, you *will not* know exactly. Just make your best guess. You can start using one particular computer for a server and later switch to a different server or make servers out of nodes that were workstations. NetWare Lite makes this reconfiguring process easy, as you will see in Chapter 5, "Installing the NetWare Lite Software." Furthermore, you can always upgrade some or all computers to add RAM or disk space. You may add new computers to the network also.

Even though you cannot be sure of your final LAN configuration, you have to start somewhere. Begin by thinking about which PCs will act as servers. Mark the servers on your PC-attribute list or, if appropriate, add to the list a computer that you need to buy. Also mark any PC that you think will be upgraded with more RAM or a bigger or faster hard disk.

Portable Computers

If you sometimes want to attach portable computers to the LAN, show these mobile computers on the list. You can add a column to the list to indicate which computers are portables, or simply indicate the portables under the "PC Type" column. Some users carry laptop computers home, burn the midnight oil, and then want to attach the computers to the LAN the next day to copy files to the shared disk drive.

Attaching a portable computer to the network requires some special hardware. One possibility is a portable LAN adapter (such as the Xircom Pocket Ethernet Adapter, explained in Chapter 9, "Sharing Other Resources"). A second approach is to use a null modem cable to connect the portable computer directly to one of the PCs on the network. The connection is made through the serial or parallel ports of each computer. LapLink and Brooklyn Bridge, discussed in Chapter 1, are two leading products of this type.

DOS Version

To find out which version of DOS is on a PC, use the VER command.

What version of DOS is installed on each PC? NetWare Lite requires version 3.1 or higher (or DR DOS 6). If some of your computers still run DOS 2.1, include in your plan the need to upgrade to a newer version of DOS. Add a "DOS Version" column to your list. If a PC that needs upgrading has an 80286 or higher processor and also has more than 640K of RAM, DOS 5 or DR DOS 6 is worth having. DOS 5 can use RAM above the 640K address mark for some DOS and LAN functions. The result is more usable RAM in the limited DOS 640K address space. (Although understanding the 640K memory barrier is not critical, you can learn more about DOS and memory usage from any of several books on using DOS.)

ROM BIOS

If you have some older PCs in the workgroup, check the date of the ROM BIOS. The *ROM BIOS* (Read-Only Memory, Basic Input/Output System) is a chip inside the PC which contains some programmed instructions essential to the PC's operation. For some manufacturers, older ROM BIOS chips may be incompatible with LAN requirements. Check with the manufacturer or Novell if a PC has a ROM BIOS older than 1986. You may want to add to your list a "ROM BIOS" column for the dates.

For many computers, the ROM BIOS information is displayed onscreen during the boot process (that is, when you turn on the computer). Also, utility programs such as PC Tools and Norton Utilities have options to display the ROM BIOS information.

In some cases, you may need to buy a new ROM BIOS chip, either from the PC's manufacturer or from an independent vendor. If local

Planning a NetWare Lite LAN

computer stores don't sell ROM BIOS upgrades, you can buy them from major mail-order companies.

Available Card Slots

Each desktop computer you connect to the LAN must have an internal card slot available to accept the LAN card. If you have any doubt, you must open the computer and check inside to be sure that a slot is available. Either an 8-bit or 16-bit slot will work, although performance is a little slower with an 8-bit slot. For more information about PC card slots, including how to open a PC and check for 8-bit and 16-bit slots, see Chapter 4, "Installing the LAN Hardware."

If you like, add a "Card Slot" column to your PC-attribute list. For each computer, either show the number of available card slots, or just indicate "yes" or "no."

Macintosh Connection

If your office has one or more Macintosh computers in addition to PC compatibles, determine what you plan to do. The following list indicates your most likely choices:

- ✦ Consider the PCs and Macs as separate worlds and don't try to exchange data between them.

- ✦ Use a non-LAN connectivity solution. For example, you can convert files on one computer, say an IBM, to a compatible data format (such as ASCII) that can be copied to a floppy disk and subsequently read by a different computer, say a Macintosh.

- ✦ Get a network merging product, such as Miramar Systems' MACLAN Connect. This software product turns a NetWare Lite workstation into a *gateway* (a connection between two unlike networks) between a Macintosh LAN and a NetWare Lite LAN. You need to buy also a second LAN card for the workstation, in addition to the NetWare Lite card. The MACLAN software turns the PC into a dedicated gateway through which workstations on a Macintosh LAN can use Apple's Appleshare software to access NetWare Lite servers.

◆ Get an entirely different type of LAN, such as Novell Netware 3.11, that supports both PC and Macintosh computers on the same network. Such LANs are much more complex than NetWare Lite, and the software is much more expensive.

Number and Types of Shared Peripherals

The "Peripherals" column of your PC-attribute list shows you who uses which devices. With this information, you can explore the sharing possibilities. Start the column with currently installed devices, then add planned future devices. The most common peripheral device is a printer. Other devices are modems, plotters, and CD-ROM disk drives.

Tape backup devices cannot be shared over the LAN. That is, you cannot place a tape backup unit on a server and have a client node access the device. A tape backup is still appropriate for the attribute list, however. You can use a tape backup drive attached to a workstation to back up files that reside on the server's hard disk.

Generally, there's no need to list input devices, such as mice, digitizers, and scanners. Input devices rarely work out as shared devices.

Printers

A printer is the most common peripheral. For the workgroup represented by Table 3-1, the LaserJet printer is the obvious candidate for sharing. You might want to share the Epson 286 printer also, or perhaps leave that printer as an unshared device attached to the AT.

To establish the current printing needs of each workgroup member, talk to everyone. In most workgroups, as soon as people find out how easily they can get fast, clear laser printer output over the LAN, their own personal dot-matrix printers begin gathering dust.

But beware! A personal printer can be an emotional issue. If you, the LAN planner, tell members of the workgroup that they are going to lose their cherished personal printers and instead start sharing a printer on this mysterious new LAN, you may cause panic. If not panic, at least count on some ruffled feathers. The smoothest transition usually occurs when people are allowed to continue using their personal printers as well as the shared laser printer. A few months after the LAN is installed, when they realize that they use only the laser printer, they won't mind giving up their personal dot-matrix printers. In fact, some will probably demand that their old (now unused) printers be removed, so that they can reclaim some precious horizontal table space.

Modems

Modems in a NetWare Lite environment can be used in two ways. First, the modem can be used as if the LAN were not there. You can use a modem from a LAN workstation in the same way you would without the LAN. Install the modem in a PC, connect the modem to a telephone line, and run your communications software independently of the LAN. The modem is used only by the person using the PC in which the modem is installed, not through the LAN or by other LAN users.

Second, you can share modems with the LAN. Instead of installing a separate modem in each PC, everyone can use one or more modems shared across the LAN. Chapter 9 explains how modem sharing works. Unless you have a real need for high-speed modems (such as 9600 bits per second (bps) models), however, modem sharing may not be cost effective. Costs have dropped so much for 2400 bps modems (you can buy each PC user a personal 2400 bps internal modem for $50 or so) that the only cost savings realized by modem sharing comes from reducing the number of telephone lines the workgroup requires. More expensive modems with extra flexibility features or that transfer data at higher speeds change the cost comparison. To share a modem on the LAN you need to buy special modem-sharing software from a third-party vendor. Modem sharing is not a standard feature of NetWare Lite. (Novell does not market modem-sharing software.)

Modem sharing can reduce the number of modem telephone lines required by a workgroup.

Plotters

Plotters have characteristics both of printers and, surprisingly, modems. Basically, a plotter is a special type of printer—it produces printed output. Some plotters require two-way communication with the computer, however, and may use a serial port and require LAN software that treats the plotter like a modem. As is the case for modems, you need independent software to support plotters that require two-way communication. For planning purposes, if you want to share a plotter, find out whether it requires two-way communication or is an output-only device. For the former, you must plan to buy the appropriate software. (Some serial printers have this two-way requirement also.)

CD-ROM Disk Drives

Chapter 2 explained some CD-ROM applications and databases you may want to consider for your workgroup. NetWare Lite has built-in CD-ROM-sharing capability. If you want to share a CD-ROM drive over NetWare Lite, be sure to add the cost of the CD-ROM drive. No extra hardware is necessary for it to work with NetWare Lite. In most cases, no extra software is needed either, except whatever CD-ROM application titles you plan to purchase. (For details of CD-ROM sharing, see Chapter 9.)

Understanding Hardware Alternatives

When you are planning a new LAN, one of the most important early decisions is to select the type of connecting hardware your LAN will use. You must choose from a variety of LAN cards, cables, and cabling schemes. Your decisions affect many factors, including LAN performance, cost, reliability, physical layout, and future expandability.

NOTE: If your planned LAN is suitable for a NetWare Lite starter kit, you have available a straightforward solution to your hardware choices. Simply buy a starter kit for the first two PCs, and an add-on kit for each additional PC. Be sure to purchase the ISA or MCA versions, as appropriate. You can scan the remainder of this chapter to understand various hardware alternatives. Pay attention to the sections that discuss starter kits.

Chapter 1 introduced some of the hardware components used to connect PCs: LAN cards, cables, connectors, and terminators. The following discussion focuses on the hardware issues relevant to LAN planning. Chapter 4, "Installing the LAN Hardware," provides even more information about different hardware alternatives.

Physical LAN Topologies: Bus, Star, and Ring

The way individual nodes of a network are physically connected is called the LAN's *topology*. The word "topology" is borrowed from mathematics; it refers to the properties of geometric shapes and configurations. Three types of LAN topology are popular today: bus, star, and ring.

Bus Topology

The simplest and most common topology is the *bus*, sometimes called a *linear bus* or *daisy-chain* topology. The bus is in effect one long cable to which all nodes attach. A NetWare Lite LAN based on thin coaxial cable uses a bus topology.

The vast majority of newly installed NetWare Lite LANs use the bus design. NetWare Lite starter kits contain thin coaxial cables and the associated hardware to create a bus LAN. The bus design is most appropriate for small LANs of two to six PCs—exactly the type of LAN most suitable for NetWare Lite.

In reality, thin-coax LANs do not use a single long cable. Rather, a separate cable connects each node to the next node. The computer in the middle of the chain is attached to the two adjoining nodes by two cables that attach to the BNC T-connector on the computer's LAN card; one cable goes to each adjoining node. Because these cables all connect end-to-end through the BNC T-connectors, the effect is the same as one

---

LAN Bus Versus Computer Data Bus

The word "bus" has multiple meanings in computer jargon. Don't confuse a bus topology with a computer's data bus. When referring to the physical layout of a LAN, a bus is simply one of several possible topologies. On the other hand, the data bus of a computer refers to the design and signalling method by which data transfers between components of a computer. Examples of data buses are the 8-bit XT bus or the 16-bit AT bus.

Bus topology
Figure 3-1.

Bus Topology

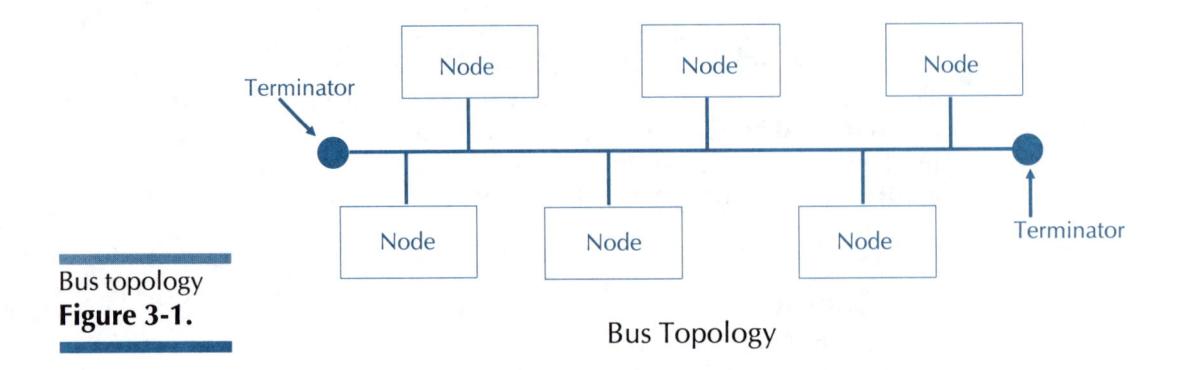

long cable. A terminator attaches to the open end of the T-connector on the node on each end of the chain. Figure 3-1 depicts a bus topology for a LAN with six nodes.

In a bus-topology LAN, a node that sends a message out to another node really broadcasts the message across the linear cable to all nodes on the LAN. The network software controls each node to receive only the messages specifically addressed to it.

If a cable between two nodes breaks or becomes disconnected, communication is jeopardized between *any* two nodes on the LAN. In a few cases, a node on one of the two separated sections can continue communicating with other nodes on the same section, but because each of the sections lacks a terminator, the chances of the whole LAN going down are high. Sometimes finding the point of failure for a bus LAN is difficult, but if you are reasonably careful where you route the cables, failures caused by damaged cables are relatively rare.

Star Topology

The *star* topology, shown in Figure 3-2, has a central *hub* to which all nodes are connected. Because the cable that connects a node to the hub is actually a pair of cables that form a loop between the hub and node, no terminator is needed. LANs based on twisted-pair cabling typically use the star topology; also many ARCnet LANs use the star topology. Any signal broadcast between nodes must pass through the hub.

Planning a NetWare Lite LAN

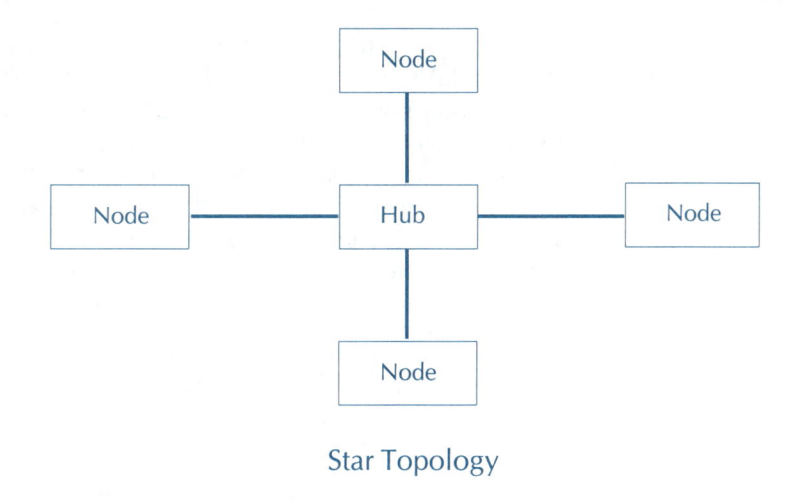

```
            Node
             |
   Node —— Hub —— Node
             |
            Node
```

Star topology
Figure 3-2.

Star Topology

You should consider using a hub-based LAN in the following situations:

◆ Your computers are relatively far apart (more than 30 feet, for instance).

◆ The computers may be moved fairly regularly to new locations.

◆ You want to connect more than six computers.

◆ You expect your LAN to grow to more than six nodes in the foreseeable future.

Although you can use a hub design with as few as two nodes, the extra expense of the hub (compared to a bus LAN, which has no hub) and the potentially more complicated wiring, makes a bus LAN the better choice for smaller networks. You can install a hub-based LAN yourself, but if you plan to connect more than six nodes, or have potentially complex cabling requirements (such as from one office to another through walls, floors, or ceilings), consider talking to a LAN consultant before you begin.

A hub can have one of several forms. Normally the hub is a box-like device, separate from any computer, which acts as a central wiring receptacle. Another type of hub is the internal, computer-based hub. You insert a special adapter card into an available computer slot and then attach cables from other nodes directly to this card.

Yet another form of hub may be found in modern office buildings that are prewired for LANs (and other cable communications). Existing cables route through walls, floors, and ceilings into a central wiring closet. Inside the wiring closet, you can connect various cables together with a routing device known as a *punchdown block*. In effect, the punchdown block creates a network hub. To be sure you understand the cable routes and to verify that your proposed LAN conforms with local building and safety regulations, check with your building engineer. A LAN consultant is recommended also.

The simplest star topology has one hub and from 2 to 20 connected nodes. (More complicated designs use a hierarchy of hubs, in which each hub connects not only to PC nodes, but also to one or more other hubs.)

The star (or hub-based) topology has some advantages over a bus topology. These advantages are as follows:

- If the cable connecting a node and the hub fails, only that node loses the ability to communicate over the LAN. All other nodes are unaffected.
- Unshielded twisted-pair cable, suitable for hub-based LANs, costs less per foot than the thin coaxial cable typically used on linear-bus LANs.
- Some buildings are prewired with twisted-pair cabling and wall sockets, making LAN installation easy.
- If nodes must be physically relocated or extra nodes are added to the LAN, recabling the LAN is usually simpler with a star topology than with a bus.

Unfortunately, these advantages are offset by the following disadvantages:

- Even though a single cable failure affects only one node, failure of the hub causes the entire LAN to fail.
- Failure of a cable that connects two hubs cuts off communication between any two nodes connected to the different hubs.

Planning a NetWare Lite LAN 57

+ To use the star topology you must purchase a hub. External hubs cost upwards of $400. As a result, even though a hub-based LAN uses less expensive cable than a bus LAN, the added cost of the hub makes a hub-based LAN more expensive than a bus LAN.

+ Unshielded twisted-pair cable is more susceptible than thin coax to electrical interference from external equipment emitting strong electrical or magnetic fields. In most office environments this is not a problem, but in some cases the result is less reliability.

Ring Topology

The ring topology, shown in Figure 3-3, physically connects all nodes in a big circle, again avoiding the need for terminators. Although the shape formed by the cable is seldom close to being a true circle, it is a closed loop. Each node is connected to exactly two other nodes.

For technical reasons, the ring topology leads to data-transfer rates that are a little faster than the rates achieved with bus or star topologies. The ring topology is seldom used with NetWare Lite LANs, however, because the electronics required on the LAN card to support ring designs result in higher cost.

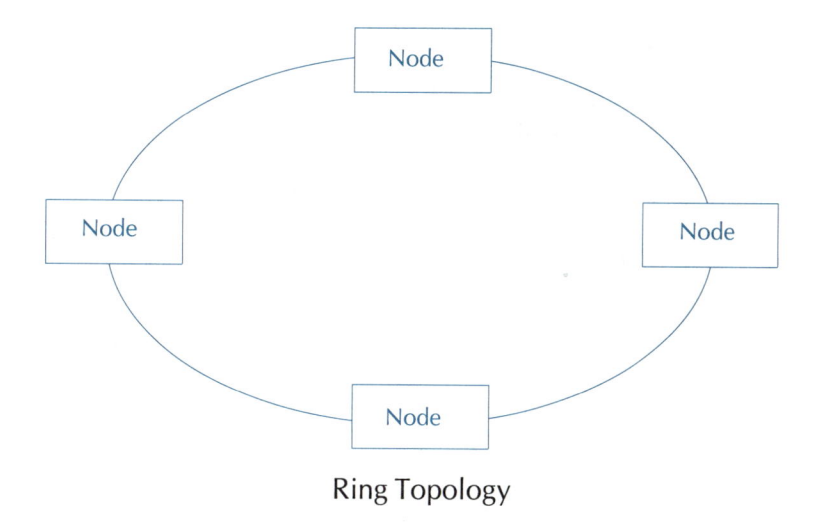

Ring topology
Figure 3-3.

Ring Topology

LAN Signalling Methods: Ethernet, Token Ring, and ARCnet

Choosing a LAN topology is a big step toward making the PCs on a LAN communicate, but it is only a beginning. Even though the method of physical connection is established, the logical communication process is not.

Consider a parallel situation with the telephone system that connects your home to virtually every other home in your neighborhood. When the telephone company installs a telephone cable leading to your home, that is only the beginning of neighborhood communications. Many other issues must be decided, either by the designers of the telephone system or by you, the telephone user.

First, everyone needs a unique telephone number. You and your neighbors have to know each other's numbers. What happens if you call someone but no one answers, or the telephone is being used? You also must decide how fast to talk, what language to speak, and what to do if both parties try to talk at the same time. Rather than stretch this telephone and LAN analogy too far, just bear in mind that communication is not a simple process, either with telephones or across a LAN.

With regard to LAN design, experts have addressed problems similar to those mentioned in the telephone analogy. Standards are established so that manufacturers know the answers to these problems and can create products accordingly.

Most LAN products adhere to standards adopted by the Institute of Electrical and Electronics Engineers (IEEE). These standards are described fully, numbered, and published so that any manufacturer can design products that comply with the standards and will work when connected to other standard products. The names and numbers of these standards frequently appear in product descriptions and in the computer press.

The hardware standards you adopt for your LAN determine which components you need to purchase. Different standards require different LAN cards and cables. The following sections briefly explain the most common standards.

IEEE 802.3: Ethernet

By far the most popular type of LAN conforms to one of the *Ethernet* standards. (These standards fall under IEEE's definitions labeled 802.3.) The Ethernet family includes several particular specifications, the most widely used of which are thick Ethernet, thin Ethernet, and twisted-pair hub. (Separate explanations of each type follow shortly.)

A problem that all these standards must solve is contention for the shared LAN communications channel. *Contention* occurs when two or more nodes simultaneously want to send a message on the LAN. The LAN is a single communications channel—only one message can be in transit at any given moment. Somehow, one node must send its message and the other nodes must wait. Each LAN standard uses some well-defined *access method* that specifies exactly how each node accesses the LAN.

All 802.3 standards use an access method called *carrier sense multiple access with collision detection (CSMA/CD)*. The CSMA portion of this imposing-looking name means that before any node tries to use the LAN, it must first sense (listen) whether the LAN is already in use. If so, the node must wait. If the communication channel is free, the node can go ahead and send a message. That method sounds fine—but if two nodes listen, hear that the channel is available, and both try to transmit a message at the same time, a *collision* of the two messages results.

This is where collision detection comes into play. The electronic circuitry built into each LAN card detects the collision, and therefore also detects that the message was not sent successfully. Both nodes wait and try again. To reduce the chance of a second collision, each node waits a random length of time before retrying.

The CSMA/CD access method works best when the LAN is lightly loaded with message traffic. The busier the traffic load, the higher the chance of multiple collisions before messages are sent successfully. In practice, CSMA/CD works well and is simple and cheap to implement electronically.

The 802.3 standard is subdivided into three additional classifications: 10BASE5 (Thick Ethernet), 10BASE2 (Thin Ethernet), and 10BASET (Twisted-Pair Hub). All three specifications use CSMA/CD, but each has individual cable and electrical specifications.

10BASE5 (Thick Ethernet)   The original type of Ethernet LAN is now called "thick Ethernet," because of the thick, inflexible coaxial cable used for connections. Not many new LANs use thick Ethernet, because of the relatively high cost of components and the awkwardness associated with installation and maintenance. 10BASE2 and 10BASE-T are considerably more dominant in the marketplace. Many LAN cards support thick Ethernet as well as thin Ethernet. NetWare Lite works with thick Ethernet but very few customers use the thick cabling.

10BASE2 (Thin Ethernet)   Thin Ethernet uses BNC T-connectors and RG58 coaxial cable, a thin, flexible cable that is widely available. The name 10BASE2 describes the key attributes of thin Ethernet (other than the cable type itself): 10 megabits per second, baseband signals, and 200 meters maximum segment length.

Baseband means that the cable is used for one communications channel. (A more technical way to say this is that one signal takes up the cable's entire band width.) Another method, called *broadband*, modulates a radio frequency signal and permits multiple communications channels on the same cable, but requires extra circuitry and results in more expense. NetWare Lite products use baseband signalling.

A group of nodes daisy-chained together is called a *segment*. The total cable length of a segment cannot exceed 185 meters (roughly the 200 meters in the 10BASE2 name), which is about 607 feet. What if you need more than 607 feet? Several solutions are possible. The simplest is to add a device called a *repeater*, which amplifies and regenerates the LAN signals. A repeater can connect two segments. You can chain together as many as four segments, using a repeater each two segments. Other solutions to exceeding the 607-foot limit are discussed later in this chapter.

Thin Ethernet is the most popular choice for NetWare Lite LANs. Compared to the alternatives, thin Ethernet offers an attractive combination of simplicity, performance, economy, and reliability. That is why the NetWare Lite starter kits contain LAN cards, cables, and connectors which use thin Ethernet. Figure 3-4 shows the contents of a two-node NetWare Lite starter kit.

10BASE-T (Twisted-Pair Hub)   10BASE-T is based on the star topology. Unshielded twisted-pair cable connects nodes to the hub.

Planning a NetWare Lite LAN

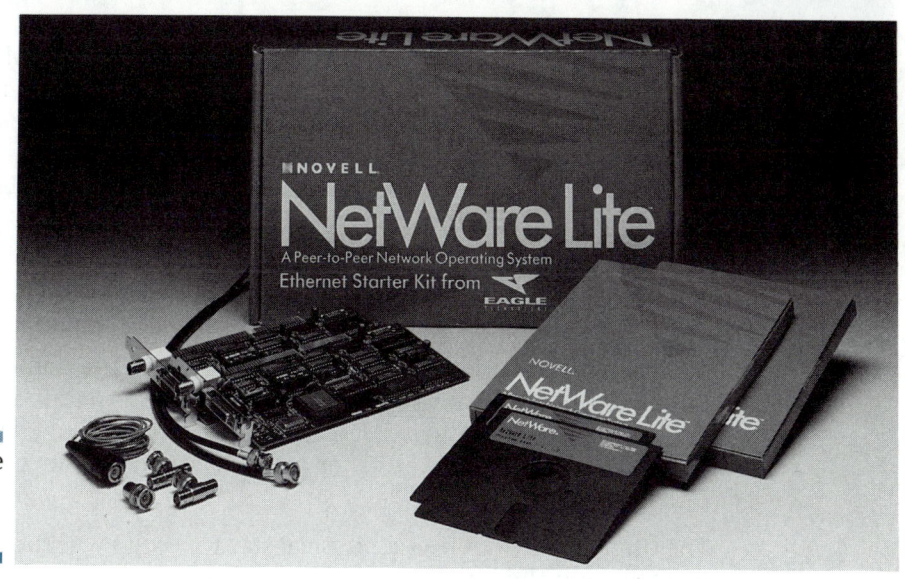

A NetWare Lite starter kit
Figure 3-4.

(The *T* in 10BASE-T is for "twisted pair.") The maximum length of a cable between the hub (sometimes called a *concentrator*) and each node is 100 meters (328 feet). Hubs can be connected together, but a maximum of four hubs is allowed between two nodes.

Even though advertisements often claim that 10BASE-T uses "ordinary telephone wire" and "modular plugs", you cannot use common flat telephone cable (often called "silver satin") or the small modular plugs frequently used on telephones. The cable must meet 10BASE-T specifications (AT&T 104, 205, 315, or Belden 1227A, for example) and the modular plugs are really large RJ45 connectors.

IEEE 802.5: Token Ring

Another family of LAN products is called 802.5, or *token ring*. Despite the name, token ring uses a star topology, not a ring. The token ring name comes from the way nodes interact on the LAN. A special message called a *token* is passed continually from one node to the next in a circular (or ring) sequence around the LAN. To send a message, a node waits for the token and then attaches the message to the token.

Compared to other standards, token-ring LANs are a bit more predictable in LAN throughput when several nodes try to communicate simultaneously, but they are expensive to implement. IBM has been the biggest proponent of token ring. Token-ring LANs are not nearly as widely accepted as Ethernet LANs, due primarily to higher cost and the fact that Ethernet was established first in the marketplace. Although very few NetWare Lite LANs use token ring, the NetWare Lite software does support token-ring LAN cards.

ARCnet

Although ARCnet is not an IEEE-accepted standard, it has been around so long that it is a de facto standard. The ARC in the name stands for Attached Resource Computing, an architecture developed originally by Datapoint. ARCnet is slow (2.5 megabits per second), but cheap. You can buy ARCnet LAN cards at lower prices than any other kind of LAN cards.

The original ARCnet uses a physical star topology with nodes connected to the hub by RG62 coaxial cable. More recent products also support a bus-type topology using unshielded twisted-pair cable or thin coax. ARCnet's access method, a token-passing scheme, is different from the token-ring standard. With ARCnet, each node is assigned an identification number and must wait for this number to be called before transmitting.

The main advantage of ARCnet is its price. ARCnet LAN cards typically are less expensive than other cards. Because of the slow speed and unofficial status, however, ARCnet is not a good choice for new LAN implementations unless rock-bottom cost is paramount. With the increasing speed at which PCs and hard disk drives are able to send and receive data, a 2.5 megabit-per-second LAN just isn't a good long-term investment.

Formulating the Hardware Plan

Armed with an understanding of hardware alternatives, you can formulate a specific plan for the hardware installation. You must take into account the physical layout of your office as well as the specific cabling topology and the hardware you choose.

Planning a NetWare Lite LAN

Locations of Computers and Printers

The physical locations of computers, printers, and other devices often become critical considerations in LAN planning. Even without a LAN, the jumble of wires in your office may resemble strands of spaghetti. PCs require so many power and data cables between the system units, monitors, printers, modems, and other devices that wiring messes are inevitable. But at least these messes are localized, usually to one or more Bermuda-triangle areas between each PC, printer, and power outlet.

The installation of a LAN adds another level of complexity to the cabling, especially if the LAN cables route between offices. Now, instead of a local jumble you can push under each desk, the jumbles are connected.

Furthermore, some people constantly want to rearrange furniture and computer locations. If rearrangements happen often, the LAN cables have to connect to a moving target. If at all possible, get each person in the workgroup to agree to a *permanent* (or as permanent as possible) location for his or her PC. The time to move PCs is *before* you plan the LAN, not after.

Even if your office has no cable jumbles, the soon-to-be installed LAN cables present new problems. These cables have to be put somewhere, and many offices are not designed with LANs in mind.

The answers to cabling problems are many and varied. Every LAN consultant has a favorite solution or two, depending on the office environment, user needs, and personal bias. The answers can significantly affect which cables to buy and how they are installed. The following list shows the possible answers to cabling problems, roughly in decreasing order of real-world occurrence.

♦ *Let the chips (cables) fall where they may (must).* Tuck the LAN cables (and external hubs if you're using 10BASE-T) into the safest available spaces. For small LANs using starter kits, the cables generally run across desktops just behind the computer equipment. Between desks, cables usually run along the floor or taped to a wall.

If you need to connect computers in separate offices, cables may have to be routed through ceiling tiles, under carpeting, through walls, or whatever the office layout dictates. Consider professional help for these more complex cabling situations.

Avoid running cables near strong sources of electromagnetic interference, such as fluorescent lights or air conditioners. Any devices directly attached to a computer, such as monitors or printers, generally are *not* a source of significant interference.

> **CAUTION:** The biggest concern is to avoid having cables out where they will be tripped over, stepped on, rolled over by chairs, or damaged by other contact. Unless the cables are suitably protected, make sure that no cables run under carpeting or across aisles or other walkways. Otherwise you can count on three problems: lawsuits from people who trip, LAN downtime from damaged cables, and electrical shorts that burn down the building.

◆ *Use existing conduit.* Many offices are designed to handle cables (for the electrical, telephone, or other wiring systems) between different office locations. The conduits through which these cables run often have room for additional cables. In some cases, completely unused spare conduit is available. As long as the conduit leads to the specific locations you need, you can install well-protected cables without much difficulty. If you have doubts, hire a LAN consultant *before* you begin.

Be aware that routing cables through conduit often requires that cables be much longer than the line-of-sight distance between two computers. Depending on the conduit layout, 10BASE-T may be more appropriate in such cases than thin Ethernet because of cable length restrictions. For only a few PCs, either method should work.

◆ *Use existing cabling.* Some office buildings, especially newer buildings, were designed to accommodate computer cabling. Such buildings already have extra thin coaxial cable or unshielded twisted-pair cable routed to all offices, complete with convenient plugs and jacks. If existing cable meets the IEEE specifications, you

Planning a NetWare Lite LAN

can save a great deal of time, trouble, and money by using the built-in cables. Along with preexisting cabling, such office buildings often have wiring closets with punch-down blocks. If you choose, you may be able to install external 10BASE-T hubs in a wiring closet. Check with the building engineer, contractor, or architect to determine the locations of wiring closets and the specifications of the preinstalled cable. Again, a LAN consultant may make this process easier for you.

✦ *Install a wireless LAN.* Chapter 1 mentioned wireless LANs. If you are willing to pay a great deal more and risk the dangers of using technology not quite as mature as cable-based LANs, you can eliminate cabling problems. Several vendors now offer wireless LAN systems.

The Floor Plan

To get a handle on the scope of your cabling needs, make a drawing of your office layout, marking the locations of planned LAN-connected PCs. Use a real floor-plan blueprint, if possible, but if a formal floor plan isn't available, make your own rough sketch. Show all offices, closets, and walls, as well as major furniture—desks, file cabinets, computer tables, and so on. Needless to say, a blueprint that shows electrical and other conduit is ideal as a starting point for this drawing.

NOTE: Planning your LAN layout with a formal floor plan is not critical for a simple two- or three-computer LAN, but for larger LANs, the process can be a lifesaver.

If you plan to share peripheral devices, mark their most likely locations also. A shared printer is important in most work groups. When you plan the printer location, keep in mind that a shared printer generates a great deal of nearby foot traffic as people come to pick up their printed output. Also, a printer needs care and feeding—someone must refill paper trays and unclog paper jams. The best printer location is at the center of all the users, near someone who can do the occasional maintenance. Because the foot traffic can be disrupting in the area immediately adjacent to the printer, placing a busy shared printer inside someone's office seldom works out well. Make sure that the printer cable stretches between the server PC and your planned printer location. Measure ahead of time so that if you need a longer printer cable, you won't have to rush out to buy it on LAN installation day.

Now study your sketch to determine how to connect cables between computers. Unless you already have decided between thin Ethernet and 10BASE-T, draw different-colored lines for each topology. Incorporate existing cables or available conduit, if possible.

Thin Ethernet Cable Planning

Although a thin Ethernet LAN is easier than 10BASE-T to design (and in most cases, less expensive), planning the cable for 10BASE-T is sometimes easier in a given office environment. To plan cabling for thin Ethernet, play "connect the dots" on your floor plan. In this case, the dots are the nodes of the proposed LAN. Because thin Ethernet uses a bus topology, you connect the PCs in one long jagged line. Each PC connects to exactly two others, except the PC at each end, which connects to only one other. You have to decide which connection sequence to use. The best sequence is not only the easiest to cable physically, but also the least expensive.

Start by drawing connection lines from one end of the chain of PCs to the other, in the longest dimension of your office. If your office layout is short and wide, for example, start at the far left and, moving from left to right, connect each PC to the next, ending with the one farthest to the right. If the floor plan is tall but narrow, start at the top and proceed to the bottom. When all the PCs in your drawing are connected, you have created one possible cabling scheme.

Is this the *best* possible cabling sequence? Unless you have only two or three computers, probably not. The important question is whether your first scheme is *acceptable*. Two factors make a scheme acceptable:

- A way to run a cable between each connected PC must exist
- The total length must not exceed the thin Ethernet limit of 185 meters (607 feet)

Planning a NetWare Lite LAN 67

Notice that the important factor here is not the total length of the lines you have drawn. Real cable lengths are what matters. If you route the cables through conduit, up through ceiling tiles, or down through false floors, how long must the cables be?

If you are working with a good floor plan, you can make good estimates from the drawing. Redraw the lines and show the paths you expect the cables to take. Add the up-and-down distances for the portions that turn up through the ceiling or turn down under or along the floor. Then add at least an extra five feet as "slop," to ensure that a small curve or two doesn't leave you a foot short. An extra ten feet is even safer. If you need to allow users the freedom to move the PCs in their offices, be sure to provide plenty of extra cable length. By using cables that are much too long, you add to the cable-jumble problem and increase the chances of exceeding the maximum allowable total cable length at some point.

To check cable lengths and routes, cut rope or string to common cable lengths (25, 50, or 100 feet) and try them out.

Next, drawing in hand, go to the planned LAN area. Verify that each cable can run as indicated in the sketch; modify the drawing, as necessary. See whether changing the connection sequence simplifies the cabling. Two of the PCs, for example, may be close together but have a major obstacle—a bank vault, a refrigerator, or an elevator shaft—between them. Instead of connecting the two PCs directly, cabling may be easier if you connect the first PC to a third PC, off to the side of the obstacle, and then connect that one to the second PC. Follow the cabling path of least resistance.

10BASE-T Cable and Hub Planning

Generally, 10BASE-T LAN cards and cables are better than thin Ethernet in offices in which PCs are spread out or rearranged often. Thin Ethernet is better where the PCs are close together and don't move often. The definitions of "spread out" and "close together" are fuzzy; a large gray area exists between the two extremes.

For 10BASE-T, you need to pick one or more tentative hub locations before you look at cable paths. If you anticipate internal card-based hubs located inside PCs, mark which computers will contain hubs; then show the cable connections to each PC. If you use other standard IEEE 802.3 10BASE-T hub products, you can install a hub in a closet or wall cabinet. Although these external hubs may enable you to connect more computers than you can with internal hubs, chances are good that the external hubs are much more expensive than the internal ones. Add to your drawing a set of different-colored lines (from the thin Ethernet lines) that show how the hub connects to each PC.

Now, as you did for thin Ethernet, go to the workgroup area and determine exactly where the cables will be located. Allow extra length, if necessary, for conduit routes or up-and-down runs through ceilings and floors. Again, allow five or ten extra feet to be safe. Providing extra cable length is less of a problem for 10BASE-T than for thin Ethernet because the maximum length of 100 meters applies to each connection between hub and computer, not the total length of all cables. Change the drawing, if necessary, to reflect the cable locations you select.

Because unshielded twisted-pair cables are more susceptible than thin coaxial cable to electromagnetic interference, you must plan more carefully for 10BASE-T LANs. Try to avoid installing UTP cables near large electric motors, fluorescent lights, air conditioners, and other possible electronic hazards. Even telephones produce potentially harmful electromagnetic fields. If such exposures cannot be avoided, consider using shielded twisted-pair wiring in these areas to reduce the risk.

Office Environment

Surge protectors provide inexpensive protection for your PC.

When you plan your network, keep in mind the workgroup's office environment. The quality of the electrical supply is a fundamental issue. Can you expect frequent power failures, brownouts, or electrical surges? Most commercially provided power is not pure and regular. Inexpensive electrical surge suppressors and filters are well worth the cost as a first line of protection. For less than $20 you can buy a six- or eight-outlet surge suppressor/filter to reduce the chances of your PCs being damaged by irregularities. Whether you have a LAN or not, you should have this cheap insurance.

If your workgroup experiences frequent power failures or your planned usage of the LAN and its computers is especially critical, consider an *uninterruptable power system* (UPS). A UPS provides an independent source of power. Find out whether your building already has a UPS installed in some or all areas. If not, investigate small UPS products for your workgroup. A UPS product can keep your computers running for a

Planning a NetWare Lite LAN

few minutes (or longer) after a power failure, allowing you to perform a few critical tasks and gracefully shut down your workstations and servers. NetWare Lite supports many UPS products (for details, see Chapter 13, "Troubleshooting").

Other environmental hazards exist in most office environments. As long as you are planning for a LAN, this is a good time to look at your exposure to other risks, such as excessive dust, water leakage, inadequate building security, and anything else that might cause damage to your LAN, computers, data, and other valuables.

Sources of LAN Equipment

You have a wide variety of hardware components from which to choose when planning your LAN. Novell licenses several hardware vendors to market starter kits based on thin Ethernet cards and cables. Many vendors manufacture 10BASE-T cards and cables. And most token-ring and ARCnet products are compatible with NetWare Lite.

Having decided what to buy, you must choose whether to buy from a local computer dealer who sells NetWare-Lite-compatible products, a local consultant, or a mail-order dealer. How do you decide?

Who you purchase your equipment from depends on your experience and comfort levels.

Much of the answer depends on what makes you comfortable. Some people love to buy by mail order to get the lowest prices, others would never buy without local support. Some people want a technical expert to configure and install everything, others want to do it themselves and learn from direct involvement. You undoubtedly have a preference already, but the following information may clarify some issues.

A small, simple, NetWare Lite Ethernet starter kit is really not difficult to buy, install, and run. As you have seen, the starter kit has all the hardware and software you need to connect the first two computers: two Ethernet LAN cards, two BNC T-connectors, two terminators, a connecting cable, and two copies of the NetWare Lite operating system software. An add-on kit provides everything you need to add a single node to the network. Typically, the cables in these kits are 20 or 25 feet long; you may need to buy a separate cable if your PCs are more than 20 feet apart.

Be sure to buy kits with LAN cards appropriate for the internal data buses of your computers (ISA or MCA). For more information about

Ethernet starter kits and the different kinds of NetWare-Lite-compatible LAN cards, see Chapter 4, "Installing the LAN Hardware."

If you have a small workgroup for which installing the LAN will not present major cabling or hardware problems (as described in this chapter), you undoubtedly can buy the equipment and do the installation yourself. Shop around for the best price. If you cannot make the LAN work, *then* you can call a Novell dealer or consultant to help you. (Of course, if you don't feel confident about installing the LAN yourself, hire a consultant before you begin.)

If your LAN needs are complicated, and you are not comfortable taking on a big project by yourself, bring in someone with expertise. Many computer dealers have experience with these matters. If not, the dealer can probably refer you to a local consultant who can help.

To minimize costs, you may like the idea of buying the LAN cards, cables, and software from different sources. This approach can work just fine, but clearly is a little more complicated than getting everything from a single dealer or mail-order house. Again, go with the approach that makes you comfortable. If you want to play it safe, get everything from one local dealer.

Important Software Applications

For many people, the central issue when planning a LAN concerns specific software applications. You install a LAN to solve problems for your workgroup, as discussed in Chapter 2. If your LAN objectives are simply to share a printer and be able to copy files to and from a shared disk, you may not care about particular LAN applications.

The software you want to use is an important consideration in planning, installing, and using your LAN.

If you *do* want to use special LAN applications (such as e-mail or resource schedulers) or LAN versions of word processors, spreadsheets, or databases, itemize your needs. The LAN hardware, LAN NOS, and application software must work together to produce a smoothly running LAN. Analyze your workgroup needs to see how the LAN and the application software address those needs.

If you have not yet picked the application software, study the alternatives and verify NetWare Lite compatibility. Analyze who in the group does what (and how, and why, and when). Be open to new ways of doing things, but recognize that many people do not adapt well to

Planning a NetWare Lite LAN

change. Talk to people who use the candidate products to be sure that the products really do what you need and that advertisers' claims are accurate.

Chapter 10, "Using Application Software on the LAN," surveys major applications for compatibility with NetWare Lite. Determine which applications best fit your workgroup, and plan to acquire and use these products.

Unless you plan a large LAN (more than 15 users) across which everyone pushes a great deal of data (constant database searching, for example), 10 Mbps (megabits per second) Ethernet LANs should have plenty of capacity for your needs. Other components, particularly server PCs and their hard disks, may be stretched to their maximum capacities, but the speed of the LAN itself is almost never the constraining factor. If you use 2.5 Mbps ARCnet cards, however, LAN throughput may be a problem.

Keep in mind that a LAN, along with its servers and server peripherals, is a shared resource. Whenever people have to share things, conflicts are possible and problems can arise. Try to plan in advance exactly who is going to use what, and how often. Be prepared to expand your resources (hard disk size, server speed, number of shared printers, and so on), if necessary. The more critical the applications you share on the LAN, the greater the need for careful planning.

Your Available Budget

Budget constraints may override all other LAN-planning issues. If minimal cost is essential, ARCnet LAN cards and cables are your best bet. As explained earlier in this chapter, thin Ethernet provides good performance and features at a modest price. For extravagant budgets (if there is such a thing), a wireless LAN is feasible. Try to estimate costs accurately and carefully.

Planning Checklists

Appendix B, "Checklists for Planning a LAN," contains a series of checklists that summarize the planning issues discussed in this chapter. You can use these lists as the backbone of your network plan.

CHAPTER

4 INSTALLING THE LAN HARDWARE

Having formed a solid plan for your NetWare Lite LAN, you are ready to install the necessary hardware and software. This chapter focuses on the hardware installation: inserting a LAN card in each computer and connecting the computers together with cables and terminators. Chapter 5 covers the installation of the NetWare Lite software.

As you have seen, NetWare Lite works with a variety of cabling hardware and topologies, including thin and thick Ethernet, twisted-pair

10BASE-T configurations, token ring, and ARCnet. Providing detailed installation instructions for the great variety of available LAN cards and cabling schemes is not the purpose of this book. Instead, this chapter concentrates on installing the most popular configuration for new NetWare Lite LANs: thin Ethernet cards and cables. Some details of installing 10BASE-T cards are provided also. If you intend to install LAN hardware not covered in this chapter, consult the documentation supplied with your hardware or get expert help.

Perhaps your LAN hardware is installed already. You may have had a consultant do professional installation or you may be using existing hardware installed for another LAN. If your LAN hardware is already in place, you may skip ahead to Chapter 5, "Installing the NetWare Lite Software." Be sure that you know what LAN cards are installed in your computers.

One comforting thought for the do-it-yourselfer before you begin: Don't be afraid. The long lists of installation details may seem intimidating at first glance, but each step is quite simple. Read each step carefully and you will see that you can, if you choose, easily install the hardware (and software) for a small NetWare Lite LAN. For a two-computer LAN, you can probably complete the entire process in less than an hour.

If the idea of removing a computer's cover to install a LAN card is too frightening to even consider, then by all means have someone else install the hardware. You can get professional help installing the software also. This chapter and the next explain details of the installation process so that you can decide.

Ethernet LAN Products

Before installing each LAN card, make sure the card is appropriate for the computer bus of the intended PC. You need ISA cards for ISA-bus computers and MCA cards for Micro Channel PS/2 computers.

NetWare Lite works with LAN cards supplied by many vendors. You can be sure that NetWare Lite supports your LAN card if the card sports the Novell name. Note that Novell does not manufacture any LAN cards but rather licenses several hardware vendors to manufacture products under the Novell name. The most prominent of these hardware

Installing the LAN Hardware

> ### The Difference Between Installing and Starting the Network
>
> Note that the installation of the LAN hardware and software does *not* actually start the communication process between the connected computers. After installation, you must *start* NetWare Lite in order to share resources or communicate across the LAN. The situation is analogous to a software application, say a word processor, that you have stored on a hard disk. The simple process of installing the word processor on the hard disk does not actually invoke the application. You still have to start the word processor to do useful work. Similarly, as explained in the next chapter, when you finish the installation of NetWare Lite, you must start NetWare Lite to begin resource sharing.

vendors is Eagle Technology, which has worked closely with Novell for several years.

Here is a quick look at the Novell/Eagle line of Ethernet LAN products appropriate for NetWare Lite. These products transmit data over the LAN at 10 megabits (10 million bits) per second and adhere to the IEEE 802.3 standards. Quoted prices represent current retail and are subject to change. Substantial discounts are available from many dealers.

Ethernet LAN Adapter Cards

Four different Novell/Eagle LAN cards occur commonly in Ethernet NetWare Lite LANs: NE2000 (16-bit ISA), NE1000 (8-bit ISA), NE/2 (16-bit Micro Channel), and NE2000T (16-bit 10BASE-T). Each card is designed for a particular computer bus and cabling scheme.

NE2000 16-Bit ISA Ethernet Adapter

The NE2000 is designed for the 16-bit bus of *Industry Standard Architecture* (ISA) computers, also known as the AT bus. The target computers are the IBM-compatible models with 80286, 386, or 486 processors. The NE2000 works on *Extended Industry Standard Architecture*

(EISA) machines as well. A BNC connector on the back of the card supports standard thin Ethernet coaxial cabling. The card can support thick Ethernet cabling also, but most new LAN installations use thin Ethernet. The retail price of this card is approximately $235.

NE/2 16-Bit Micro Channel Ethernet Adapter

A Micro Channel version of the NE2000, the NE/2 is designed for IBM PS/2 computers that use the Micro Channel Adapter (MCA) architecture. This card supports thin and thick Ethernet cabling. Be aware that some PS/2 computers (mostly the lower-numbered models) do *not* use the Micro Channel card type, but instead use the old AT-type, or ISA, cards. The NE/2 costs approximately $80 more than the NE2000.

NE1000 8-Bit ISA Ethernet Adapter

An 8-bit version of the NE2000, the NE1000 works on the 8-bit bus of the IBM PC, PC XT, and compatible computers. The card supports both thin and thick Ethernet cabling. The cost is approximately $30 less than that of the NE2000.

NE2000T 16-Bit ISA 10BASE-T Adapter

A variant of the NE2000, this card supports 10BASE-T unshielded twisted-pair cabling. Cables route directly from this card to a 10BASE-T hub. You may use these cards if your office is already wired for twisted-pair cabling. The NE2000T is priced the same as the NE2000.

Ethernet Starter Kits

Starter kits based on either the NE2000 or the NE/2 LAN cards are available. Each starter kit contains all the hardware and software you need to construct a two-node LAN (two LAN cards, cable, terminators, two copies of the NetWare Lite operating system, and manuals). The simplest way to install, say, a five-node LAN, is to buy a LAN starter kit as well as three additional LAN cards and three more cables of the same type. Add-on kits, designed to extend an existing LAN with an additional node, include a single LAN card, cable, and one copy of NetWare Lite. The best-selling starter kit uses the NE2000 card and thin coaxial cable.

NE2000 Starter Kit (ISA)

This starter kit includes two NE2000 cards, a 20-foot coaxial cable, two terminators, and two copies of NetWare Lite. If you want to connect two ISA computers located no more than about 15 feet apart, this kit has all you need. The retail cost is approximately $600.

NE/2 Starter Kit (MCA)

The Micro Channel version for thin Ethernet, this starter kit includes two NE/2 LAN cards, connecting cable, terminators, and two copies of NetWare Lite.

Purchasing Hardware

You can obtain LAN hardware from many sources and in many configurations. Three general approaches are possible:

1. NetWare Lite starter and add-on kits. The simplest way to buy hardware (and software) is to buy a NetWare Lite starter kit and sufficient add-on Kits. The starter kit includes all the proper components for the first two computers. If you want to connect more than two computers, buy NetWare Lite add-on kits as necessary. You get everything you need in convenient packages.

2. NetWare Lite software and independent hardware components. You don't have to buy any hardware from one of Novell's licensed hardware vendors. You can choose to buy other manufacturers' LAN cards, cables, connectors, terminators, hubs, and any other hardware you need. You will need to buy a copy of the NetWare Lite software for each node of your LAN, however.

3. A combination of the first two approaches. You can mix the two approaches in countless ways. One example is to buy a starter kit for the first two nodes, then buy low-cost independent LAN cards and NetWare Lite software for additional nodes. Another example is to buy a starter kit plus all the NetWare Lite LAN cards you need, but use cable that is prewired in the building. Even with starter and add-on kits, you may need to buy cables longer than the 20-foot cables supplied with the kits.

As you can see, you can acquire your hardware from one of Novell's licensed NetWare Lite vendors or from an independent company.

Installation issues vary, depending on the hardware you use. This chapter first examines the standard Novell-licensed hardware, and then looks at installation issues concerning hardware from independent vendors.

Installation Overview

This section, an introduction to hardware installation, offers a step-by-step overview of the installation process. Detailed instructions are in the "Installation Details" section, which follows.

Because the NE2000 is the most popular LAN card for new NetWare Lite LANs, the instructions in this chapter focus on the installation of a thin Ethernet LAN, using the NE2000 starter kit. The instructions are much the same for installations based on NE/2 cards and on LAN cards from various manufacturers. Throughout the "Installation Details" section, notes explain installation issues that arise with other LAN cards (whether from Novell or another manufacturer) and other cabling.

Follow these steps to install Netware Lite hardware:

1. Verify that the settings for each LAN card do not conflict with other devices in the PCs. If necessary, change the card settings as appropriate for each computer.
2. Turn off the power to each computer and remove the cover from each PC.
3. Install the NE2000 LAN card in each PC.
4. Attach a BNC T-connector to the appropriate socket on the back edge of each LAN card.
5. Reinstall the computer covers.
6. Connect the PCs together by attaching thin coaxial cables to the T-connectors on the back of the LAN cards.
7. Route the cables to safe, protected locations between the computers.
8. Attach terminators to the unused sides of the two BNC T-connectors at each end of the daisy chain of cables.
9. Turn on the power to each computer. Verify that the computers still work as before. Until you install and start the LAN software, you should notice no difference in computer operation.

Installing the LAN Hardware

Installation Details

This section examines in depth the installation steps outlined in the preceding section. The instructions focus on the installation of an NE2000 starter kit, but comments pertaining to other cards are included.

Each starter kit contains two LAN cards. If you are installing a LAN with more than two nodes, buy an extra LAN card and cable for each additional PC. An add-on kit contains a single LAN card and cable (and software) in one convenient package.

Verify Card Settings

Certain options on Novell's LAN cards are preset. These settings are called the *default settings*; you choose them by default if you take no action. Although in most cases the default settings are exactly what you want, some situations call for other settings. Also, to be sure of no mistakes, you should examine each LAN card to verify that the factory correctly set the defaults to what you expect. For both reasons, you should review the following explanations with the LAN cards in front of you.

Like most LAN cards, the NE2000 makes use of tiny double-slot devices called jumpers to set options. A *jumper*, which is rectangular and about the size of a contact lens, makes a connection between two protruding *pins* (pairs of prong-like wires that occupy areas on the card). You select different card settings by sliding the jumper off one pin pair and onto another. You can grab a jumper with your fingers or needle-nosed pliers (carefully) and pull the jumper away from the card. Then attach it to the pin pair you want by pushing the jumper onto the pins. Compare your newly attached jumper with other jumpers on the card to be sure that you have the jumper properly aligned and pushed down all the way.

CAUTION: Handle a LAN card carefully to avoid damage to the card. Before you touch the card, touch a grounded piece of metal to discharge your body's buildup of static electricity. (Your computer case is grounded if the power cord is plugged into a grounded outlet.) Handle the card by the edges—don't touch the delicate chips. When you move jumpers, put the card on a sheet of the packing foam that protected the card in the box.

Default Settings and Default Values

The installation instructions in this chapter, and many other computer-related hardware and software instructions, refer to *default settings*, *default values*, or just *defaults*. These terms (used pretty much interchangeably) refer to a selection you make by default if you don't override or change a factory preset selection. In other words, you give tacit approval to the choice unless you take an action to change it.

On the NE2000 card, for example, the default value for the IRQ selection is 3. (IRQ is explained in this section.) This means that unless you change the IRQ setting by moving a little connector called a *jumper*, you choose to use IRQ 3 by default.

Similarly, the installation process for many software applications shows (onscreen) certain settings preset to particular values. A word processor, for example, might preset the effect of the [Ins] key to insert characters rather than overtype. You can change the preset values; if you don't, you are in effect accepting these default values.

In computer jargon, the term "default" does not have the negative connotation associated with "defaulting" on a loan or winning a contest by default (forfeit). Don't lose any sleep over accepting a default value—it's just a convenience, designed to facilitate your selection of a common choice. Just make sure that the value is what you want. Most of the time it will be.

For the NE2000 card, two jumper selections must be made: the IRQ number and the I/O Base Address. Although the factory defaults for these values probably are exactly what you want, you may have to change these defaults, depending on your system configuration.

Verifying these jumpers is the trickiest part of LAN hardware installation. The IRQ and I/O Base Address jumper blocks are located near the middle of the NE2000 card. To find the jumpers, consult the documentation that comes with the board.

Installing the LAN Hardware

> **NOTE:** If your LAN does not work when first tested after installation, a conflict in the IRQ or I/O Base Address settings is the most likely cause.

Note that NE/2 and other Micro Channel LAN cards do not require that you set these jumpers. The MCA bus does not use IRQ and I/O Base Addresses.

IRQ

The IRQ jumper selects the interrupt request (IRQ) line the LAN card uses to communicate with the computer's processor. The LAN card often needs the computer's main processor to take action on behalf of the LAN. The processor interrupts its current work, takes the action, and then resumes work. An *IRQ line* is the communications channel by which the processor permits these "shoulder tap" interrupts from connected devices.

Besides the LAN cards, other hardware devices in the computer also use IRQs. If two devices try to use the same IRQ number, a conflict arises. This type of conflict may cause unpredictable results, such as one or both devices not working properly or the computer locking up and refusing to respond. You need to be sure that your LAN card's IRQ number is not used by some other device in the computer. On the NE2000 card, the default IRQ selection is 3.

PC AT-class computers (286 or higher processors) have 16 IRQ lines, numbered from 0 to 15. PC XT-class computers (with an 8088 or 8086 processor), have only eight IRQ lines, numbered from 0 to 7.

The NE2000 card permits an IRQ setting of 2, 3, 4, or 5. (This is relatively restrictive. Boards from other manufacturers often permit the IRQ number to be selected from 2 to 15.) The default IRQ of 3 usually does not conflict with other devices installed in the PCs. Sometimes there is a conflict from a device attached to the COM2 port. Be aware that a bus mouse, sound card, or other device may use any IRQ; check the device's manual to see whether a conflict with IRQ 3 exists. Also, some utility programs such as Norton Utilities and PC Tools have options to display the IRQ settings in use. If a conflict exists, you must reset the IRQ number on the LAN card (or on the card of the conflicting device).

The IRQ jumper block consists of four pin pairs, across one of which the jumper must be set. To locate the IRQ block on the LAN card, consult your card's documentation. Figure 4-1 shows the jumper settings corresponding to the available IRQs.

I/O Base Address

An *I/O* (Input/Output) *port address* provides a data area used by the processor and peripheral devices (such as LAN cards) to send data back and forth. Different devices must not try to use the same I/O port address numbers. The NE2000 card uses a series of I/O port addresses, starting with a number called an *I/O Base Address*. The default base address is 300H. By convention, the addresses are specified in *hexadecimal notation* (which is what the H in "300H" represents). Because the NE2000 needs 32 addresses (20H), the default 300H uses up the address range from 300H to 31FH.

On the NE2000 card, the jumper block for the I/O Base address is located next to the IRQ jumper block. You must select one of four available base addresses: 300H, 320H, 340H, or 360H. The I/O Base block consists of three pairs of pins onto which none, one, or two jumpers must be attached to choose one of the four possible

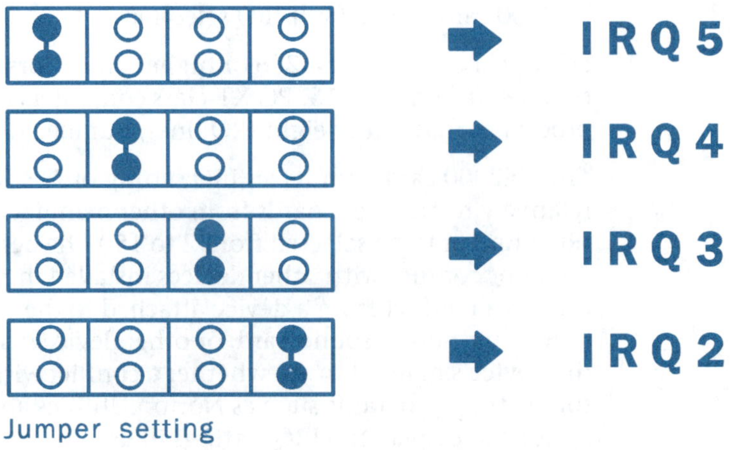

Jumper settings on the NE2000 IRQ block
Figure 4-1.

Jumper setting → IRQ 5, IRQ 4, IRQ 3, IRQ 2

Installing the LAN Hardware

base-address values (see Figure 4-2). The default setting of 300H requires two jumpers to be set on the two leftmost pairs of pins. If no jumpers are engaged, the base address is 360H.

Power Off and Remove Cover

Before you remove the cover from any computer so that you can work inside the machine, turn off the power switch. Also turn off any devices attached to the computer, such as monitors or printers. Discharge the static electricity from your body by touching a grounded piece of metal. (Your computer case is grounded if the power cord is attached to a grounded outlet.)

For extra safety, disconnect the computer's power cable. This step protects both you and the computer from potential damage.

With the power off, remove the computer's cover to gain access to the inside. If you are unfamiliar with this process for your computer, check your PC's *Guide to Operation* (or whatever the title of its hardware reference manual may be). First, remove anything resting on top of the computer (such as a monitor). From the back of most computers, you must remove from two to six screws (five is common). Many computers also have screws on the back that you should *not* remove. Check your manual to avoid a mistake. After you remove the screws, you can remove the cover by sliding it to the front, sliding it to the back, lifting

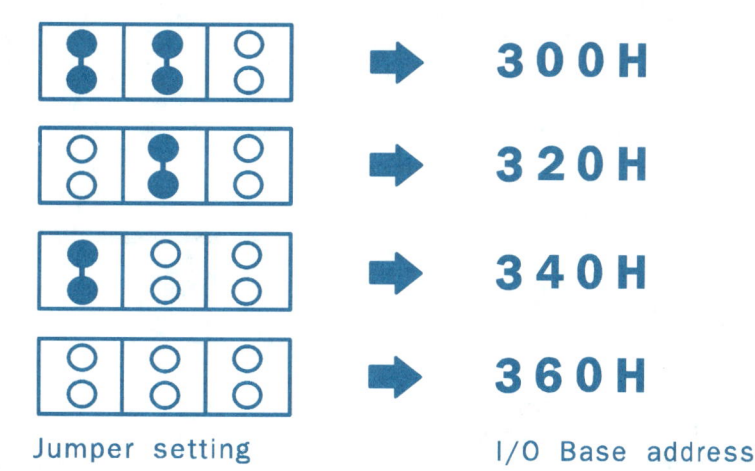

Jumper settings on the NE2000 I/O Base Address block
Figure 4-2.

Jumper setting	I/O Base address
●● ●● ○○	300H
○○ ●● ○○	320H
●● ○○ ○○	340H
○○ ○○ ○○	360H

it, or a combination of movements (depending on the computer). Typically you slide the cover toward the front of the computer, as shown in Figure 4-3. Remove the cover slowly, being careful not to snag any internal cables. Put the cover out of the way for the moment. Don't lose the screws.

Choose Slot and Remove Cover Plate

Choose any unused expansion slot to receive the LAN card. For most computers, any slot will work. For AT-class computers (286, 386, or 486 processors), slots are either 8- or 16-bit. (XT-class computers have 8-bit slots only. Some 386 and 486 computers also have one or two 32-bit slots. Special cards are required for 32-bit slots; don't use a 32-bit slot for the LAN card.) Eight-bit slots are shorter than 16-bit slots. That is, the slot into which you insert the card's edge connector is shorter; the overall length of the space allotted for the card is usually the same. Some computers have one or two slots that have room only for short expansion cards, usually called *half-cards*. These short spaces may use either 8- or 16-bit slots (look at the expansion slot), but usually are 8-bit. Check your hardware manual if you have any doubt about which slots are 8-bit and which are 16-bit slots.

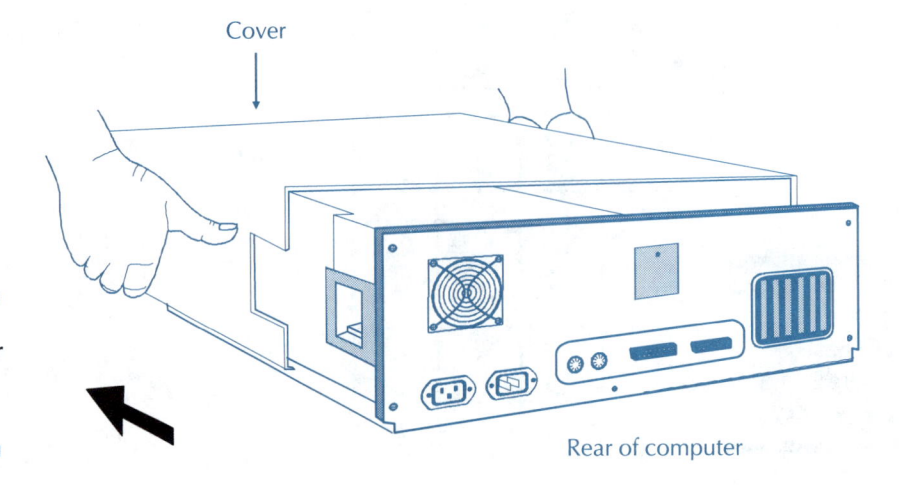

Sliding the computer cover forward
Figure 4-3.

Installing the LAN Hardware

To install a 16-bit card such as the NE2000, you must use a 16-bit slot. An 8-bit card such as the NE1000 will work in either an 8- or 16-bit slot. If you are installing an 8-bit card and have a choice between an 8-bit or 16-bit slot, you may as well choose the 8-bit slot in case you later need the 16-bit one for a 16-bit card.

Try to position your computer cards for ease of access.

If your computer has several unused slots (an uncommon luxury), pick the slot isolated as much as possible from the already-occupied slots. Don't squeeze all the expansion cards close together. By spreading out your cards, you give yourself easier access to each of them, in case you need to remove a card or change a jumper on the card. Another advantage is that cables which come out the back of the computer are spread apart from each other, reducing knuckle scrapes and profanity. Also, spreading apart your cards provides each card with more ventilated air space, which reduces the chance of damage from overheating.

The NE2000, NE1000, NE/2 and most thin Ethernet cards often are packaged with the BNC T-connector attached to the back edge of the card. If your card is packaged this way, you probably need to remove the T-connector before you install the card in your computer. Grab the ridged ring around the T-connector (*not* the crossbar part of the T-connector) and turn the ridge one-quarter turn counterclockwise. This loosens the connector so that you can slide the T-connector off the card. The NE2000T (10BASE-T twisted-pair) card has no protruding connector, just a socket for an RJ45 plug.

On the back of the computer, behind each expansion slot, is a cover plate that seals the rear of the computer when the expansion slot is empty. Before inserting the LAN card, you must take out the cover plate protecting the slot you want to use. Remove the screw that holds the plate in place and lift the plate (see Figure 4-4). Save the plate, in case you remove the card some day. (Some people use the plates as letter openers.) Keep the screw handy to attach the LAN card you are about to install.

Install the LAN Card

To insert the LAN card into the slot, hold the card by the top of its chrome mounting bracket with one hand and on the opposite edge with the other hand. The chrome edge goes toward the rear of the

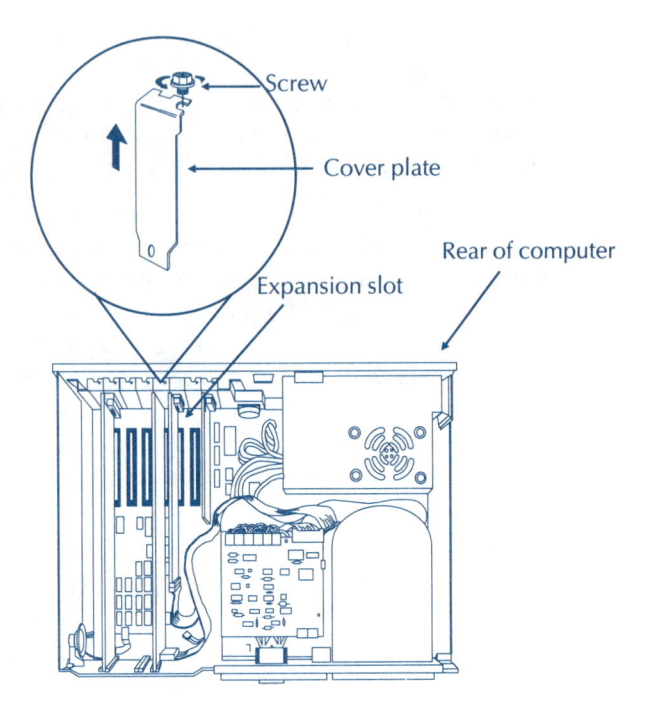

Figure 4-4. Removing the cover plate

computer; the gilded edge connector, toward the empty expansion slot (see Figure 4-5). Gently move the card down toward the slot while watching to make sure that the edge connector fits properly into the slot on the computer motherboard. When the card is in place, push down on the mounting bracket and top edge of the card until the card clunks into place. (It doesn't quite click, snap, or slide. It clunks.) Don't force it. If necessary, rock the card back and forth slightly by pressing on the top of the card near the front and back ends. When properly seated in the slot, the card stays firmly in place and the screw hole on the top back edge of the computer aligns with the notch on the card's mounting bracket. To attach the LAN card's mounting bracket to the computer, use the screw you removed with the cover plate.

Attach BNC T-Connector

Reattach the BNC T-connector to the rear of the LAN card. (You can skip this step with 10BASE-T cards using twisted pair cables because

Installing the LAN Hardware

Figure 4-5. Aligning the LAN card for installation

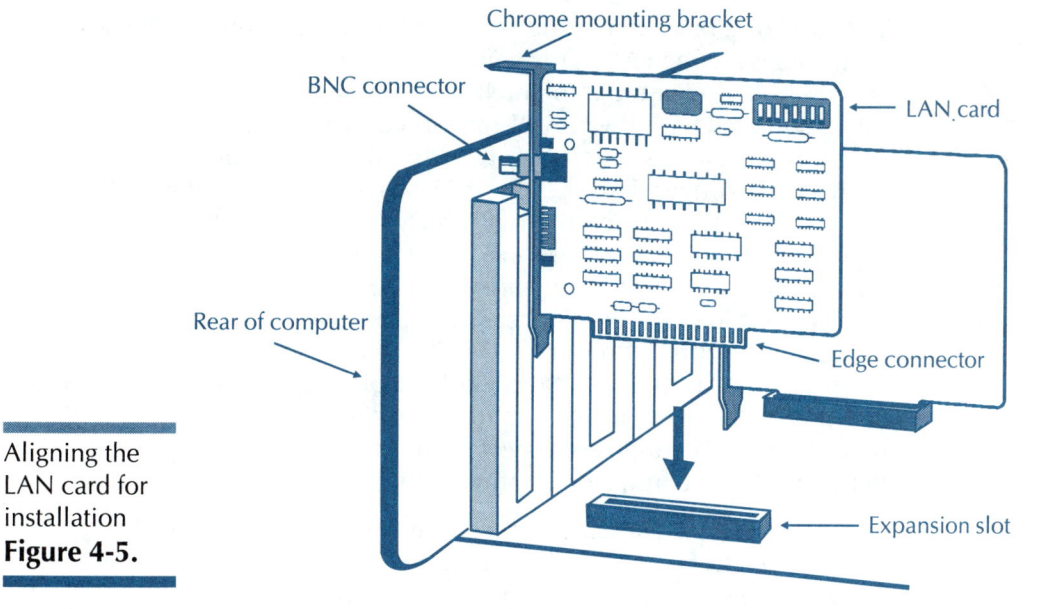

[Diagram labels: Chrome mounting bracket, BNC connector, LAN card, Rear of computer, Edge connector, Expansion slot]

those cards don't use BNC connectors.) Align the T-connector's slotted openings with the pins on the connector that protrudes from the rear of the LAN card. Push the T-connector over the protruding connector and twist the ridged ring one-quarter turn clockwise. The BNC T-connector clicks into place (not a clunk this time) and remains extended out beyond the rear of the computer. Note that you can easily rotate the T-part of the connector that extends beyond the ridged ring.

Reinstall the Computer Cover

Reinstall the computer cover and screw it in place. Be careful not to snag any internal computer cables when you attach the cover.

Attach Cables

Depending on your office layout, you may want to do the next step (routing and protecting cables) before attaching the cables. In some cases you can better manipulate the cables if they are not attached to anything. At other times, you can attach the cables to the cards and then move the spans of cable to your planned locations. Do whatever is best for your office environment.

Selecting a high-quality cable is critical to sucessful LAN operation.

This is a good place to remind you to be absolutely sure you have the right cables for the LAN cards you are using. Just any old thin coaxial cable is not good enough for a reliable thin Ethernet LAN. Of course, cables supplied with the Novell-sponsored starter kits are satisfactory. Even with a starter kit, you may need to purchase other cables if you need a cable longer than the 20- or 25-foot cable included with the kit. Make sure that any thin Ethernet cable you use meets the RG58 A/U specifications. Look for the words "Novell" or "RG58 A/U" printed directly on the cable. Cables marked "RG58 C/U" should be okay, but don't accept RG58/U or RG58 cable. Use one cable type from a single manufacturer throughout the LAN. The larger the LAN, the more important this is. Be sure that the total cable length does not exceed the 185-meter (607-foot) maximum for a NetWare Lite LAN segment. Also, do not directly juxtapose connected computers. The minimum length between BNC T-connectors is one-half meter (1.6 feet).

Similarly, for twisted-pair cable, be sure to comply with the LAN card's specifications. If you have the slightest doubt, contact your dealer or Novell to be sure. Appropriate unshielded twisted-pair cabling is 22, 24, or 26 gauge. The maximum segment length is 100 meters (328 feet) between each LAN card and its hub. Set up and configure the hub the way the hub manufacturer recommends.

For a thin Ethernet LAN, you can rotate each computer's BNC T-connector to route the one or two cables you attach in whatever direction work best. Do not turn the ridged ring; turn the crossbar part of the T.

Attaching the cables to the T-connector is a straightforward process. At the ends of each cable, a BNC connector attaches directly to the T-connector. Simply push the end of the cable over the T-connector, align the slots on the cable's connector with the pins on the T-connector, and turn the cable one-quarter turn clockwise. The BNC connectors click into place.

For a 10BASE-T LAN, insert an RJ45 plug at one end of a cable into the LAN card's RJ45 socket until it clicks into place. The RJ45 plug at the other end of the cable connects to an RJ45 socket on a hub or *concentrator* (a wiring hub such as a punch-down block in a building's electrical closet).

Installing the LAN Hardware

Route and Protect Cables

Chapter 3 discussed the need to route cables to avoid damage and tripping accidents. Follow the steps outlined in that chapter. If you need professional help, don't hesitate to get it. Any time or money you spend on proper cabling and hardware installation is bound to pay substantial dividends in preventing potential problems later.

Attach Terminators

Thin Ethernet cabling with NE1000, NE2000, and similar LAN cards, requires a terminator plug at each end of the daisy chain of cables. No matter how many computers you connect, the daisy chain of cables has exactly two ends. The T-connector at the back of each LAN card has two BNC connectors, each of which must be attached to a cable routed to the adjoining computer or to a terminator sealing the end of the network chain. Figure 4-6 shows the cabling and terminator connections for a three-computer network.

Terminators can be grounded or ungrounded. For NetWare Lite thin Ethernet LANs, at least one of the two terminators should be grounded. Novell starter kits include one grounded and one ungrounded terminator. A 10BASE-T LAN uses no terminators—each cable between a LAN card and a hub is actually a loop (dual twisted-pair), not a two-ended cable.

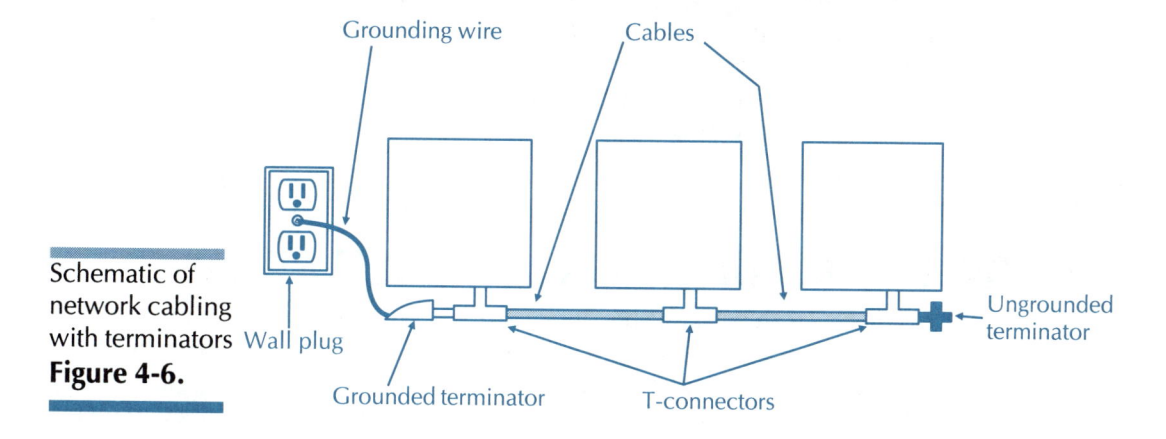

Schematic of network cabling with terminators
Figure 4-6.

A BNC connector attaches on one end of an ungrounded terminator. The other end, which usually has a short rod sticking out or is flat, can appear in various shapes. Grounded terminators are similar, but a grounding wire protrudes from the nonconnector end of the terminator. Also, grounded terminators usually are encased in a rubberized protective sheath.

Terminators attach to the BNC T-connectors in exactly the same way as cables attach. To attach an ungrounded terminator, push it over the T-connector and turn it clockwise into place. The grounded terminator attaches the same way; to facilitate the connection, however, you may have to slide the protective sheath a short distance (temporarily) to expose the metal connector. Attach the grounding wire to a nearby grounding source. A good grounding choice is the metal screw usually found on the wall plug of electrical sockets.

Reattach Power Cords

Reattach the power cords to each computer and to other connected devices. This is a good time to verify that the power cord for each computer is attached to an electrical surge protector and power filter. If you don't have a surge suppressor, you should. It's cheap insurance against a fried computer (and LAN card) in the event of a severe power fluctuation. You can buy electrical surge suppressors at most computer stores and electrical supply stores.

Turn On the Computers

Turn on each computer, one at a time, and verify that each still works as before. Until you install and start the LAN software, you should notice no difference in computer operation. Simply installing the LAN card and cable shouldn't change anything unless something is seriously wrong with the card.

Installation of Independent Hardware

If you buy independent hardware rather than Novell-sponsored products, the installation process is almost the same as that for the NE2000 card. Because other LAN cards may have other jumpers (or adjustable switches) with options different from those described earlier

Installing the LAN Hardware

in this chapter for the NE2000 card, the range of permissible IRQ and I/O Base Addresses may be different.

You are responsible for determining whether other LAN cards offer the features you need. As long as you verify that the cards you choose have software drivers compatible with NetWare Lite, you should at least be able to make the LAN work. (Software drivers are discussed shortly.)

Another big concern if you buy independent hardware is to be sure that you buy all the necessary components, and that the components all work together properly. Doing so is not difficult, but be sure not to overlook anything or make a wrong assumption. Be sure the cable meets specifications. Be sure you can return the LAN cards if they prove unsatisfactory. Don't forget to buy terminators for thin Ethernet. Be sure that a 10BASE-T hub meets 802.3 specifications and has enough ports for the number of nodes you plan. Buy from vendors who guarantee satisfaction and have a track record of stability.

Finally, perhaps your biggest worry is what happens if you buy all the parts, put everything together, and then cannot get the LAN to work. Unless you hire a single consulting firm to buy and install everything, and the firm stands behind its work, you may soon learn the true meaning of passing the buck. Each supplier will claim its products work fine, and your problem must be that one of the other guys sold you some bad equipment. The advantage of getting everything from a single source is that you can go to that source and say, "Look, you sold me all this stuff, so what's wrong. Please fix it!"

Fortunately, this problem isn't too likely if you just exercise a little care to ensure that all parts meet specifications and are compatible with NetWare Lite. Read the chapter on troubleshooting (Chapter 13) to see how you can isolate whatever problems you encounter. If all else fails, or if you don't want to take the time to fix a problem, you can call the nearest Novell dealer or an independent consultant who has worked with NetWare Lite. You may spend some extra money, but you should be up and running quickly.

Verifying the Hardware Drivers

Before moving on to software installation in the next chapter, you should ensure that NetWare Lite offers software drivers that support the LAN cards you have installed. A *driver* is a software program that acts as an interface between a main piece of software and a hardware device. In this case, the driver enables the main NetWare Lite software to make the LAN card respond appropriately to various requests.

NetWare Lite ships with drivers for several LAN cards. Table 4-1 lists the drivers and the supported cards for NetWare Lite version 1.1. If you are using version 1.0, you will not have the NE1500T.COM or NE2100.COM drivers. During the software-installation process, you must select the proper driver from the available choices. Chapter 5 explains how.

If your LAN card is not on this list, all may still be well. Many vendors make LAN cards that are compatible with the drivers on this list. For example, several vendors make 16-bit ISA Ethernet cards compatible with the NE2000.COM card and driver. If you are not sure, check your card's documentation or contact the manufacturer.

If your card does not use one of the standard NetWare Lite drivers, you must get a NetWare-Lite-compatible driver for your LAN card. Many cards come with their own software drivers. Again, check with the card's manufacturer if you are in doubt.

Software Drivers and Supported LAN Cards
Table 4-1.

Driver Name	Supported LAN Cards
NE2000.COM	Novell/Eagle NE2000 Artisoft AE-2
NE1000.COM	Novell/Eagle NE1000
NE2.COM	Novell/Eagle NE/2
NE1500T.COM	Novell/Eagle NE1500T
NE2100.COM	Novell/Eagle NE2100
3C503.COM	3Com EtherLink II
3C523.COM	3Com EtherLink/MC
PCN2L.COM	IBM PC Network Baseband adapters
TOKEN.COM	IBM Token-Ring adapters

C H A P T E R

CHAPTER

5
INSTALLING THE NETWARE LITE SOFTWARE

With the LAN hardware in place, you can install the NetWare Lite software. The process is relatively straightforward. You install a separate copy of NetWare Lite on the hard disk of each computer. (For machines without a hard disk, you can install NetWare Lite on a floppy disk.)

This chapter takes you, step by step, through the software installation process, which concludes with a test to verify that the nodes are correctly connected and able to communicate. In the next chapter, you initiate NetWare Lite and begin true networking.

CAUTION: You must install a separate copy of the NetWare Lite software on each node of the network. Novell licenses you to install one copy of NetWare Lite on a single machine. You violate the license if you use the same Novell disk to install NetWare Lite on more than one machine. Novell safeguards this license by transferring to the installed software unique identification information stored on each NetWare Lite disk. When the network is up and running, NetWare Lite tracks each node by its particular identification information. If multiple copies of a particular ID are found, an error message warns you of software license violations. Respect Novell's licensing rights and buy a separate copy of NetWare Lite for each node of your network.

Prerequisites for Software Installation

Before you start installing the software, you need to answer the following questions about each node of your network:

- What LAN card is installed in the machine?
- What IRQ and I/O Base Address are set on the LAN card?
- Do you want the node to be a server, a client, or both?

These three questions raise some important issues relevant to the installation process.

The LAN Card

You need to know what kind of LAN card is installed in each machine to know which software driver is required for that LAN card. During the installation of NetWare Lite, you will indicate the proper driver for the LAN card installed on each machine.

NetWare Lite comes with drivers for the most popular LAN cards. Table 4-1 lists these drivers and the LAN cards each driver supports. If your card is on this list, just select the appropriate driver when prompted during the installation process.

Installing the NetWare Lite Software

If your LAN card is not on the list, two solutions are possible:

1. Your LAN card may work with one of the drivers supplied with NetWare Lite. Many LAN cards are compatible with one of the cards listed in Table 4-1. Most likely, the documentation supplied with your LAN card indicates such compatibilities. If you are not sure, contact your card's manufacturer. If you have a compatible card, you can simply select the compatible driver during the installation process.

2. You have a software driver for your LAN card. Some card manufacturers supply a driver (on disk) with the LAN card. If you have a driver for your LAN card, you can install the driver during the installation of NetWare Lite. The process of installing an outside driver is explained later in this chapter.

If you are still unsure about the correct driver, contact your hardware dealer or the manufacturer of your card. There is no way around the driver requirement. To install NetWare Lite successfully, you must know the proper driver for each LAN card.

The IRQ and I/O Base Address

In addition to knowing the appropriate driver for each LAN card, you must also know the IRQ and I/O Base Address set on each card. Chapter 4 explains how to determine and set the proper values of the IRQ and the I/O Base Address. During the installation of NetWare Lite, you must indicate the values of the IRQ and I/O Base Address.

For some LAN cards, the IRQ and I/O Base Address are not adjustable and this step is not required. Token ring cards and cards for PS/2 computers with the MCA architecture do *not* use IRQs or I/O Base Addresses, for example, but the common Ethernet LAN cards for ISA bus computers *do* require IRQs and I/O Base Addresses.

Some cards have a third setting, called the *Base Memory Address*, which is not adjustable on the Novell-sponsored NE1000 and NE2000 LAN cards. If your LAN card has a jumper to adjust the Base Memory Address, however, you are prompted for the value set on the card during the installation of NetWare Lite. See your card's documentation for the available jumper settings and how to select and set a value for the Base Memory Address.

NOTE: An incompatible IRQ or I/O Base Address is the most likely culprit should your LAN fail to install properly. For each computer, you must know the IRQ and I/O Base Address values set on the LAN card and you must be sure that these values do not conflict with other cards (and devices) installed on the machine. The documentation supplied with your LAN card should show you which values you can select for the IRQ and I/O Base Address and how to change the values on the LAN card. Chapter 4 explains the IRQ and I/O Base Address and how to choose the proper values for your computers.

Choosing a Server, a Client, or Both

When you install NetWare Lite on each computer, you must decide whether that node will function as a server, a client, or both. A server can offer its resources across the LAN. A client can utilize resources supplied by the servers. Naturally enough, a machine that is both a server and client can act in both capacities.

At least one of the nodes on your network must have serving capability. That is, you must make at least one machine a dedicated server or both a client and server. Having read Chapters 2 through 4, you should have a good idea about how you will use your LAN and which computers will act as servers. You may want two nodes—or perhaps all nodes—to have server capability. If you are still undecided, designate each computer as both a server and client. This choice gives you maximum networking flexibility but requires the most RAM. Whatever you choose, you can easily change the configuration. This reconfiguring process is described in this chapter's "Reconfiguring an Individual Node" section.

Installation Overview

Here are the major steps in the software installation process. Each step is explained in detail later in the chapter.

1. Place a copy of the NetWare Lite PROGRAM disk in drive A of one PC.
2. Type **a:install** and press [Enter].

Installing the NetWare Lite Software

3. Follow the onscreen directions to select various options. You must take the following actions:

   a. Designate the node as a server, a client, or both.
   b. Select and install the proper driver for the LAN card.
   c. If necessary, indicate the IRQ, I/O Base Address, and Base Memory Address for the LAN card.
   d. For a server, choose the name which identifies that node across the LAN.

4. Press [Esc] to exit the installation program.
5. Remove the Novell installation disk from the floppy drive. Label the disk with a description of the node on which that copy of the NetWare Lite software is installed.

Repeat this process for each node on your network. Remember that you must use a separate copy of NetWare Lite for each PC.

After NetWare Lite is installed on each PC, you need to verify that the network hardware and software are properly installed. As explained later in this chapter, the Novell installation disks have a special option for verifying that the network is properly connected.

Installation Details

The detailed instructions that follow elaborate on the instructions presented in the Installation Overview. For most installations, you select default choices and respond to a few prompts.

NOTE: The instructions in this chapter explain the installation process for version 1.1 of NetWare Lite. If you are installing version 1.0, the process is similar and the same principles apply. The installation program for version 1.0 prompts you for the same information as does version 1.1, but in a different order. Skim this chapter for information about the various options. Better yet, upgrade to version 1.1 which contains some new features and performance enhancements.

Verify that You Have the Appropriate Installation Disks

The NetWare Lite software comes on either 5 1/4-inch or 3 1/2-inch disks. On computers with more than one floppy drive, you can install NetWare Lite from drive A or drive B. Because Novell supplies disks of only one size (5 1/4-inch or 3 1/2-inch) with each copy of NetWare Lite, make sure that you have the proper size for the floppy drive(s) on each computer.

The 5 1/4-inch version is on two disks, one labeled PROGRAM and the other labeled DRIVER. The 3 1/2-inch version comes on a single disk labeled PROGRAM and DRIVER. On these disks are all the programs and information you need to install and run NetWare Lite.

Back Up the Installation Disks

Making backups of important disks is always a good idea. The NetWare Lite disks are not copy protected. You can make a backup copy of each NetWare Lite disk by using the DISKCOPY command from DOS. Consult your DOS documentation if you need help with the command.

NOTE: You may install NetWare Lite from the original disks or from your backup copy. Novell authorizes you to make disk copies for backup and archival purposes. You cannot bypass the Novell licensing restrictions by making multiple copies of a NetWare Lite disk and installing one copy on each node. You must purchase a separate copy of NetWare Lite for each networked PC.

All the NetWare Lite files fit on a single high-density (1.2 MB) 5 1/4-inch floppy or one 3 1/2-inch floppy. If you purchased the 5 1/4-inch version of NetWare Lite, which comes on two 360K disks, and you have a high-density 5 1/4-inch drive, you can copy all the files from the two Novell disks onto your single high-density backup disk and install NetWare Lite from this backup copy. By consolidating the two Novell disks into a single disk, you eliminate having to swap disks during the installation process.

Installing the NetWare Lite Software

Also, you can change the disk format size by copying all the files from a Netware Lite disk to a disk of a different size. You might copy the files from a 3 1/2-inch NetWare Lite disk to a high-density 5 1/4-inch disk, for example. Use the COPY or XCOPY command from DOS to copy files from one disk to another.

Insert the Installation Disk

Place the PROGRAM disk into the floppy drive. For 5 1/4-inch versions, use the disk labeled PROGRAM. (If you made a single high-density 5 1/4-inch backup disk, you can use that disk.) For 3 1/2-inch versions, use the single disk labeled PROGRAM and DRIVER. On machines with two floppy drives, you may use either drive A or drive B.

Activate the drive containing the installation disk. If you inserted the installation disk into drive A, for example, type **a:** at the DOS prompt and press Enter.

If your disk is in drive B, type **b:** instead of **a:**.

Review README.TXT

Check to see whether your installation disk contains a file named README.TXT. Type the following command at the DOS prompt:

dir *.txt

to display a list of all files with the .TXT file extension. Look for a file named README.TXT (which is probably the only file you will see listed). If you don't see the file, you can skip ahead to the "Start INSTALL" section of this chapter.

The README.TXT text file contains updates to the information in the NetWare Lite manual. Included in this file are corrections to the manual, supplemental information, solutions to problems, and software changes Novell made too late to include in the manual.

Tips on installing and using NetWare Lite may be included also. Scan the file, looking for anything related to the installation process.

> **NOTE:** Much of the information in README.TXT is quite technical, but you can scan the file for any updated instructions on installing NetWare Lite.

The information in README.TXT takes precedence over anything in the NetWare Lite manuals or this book. The only sources of information to usurp README.TXT are a loose errata sheet inserted into the manual to show a late change, or information you might receive from Novell's Technical Support group.

You can view README.TXT in a variety of ways. You can use your favorite utility to browse through the text file or you can load README.TXT into your word processor and read it that way. If you want to print the file, and a printer is attached to parallel port LPT1, type the following command and press [Enter]:

copy readme.txt lpt1:

If you have DOS 5, you can browse through the file with the DOS text editor. Type the following command and press [Enter]:

edit readme.txt

Start INSTALL

To begin installing NetWare Lite on your hard disk, type **install** and press [Enter]. Figure 5-1 shows the opening screen.

As you can see, the Main menu on this opening screen presents five options, with the highlight on `Make this machine a client`. You can move the highlight through the options with the up and down cursor keys. To select an option, move the highlight to that option and press [Enter]. If you want to exit the installation program, press [Alt]-[F10] to pop open the Exit box and then press [Enter] to confirm that you want to exit.

Installing the NetWare Lite Software

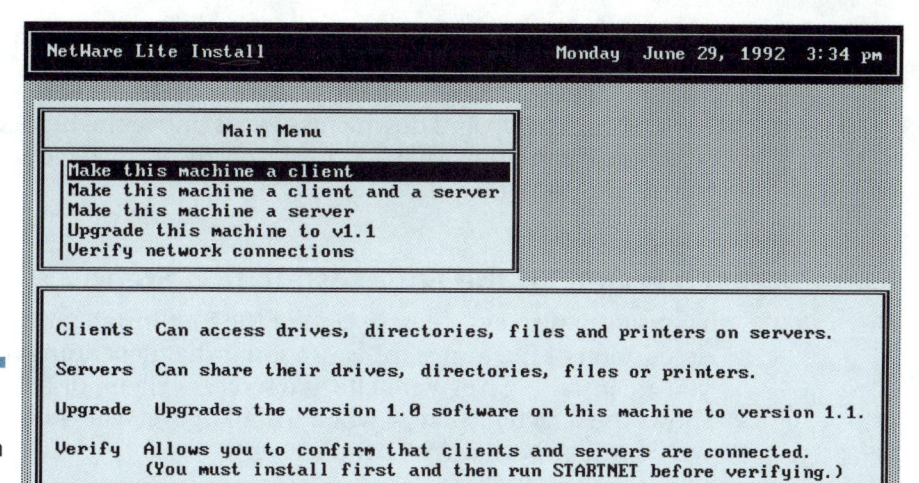

```
NetWare Lite Install                Monday  June 29, 1992  3:34 pm

                        Main Menu
            ┌─────────────────────────────────────────┐
            │ Make this machine a client              │
            │ Make this machine a client and a server │
            │ Make this machine a server              │
            │ Upgrade this machine to v1.1            │
            │ Verify network connections              │
            └─────────────────────────────────────────┘

  Clients  Can access drives, directories, files and printers on servers.

  Servers  Can share their drives, directories, files or printers.

  Upgrade  Upgrades the version 1.0 software on this machine to version 1.1.

  Verify   Allows you to confirm that clients and servers are connected.
           (You must install first and then run STARTNET before verifying.)

Esc-exit install    Enter-select
```

The INSTALL program's opening screen **Figure 5-1.**

NOTE: The installation program does not support a mouse. You must select all options from the keyboard.

Upgrading to Version 1.1

If you are already running version 1.0 of NetWare Lite and are now upgrading to version 1.1, move the highlight to the option labeled Upgrade this machine to v1.1 and press Enter. Your network software will be upgraded. When presented with the option of installing the NetWare Lite cache, the simplest course is to respond "No". For information about the cache, see the material in this chapter and in Chapter 14, "Optimizing LAN Performance." If you wish to install the cache at a later date, you can run the NLCINST.EXE program as described in Chapter 14.

Make the Node a Client, Server, or Both

Your first decision is whether to make the node a client, a server, or both. Using the up and down cursor keys, move the highlight to your selection. Then press ⌜Enter⌝. A screen now displays the four main steps in the installation process.

Overview of the Four Installation Steps

Your screen displays a description of the four installation steps. The description of the four steps varies somewhat depending on whether you are installing NetWare Lite as a server, a client, or both. Figure 5-2 shows the screen displayed when installing NetWare Lite on a node which will be both a server and a client.

Step 1 varies depending upon whether the node will be a server or a client. Steps 2 through 4, however, are the same for all installations. A short description of each step now follows. Detailed instructions follow after the descriptions.

Step 1 for a server (or a server and client)   You provide a name by which the server will be known across the network.

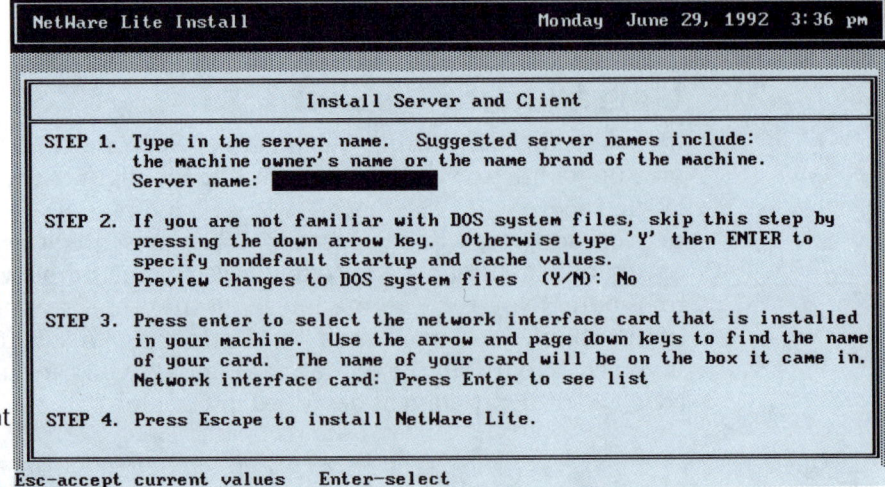

```
NetWare Lite Install                       Monday  June 29, 1992  3:36 pm

                       Install Server and Client

    STEP 1. Type in the server name.  Suggested server names include:
            the machine owner's name or the name brand of the machine.
            Server name: ▮

    STEP 2. If you are not familiar with DOS system files, skip this step by
            pressing the down arrow key.  Otherwise type 'Y' then ENTER to
            specify nondefault startup and cache values.
            Preview changes to DOS system files   (Y/N): No

    STEP 3. Press enter to select the network interface card that is installed
            in your machine.  Use the arrow and page down keys to find the name
            of your card.  The name of your card will be on the box it came in.
            Network interface card: Press Enter to see list

    STEP 4. Press Escape to install NetWare Lite.


 Esc-accept current values    Enter-select
```

The four major steps for a PC configured as a server and client
Figure 5-2.

Installing the NetWare Lite Software

Step 1 for a client   You specify a path to the directory where the NetWare Lite software will be stored.

Step 2   You indicate which modifications, if any, the installation program will make to the DOS system files AUTOEXEC.BAT and CONFIG.SYS.

Step 3   You specify the LAN card driver and the IRQ and I/O Base Address for the LAN card.

Step 4   With steps 1 through 3 complete, you install the NetWare Lite software and complete installation.

Completing the Four Steps

To complete the four steps, you move the highlight to each step and provide the requested information. When you complete a step, the highlight moves to the next step. If you wish to change a value in a previous step, you can use the up and down arrow keys to move the highlight to any step. The following discussion explains each step in detail.

Step 1 for a Server—Specifying the Server Name

If the node is a server (a dedicated server or both a server and client), step 1 prompts you to enter a server name. If the node is a client only, skip this step and advance to the section titled "Step 1 for a Client—Choosing the NetWare Lite Directory."

NetWare Lite uses the server name to identify this computer to the people at the network's other nodes. Each server on the network should have a unique server name.

A server name can be up to 15 characters long. Because other LAN users refer frequently to these names, be sure to pick short, simple names that are easy to remember. The most common type of server name, especially in a small office, is the PC user's first name. Such names tend to be short and familiar to everybody and this approach is fine, as long as all names are different. If you have two Daves in the office, add last initials or use nicknames—whatever makes each name unique (DAVEJ,

DAVE_T, BIGDAVE). Avoid punctuation characters. The installation program converts each blank space you type to an underscore character.

When you decide on a name, type it in and press [Enter]. Names are displayed in uppercase letters, even if you type lowercase letters. In Figure 5-3, the server name JUANITA has just been typed.

If you don't want to use first names (maybe the office has four Daves), use another simple naming scheme. You can assign sequential names to each server (SERVER1, SERVER2, SERVER3) or use organizational names (SALES, ACCOUNTING, SHIPPING). If the characteristics of each computer or its peripherals are important, use descriptive names (486SERVER, SRV300MB, CDROM1). The danger of this approach is that the names become obsolete if you change the computer configurations. You can use functional names that reflect how each server is used (FILESERVER, PRINTSERVER, DB1) or simply use the brand and model name of the computer (AST286, INFINITI486). Finally, you can use whimsical names and let your creativity run wild (JAWS, BIG_BROTHER, FROG, WATERCOOLER).

Of course, you can combine these naming schemes. If you plan to have servers dedicated to serving only (not doubling as workstations), you

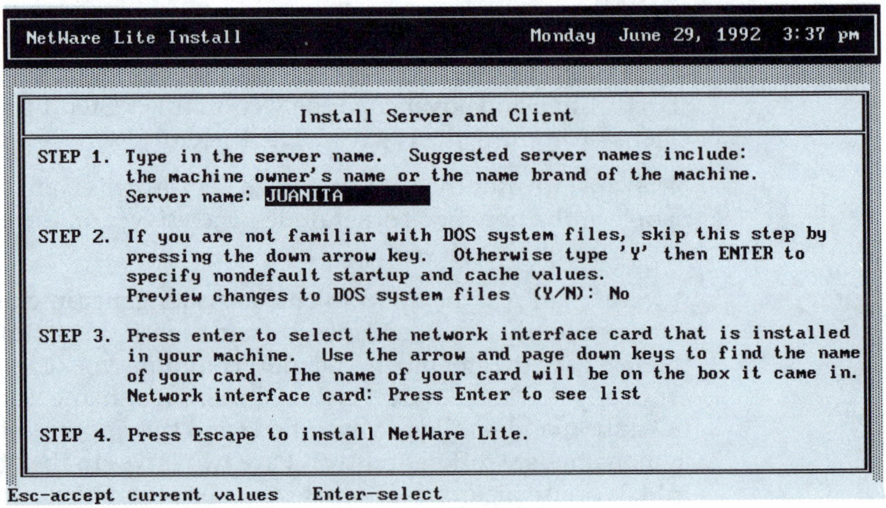

The server name is JUANITA
Figure 5-3.

```
NetWare Lite Install                    Monday  June 29, 1992  3:37 pm

                    Install Server and Client

    STEP 1. Type in the server name.  Suggested server names include:
            the machine owner's name or the name brand of the machine.
            Server name: JUANITA

    STEP 2. If you are not familiar with DOS system files, skip this step by
            pressing the down arrow key.  Otherwise type 'Y' then ENTER to
            specify nondefault startup and cache values.
            Preview changes to DOS system files   (Y/N): No

    STEP 3. Press enter to select the network interface card that is installed
            in your machine.  Use the arrow and page down keys to find the name
            of your card.  The name of your card will be on the box it came in.
            Network interface card: Press Enter to see list

    STEP 4. Press Escape to install NetWare Lite.

Esc-accept current values    Enter-select
```

Installing the NetWare Lite Software

may want to give functional names to servers (GROUPDISK, PRINTERS) and people's names to PCs that act as clients and servers (ANGELA, RAMESH, LYNN).

Because people will use these names constantly, pick names that will endure even if you add computers to the LAN. People are amazingly good at adapting to whatever names you pick (but are upset by frequent changes). Everyone will quickly learn the difference between SERVER1 and SERVER2. If you change SERVER1 to SALES this week, and then to DATABASE next week, however, you may find yourself without lunchtime companions. Pick your names and keep them.

Step 1 for a Client—Choosing the NetWare Lite Directory

If the PC is going to be a client exclusively, step 1 prompts you to type the path to the subdirectory where the NetWare Lite software will be installed. By default, as Figure 5-4 shows, the installation program specifies the path as C:\NWLITE. Normally, you should accept this subdirectory path by pressing [Enter] to indicate approval.

```
NetWare Lite Install                    Monday  June 29, 1992  3:37 pm

                          Install Client

      STEP 1. Type in DOS directory path or the drive where you want the
              software to be installed.
              Target directory for CLIENT software:  C:\NWLITE

      STEP 2. If you are not familiar with DOS system files, skip this step by
              pressing the down arrow key.  Otherwise type 'Y' then ENTER to
              specify nondefault startup and cache values.
              Preview changes to DOS system files  (Y/N): No

      STEP 3. Press enter to select the network interface card that is installed
              in your machine.  Use the arrow and page down keys to find the name
              of your card.  The name of your card will be on the box it came in.
              Network interface card: Press Enter to see list

      STEP 4. Press Escape to install NetWare Lite.

Esc-accept current values    Enter-select
```

The directory path is C:\NWLITE
Figure 5-4.

NOTE: You don't need to create the C:\NWLITE directory yourself. The installation program creates the directory for you and copies the needed files to that directory.

You can install NetWare Lite in a different directory, however. Perhaps you simply prefer another directory name (C:\NETWORK, for example), or you want to install NetWare Lite on the D drive (D:\NWLITE), or you want to place the NWLITE directory farther down the directory path (C:\NOVELL\NWLITE). To indicate a subdirectory other than C:\NWLITE, type in the directory name and path that you prefer. Use the [Backspace] key to delete unwanted characters from the currently displayed path. When you have typed the path, press [Enter].

NOTE: If the computer will be a server, the directory path C:\NWLITE is chosen by default. You cannot alter this selection.

Step 2—Specifying Modifications to DOS System Files

During installation, NetWare Lite modifies two special system files used by DOS—the AUTOEXEC.BAT and CONFIG.SYS files. In step 2, you can accept the default modifications or specify custom modifications.

At the beginning of step 2, the highlight is on the word No in response to the onscreen query "Preview changes to DOS system files". Should you press [Enter] twice (or [↓] once), you would accept the default modifications and proceed to step 3.

However, don't accept the default modifications. Instead, you will customize the modifications that the installation program makes to your DOS files. To do so, with the highlight on No, press [Y]. The highlighted text changes from No to Yes. Press [Enter] to pop open a box labeled DOS System files modifications.

Installing the NetWare Lite Software

This box specifies various modifications that the installation program can make to your system files. The default values for each modification are indicated in the box. To change a value, use the ⬆ and ⬇ keys to move the highlight to the value you wish to change, and then type the new value. You can change values of "Yes" or "No" by simply pressing Y or N.

If you are installing NetWare Lite as both a client and server, the box displays six different modifications for which you can specify values. Table 5-1 shows the recommended values. Figure 5-5 shows the screen after the recommended values are specified.

If you are installing NetWare Lite as a client or server (but not both), the box does not display all six modifications. For a client, you see three of the modifications. For a server, you see five. The recommended value for each modification that you see, however, remains the same as that shown in Table 5-1.

> **NOTE:** The default values shown by the installation program depend on the hardware and software installed on your PC. Most likely, the only values you need to change from the shown defaults, are those for the second and third modifications shown in Table 5-1.

Recommended modifications to the DOS system files
Table 5-1.

Modification	Recommended Value
Add NWLITE directory to PATH in AUTOEXEC.BAT	Yes
Add STARTNET.BAT (loads NWLITE) to AUTOEXEC.BAT	No
Use NLCACHE and load it from STARTNET.BAT	No
Number of BUFFERS specified in CONFIG.SYS	30
Number of FILES specified in CONFIG.SYS	30
LASTDRIVE specified in CONFIG.SYS	M

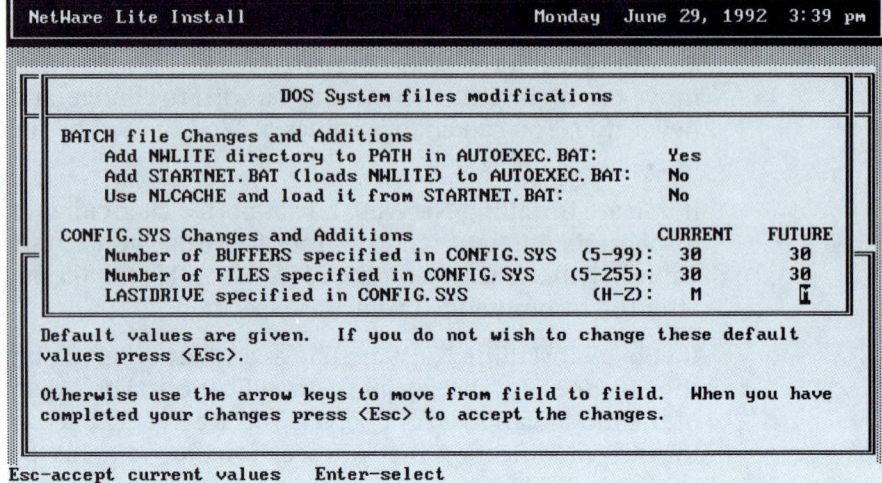

The recommended modifications to the DOS system files are specified **Figure 5-5.**

```
NetWare Lite Install                    Monday  June 29, 1992  3:39 pm

                    DOS System files modifications

    BATCH file Changes and Additions
        Add NWLITE directory to PATH in AUTOEXEC.BAT:       Yes
        Add STARTNET.BAT (loads NWLITE) to AUTOEXEC.BAT:    No
        Use NLCACHE and load it from STARTNET.BAT:          No

    CONFIG.SYS Changes and Additions                    CURRENT  FUTURE
        Number of BUFFERS specified in CONFIG.SYS (5-99):    30     30
        Number of FILES specified in CONFIG.SYS  (5-255):    30     30
        LASTDRIVE specified in CONFIG.SYS           (H-Z):    M      L

    Default values are given.  If you do not wish to change these default
    values press <Esc>.

    Otherwise use the arrow keys to move from field to field.  When you have
    completed your changes press <Esc> to accept the changes.


    Esc-accept current values    Enter-select
```

When you have specified the recommended values, press [Esc] to complete step 2 and begin step 3. The following several sections explain the modifications you can specify in step 2. If you wish, you can skip ahead to the section titled "Step 3—Specifying the Network Adapter Card and Driver." However, it's a good idea to at least skim the following material for an understanding of the special DOS system files and how they are used in NetWare Lite.

DOS Batch Files

A *batch file* is a text file that contains a series of DOS commands and/or program names. When you run a batch file, DOS executes each command or program in the batch file one at a time.

Each batch file has a name that ends with the extension BAT. For example, a hypothetical batch file might be named DOIT.BAT. To run this file, you type **doit** at the DOS prompt (you don't need to include the BAT extension) and then press [Enter]. The effect is as though you typed the first command in DOIT.BAT, then, when that first command executed and the DOS prompt returned, you typed the second command in DOIT.BAT, and so on through every command in the batch file.

Installing the NetWare Lite Software

Because a batch file is a text file, you can view and edit a batch file with any text editor or word processor. The DOS TYPE command displays the contents of a batch file. For example, to view the hypothetical DOIT.BAT file, you could type **type doit.bat** and press Enter.

For more about batch files and how to modify them, see Appendix C, "Sample Batch Files."

AUTOEXEC.BAT

AUTOEXEC.BAT is a special batch file that DOS uses each time your system is powered up or rebooted. AUTOEXEC.BAT contains a list of commands for DOS to carry out when you begin each work session. Normally, AUTOXEC.BAT is created when you install DOS. Some software programs require that certain commands in AUTOEXEC.BAT be added or modified to optimize the way DOS works with that software. For more about AUTOEXEC.BAT, see Appendix C and refer to your DOS documentation.

> **NOTE:** AUTOEXEC.BAT is not required by DOS. Though not likely, your PC may be running without an AUTOEXEC.BAT file.

Adjusting the PATH in AUTOEXEC.BAT

For most PC's, the AUTOEXEC.BAT file contains one or more PATH commands. PATH commands specify directory search lists. Whenever you invoke a program that DOS cannot find in the current directory, DOS searches for the program in the directories listed in the PATH commands.

The first option in step 2 (shown at the top of Figure 5-5) specifies whether the NetWare Lite installation program can modify your AUTOEXEC.BAT file to include a PATH command which contains the directory path to the NetWare Lite files. The option reads as follows:

```
Add NWLITE directory to PATH in AUTOEXEC.BAT:
```

Specify Yes, the recommended value, to accept this update to your AUTOEXEC.BAT file. If you don't accept this modification, DOS may not be able to find the NetWare Lite files later when you try to start the network.

STARTNET.BAT

The NetWare Lite installation program creates a batch file named STARTNET.BAT. This batch file executes several programs necessary to initialize NetWare Lite on that PC. STARTNET.BAT is discussed throughout this chapter and in Appendix C.

Executing STARTNET.BAT As Part of AUTOEXEC.BAT

Step 2 of the NetWare Lite installation includes an option to execute STARTNET.BAT as part of your AUTOEXEC.BAT file. The option reads as follows:

```
Add STARTNET.BAT (loads NWLITE) to AUTOEXEC.BAT:
```

This book's recommended value is No. That's normally the best choice when you are first installing and testing the network software.

If, instead, you accept this modification, the NetWare Lite software is initialized each time you turn on (or reboot) your computer. Loading the network software takes up some RAM that, without the network, would be available to software applications such as spreadsheets and word processors. If you plan to use your PC sometimes as a workstation not connected to the network, you should select No. However, if you plan to utilize the network every time you turn on the computer, you can select Yes.

NOTE: Anytime after installing NetWare Lite, you can modify AUTOEXEC.BAT and other system files to change the installation options. See Appendix C for more information.

Installing the NetWare Lite Disk Cache

A *disk cache* (pronounced "cash") is a software program which utilizes RAM to improve the performance of DOS when reading and writing

Installing the NetWare Lite Software

data to your hard disk. A disk cache can be useful on any node which has serving capacity (that is, a dedicated server or a server and client).

If you are installing NetWare Lite as a server or as a server and client, step 2 includes an option to load a disk cache whenever you initialize the network software. The option reads as follows:

```
Use NLCACHE and load it from STARTNET.BAT:
```

The recommended value is No. A disk cache is a sophisticated piece of software which can be installed with several different options. It's better to make sure the network works okay before adding the complexity of a disk cache. You can always add the disk cache at any later time. For more information about using the NetWare Lite disk cache, see Chapter 14, "Optimizing LAN Performance" and Appendix C.

NOTE: The disk cache feature of NetWare Lite is new to version 1.1. Version 1.0 does not include a disk cache.

CONFIG.SYS

CONFIG.SYS (the name stands for *system configuration*), like AUTOEXEC.BAT, is a special system file DOS uses when your computer is powered up or rebooted. This file contains information about how DOS should be configured on your PC, information that includes which device drivers DOS should load, how many files DOS can have open simultaneously, and similar system-level specifications. Normally, CONFIG.SYS is created when you install DOS. Some software programs require that parameters in CONFIG.SYS be added or modified to optimize the way DOS works with that software. For more about CONFIG.SYS, refer to your DOS documentation.

NOTE: CONFIG.SYS is not required by DOS. Your PC may be running without a CONFIG.SYS file.

Adjusting the BUFFERS and FILES Statements in CONFIG.SYS

If you are installing NetWare Lite as a dedicated server or as a client and server, step 2 includes the option to modify the BUFFERS and FILES statements in your system's CONFIG.SYS file. The options appear as follows:

```
Number of BUFFERS specified in CONFIG.SYS   (5-99):
Number of FILES specified in CONFIG.SYS     (5-255):
```

If you are installing NetWare Lite exclusively as a client, step 2 does not include the option to modify the FILES and BUFFERS statements.

For the server portion of NetWare Lite to work optimally, the FILES and BUFFERS statements in CONFIG.SYS should each specify a value of at least 30. By default, the installation program specifies 30 as the value for both BUFFERS and FILES (or a larger value if the CONFIG.SYS file currently has statements which specify a larger value). Normally, you do not adjust the default values. When installing the NetWare Lite software, the installation program will modify (or, if necessary, create) CONFIG.SYS for you.

Adding a LASTDRIVE Statement to CONFIG.SYS

If you have designated your machine to be a client or both a client and server, step 2 includes an option to add a LASTDRIVE statement to your CONFIG.SYS file. The option reads as follows:

```
LASTDRIVE specified in CONFIG.SYS    (H-Z):
```

The value set in the LASTDRIVE statement tells DOS the highest drive letter available for that computer. As Chapter 6 explains, various network resources are mapped into drive letters when NetWare Lite is running. The installation program's default value of M (or possibly a higher letter if your CONFIG.SYS already includes a LASTDRIVE statement) is appropriate for most networks.

Installing the NetWare Lite Software

Understanding FILES and BUFFERS

The FILES and BUFFERS statements in CONFIG.SYS specify, respectively, the number of files DOS can open simultaneously and the number of buffers DOS should create. A *buffer* is a reserved area of memory that stores information read from disk. A value of 30 for FILES and also for BUFFERS is sufficient for NetWare Lite to run efficiently.

Some software applications, such as sophisticated accounting programs, require a value greater than 30 for FILES and/or BUFFERS. If FILES or BUFFERS is set to more than 30 on any of your network nodes, no further modification is necessary for NetWare Lite.

There is a small penalty to pay as you increase the size of FILES and BUFFERS. Each incremental increase in the value of FILES or BUFFERS reduces available RAM by an amount from 1/2K to 1K. The exact amount of the decrease in memory depends on the version of DOS and the memory configuration of the machine. Also, if BUFFERS increases past 50 or so, DOS itself may slow down slightly because of increased time spent searching the buffers.

Step 3—Specifying the Network Adapter Card and Driver

Step 3 of the installation process consists of specifying which LAN adapter card is installed in your PC. The step begins with the highlight on the words `Press Enter to see list` in response to the onscreen prompt `Network interface card:`.

Press `Enter` to see the list of supported LAN cards. If you are prompted to insert the DRIVER diskette in floppy drive, do so.

Included on the installation disks are several software drivers for various network adapter cards; the adapter cards and driver names are listed in a pop-up window. You can use the cursor keys to scroll the list and to move the highlight up and down.

If your card appears on the list, move the highlight to the card's name and press [Enter]. Figure 5-6 shows the highlight on the NE2000 card. (As you may recall from Chapter 4, the NE2000 is the 16-bit Ethernet card for ISA machines, supplied in NetWare Lite starter kits produced by Eagle.)

If your card is not on the list, you have two choices. First, if your card is compatible with one of the cards listed, you can simply select the name of the compatible card from the list. (To verify compatibility, check your card's documentation or consult the manufacturer.)

Second, if you have a special driver for your LAN card, select the option *OTHER CARDS. You will be prompted to insert a disk containing your special driver into the disk drive. (Many manufacturers supply drivers with their LAN cards. The driver's file name should have a .COM or .EXE extension.) After inserting your driver disk, press [Esc] to continue.

Indicating the IRQ and I/O Base Address Set on the Adapter Card

After selecting the LAN card, the installation program may prompt you for the IRQ and I/O Base Address set on the LAN card. For some cards, these settings do not apply or cannot be adjusted, in which case the

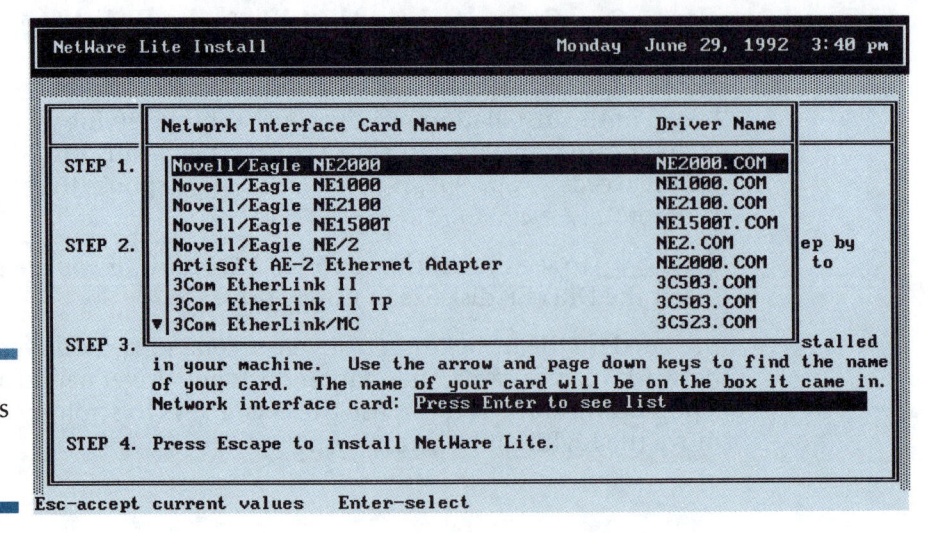

The NE2000 adapter card is selected
Figure 5-6.

Installing the NetWare Lite Software

installation program skips this step. For a few cards, the installation program may request additional address information, such as the Base Memory Address. For such additional address settings, consult the documentation for your LAN card.

The installation program must know the IRQ and I/O values you set on your LAN card. The pop-up window in Figure 5-7 enables you to specify the proper values of IRQ and I/O Base Address for the NE2000 card. The default value for the IRQ is 3; for the I/O Base Address, the default value is 300 (hex). If you did not change these default values on the LAN card, press (Esc) to continue installation.

If you reset the board jumpers for the IRQ or I/O Base Address during installation of the hardware, you must indicate the new settings now. To change the default value of IRQ, move the highlight to the option (INT) Interrupt Request and press (Enter). The window that pops open shows the possible settings. Move the highlight to the value set on the LAN card and press (Enter). To reset the I/O Base Address, move the highlight to (PORT) IO Base Address, press (Enter), and then select the correct value from the supplied list. After changing the settings to match the configuration of your LAN card, press (Esc) to resume the installation process.

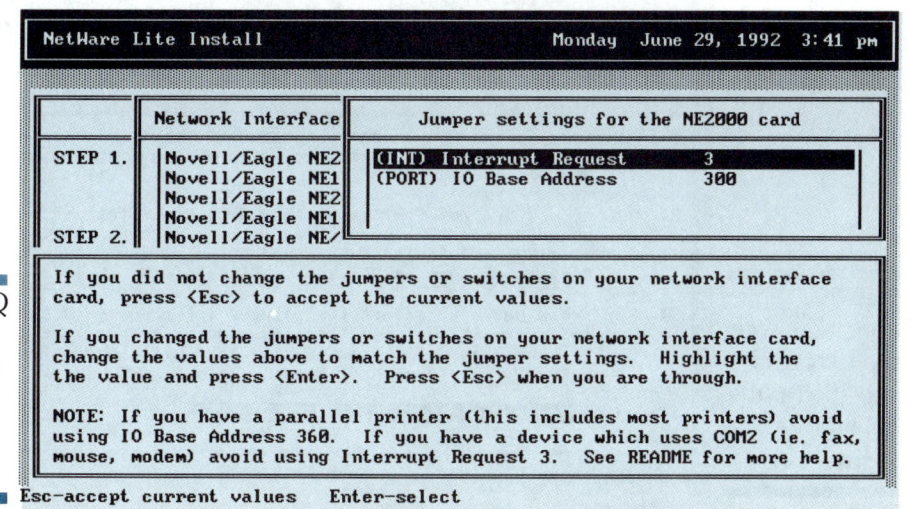

The default IRQ and I/O Base Address for the NE2000 LAN card
Figure 5-7.

```
NetWare Lite Install                          Monday  June 29, 1992  3:41 pm

              Network Interface    Jumper settings for the NE2000 card
   STEP 1.   Novell/Eagle NE2     (INT) Interrupt Request         3
             Novell/Eagle NE1     (PORT) IO Base Address         300
             Novell/Eagle NE2
             Novell/Eagle NE1
   STEP 2.   Novell/Eagle NE/

   If you did not change the jumpers or switches on your network interface
   card, press <Esc> to accept the current values.

   If you changed the jumpers or switches on your network interface card,
   change the values above to match the jumper settings.  Highlight the
   the value and press <Enter>.  Press <Esc> when you are through.

   NOTE: If you have a parallel printer (this includes most printers) avoid
   using IO Base Address 360.  If you have a device which uses COM2 (ie. fax,
   mouse, modem) avoid using Interrupt Request 3.  See README for more help.

   Esc-accept current values    Enter-select
```

The settings you choose for IRQ and I/O Base Address are written to a file (NET.CFG) stored on the hard disk. This text file lists the LAN card and driver installed on the machine, as well as the IRQ and I/O Base Address set on the card. The installation program does not create NET.CFG if the LAN card does not permit optional settings.

Step 4—Installing NetWare Lite

When step 3 concludes, the highlight moves to step 4, which reads:

```
Press Escape to install NetWare Lite
```

Note that the LAN card you specified in step 3 is now shown onscreen in the description of step 3 (Figure 5-8).

Press [Esc] to begin the installation of the NetWare Lite software.

Copying Files

The installation program now copies files from the installation disk to the hard disk. A directory named C:\NWLITE is created and the files are copied to that directory. As each file is copied, a message box onscreen indicates which file is being copied.

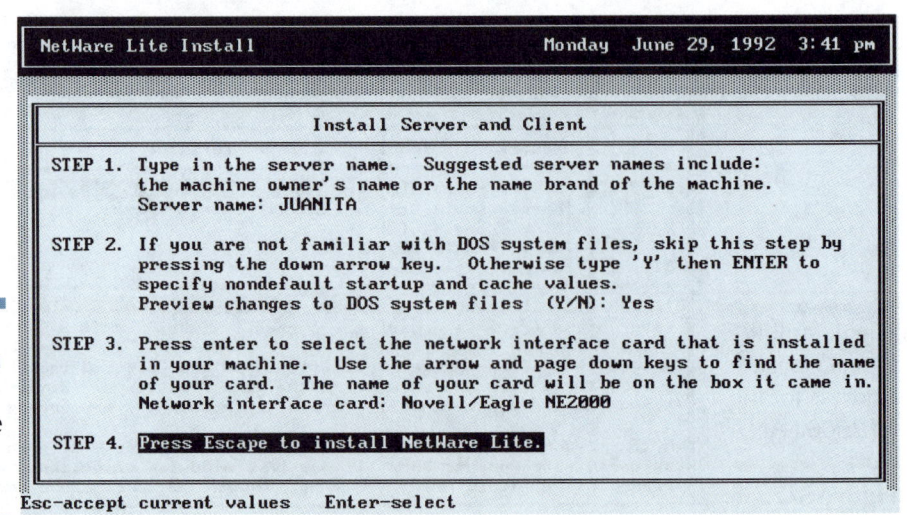

Step 3 concludes with the LAN card specified as the NE2000
Figure 5-8.

```
NetWare Lite Install                          Monday   June 29, 1992   3:41 pm

                        Install Server and Client

      STEP 1.  Type in the server name.  Suggested server names include:
               the machine owner's name or the name brand of the machine.
               Server name: JUANITA

      STEP 2.  If you are not familiar with DOS system files, skip this step by
               pressing the down arrow key.  Otherwise type 'Y' then ENTER to
               specify nondefault startup and cache values.
               Preview changes to DOS system files  (Y/N): Yes

      STEP 3.  Press enter to select the network interface card that is installed
               in your machine.  Use the arrow and page down keys to find the name
               of your card.  The name of your card will be on the box it came in.
               Network interface card: Novell/Eagle NE2000

      STEP 4.  Press Escape to install NetWare Lite.

      Esc-accept current values    Enter-select
```

Installing the NetWare Lite Software

Switch to the DRIVER Disk

If you are installing NetWare Lite from two 5 1/4-inch floppy disks, the installation program may prompt you to insert the DRIVER disk in drive A (or drive B, if you are installing from that drive). After you switch floppies as requested, press Esc to continue.

Ending Installation

The installation of NetWare Lite concludes with the screen shown in Figure 5-9. Press Esc to exit the installation program. The system returns to the DOS prompt.

Removing and Labeling the Floppy Disk

Remove the installation disk from the floppy disk drive. This disk is now associated with that particular machine; the installation process copied an identification address unique to the disk onto the NetWare Lite files on your hard disk. If you want to reinstall NetWare Lite on this computer, use the same installation disk. (You may want to

The conclusion of the installation program
Figure 5-9.

```
NetWare Lite Install                       Monday  June 29, 1992  3:43 pm

  NetWare Lite is now installed on this machine.  Follow the steps below:

  STEP 1. Remove the diskette from the A: drive.

  STEP 2. Write the machine description on the label of the Program diskette.
          Example: the machine owner's name or the machine location.
          (If you install NetWare Lite on THIS machine again you must use
          THIS diskette.)

  STEP 3. Write down the words "NET" and "SUPERVISOR".
          After you reboot your machine (STEP 4.) type "NET" then <ENTER>
          and then type "SUPERVISOR" when prompted for a user name.
          (See page 7 of your NetWare Lite manual).

  STEP 4. REBOOT YOUR MACHINE.  (press <Ctrl> <Alt> <Del> at the same time)

  If you have any further questions type the README.TXT file in the NWLITE
  directory, or contact customer support (see your NetWare Lite box).

Esc-exit install
```

reinstall NetWare Lite to change the configuration, changing a client machine into a client and server, for example.)

Label the installation disk with a description of the PC, using any name which uniquely identifies that particular machine. You might choose a descriptive name such as Carlotta's 386 or the IBM PS/2 Model 50. If your network consists of several similar computers, you might use the computer's serial number as a unique description. If you used two 5 1/4-inch disks to install NetWare Lite, label the PROGRAM disk only. You do not need to label the DRIVER disk.

CAUTION: When labeling a disk, don't write with a hard-tip pen directly on a label already attached to the disk; doing so may damage the information stored on the disk. Rather, be sure to use a felt or soft-tip pen to write directly on a label that is attached to the disk. If you have peel-and-stick labels, write on the label before attaching it to the disk.

Initializing NetWare Lite

Follow these steps to initialize NetWare Lite:

1. Reboot the computer.

   To activate the changes to CONFIG.SYS and AUTOEXEC.BAT, you must reboot the PC. Either turn off the machine and then turn it back on, or do a three-key boot by pressing [Ctrl]-[Alt]-[Del].

2. Make the NetWare directory active. Type **cd \nwlite** at the DOS prompt and then press [Enter].

3. Load the NetWare Lite software. Type **startnet** and then press [Enter]. Do this for each machine on the network.

NOTE: During installation, if you accepted the option of adding STARTNET.BAT to your AUTOEXEC.BAT file (not the recommended specification), steps 2 and 3 are done automatically for you when you reboot your computer.

Installing the NetWare Lite Software

The startnet command invokes STARTNET.BAT, a batch file which was created by the installation program. The STARTNET.BAT batch file automatically executes several programs necessary to initiate NetWare Lite. As the STARTNET batch file executes, you should see several technical messages on your screen. For more about batch files, see Appendix C.

If the final message says that SERVER.EXE or CLIENT.EXE was loaded successfully, you have reached an important milestone: the NetWare Lite software has communicated successfully with the LAN card.

But if you hear beeps and see error messages, a problem exists. Most likely, the NetWare Lite software did not communicate properly with the LAN card. The usual cause is a mismatch between the LAN card configuration you specified during the NetWare Lite installation and the jumper settings on the LAN card. If you specified an IRQ of 3 during software installation, for example, but the jumper on the card is set to IRQ 5, the hardware and software cannot communicate. The card and the software are, in effect, on different wavelengths. The same kind of mismatch can occur for the I/O Base Address or Base Memory Address. To fix this problem, you must either change the card's jumper settings (refer to the "Verify Card Settings" section in Chapter 4) or rerun the installation program to specify the card configuration correctly.

Troubleshooting

If you have a problem, first make sure that your LAN card's jumper settings are correct. Check that the jumpers are set to the values you expect and that these values do not conflict with any other card or device installed in the PC. If the problem persists, try the following troubleshooting tips. To review the hardware installation of the LAN card, reread Chapter 4.

- ◆ Make sure that the LAN board matches the machine. Use only an ISA board with an ISA machine, or a Micro Channel board with a Micro Channel machine. Use only a 16-bit card in a 16-bit slot or an 8-bit card in an 8-bit slot.

CAUTION: Before reopening your computer, turn off the machine. Before handling a LAN card, touch grounded metal or wear an antistatic wrist strap. (You can purchase an antistatic wrist strap for a few dollars from major electronic retailers such as Radio Shack.)

- Make sure that the LAN card is firmly installed in the edge connector. A loose connection prevents proper communication and can damage the LAN card.

- Make sure that you selected the proper LAN card and jumper settings during software installation. If you have any doubts, reinstall NetWare Lite on that machine.

If you are still having trouble, review the entire installation process covered in this chapter and Chapter 4. Make sure that you followed all the steps properly. Read any literature supplied with your hardware, looking for special installation instructions. Perhaps you overlooked, misinterpreted, or incorrectly followed a step. For additional troubleshooting advice, see Chapter 13, "Troubleshooting." If all else fails, you can contact Novell Technical Support or a NetWare Lite consultant for help.

Testing NetWare Lite

After you initialize NetWare Lite on each node by typing **startnet** at the DOS prompt and then pressing (Enter), you need to verify that the individual nodes can communicate with each other across the network. Follow these steps for *each* machine on the network:

1. Reinsert the PROGRAM installation disk into each machine's floppy disk drive.

2. If the disk is in drive A, type **a:install** and press (Enter).

   If the disk is in drive B, type **b:install** and press (Enter).

3. Move the highlight to `Verify network connections` and press (Enter).

4. When prompted for a workstation name, type a unique name on each PC and press (Enter). In Figure 5-10, the name NODE1 has been entered for the first machine on the network.

Installing the NetWare Lite Software

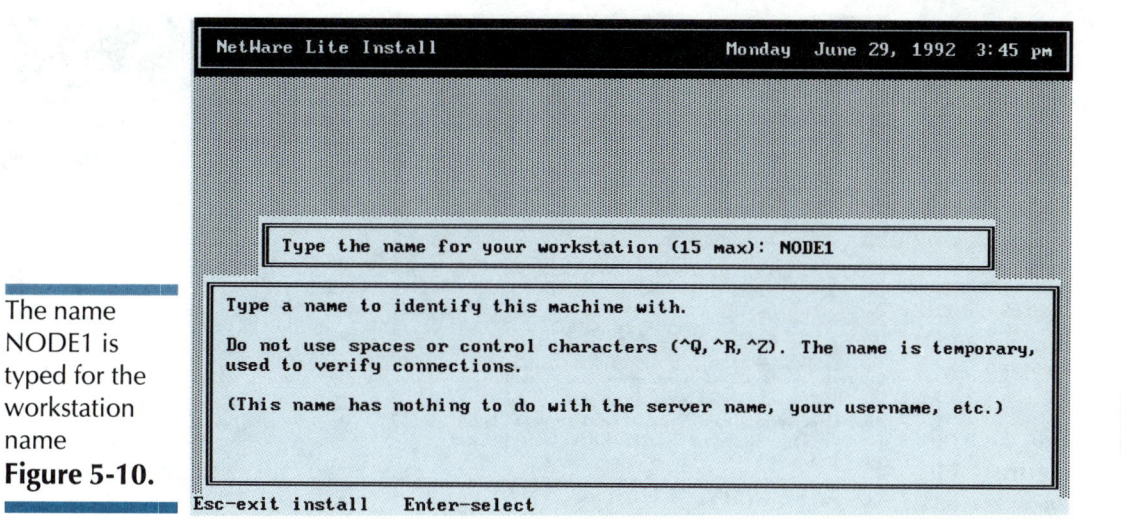

```
NetWare Lite Install                    Monday  June 29, 1992  3:45 pm


        ┌─────────────────────────────────────────────────────────────┐
        │  Type the name for your workstation (15 max): NODE1         │
        ├─────────────────────────────────────────────────────────────┤
        │  Type a name to identify this machine with.                 │
        │                                                             │
        │  Do not use spaces or control characters (^Q, ^R, ^Z). The name is temporary, │
        │  used to verify connections.                                │
        │                                                             │
        │  (This name has nothing to do with the server name, your username, etc.) │
        │                                                             │
        └─────────────────────────────────────────────────────────────┘
Esc-exit install    Enter-select
```

The name NODE1 is typed for the workstation name
Figure 5-10.

The names you type are used only during this test to identify each machine temporarily. These names are completely independent of the server names you supplied during the software installation. When you later run the network, the server names you typed during installation are used to identify serving nodes.

In the context of this test, the word "workstation" in the name prompt is an inappropriate choice by Novell. Here, "workstation" refers to any node of the network and is not meant to distinguish between a client node (sometimes called a workstation) and a server node.

Verifying the Network Connections

On each machine, a box pops up, showing the nodes connected to the network. As you type a name for each successive machine in the network, that name should appear on *every* machine tested to that point. Figure 5-11 shows the pop-up box on the computer named NODE1, after the first two nodes have been tested. (The second node is named NODE2.)

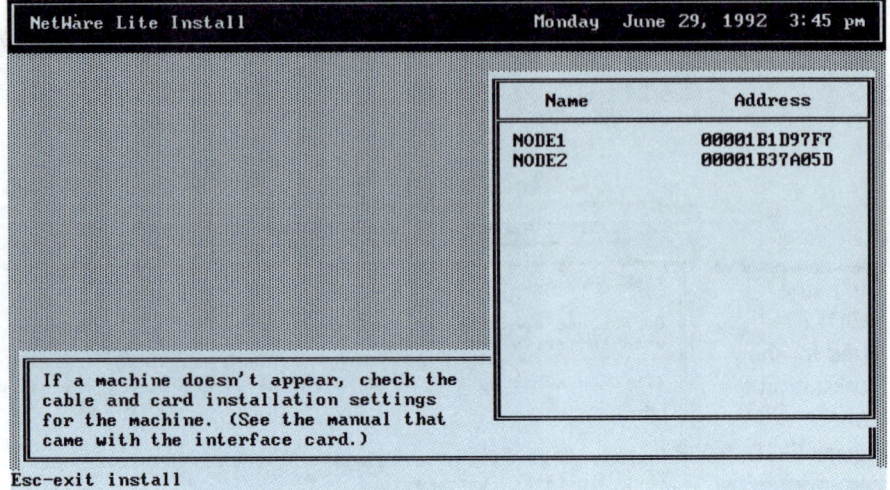

```
NetWare Lite Install                    Monday  June 29, 1992   3:45 pm


                                        ┌─────────────────────────────┐
                                        │  Name          Address      │
                                        │                             │
                                        │  NODE1         00001B1D97F7 │
                                        │  NODE2         00001B37A05D │
                                        │                             │
                                        │                             │
                                        │                             │
                                        │                             │
                                        │                             │
                        ┌──────────────────────────────────┐          │
                        │ If a machine doesn't appear, check the      │
                        │ cable and card installation settings        │
                        │ for the machine. (See the manual that       │
                        │ came with the interface card.)              │
                        └─────────────────────────────────────────────┘
Esc-exit install
```

Nodes named NODE1 and NODE2 are communicating with each other
Figure 5-11.

During this test, each node communicates with every other node. If a node name does not appear on one or more machines, a problem exists. As they say in politics, there is a failure to communicate. Make sure that the cables and terminators are properly installed. If a problem remains, use the troubleshooting tips presented earlier in this chapter's "Troubleshooting" section. Chapter 13 contains additional troubleshooting advice.

In the pop-up verification box, the address shown with each node is a unique identification address associated with the LAN card installed in the node. Like an engine's serial number identifies a particular automobile, the LAN card's address identifies a particular network node.

Ending the Verification Test

If you see every node name on all the PC screens, congratulations. You are in business and ready to do full-fledged networking.

To exit the test verification on each PC, press [Esc]. The system returns to the DOS prompt.

Reconfiguring an Individual Node

You can easily change the configuration of any network node at any time. You may find that your network's usage and needs change occasionally. Suppose, for example, that you acquire a new printer which you connect to a node that is a client only. With everyone clamoring to share the new printer, you soon will want to reconfigure the node as a client *and* server.

To reconfigure, rerun the software installation program, responding to the prompts according to the new configuration you want. The program will update the NetWare Lite files as necessary. For each node, be sure to use the same installation disk you used originally to install NetWare Lite.

Special Installation Situations

The remainder of this chapter discusses installation issues that arise under special circumstances. If your network connections verified properly, you can browse through this material. The next chapter discusses the basic principles of working with NetWare Lite.

Installing NetWare Lite on a PC Without a Hard Disk

If you want to use NetWare Lite on a PC that has no hard disk, you can install the network software on a floppy disk. A disk of any size will work because all the files required to run NetWare Lite fit on the disk with the smallest capacity—a 5 1/4-inch 360K floppy disk.

A network machine without a hard disk must be configured as a client because NetWare Lite requires a hard disk on any machine that acts a server. Expect network performance to be slow on machines that run the network from a floppy drive.

The procedure to install NetWare Lite on a floppy disk parallels the procedure used to install Netware Lite on a hard disk. When the installation program prompts you for a directory path on which to install the client, type **a:** (or **b:**) and press [Enter]. Have ready a formatted disk on which to install the NetWare Lite software. The installation program transfers files from the installation disks to your disk. From time to time during the installation process, you may be prompted to switch disks.

To initialize NetWare Lite, insert your newly created disk into the floppy drive. Type **startnet** at the DOS prompt and press Enter.

Loading SERVER.EXE and CLIENT.EXE into Upper Memory

The STARTNET.BAT batch file, which you use to initialize NetWare Lite, loads some TSR programs into the computer's RAM. In particular, SERVER.EXE and CLIENT.EXE are loaded for server and client machines, respectively. A PC configured as both a client and server uses both programs.

Because SERVER.EXE and CLIENT.EXE are loaded into *conventional memory*—the memory area below the 640K boundary—less conventional memory is available for application programs and data files after you initialize NetWare Lite. The sizes of the SERVER.EXE and CLIENT.EXE files are approximately 40K and 20K, respectively.

For some PC users, every available byte of conventional memory is precious. Each TSR program in conventional memory means less memory for large spreadsheets, multiple documents, or large application programs. If you have ever run into `out of memory` messages, you know the feeling.

On machines with a 286, 386, or 486 processor running DOS 5, TSR programs can be loaded into *upper memory*, the memory area between 640K and 1,024K.

Many newer machines with 386 and 486 processors have *extended memory* (memory addresses greater than 1,024K). TSRs can be loaded into extended memory with the aid of an extended memory manager. Several companies make extended memory managers; two leading products are QEMM386 and 386MAX.

The point of all this is that CLIENT.EXE and SERVER.EXE can be loaded into upper or extended memory, thus freeing up about 60K of conventional memory.

Installing the NetWare Lite Software

> **CAUTION:** With version 1.0 of NetWare Lite, SERVER.EXE should not be placed into upper or extended memory because the program grows somewhat after being loaded from the hard disk. Most upper memory managers reserve a fixed block of memory for a TSR program and cannot accommodate a program that grows. If you try to place version 1.0's SERVER.EXE in upper or extended memory, you risk unpredictable results. Most likely, memory conflicts will occur and your machine will freeze up and hang. However, SERVER.EXE for version 1.1 of NetWare Lite is "well-behaved" and can be placed into upper or extended memory.

To load programs into high memory you must have an upper or extended memory manager. To move SERVER.EXE and CLIENT.EXE into high memory, follow these steps:

1. Modify STARTNET.BAT by removing SERVER.EXE and CLIENT.EXE.

   Load the STARTNET.BAT batch file into a word processor or text editor (such as the EDIT utility in DOS 5), remove the batch file's final lines (SERVER.EXE and CLIENT.EXE), and then resave STARTNET.BAT.

2. Execute the modified STARTNET.BAT file.

   When you initialize the network, run the modified form of STARTNET.BAT. At the DOS prompt, type **startnet** and press [Enter].

3. Load SERVER.EXE and CLIENT.EXE into upper or extended memory.

Use your upper memory manager or extended memory manager to load SERVER.EXE and CLIENT.EXE into upper or extended memory. For DOS 5, use the LOADHIGH command. For more information about loading high, consult the documentation for DOS or for your memory manager. Note that you can place directly into the modified STARTNET.BAT file the commands needed to load SERVER.EXE and CLIENT.EXE high. See Appendix C for more about batch files and loading high directly from STARTNET.BAT.

CHAPTER

6 WORKING WITH NETWARE LITE: BASIC PRINCIPLES

At this point, you have installed the network hardware and software. Each networked computer has a LAN card in place, the computers are cabled together, and you have installed the NetWare Lite software on the hard disk of each machine (or on a floppy disk, for machines without a hard disk).

Now it's time to start NetWare Lite and begin networking. Remember that the installation process you completed in Chapter 5 just prepares the NetWare Lite software to run from each PC's hard disk. Installation does not actually begin the communication process between computers. After installation, you have to start NetWare Lite to share resources or communicate with other network nodes. Just as you cannot talk to anyone on the telephone until you dial a number, you cannot share resources on your LAN until you start the LAN software.

This chapter presents an overview of working with NetWare Lite. The following topics are discussed:

- Starting NetWare Lite with the STARTNET.BAT batch file
- Logging in to and out of the network
- Using the network menu system
- Using the NET program from the DOS prompt
- Using the NetWare Lite Help facility
- Experimenting with resource sharing by mapping a disk drive

Understanding the NetWare Lite Directory

Installing the NetWare Lite software created a C:\NWLITE directory on the hard disk of each PC on your network, unless you specified a different path and name for the directory during the installation process. (If you did specify another path and name, type that path and name whenever directions in this chapter refer to C:\NWLITE.)

The C:\NWLITE directory on each networked computer contains all the programs and files needed to run NetWare Light. To see a list of the files stored in the C:\NWLITE directory, follow these two steps:

1. At the DOS prompt, type **cd \nwlite** and press [Enter].
2. Type **dir** and press [Enter].

Working with NetWare Lite: Basic Principles

If the computer is a server, the file named SERVER.EXE is one of the files listed. For client computers, you see the file CLIENT.EXE. If the computer is both a server and a client, SERVER.EXE and CLIENT.EXE are both present.

The STARTNET.BAT batch file (created during the NetWare Lite installation) consists of a list of programs that run sequentially when you type **startnet**. As you may recall, you ran this file—by typing **startnet**—as part of the verification testing of your software installation. To initialize your network, you will run STARTNET.BAT at each PC.

To see what's in STARTNET.BAT, type the DOS command **type startnet.bat** and press Enter. A list of programs, customized for you by NetWare Lite according to the options you selected during the installation process, is displayed. The list includes SERVER (which invokes SERVER.EXE), CLIENT (which invokes CLIENT.EXE), or both. As their names imply, CLIENT.EXE and SERVER.EXE load the TSR programs necessary for the PC to act as a client and/or server.

STARTNET.BAT also runs the program that loads the software driver for the installed LAN card. A computer with the NE2000 card, for example, has a program named NE2000.COM in the NetWare Lite directory. STARTNET.BAT invokes this program with the line `NE2000`.

The contents of the STARTNET.BAT file may vary for each PC on the network, depending on the options you selected during the installation of the NetWare Lite software. In addition to CLIENT, SERVER, NE2000 (or another LAN-card program), the batch file runs other programs needed to run NetWare Lite.

Initializing NetWare Lite

Now it's time to initialize your network. To do so, you run STARTNET.BAT on each PC.

CAUTION: Before starting the network, you must reboot each PC at least once subsequent to the software installation. Booting ensures that any changes made by the installation program to your system's AUTOEXEC.BAT and CONFIG.SYS files take effect. If you have not booted a machine since installing the NetWare Lite software, either power the machine off and back on, do a three-key boot by pressing Ctrl-Alt-Del, or press the reset button if your machine has one.

Running STARTNET.BAT

To initialize NetWare Lite, type the following command at the DOS prompt and press Enter:

startnet

> **NOTE:** As explained in Chapter 5, if you have version 1.1 of NetWare Lite and you accepted the default options when installing the NetWare Lite software, the installation program (INSTALL) adds a line to your AUTOEXEC.BAT file which automatically runs STARTNET.BAT each time you turn on your computer. (As such, you do not have to type **startnet**.) However, if you did not accept this default option, or if you have version 1.0 of NetWare Lite, you must type **startnet** to initialize NetWare Lite.

You will see several on-screen messages as the various programs in the STARTNET.BAT batch file execute. After a few seconds, you should once again see the DOS prompt. The final message before the DOS prompt should indicate that CLIENT.EXE or SERVER.EXE was successfully loaded.

If the DOS error message `Bad command or file name` appears when you type **startnet**, DOS probably could not find the path to your STARTNET.BAT batch file. The batch file is located in the C:\NWLITE directory. During normal installation, NetWare Lite adds a PATH statement to your AUTOEXEC.BAT file which provides the path to this directory. If you opted during installation to not have your AUTOEXEC.BAT file updated (or if you haven't rebooted your computer since installation), you may get the error message. If the message is displayed, make the C:\NWLITE directory active by typing **cd \nwlite** and pressing Enter. Then type **startnet**.

If you get any other error messages other than `Bad command or file name` while running STARTNET.BAT, read the section titled

Working with NetWare Lite: Basic Principles

"Troubleshooting" in Chapter 5. If you need further help, see Chapter 13, "Troubleshooting."

Running Applications Outside the Network

The process of initializing NetWare Lite with the **startnet** command does not alter the way your computer works. Many first-time networkers incorrectly think that running STARTNET.BAT puts the computer in a special mode under control of the network.

In fact, at this point, everything is very much as it was before you installed the network. The notable exception is that a little less RAM is available. After running STARTNET.BAT, you see the normal DOS prompt. Your computer should work just as it did in your prenetwork days. Try running your word processor, spreadsheet program, DOS commands, or anything else you normally do from the DOS prompt. Everything should work in the customary way.

CAUTION: Although not likely, you may experience difficulties with your computer because of the reduction in available RAM. The most common problem is that a large spreadsheet file or database file no longer will load into memory. In very rare cases, your computer may lock up or not run properly while booting or just after booting. If you encounter any of these difficulties, see Chapter 13, "Troubleshooting."

Introducing the NET Command

NetWare Lite's NET.EXE program makes possible all the various forms of resource sharing across the network. With the NET command, you get access to server resources from a workstation. To use NET.EXE, type the command net. As explained in this chapter and subsequent chapters, the NET command has several forms with various optional parameters.

Much of the rest of this chapter focuses on some basic features of the NET command, using a two-node network to present examples. To follow the exercises in this chapter, choose two PCs in your network. For NODE1, choose a PC on which NetWare Lite was installed with server capability. This node can be either a dedicated server or both a

Running the Network Reduces Available RAM

Running STARTNET.BAT loads several TSR programs into RAM. As a result, less memory is available while the network software is loaded.

The reduced memory is not likely to cause any noticeable effects. But if you run applications which tax your machine's RAM limit (large spreadsheet applications, for example), you may not have enough memory to load large applications that fit before the network software was loaded. If you encounter this problem, see Chapter 14, "Optimizing LAN Performance."

If you want to find out just how much RAM the network software uses, follow these steps:

1. Before running STARTNET.BAT, type **chkdsk** and press Enter.

   The DOS command CHKDSK reports, among other things, how much RAM is available. The last two displayed lines indicate, respectively, the total amount of RAM installed in the machine and the number of RAM bytes currently unused (available). Make a note the number on the bottom line. This number is the number of RAM bytes currently unused.

2. Type **startnet** and press Enter.
3. Type **chkdsk** and press Enter.

Now look again at the number in the bottom line. This new value is the number of available memory bytes after the NetWare Lite software is loaded. Subtract this number from the number you noted in Step 1. The remainder tells you how much RAM NetWare Lite takes on that PC and, therefore, how much less memory you have for your applications because of the network software.

server and client. For NODE2, choose a PC on which NetWare Lite was installed as a client. This node may be exclusively a client or may be both a server and a client.

Logging in to the Network

To begin sharing resources on the network, you must first log in each computer to the network. A *login* is the process whereby a network node actively joins the network. To log in, you use a form of the NET command.

If you haven't done so already, run STARTNET.BAT on each node (type **startnet** and press Enter). To log in NODE1, type the following command at the DOS prompt:

net login supervisor

and then press Enter.

> **NOTE:** You can type the NET command from any active directory, as long as you accepted NetWare Lite's request to modify your AUTOEXEC.BAT file during the installation of NetWare Lite. If you did not accept the modification, you must be working from the C:\NWLITE directory.

Your computer returns to the DOS prompt after displaying the following message:

```
You are logged in to the network as SUPERVISOR.
```

Introducing the User Named SUPERVISOR

The *supervisor* parameter indicates that you are going to be known temporarily as a user named SUPERVISOR. A user named SUPERVISOR has special meaning to NetWare Lite. Any user logged in as SUPERVISOR has privileges to create user accounts and, in general, oversee the operation of the network.

By default, any user can log in as SUPERVISOR. For small office networks, (the primary market for NetWare Lite), you typically want all users to be peers with equal network privileges. As your network grows, or in situations in which security is important, you may want to restrict various network privileges to certain users. For more on security issues, see Chapter 11, "The Role of the LAN Administrator," and Chapter 12, "Securing the Network."

NetWare Lite Made Easy

In this chapter, each network node will log in as SUPERVISOR. The following chapter explains how to log in to the network with individual user names and accounts.

Starting the NET Menus

The easiest way to share resources and perform other network tasks is to use the NET menu system. At NODE1, invoke the NET hierarchical menu system by typing **net** (the command only, with no parameters) and pressing Enter. Your screen should look like Figure 6-1.

Using the Menu System

The NET menu system works like most pop-up menu systems. From the Main menu, use the ↑ and ↓ keys (the cursor keys) to move the highlight to any of the options. Alternatively, you can press the first letter of an option to move the highlight immediately to that option. When the highlight is on your choice, press Enter. A secondary screen pops open to show or request additional information. The secondary screen may present further options that yield tertiary screens. At any point, you can press Esc to go back one level in the menu hierarchy.

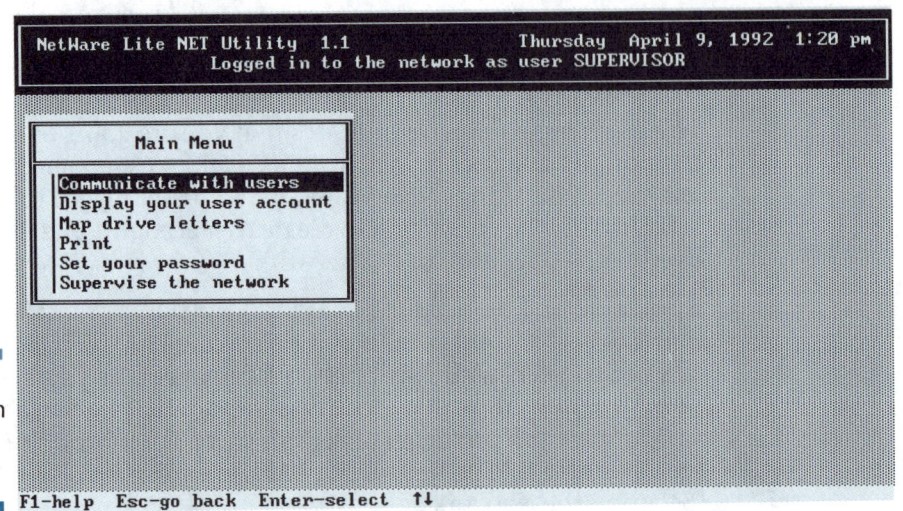

```
NetWare Lite NET Utility  1.1              Thursday April 9, 1992  1:20 pm
                 Logged in to the network as user SUPERVISOR


              ┌──────── Main Menu ────────┐
              │ Communicate with users    │
              │ Display your user account │
              │ Map drive letters         │
              │ Print                     │
              │ Set your password         │
              │ Supervise the network     │
              └───────────────────────────┘




 F1-help  Esc-go back  Enter-select  ↑↓
```

The NET program's Main menu
Figure 6-1.

Working with NetWare Lite: Basic Principles

> **NOTE:** The NET menu system does not support a mouse. You must select all options and navigate through the menu system from the keyboard.

The bottom line of the screen acts a keystroke indicator. This line lists the active keys as well as the action each performs. As you move through the menus you will see this bottom line change as different keys become active. As you can see from the bottom line in Figure 6-1, the following keys are active from the Main menu:

Key	Action
F1	Provides context-sensitive help
Esc	Goes back one menu level
Enter	Selects the currently highlighted option
↑	Moves the highlight up one option
↓	Moves the highlight down one option

Overview of the Main Menu

The Main menu presents six options, each of which opens secondary menus or pop-up boxes. Table 6-1 summarizes the options available from the Main menu. (The numbers in the second column refer to chapters in which the menu option is discussed in detail.)

Trying Out the Menu System

Follow these steps to familiarize yourself with the operation of the NET menu system:

1. Press the ↑ and ↓ keys a few times to move the highlight up and down the Main menu.
2. With the highlight on an option other than Print, press **P** and then press Enter. Note how the highlight jumps immediately to the Print option.

Table 6-1.
Options Available from NET's Main Menu

Option	Chapter Reference	Description
Communicate with users	9	Send and receive text messages to and from other users
Display your user account	12	Show detailed account information
Map drive letters	7	Capture another user's hard disk to share data and programs
Print	8	Share printers and manage print jobs
Set your password	12	Set or change your security password
Supervise the network	11	Perform various network-management functions

3. Move the highlight to `Display your user account`. Press [Enter] to select this option.

4. A box pops open, displaying information about your network account (see Figure 6-2). The different parameters in this account information box are discussed in Chapter 12, "Securing the Network."

   Note that the bottom line now shows the [F1] and [Esc] keys as active. The [Enter] key and arrow keys are not currently active. Press [Enter] a few times and notice that nothing happens.

5. Press [F1] to activate the NET help facility. A window pops open with information about user accounts. Press [Pg Dn] a few times to browse through text screens containing information about the account information box. Press [Esc] to close the help system. For more about help, see "Using the NET Help System" later in this chapter.

6. Press [Esc] to return to the Main menu.

7. Move the highlight to "`Supervise the network`" and press [Enter] to pop open a Supervise the Network secondary menu.

Working with NetWare Lite: Basic Principles

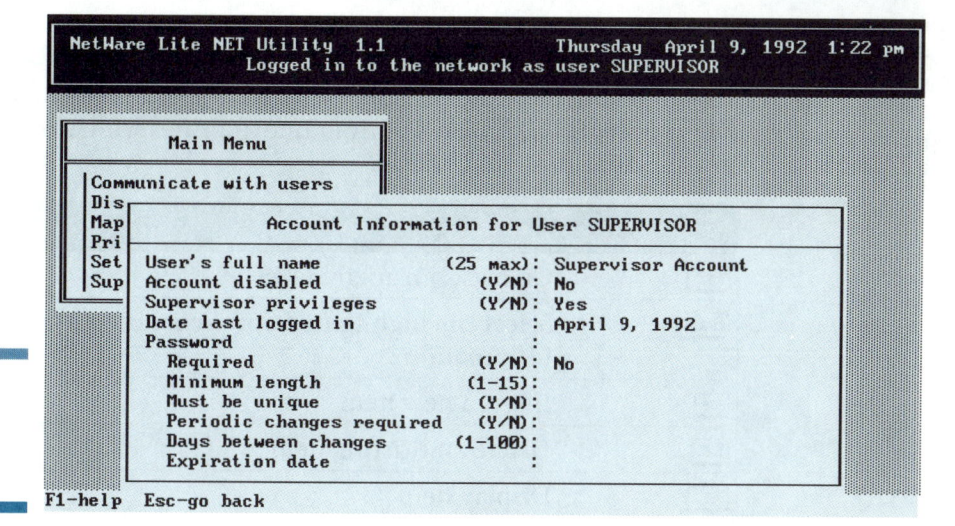

The account information screen
Figure 6-2.

```
NetWare Lite NET Utility 1.1              Thursday April 9, 1992 1:22 pm
            Logged in to the network as user SUPERVISOR

           Main Menu
      Communicate with users
      Dis┌─────────────────────────────────────────────────────────┐
      Map│         Account Information for User SUPERVISOR         │
      Pri│                                                         │
      Set│ User's full name         (25 max): Supervisor Account   │
      Sup│ Account disabled             (Y/N): No                  │
         │ Supervisor privileges        (Y/N): Yes                 │
         │ Date last logged in               : April 9, 1992       │
         │ Password                          :                     │
         │   Required                   (Y/N): No                  │
         │   Minimum length           (1-15) :                     │
         │   Must be unique             (Y/N):                     │
         │   Periodic changes required  (Y/N):                     │
         │   Days between changes     (1-100):                     │
         │   Expiration date                 :                     │
         └─────────────────────────────────────────────────────────┘
      F1-help  Esc-go back
```

8. Move the highlight to Server status and press [Enter]. A third window pops open, showing the active servers on the network. Your screen should be similar to Figure 6-3; the name "JUANITA" appears in Figure 6-3, but your screen will display the server name you specified when you installed NetWare Lite on NODE1.

9. Press [Esc] twice to return to the Main menu.

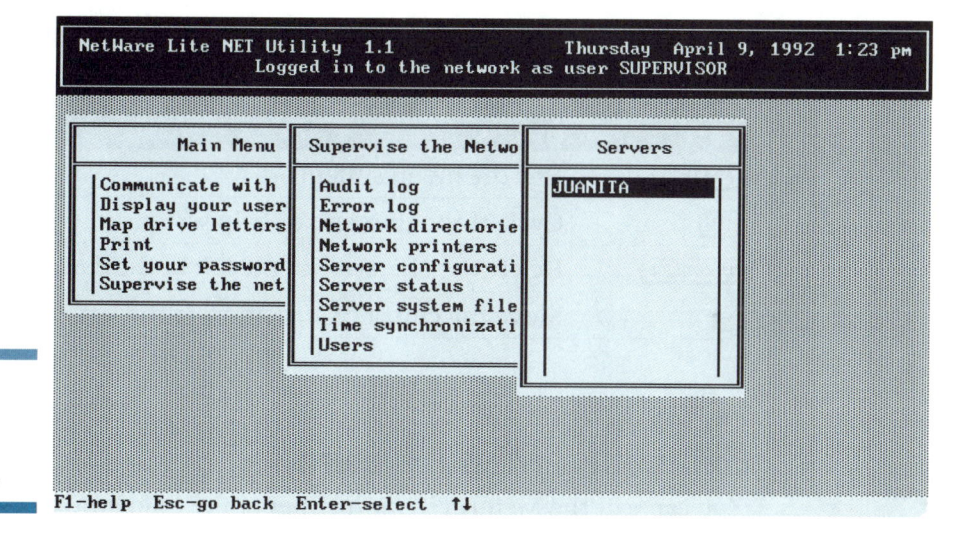

The server name is displayed
Figure 6-3.

```
NetWare Lite NET Utility 1.1              Thursday April 9, 1992 1:23 pm
            Logged in to the network as user SUPERVISOR

         Main Menu        Supervise the Netwo       Servers
      Communicate with    Audit log              ┌─────────┐
      Display your user   Error log              │ JUANITA │
      Map drive letters   Network directorie     └─────────┘
      Print               Network printers
      Set your password   Server configurati
      Supervise the net   Server status
                          Server system file
                          Time synchronizati
                          Users

      F1-help  Esc-go back  Enter-select  ↑↓
```

Using Function Keys and Other Special Keys

The following table shows which keys have special meanings in the menu system. The screen's bottom line indicates which keys are active in your current menu context.

Key	Use
Esc	Go back one menu level
Enter	Select the highlighted option or accept typed information
Ins	Insert a new item
Del	Delete an existing item
F1	Display help
F3	Modify or edit an existing item
F5	Toggle an option between two choices
F7	Cancel an option or edit typed changes
F9	Change modes
↑	Move highlight up one line
↓	Move highlight down one line

The following table shows keys that are never displayed in the screen's bottom line but perform specific actions.

Key	Action
Alt-F10	Exit the menu system
Tab	Cycle through menu or help screens
Backspace	Delete the character to the left of the cursor
←	Move the cursor one position to the left

Exiting the Menu System

You can exit the Menu system in either of the following ways:

Working with NetWare Lite: Basic Principles

- Press [Esc] while at the Main menu
- Press [Alt]-[F10] from any level of the menu system

Press [Esc] now to exit the NET program. When a box pops up asking for confirmation that you want to exit, press [Enter]. The system returns to the DOS prompt and you can do any work you normally would do from the DOS prompt.

Introduction to Resource Sharing

It's time to try sharing a resource across the network. This example takes you through the process of accessing the hard disk of a server from a client machine. You will use the hard disk of NODE1 while working at NODE2.

The purpose of this exercise is for you to experiment with networking and learn more about the NET facility. Only the simplest form of disk drive sharing is covered in this chapter. For a detailed discussion of sharing hard disks, see Chapter 7, "Sharing Disks and Directories."

Log in to the Second Computer

Go to NODE2, the machine with client capability. If you haven't done so already, run STARTNET.BAT on this machine. Log in to the network as a supervisor, exactly as you did with NODE1. Type **net login supervisor** and then press [Enter].

Map a Drive Letter

From a client, you access the hard disk on a server by mapping a drive letter. *Mapping* a drive letter means that you assign a previously nonexistent drive letter on the client to correspond with a specific directory on the server's hard disk. The drive letter mapped on the client is *not* a hard disk that physically exists; rather, a fictitious drive letter on the client is mapped, or equated, with an actual directory on the server's hard drive. By using the mapped drive letter on the client machine, the client node can access the server's hard disk. The following example should make this process clear.

On NODE2, the client machine, activate the NET menu system. (Type **net** and press [Enter].) Then follow these steps to map drive letter J on NODE2 with drive C on NODE1:

1. At the Main menu, move the highlight down to `Map drive letters` and press [Enter].

    A Network Directory box that contains a list of drive letters pops open (see Figure 6-4). The highest drive letter displayed in this box corresponds to the LASTDRIVE= statement in your CONFIG.SYS file. If you accepted the normal NetWare Lite installation options, you see drive letters from A to M.

2. Move the highlight to `J:` by pressing **J** or using the [↓] key.
3. Press [Enter].

    A third box, which displays the default drives available to be mapped, pops open (see Figure 6-5). As you can see, a single server drive is available in this example. By default, NetWare Lite lists drive C of all servers logged into the network. In this example, CDRIVE is available on the server JUANITA. (If you see more than one server name on your screen, move the highlight to the line that specifies the server name corresponding to your NODE1.)

4. Press [Enter] to accept the drive mapping.

    The third box closes. The second box now reveals the mapping assigned to drive J (see Figure 6-6).

5. Exit NET.

    Instead of pressing [Esc] twice to go back through the menus, press [Alt]-[F10] as a kind of "express" exit. When the confirmation box appears, press [Enter] to accept the exit from NET.

Testing the Drive Mapping

Now for the moment of truth. From the client, you will access drive C on the server.

At the DOS prompt on the client, type **J:** and press [Enter]. You should see the following DOS prompt on your screen:

```
J:\>
```

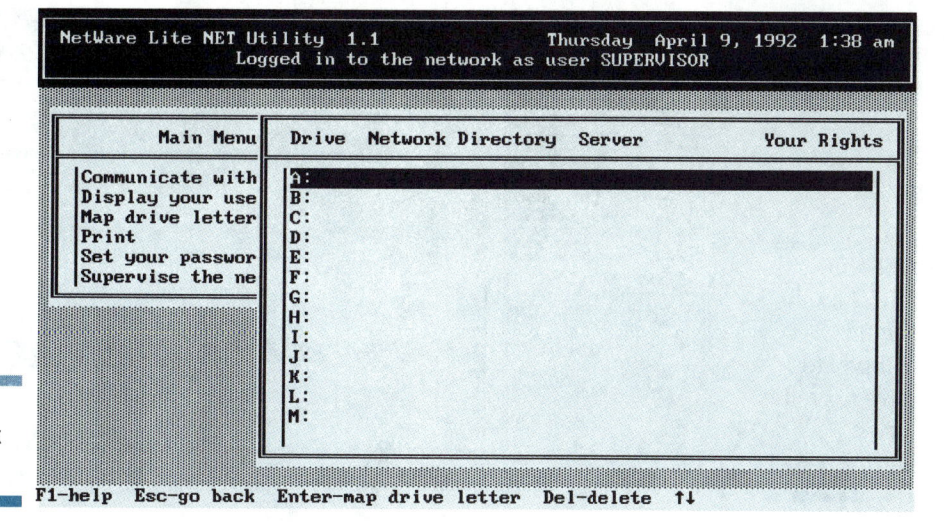

Working with NetWare Lite: Basic Principles

```
NetWare Lite NET Utility  1.1              Thursday  April 9, 1992  1:38 am
               Logged in to the network as user SUPERVISOR

         Main Menu     Drive  Network Directory   Server        Your Rights
    Communicate with    A:
    Display your use    B:
    Map drive letter    C:
    Print               D:
    Set your passwor    E:
    Supervise the ne    F:
                        G:
                        H:
                        I:
                        J:
                        K:
                        L:
                        M:

 F1-help  Esc-go back  Enter-map drive letter  Del-delete  ↑↓
```

The Network Directory box
Figure 6-4.

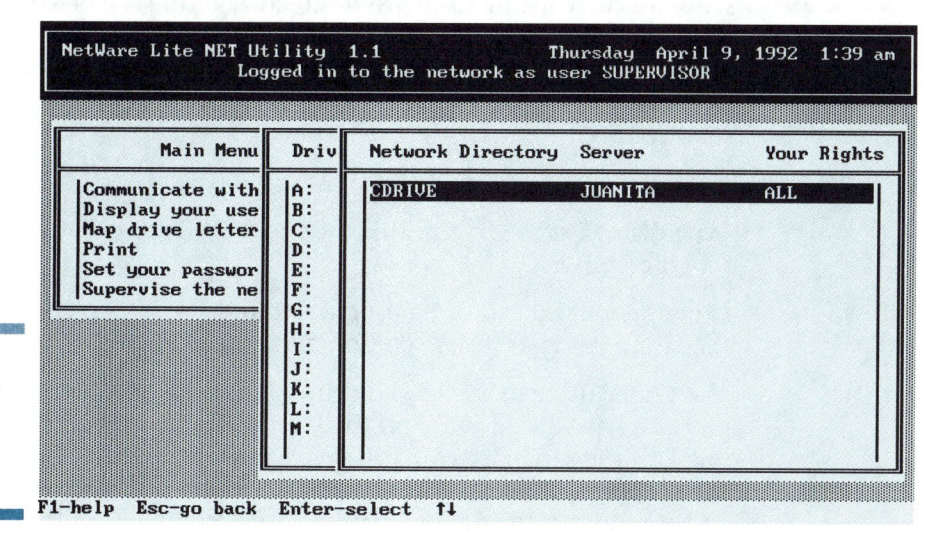

```
NetWare Lite NET Utility  1.1              Thursday  April 9, 1992  1:39 am
               Logged in to the network as user SUPERVISOR

         Main Menu    Driv   Network Directory   Server        Your Rights
    Communicate with  A:     CDRIVE              JUANITA        ALL
    Display your use  B:
    Map drive letter  C:
    Print             D:
    Set your passwor  E:
    Supervise the ne  F:
                      G:
                      H:
                      I:
                      J:
                      K:
                      L:
                      M:

 F1-help  Esc-go back  Enter-select  ↑↓
```

NET displays the disk drive available for mapping
Figure 6-5.

The exact DOS prompt displayed depends on the PROMPT statement in your AUTOEXEC.BAT file. On most computers, `prompt $p$g` or a similar statement is in the AUTOEXEC.BAT file. Such a statement results in the active drive, J in this case, showing as the DOS prompt.

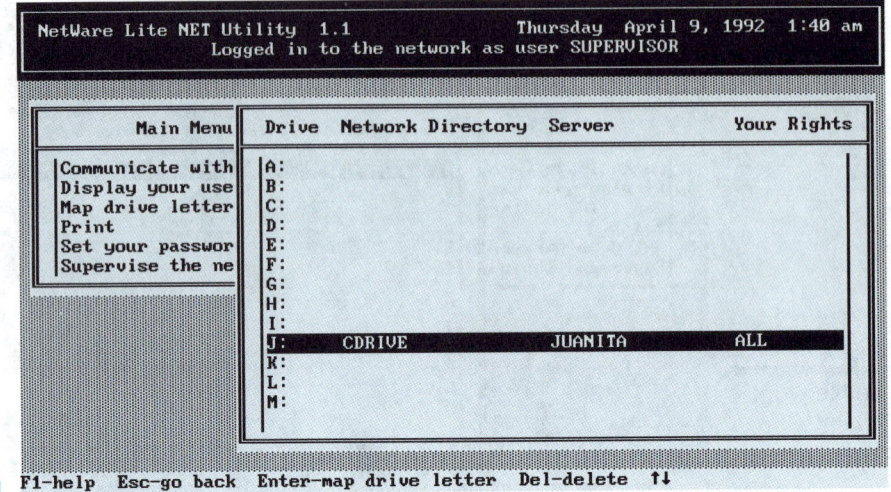

```
NetWare Lite NET Utility  1.1           Thursday  April 9, 1992  1:40 am
              Logged in to the network as user SUPERVISOR

         Main Menu    Drive  Network Directory    Server        Your Rights
      Communicate with  A:
      Display your use  B:
      Map drive letter  C:
      Print             D:
      Set your passwor  E:
      Supervise the ne  F:
                        G:
                        H:
                        I:
                        J:     CDRIVE              JUANITA          ALL
                        K:
                        L:
                        M:

F1-help   Esc-go back   Enter-map drive letter   Del-delete   ↑↓
```

NET shows that drive J on the client is mapped to drive C on the server
Figure 6-6.

You now have access to the root directory on the server's hard disk. To see a directory listing of the root directory of the server's drive C, type **dir**. You can use the CD command to access subdirectories. If, for example, you type **cd \nwlite** and press Enter, you see the following DOS prompt, which indicates that you are now in the server's NWLITE subdirectory:

J:\NWLITE>

Type **dir** to list the files in this subdirectory. Type **cd** to return to the root directory.

Experiment. You can run a program found on the server's hard disk by executing the appropriate command at the client.

The virtual drive (denoted J) on the client is mapped (equated) to the physical hard disk drive C on the server. The two disk drives act as one-and-the-same drive. If you save a new file on drive J of the client, the file is actually saved on drive C of the server. Similarly, if you erase a file on drive J, the file is actually erased on drive C of the server. Needless to say, be careful about erasing any files that the server's owner may covet.

If you need more proof that the two disk drives are mapped, try the following exercise. Go to the server machine. Create a short text file

Working with NetWare Lite: Basic Principles

containing a message such as "Hello out there from the server." To create the file, use a text editor such as EDLIN in DOS, the EDIT command in DOS 5, any text editor, or word processor. Save the file directly on the server in the root directory of drive C with the name TESTNET.DOC. Return to the client machine. Currently, the DOS prompt J:\> should be displayed. If not, type **cd** to return to the root directory. Type **type testnet.doc** and press [Enter].

You should see on the client whatever message or text you saved in the file on the server. To erase the file on the server's hard disk, type **erase testnet.doc** and press [Enter].

At the client, type **C:** and press [Enter]. The DOS prompt becomes C:\> (referring to drive C of the client, not drive C on the server). Remember that the server's drive C is mapped into drive J on the client. Drive C on the client remains intact and has nothing to do with drive C on the server.

Verifying the Mapping

Another way to confirm the mapping is to type **net map** at the DOS prompt and then press [Enter].

NetWare Lite responds with a short table titled "Current Drive Mappings." The table indicates that drive J has been mapped into the network directory CDRIVE on the server JUANITA. (Your server name will vary.)

> **NOTE:** The net map command is another example of using a NET command directly from the DOS prompt. Recall that you previously invoked a NET command from the DOS prompt by typing **net login supervisor** to log in to the network. For more about using NET commands at the DOS prompt, see "Using NET from the DOS Prompt" later in this chapter.

Terminating the Mapping

To cancel the drive mapping, follow these steps:

1. From the client, activate the NET menu system. (Type **net** and press [Enter].)

2. Highlight `Map drive letters` and press [Enter]. The Network Directory list displays.

3. Move the highlight down to the J: line.

4. Note that the bottom screen line indicates that the [Del] key is active to delete entries. Press [Del].

5. A confirmation box pops open. Press [Enter] to confirm that you want to delete the mapping. The server name and directory are deleted from the J: drive line.

6. Exit NET by pressing [Alt]-[F10] followed by [Enter].

You have terminated the map, or link, between the client's drive J and the server's drive C. Now when you type **J:** and press [Enter], you see the following (undoubtedly familiar) DOS error message:

```
Bad command or file name
```

Using NET from the DOS Prompt

Even though using the NET menu system is easy, you can accomplish most of the same results without using the interactive menus. Instead, you type at the DOS prompt the various forms of the NET command that specify the complete action you want taken.

As you've seen, to invoke NET's menu system, you type **net** and press [Enter]. To bypass the menu system and use NET in an "express" mode, you type **net**, followed by appropriate parameters, and then press [Enter]. You used this express form of NET when you typed **net login supervisor** to log in to the network and when you typed **net map** to list the current drive mappings.

Although most of the NET functions available in express mode can be invoked also from the menu system, some express-mode commands *cannot* be duplicated from the menus. Table 6-2 shows the NET commands available in express mode. The Name column indicates the parameter you type immediately following **net**. Scan the table to get an idea of what you can accomplish with express-mode NET commands. Each of the commands in Table 6-2 is discussed in depth later in the book.

To complete most of the commands listed in Table 6-2, you must also type one or more additional parameters before you press [Enter]. For

Working with NetWare Lite: Basic Principles

Name	Chapter Reference	Menu Equivalent	Description
audit	12	No	Writes an entry to the network audit log
capture	7	Yes	Sends a print job to a network printer
help	6	Yes	Displays help text
info	12	No	Displays user-account information
login	6	No	Logs a node in to the network
logout	6	No	Logs a node out of the network
map	7	Yes	Maps drive letters
ndlist	7	Yes	Lists available network directories
nplist	8	Yes	Lists available network printers
print	8	Yes	Prints a file on a network printer
receive	9	Yes	Controls message reception from other users
save	7	No	Saves a record of your node's current configuration
send	9	Yes	Sends text messages to other users
setpass	12	Yes	Sets a password for your node
slist	16	Yes	Lists the servers connected to the network

NET commands available from the DOS prompt
Table 6-2.

Table 6-3.
NET commands available from the DOS prompt

Name	Chapter Reference	Menu Equivalent	Description
time	15	Yes	Synchronizes clock time between a client and a server
ulist	7	Yes	Lists the users on a network

instance, **net map** is a valid command by itself but **net login** accepts an additional parameter identifying the user's name. In this chapter, you used the name "supervisor" as the additional parameter. The next chapter explains how to log in with an individual user's account name.

> **NOTE:** One important use of NET from the DOS prompt is to insert NET commands into batch files. For example, you can modify STARTNET.BAT to initialize the network according to your preferences. Perhaps you want to always start your network with particular drive mappings in effect. You can also create customized batch files that perform a standard series of network chores. For more about creating and modifying network batch files, see Appendix C, "Sample Batch Files."

Using the NET Help System

NetWare Lite provides several screens of help information to assist you with NET. Help is available from within the menu system or directly from the DOS prompt.

Getting Help from the Menu System

While in the menu system, you can get help at any time by pressing **F1**. A box containing help text pops open. In most situations, you can use the (Pg Up) and (Pg Dn) keys to see boxes of related information. Press (Esc) to close the help system.

Getting Help from the DOS Prompt

To enter the help system while at the DOS prompt, use the net help command. Type **net help** followed by the name of the command for which you want help. For example, to see help about logging into the network, type **net help login** and press Enter.

If you type **net help** or **net ?** and then press Enter, NetWare Lite displays the following list of available net help commands:

```
net help audit
net help capture
net help info
net help login
net help logout
net help map
net help ndlist
net help nplist
net help print
net help receive
net help save
net help send
net help setpass
net help slist
net help time
net help ulist
```

Shutting Down the Network

If net login is the command to log you in to the network, it makes sense that net logout is the command to log you out of the network.

When you type **net logout** and press Enter, you remove your node from the active network. Mapped drives and other networking links established at your node are canceled. For more about logging in to and out of the network, see Chapter 7, "Sharing Disks and Directories."

Shutting Off a Network Computer

The most dramatic way to remove a network node from the active network is to power off the computer. Or reboot your computer, either with the Ctrl-Alt-Del keypress combination or by pressing a reset button if your computer has one.

CAUTION: Before you turn off a server, be sure that no other computers are using the server's resources. If you press a reset button or turn off the server's power, you might lose disk data or corrupt data files if any users have disk files open on the server. As explained in Chapter 7, you can use NET to determine which nodes, if any, are actively accessing server resources.

If you use Ctrl-Alt-Del on a server, NetWare Lite intercepts the command, sounds three quick beeps, and pops open a Server Shut-Down box. As indicated in the box, you can now select one of three continuation options, as follows:

◆ Press **1** to disable the server without rebooting. NetWare Lite removes the SERVER.EXE program from memory.

◆ Press **2** to reboot the computer. Use this option to proceed with the rebooting.

◆ Press Esc to cancel the reboot process and return to the DOS prompt.

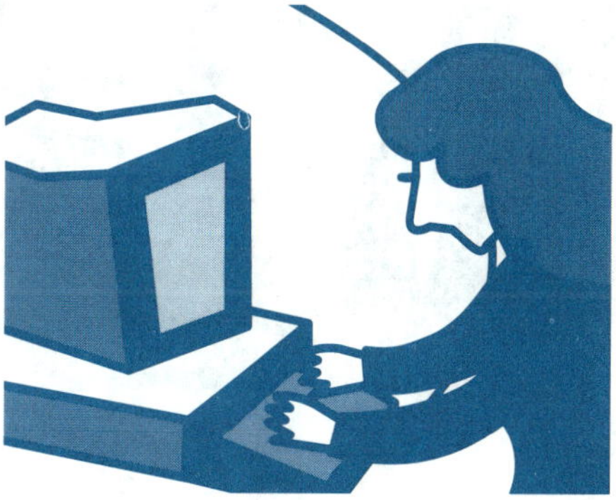

CHAPTER

7
SHARING DISKS AND DIRECTORIES

The previous chapter introduced disk sharing. You learned how to map a drive letter on your workstation to drive C on a server's hard disk. This chapter further examines the process of sharing hard disk drives and directories. You can share drives other than drive C and also share specific directories. You will learn the following techniques:

✦ *Offering, from a server, a specific drive or directory for sharing*

- Mapping, from a workstation, a local drive letter into any drive or directory offered by a server
- Canceling, from a workstation, an existing mapping
- Discontinuing, from a server, the offering of a drive or directory

Files and Directories in DOS

As a user of NetWare Lite, you are necessarily involved with DOS, the operating system used on IBM PCs and compatibles. Your computers may be running PC DOS, MS-DOS, or DR DOS. These versions of DOS all treat files and directory structures in a similar way.

To use the NetWare Lite disk-sharing features, you should be familiar with the basic principles of working with DOS files, directories, and paths. You don't need to be a DOS wizard; a knowledge of how DOS organizes files into directories is sufficient. In the interests of establishing common terminology and introducing the basic concepts, a brief tutorial is included here. Should you want more information, consult your DOS documentation or one of the many excellent books on DOS, such as *DOS 5 Made Easy*, by Herbert Schildt, published by Osborne/McGraw-Hill.

Your computer has one or more disk *drives*, each designated by a letter. Floppy disk drives are designated drive A and drive B. (Machines with one floppy drive have drive A but no drive B.) You insert (and remove) floppy disks into (and from) the floppy disk drives. A hard disk drive usually is designated drive C. Some machines have more than one hard drive, in which case the additional drives are called drive D, drive E, and so on. Each hard disk is permanently mounted inside a hard disk drive. Another name for a hard disk is *fixed* disk.

Each disk (whether hard or floppy) is organized in a *directory* structure, which may have a single level or several levels. The base directory, called the *root*, may spawn one or more subdirectories, each of which may also have further subdirectories, and so on. (The terms *directory* and *subdirectory* are used interchangeably in practice.)

A *file* is a collection of *bytes* (computer data) given a name and stored in a directory. A directory can contain no files, one file, or several files. Two different directories may contain files with the same name. Such

Sharing Disks and Directories

files, however, are independent and may contain completely different data.

A path is used to indicate the logical location of a file on a disk.

To uniquely identify a file, you must specify not only the name of the file, but also the path to the file. The *path* consists of the drive letter and the chain of directories from the root to the directory containing the file.

A path name begins with the drive letter followed immediately by a colon. The directory chain follows, beginning with a backslash character (\) to indicate the root directory. Directory names, which can be from one to eight characters long, are separated by backslashes.

Here are some examples of directory paths:

A:\

B:\DOCUMENT

C:\SALES\REPORTS\DOCUMENT

The first sample path specifies the root directory on drive A. The second specifies a directory named DOCUMENT located immediately below the root directory of drive B. The third example specifies a directory chain three levels deep on drive C.

Filenames, which also have from one to eight characters, can include an optional extension of one to three characters. If included, the extension is separated from the rest of the name by a period. RESUME.ME, CLIENT.EXE, and CHAPTER7.DOC, for example, are all valid filenames. When you specify a file or directory name, DOS treats upper- and lowercase letters equivalently: RESUME.ME and resume.me refer to the same file.

To indicate a specific file in a specific directory, you add the filename after the path designation (using a backslash to separate the two). To illustrate: B:\DOCUMENT\RESUME.ME specifies the file named RESUME.ME located in the directory named \DOCUMENT on drive B. Such a complete specification, which includes the filename and the path to the file, is called a *filespec*.

At all times, DOS maintains a default drive and a default directory on each drive. When you first turn on a computer, the default directory on each drive is the root directory (unless an AUTOEXEC.BAT command alters this default). To change the default drive, you type a drive letter followed by a colon and then press (Enter). For example, if you type **a:** and press (Enter), the computer makes drive A the default drive (the DOS prompt changes to A:\>). You can change the default directory on a drive by using the CHDIR command in DOS. (CHDIR stands for "Change Directory"; the short name for the command is CD.) If you type **cd \document** and press (Enter), for example, the computer makes the \document directory the default directory (the DOS prompt changes to A:\DOCUMENT>).

Overview of Disk Sharing

Before you can share a server's hard disk or directory from a workstation, you must take the following steps:

1. On the server, declare the disk or directory to be available. This is called *creating a network directory*.
2. On the workstation, map a drive letter to the available disk or directory.

To accomplish each of these steps, you use NET (either with the menu system or by commands at the DOS prompt). After the disk directory is mapped, the workstation user typically exits the NET program. The DOS prompt appears onscreen, and the user can do normal work such as word processing, spreadsheet calculations, or other applications. The big difference is that the server's disk is now available to you while you work in an application. While working in your word processor at a workstation, for example, you can load a document stored on the server's mapped hard drive.

To share any network resource, NetWare Lite uses the principle of associating a device name on the workstation with the actual shared resource on the server. For disk drives, as explained in this chapter, you map a drive letter on the workstation to the server's disk. For printer sharing, as you will learn in Chapter 8, you capture a workstation's printer port to the server's printer.

In networking terminology, the process of routing a device request from the workstation to the proper device on the server is called *redirection*. The workstation user acts as though the mapped disk or

Sharing Disks and Directories

captured printer exists locally on the workstation. After a drive letter has been mapped, for example, a file saved on the workstation's mapped drive is redirected to the server's hard disk (where the file is actually stored). Also, after a shared printer has been captured, print jobs created at the workstation are redirected to the printer physically attached to the server.

NOTE: Even though you now have a network, you will spend most of your computer time as you did in prenetwork days. After you initialize the network, log in, and redirect the resources you want, you return to the DOS prompt. You can run application programs, Windows, or anything else you ran before you installed NetWare Lite. Although you occasionally will run NET to use a network feature, most of your working time is spent running your familiar applications.

Network Directories

When you install NetWare Lite on a server, drive C automatically is made available for sharing. In Chapter 6 you learned how to map drive C on a server to a drive letter on a workstation.

You have the option of sharing, from the server's hard disk, entire disk drives (such as drive C or drive D) or specific directories. To share a drive or directory, you first use NET to designate the drive or directory a *network directory*. Then you can map a workstation's drive letter to the server's network directory. At that point, the workstation can access any files in the server's network directory.

Each server can stipulate multiple network directories. It's not uncommon for a server to define five or more network directories.

NOTE: You can designate an entire disk drive—drive C, for example, or drive D (if the server has a drive D)—or a specific directory—such as C:\SALES or C:\SALES\REPORTS—as a network directory. When considered as a network directory, drive C means the root directory (on drive C).

A Sample LAN Configuration

The examples in this chapter assume a three-node LAN consisting of two servers (JUANITA and MAXWELL) and a workstation. (Remember—each server must be given a name during installation.) Each server is configured to be both a server and a client.

All three nodes are initialized with STARTNET.BAT (as described in Chapter 6) and logged into the network with the command **net login supervisor**. (Chapter 9 explains how to set up customized user accounts and log into the network with separate named accounts.)

NOTE: If all nodes are logged into the network as SUPERVISOR, every node has access to all the network directories and other network resources. As you will learn from Chapter 12, by setting up individual user accounts you can restrict access to particular resources by specific users.

Figure 7-1 depicts the directory structure of drive C of the server JUANITA. The root branches to three subdirectories named DOS, SALES, and NWLITE. SALES branches to three subdirectories: CHARTS, REPORTS, and BUDGETS. REPORTS has two subdirectories: DOCUMENT and GRAPH. This chapter's "Creating a Network Directory" section explains how to make C:\SALES\REPORTS a network directory.

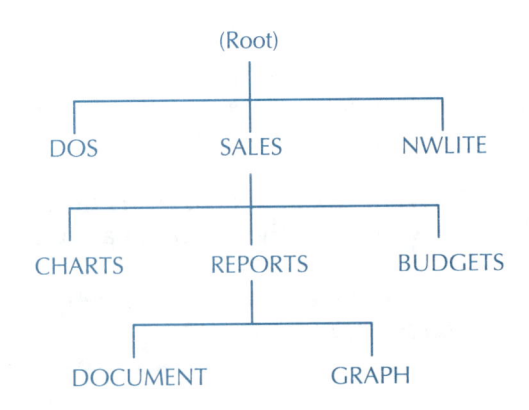

Directory structure of drive C on the server JUANITA
Figure 7-1.

Sharing Disks and Directories

The simple directory structure of JUANITA is used here for illustration. Directory structures on your PCs are likely to be more complicated.

The Scope of a Network Directory

When a workstation maps a drive letter to a network directory, the workstation gains access to all files in subdirectories below the network directory as well as to all files in the network directory. In other words, the workstation can access all subdirectories whose path includes the network directory.

The range of available directories is referred to as the *scope* of the network directory. If C:\SALES\REPORTS is made a network directory on the server JUANITA, the shaded area in Figure 7-2 shows the scope of this network directory. A workstation that maps a drive letter to this network directory has access to all files contained in the directories included in the shaded area. In the example of Figure 7-2, the workstation has access to files in the directory C:\SALES\REPORTS\DOCUMENT but cannot access files in C:\SALES or in C:\SALES\BUDGETS.

The ability to restrict scope explains why a server might choose to offer a specific directory rather than an entire disk drive. Remember that, by default, NetWare Lite makes drive C of each server a network directory. With this default network directory, a workstation can access every

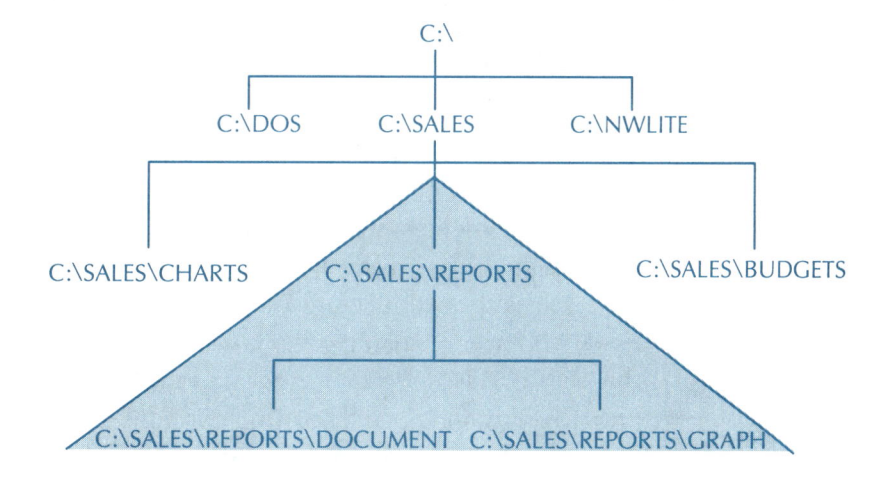

Scope of the network directory C:\SALES\REPORTS
Figure 7-2.

directory and every file on drive C. If the network directory is instead a specific directory down the directory chain, the workstation can access only that directory and its subdirectories.

For two common reasons—security and simplicity—a server may want to limit scope by offering a specific directory rather than the entire drive.

Security   Frequently, the server may not want workstations to have access to files in the root directory (or to files in directories outside the scope of a network directory). Perhaps certain files contain sensitive information not intended for use by the entire network. And if access to critical files is denied, a workstation user cannot accidentally modify or erase an important file. By making important files off-limits to workstations, a degree of security is obtained.

Simplicity   If a workstation user wants to access a particular directory on a server, mapping a drive letter directly to that directory is more convenient for the user than mapping a drive letter to the root directory. If the root directory is mapped, the workstation user must later (after exiting NET) specify directory paths to gain access to the desired directory.

Creating a Network Directory

You can create a network directory while working at any node in the network. (That is, to create a network directory on a server, you don't have to be working on that server—you can be working at another server or at a workstation.) To create the network directory, follow the steps in this section. In this example, the server JUANITA makes C:\SALES\REPORTS a network directory.

1. Activate the menu system by typing **net** and then pressing [Enter].
2. At the Main menu, move the highlight down to Supervise the network, as shown in Figure 7-3.
3. Press [Enter] to pop open the "Supervise the Network" menu. Move the highlight to Network directories, as in Figure 7-4.
4. Press [Enter] to pop open a box that contains a list of the existing network directories, shown in Figure 7-5.

Sharing Disks and Directories

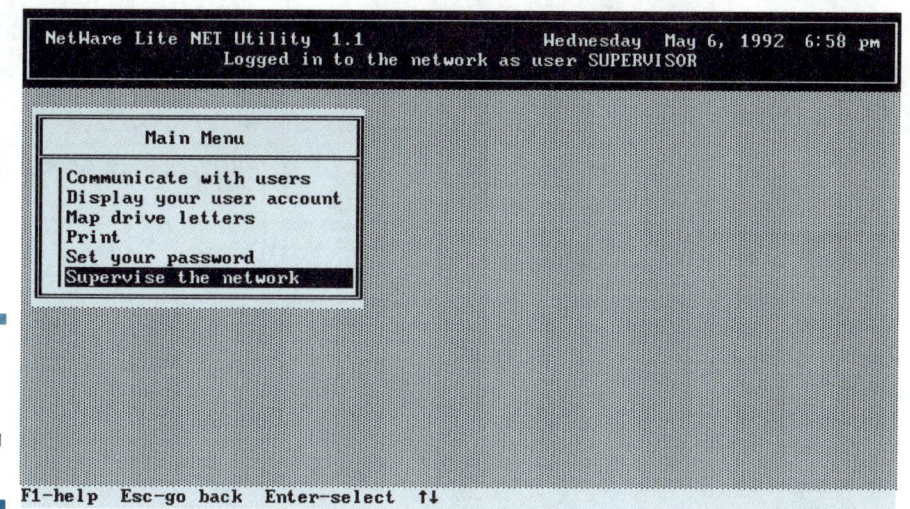

```
NetWare Lite NET Utility 1.1          Wednesday  May 6, 1992  6:58 pm
              Logged in to the network as user SUPERVISOR

              ┌──────── Main Menu ────────┐
              │ Communicate with users    │
              │ Display your user account │
              │ Map drive letters         │
              │ Print                     │
              │ Set your password         │
              │ Supervise the network     │
              └───────────────────────────┘




F1-help  Esc-go back  Enter-select  ↑↓
```

"Supervise the network" is selected from the Main menu
Figure 7-3.

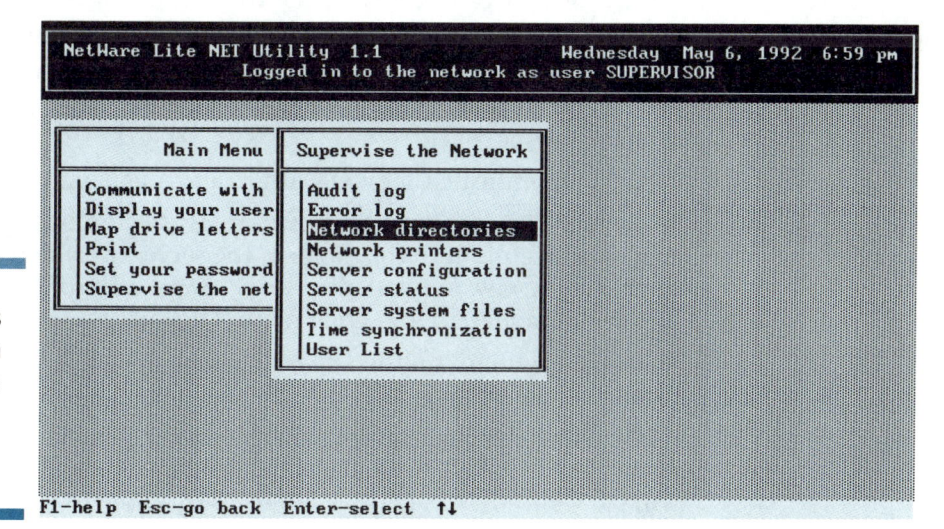

```
NetWare Lite NET Utility 1.1          Wednesday  May 6, 1992  6:59 pm
              Logged in to the network as user SUPERVISOR

         ┌──── Main Menu ─────┬──── Supervise the Network ────┐
         │ Communicate with   │ Audit log                     │
         │ Display your user  │ Error log                     │
         │ Map drive letters  │ Network directories           │
         │ Print              │ Network printers              │
         │ Set your password  │ Server configuration          │
         │ Supervise the net  │ Server status                 │
         └────────────────────│ Server system files           │
                              │ Time synchronization          │
                              │ User List                     │
                              └───────────────────────────────┘

F1-help  Esc-go back  Enter-select  ↑↓
```

"Network directories" is selected from the Supervise the Network menu
Figure 7-4.

This "Network Directory" box shows not only the name given to each network directory but also the name of the server on which the directory is located. When you install NetWare Lite, the installation program sets up drive C on each server as a network directory. As you can see from Figure 7-5, drive C on JUANITA and

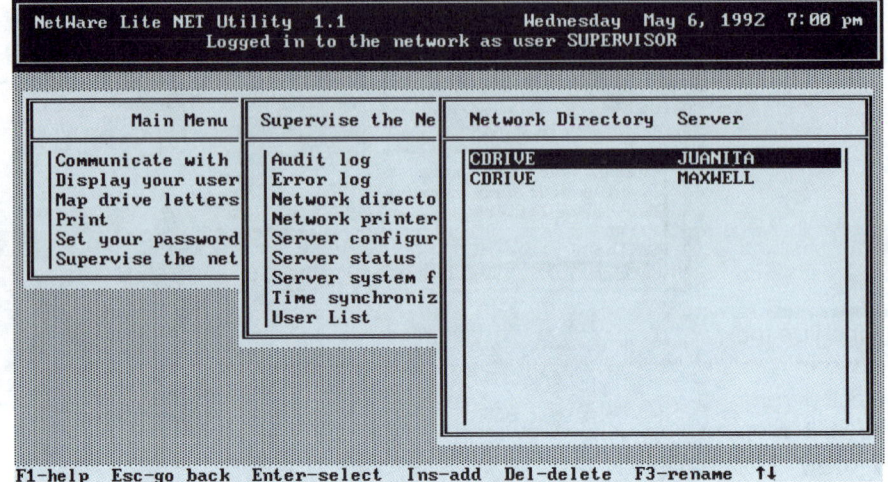

By default, drive C on each of the two servers is a network directory
Figure 7-5.

```
NetWare Lite NET Utility 1.1           Wednesday  May 6, 1992  7:00 pm
              Logged in to the network as user SUPERVISOR

        ┌───── Main Menu ─────┬── Supervise the Ne ──┬── Network Directory  Server ──┐
        │ Communicate with    │ Audit log            │ CDRIVE            JUANITA     │
        │ Display your user   │ Error log            │ CDRIVE            MAXWELL     │
        │ Map drive letters   │ Network directo      │                               │
        │ Print               │ Network printer      │                               │
        │ Set your password   │ Server configur      │                               │
        │ Supervise the net   │ Server status        │                               │
        │                     │ Server system f      │                               │
        │                     │ Time synchroniz      │                               │
        │                     │ User List            │                               │
        └─────────────────────┴──────────────────────┴───────────────────────────────┘
 F1-help  Esc-go back  Enter-select  Ins-add  Del-delete  F3-rename  ↑↓
```

drive C on MAXWELL were given the name CDRIVE. Later in this chapter, you will learn how to delete these default network directories.

Note that the screen's bottom line indicates some newly active keys. You can press [Ins], [Del], or [F3] to add, delete, or rename a directory, respectively.

5. Press [Ins] to indicate that you want to add a new network directory.

   A "Servers" box like the one shown in Figure 7-6 pops open. You move the highlight to the name of the server on which you want to define the new network directory. In this example, the network directory is added to the server named JUANITA.

6. With the highlight on the server you want (JUANITA, in this example), press [Enter].

   A box pops open, prompting you to provide a name for the new network directory. This name is the descriptive name client nodes will see when they map drive letters to this directory. Select a name that clients will readily identify with the contents of the directory. Note that this name is not the actual name of the directory on the server's hard disk (although you can use that name if you want to).

7. Type a descriptive name. TEXT_DOCUMENTS, the name typed in this example, is shown in Figure 7-7.

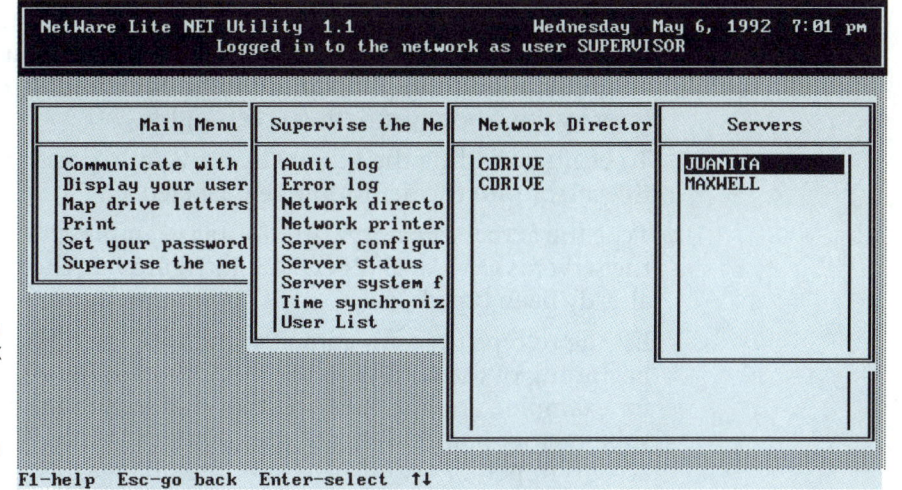

Sharing Disks and Directories

```
NetWare Lite NET Utility 1.1              Wednesday  May 6, 1992  7:01 pm
          Logged in to the network as user SUPERVISOR

       Main Menu        Supervise the Ne   Network Director        Servers
    Communicate with    Audit log          CDRIVE               JUANITA
    Display your user   Error log          CDRIVE               MAXWELL
    Map drive letters   Network directo
    Print               Network printer
    Set your password   Server configur
    Supervise the net   Server status
                        Server system f
                        Time synchroniz
                        User List


F1-help  Esc-go back  Enter-select  ↑↓
```

The Servers box opens
Figure 7-6.

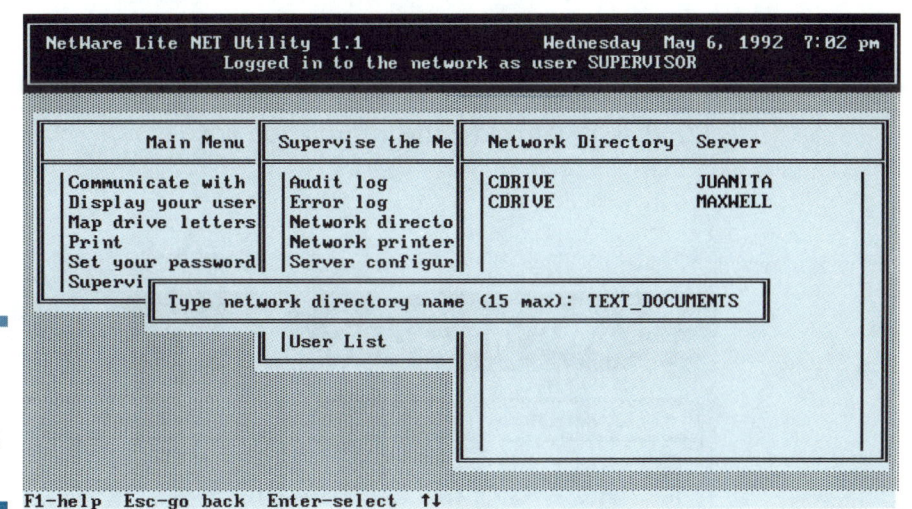

```
NetWare Lite NET Utility 1.1              Wednesday  May 6, 1992  7:02 pm
          Logged in to the network as user SUPERVISOR

       Main Menu        Supervise the Ne   Network Directory    Server
    Communicate with    Audit log          CDRIVE               JUANITA
    Display your user   Error log          CDRIVE               MAXWELL
    Map drive letters   Network directo
    Print               Network printer
    Set your password   Server configur
    Supervi
           Type network directory name (15 max): TEXT_DOCUMENTS

                        User List


F1-help  Esc-go back  Enter-select  ↑↓
```

The network directory is named TEXT_DOCUMENTS
Figure 7-7.

NetWare Lite accepts names up to 15 characters long. Letters must be uppercase; any lowercase letters you type are converted to uppercase. Also, any blank spaces are converted to underscore (_) characters.

8. Press `Enter` to pop open a box that prompts you for information about the network directory.

The main information you must provide is the directory path to this new network directory. The box also enables you to restrict access to this directory in various ways. See Chapter 12 for more information about restricting access rights.

9. To begin providing the actual directory path, press [Enter] to move the cursor into the definition field labeled `Actual directory path`.

10. Type the actual directory path. In this example, the actual path on the server is C:\SALES\REPORTS. In Figure 7-8, the path has already been typed.

    Be sure to type the path correctly. Indicate the physical drive at the beginning of the path with the drive letter followed by a colon (C:, for example), and use the backslash character (\) to separate subdirectory names. When you type the path, NetWare Lite accepts upper- or lowercase letters interchangeably.

11. After typing the path correctly, press [Enter].

    The highlight moves down to the field labeled `Default access rights`. See Chapter 12 for a discussion of restricting access rights and other security issues.

12. Press [Esc] to close the information box.

```
NetWare Lite NET Utility 1.1                    Wednesday  May 6, 1992  7:03 pm
              Logged in to the network as user SUPERVISOR

        Main Menu    │ Supervise the Ne │ Network Directory   Server
   Communicate with  │ Audit log        │ CDRIVE              JUANITA
   Display your user │ Error log        │ CDRIVE              MAXWELL
   Map drive letters │ Network directo
   Print             │ Network printer
   Set your password │ Server configur
   Supervise the net │ Server status
                     │ Server system f
                     │ Time synchroniz
                     │ User List

   Information for Network Directory TEXT_DOCUMENTS on Server JUANITA
   Actual directory path  (40 max):  C:\SALES\REPORTS
   Default access rights           : ALL
   Users with nondefault rights    : (Press Enter to see list)
   F1-help   Esc-go back   Enter-select   ↑↓
```

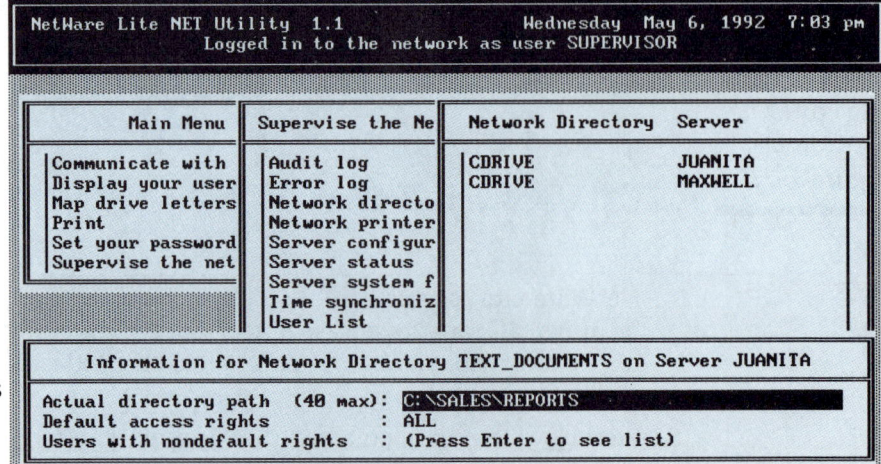

The actual directory path is entered
Figure 7-8.

Sharing Disks and Directories

A confirmation box labeled "Save changes" pops open. You can select Yes or No. The highlight is on Yes.

13. Press [Enter] to select Yes from the confirmation box.

   By selecting Yes, you indicate that the directory path is typed correctly and that you want NetWare Lite to retain a record of the new network directory.

   After you press [Enter], the information box and the confirmation box close. As Figure 7-9 shows, the Network Directory box now indicates that TEXT_DOCUMENTS is a network directory.

14. Press [Alt]-[F10] and then [Enter] to exit the NET menu system and return to the DOS prompt.

Mapping a Drive Letter to a Network Directory

Now consider a workstation user who wants to access a server's network directory. In the preceding chapter, you learned how to map a drive letter. You mapped virtual drive J on a client machine to drive C on a server machine. In general, you can map a drive letter on a workstation to any network directory offered by a server.

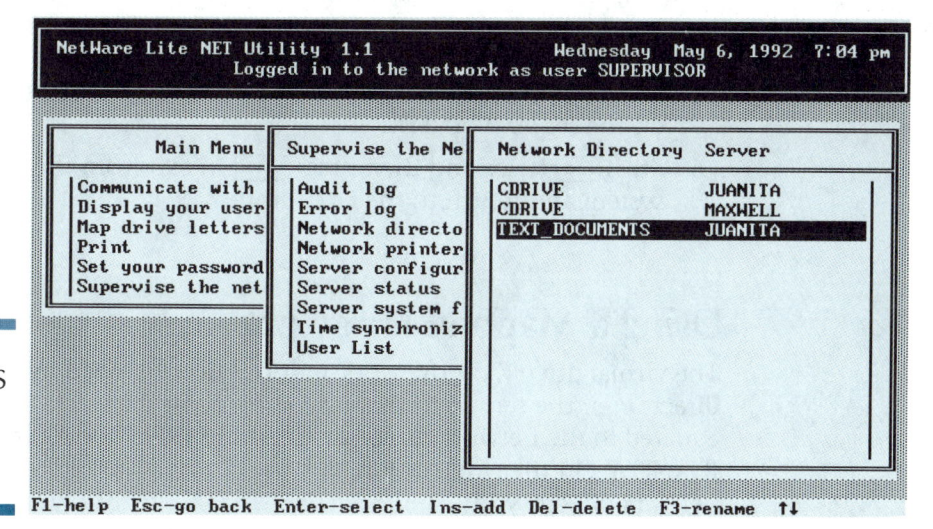

TEXT_DOCUMENTS is a network directory
Figure 7-9.

Creating a Mapping

The following example maps drive K on a workstation to the network directory named TEXT_DOCUMENTS (the one you just created). Remember that the network directory is offered on the server named JUANITA and the path on the server for this directory is C:\SALES\REPORTS.

Follow these steps to map drive K on a workstation to the network directory named TEXT_DOCUMENTS:

1. On the workstation, at the DOS prompt, type **net** and press [Enter] to invoke NetWare Lite's Main menu.
2. Move the highlight to Map drive letters and press [Enter].
3. At the Network Directory box, move the highlight down to K:.

    You are now prepared to map drive K on the workstation to a network directory.

4. Press [Enter] to see a list of the available network directories. The screen should look like Figure 7-10.

    Three network directories are available: CDRIVE on both servers and TEXT_DOCUMENTS on the server JUANITA.

5. To establish the mapping, move the highlight down to TEXT_DOCUMENTS and press [Enter].

    The screen should look like Figure 7-11. The Network Directory box indicates that NetWare Lite has mapped drive K of the workstation to the network directory TEXT_DOCUMENTS located on the server JUANITA.

6. Press [Esc] twice and then press [Enter] to exit from the NET menu system and return to the DOS prompt.

Using a Mapped Directory

The virtual drive K on the workstation is now mapped into the network directory of the server. In this case, drive K on the workstation is equated to the network directory C:\SALES\REPORTS on the server JUANITA. On the workstation, any use of drive K is redirected to the network directory.

Sharing Disks and Directories

CAUTION: Don't get confused between physical and redirected device names. When you choose K: as your local name for the server's network directory, that name applies only to you. Someone at a different workstation may use H: or M: to refer to the same network directory. Someone working at the server's keyboard continues to use C: for the drive that contains the network directory.

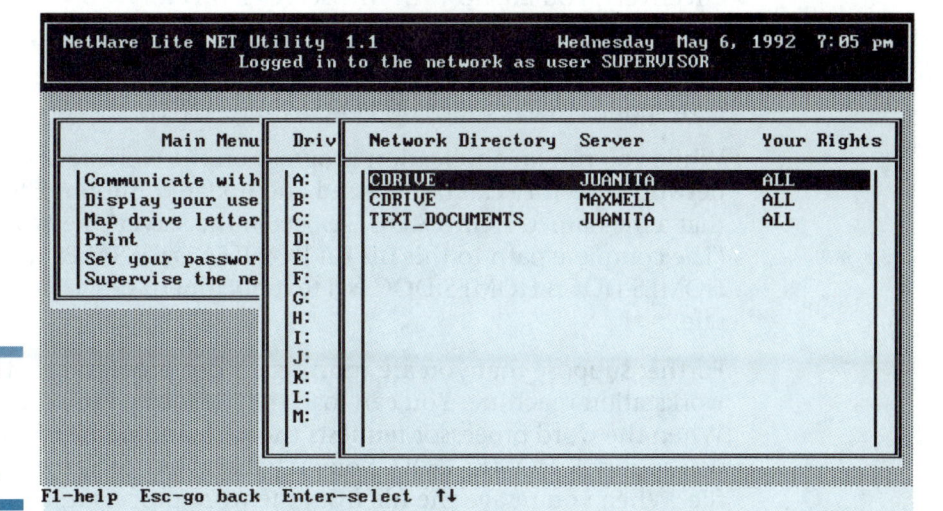

```
NetWare Lite NET Utility 1.1              Wednesday  May 6, 1992  7:05 pm
              Logged in to the network as user SUPERVISOR

         Main Menu      Driv  Network Directory   Server        Your Rights
      Communicate with  A:    CDRIVE              JUANITA       ALL
      Display your use  B:    CDRIVE              MAXWELL       ALL
      Map drive letter  C:    TEXT_DOCUMENTS      JUANITA       ALL
      Print             D:
      Set your passwor  E:
      Supervise the ne  F:
                        G:
                        H:
                        I:
                        J:
                        K:
                        L:
                        M:

F1-help  Esc-go back  Enter-select  ↑↓
```

The available network directories
Figure 7-10.

```
NetWare Lite NET Utility 1.1              Wednesday  May 6, 1992  7:06 pm
              Logged in to the network as user SUPERVISOR

         Main Menu      Drive  Network Directory   Server        Your Rights
      Communicate with  A:
      Display your use  B:
      Map drive letter  C:
      Print             D:
      Set your passwor  E:
      Supervise the ne  F:
                        G:
                        H:
                        I:
                        J:
                        K:    TEXT_DOCUMENTS      JUANITA       ALL
                        L:
                        M:

F1-help  Esc-go back  Enter-map drive letter  Del-delete  ↑↓
```

Drive K is mapped to the network directory TEXT_DOCUMENTS on server JUANITA
Figure 7-11.

To demonstrate the redirection, at the workstation, type **k:** and press
Enter. The DOS prompt K:\> appears. If you type **dir** and press Enter,
you see a list of all files in the server's network directory.

You can type **cd document** to access the DOCUMENT subdirectory
(refer to Figure 7-1 for the directory tree). The DOS prompt changes to
K:\DOCUMENT>. Now if you type **dir**, you see a list of all files in
JUANITA's directory with the path C:\SALES\REPORTS\DOCUMENT.
Effectively, you are now "in" the server's directory.

If you type **cd** and press Enter, the DOS prompt returns to K:\>. You
have returned the workstation to the root directory of drive K, which
corresponds to C:\SALES\REPORTS on JUANITA.

While you run an application program on the workstation, files in the
network directory can be accessed and updated. Suppose, for example,
that a file named HOMES.DOC exists in the server's network directory.
(The complete path to this file on JUANITA is C:\SALES\REPORTS\
HOMES.DOC.) HOMES.DOC is a text document describing homes for
sale.

Further suppose that you are running a word processor on the
workstation machine. You can load the file into your word processor.
When the word processor requests the path and name of a file to load,
you specify K:HOMES.DOC. You may then view or perhaps modify the
file. When you resave the file from the word processor, the file is
updated on the server's machine. Other users who access the file will
get the updated version.

Another important way to use file sharing is to share programs and
executable files. From a workstation, you can run a program stored on
the server's hard disk. Suppose that a loan calculation program named
LOAN.EXE is stored in the server's network directory, and that you map
drive M on a workstation to that network directory. At your workstation,
you can then type **m:loan**, press Enter—and there you are, running the
loan program. Major application programs can be shared in the same
manner. For more about sharing applications, see Chapter 10.

CAUTION: Avoid redirecting one of your workstation's physical
drive letters to a network directory. Don't map C: on your
workstation to a network directory, for example. If you do, from that
point on, drive C on your workstation refers to the network directory

Sharing Disks and Directories

and not to your actual drive C. The results are confusion and the inability to access your own hard disk. You can regain access to your drive C by canceling the mapping.

Canceling NetWork Directories and Mapped Drive Letters

You can cancel the redirection of a mapped drive letter to a network directory from a workstation or from a server. From a workstation, you cancel a drive letter's mapping to a network directory; from a server, you withdraw the offer of a network directory. The following sections explain both techniques.

Canceling an Existing Mapping

After mapping a drive letter to a network directory, you may want to terminate that mapping. Another way to say this is that you want to *cancel redirection* to the disk drive, or break the virtual connection.

You may recall from Chapter 6 that to cancel an existing mapping you first type **net** and press [Enter] to invoke the NetWare Lite menu system. From the Main menu, select Map drive letters. NetWare Lite displays the list of mapped drive letters and the network directories to which the drive letters are mapped. Move the highlight down to the drive letter you want to cancel. Then press [Del]. The NET program prompts you to verify that you want to delete the mapping. Press [Enter] to select Yes. The mapping is canceled. The Network Directory box now shows no mapped network directory for the drive letter just canceled. To exit NET, press [Alt]-[F10] and then press [Enter].

The four common reasons you may want to cancel an existing mapping are as follows:

To remap that same drive letter to a different network directory

In most cases, when your workstation needs access to an additional network directory, you can simply map an unused drive letter to the needed network directory. In that way, you have access to the new network directory and still retain access to all the currently mapped directories. Application software (such as a word processor) installed on your workstation's hard disk, however, may expect data files to be on a particular drive. If you specify in the word processor that data files are found by default on drive K, for example, you may want drive K to always be mapped into whichever directory on the server contains the data file currently in use. If you need data files located on different network directories, remapping the directories to drive K may be the most convenient approach. You may also have batch files or other procedures that expect to find programs or data files in a particular drive, such as drive K.

To "clean up" and prevent accidents while manipulating data on the server's hard disk   As long as you retain an active mapping to the server's disk, you risk absentmindedly copying or deleting files from the wrong disk. Suppose that you want to clean up your workstation's drive C by deleting some files and copying other files to floppy disks. To be safe, you should first cancel your access to a server's disk to avoid accidental use of the mapped drive letter while deleting or moving files. Clearly, if your cleanup process involves the network directory, you need to retain the mapping. Just be careful, as usual, to specify the proper disk drive with each DOS command.

To remove the default assignment of drive C as a network directory
By default, as you have seen, NetWare Lite offers drive C on each server as a network directory. For security reasons, you may not want workstations to have access to the entire drive. Simply cancel drive C as a network directory and offer one or more specific subdirectories for sharing.

To free a drive letter   As you continue mapping different drive letters, you may run out of available drive letters. To map to another network directory, you may have to cancel an existing mapping to free a drive letter. (As explained in Chapter 14, you can adjust the number of available drive letters by modifying the LASTDRIVE parameter in your CONFIG.SYS file.)

CAUTION: Be careful if you cancel the mapping of a drive letter while that drive letter is your current drive. (Suppose, for example, that you have mapped drive K and subsequently invoke the NET menu system from the K:\> prompt. K: is your current drive. From the menu,

Sharing Disks and Directories   171

you then cancel the mapping of drive K.) When you end NET and return to the DOS prompt, DOS displays the message `Current drive is no longer valid`. You have to type **C:** and press [Enter] to restore drive C as the current drive.

Deleting a Network Directory

You can delete a network directory so that it is no longer available for sharing. To do so, first activate the menu system (type **net** and press [Enter]). You do not have to be working on the server; you can delete a network directory from any node that has supervisor privileges. From the Main menu, move the highlight to `Supervise the network` and press [Enter]. Select `Network directories` and press [Enter]. NetWare Lite lists the existing network directories. Move the highlight to the directory you want to cancel and press [Del]. In the box that asks for confirmation that you want to delete the network directory, select `Yes` and press [Enter]. The network directory is deleted and no longer available for clients to map.

If you define one or more specific subdirectories on a server as network directories, you may want to delete the default network directory named CDRIVE. Remember that when you install NetWare Lite, the installation program defines drive C of each server as a network directory named CDRIVE. By deleting the CDRIVE network directory, you prevent any workstation from having access to the server's entire drive C.

NOTE: Deleting a network directory does not delete any actual files or directories on the server's hard disk. All that is canceled is the ability of client nodes to map drive letters to the former network directory.

CAUTION: Be careful not to delete a network directory while a client is mapped to that directory. If you do, the client may experience DOS errors and unpredictable results.

Logging Out of the Network

If you log a workstation out of the network, mapped drive letters are lost. When you later log the workstation back into the network, you must remap drive letters to reestablish sharing. As you will learn from this chapter's "Saving a Record of Existing Mappings" section, however, you can store a record of your mapped drives for later retrieval.

If you log a server out of the network, you do not cancel existing mappings. Clients currently accessing the server's resources can continue to do so.

Shutting Down a Server

Logging a server out of the network (with the DOS **net logout** command) is one thing; shutting down a network server is quite another. If you reboot a server or turn off the machine entirely, you sever all mappings. Any client currently using a server's resources will experience errors and unpredictable results. The client's computer may lock up and data files may become lost or corrupted.

Before shutting down a server, be sure that no clients are using the server's resources. To see a list of users currently logged into the network, type **net ulist** at the DOS prompt and then press Enter. Although you cannot tell from this list whether any of the listed users are sharing resources, you can at least determine who is active on the network.

Shutting down a server does not delete network directories. NetWare Lite saves on the server's hard disk a record of the network directories and other resources that a server has offered for sharing. When you shut down a server for the day, you do not lose this record. As a result, when you later turn on the server again and log into the network, previously defined network directories still exist. You do not have to constantly redefine network resources.

Issuing Commands at the DOS Prompt

Even though using the NET menu system is easy, you can also issue various NET commands directly from the DOS prompt. Many of the commands available from the DOS prompt duplicate actions available from the menu system. You may find that issuing some commands

Sharing Disks and Directories

from the DOS prompt is simpler and faster than activating the menus. Furthermore, some NET commands from the DOS prompt perform actions you cannot accomplish from the menu system.

One benefit of commands from the DOS prompt is that you can place such commands in batch files. You can create your own specialized batch files or modify STARTNET.BAT. Customized batch files provide you with a convenient way to configure the network to your preferences each time you start the network. For more about batch files, see Appendix C.

This following section examines several NET commands, each of which begins with the word *net*. You can type any of these commands in upper- or lowercase letters. After you type a command and press Enter, NetWare Lite displays a message which either confirms that the command was executed successfully or indicates that a problem occurred.

Displaying a List of Network Directories

To see a list of the currently available network directories, type the following command at the DOS prompt and press Enter:

    net ndlist

The list includes only directories a client could currently map. Network directories on servers not presently connected to the network (or on servers not turned on) are not listed.

Displaying a List of Current Mappings

To see a list of the currently mapped drive letters, type the following command and press Enter:

    net map

NetWare Lite displays the mapped drive letters and the network directories to which each drive letter is mapped. This command works with each individual workstation and shows only the mapped drive letters for that workstation.

Mapping a Drive Letter

To map a drive letter, you use a variation of the **net map** command. Include the drive letter and the network directory you want to map. The following command, for example, maps drive letter K to a network directory named UTILITY:

    net map k: utility

You must include the colon after the drive letter. If your network has the same network directory name defined on two or more servers, include the server name at the end of the command. Suppose, for example, that CDRIVE is defined as a network directory on the server JUANITA and on the server MAXWELL. The following command maps drive K to CDRIVE on MAXWELL:

    net map k: cdrive maxwell

If you substitute the word *next* for the drive letter, NetWare Lite maps the first available drive letter and makes it the currently active drive. (That is, the DOS prompt changes to that drive letter.) On a machine with a drive C and a drive D, for example, the following command maps drive E to the network directory CDRIVE:

    net map next cdrive

Canceling an Existing Mapping

To cancel the mapping of a drive letter, use **del** followed by the drive letter you want to cancel. The following command, for example, cancels the mapping of drive E:

    net map del e:

Don't forget to include the colon after the drive letter.

Saving a Record of Existing Mappings

The *net save* command creates a file that stores a record of the currently mapped drive letters and the network directories to which the drive letters are mapped. This file—a batch file named NLLOGIN.BAT—is saved by default in the current directory on the hard disk of the workstation that issues the command. The file includes not only the mapped drive letters, but also captured printer ports and the user's *net login* command, complete with the user name.

By running NLLOGIN.BAT after running STARTNET.BAT, you log into the network and reestablish the previous drive letter mappings and captured printer ports.

If you type **net save** and press [Enter], NetWare Lite saves the NLLOGIN.BAT file on the current default drive and directory. Optionally, you can specify a complete path and filename as part of the *net save* command. The following command, for example, creates the file MYCONFIG.BAT on the \NWLITE directory:

    net save \nwlite\myconfig.bat

A workstation can run MYCONFIG.BAT at the beginning of a work session just after running STARTNET.BAT. That is, the user powers on the computer, types **startnet** (and presses [Enter]), and then types **myconfig** (and presses [Enter]). The user is logged onto the network and drive mappings are reconstructed. In this manner, a common network configuration can easily be reconstructed with each new work session.

NOTE: The net save command is new for version 1.1 of NetWare Lite. The command does not exist in version 1.0.

CHAPTER

8 SHARING PRINTERS

With your workgroup's PCs connected on the network, you can share printers across the LAN. Most NetWare Lite LANs have one or more shared printers physically connected to a server. Individual local printers may be attached to some workstations.

A common LAN configuration includes one shared printer (often a laser printer) as well as one or two dot-matrix printers (located at different workstations). Clearly, many different configurations are possible. Some LANs have no shared printers; other LANs have upwards of five shared printers.

Overview of Printer Sharing

With NetWare Lite, the process of sharing a printer is similar to the process of sharing disks and directories. Just as you create a network directory on a server to offer disk sharing, you create a *network printer* on a server to offer printer sharing.

After the network printer has been defined, you *capture a port* on your workstation to access the printer. This process is analogous to mapping a drive letter when you access a network directory.

Capturing a port creates a virtual port on the workstation. From the point of view of the workstation, once the port is captured, print jobs directed to the workstation's local virtual port are redirected to the actual port on the server. Because the printer is connected to the server's port, the printed output is sent to the network printer.

Prerequisites to Creating a Network Printer

Before you can use NET to define a network printer, you must perform the following steps:

1. Determine to which port on the server the printer is attached.

   Typically, the port is LPT1, but the server's printer may instead be connected to COM1, COM2, LPT2, or LPT3. If you are unsure, consult your PC documentation for information about the physical port to which the printer is attached. And some third-party utility programs, such as PC Tools, have options to indicate the ports in use.

2. Choose a name for the network printer.

   Just as you must choose a descriptive name for a network directory, you must choose a descriptive name for each network printer. A useful name describes the printer unequivocally for the workstation users. Brand names, such as EPSON_DOT or OKIDATA, are often good choices. To describe the only laser printer in a network, you might use LASER or LASERJET.

Printer Ports: A Brief Tutorial

A PC must often send and receive data from various devices attached to the computer. A computer must receive input from a mouse or keyboard, for example, and send output to a video monitor or printer. The communication channels through which data passes between a computer and external devices are called *I/O* (Input/Output) *ports*, or simply *ports*.

Ports are physical devices that usually are accessible at the rear of the computer. Two types of ports are common on PCs: *serial* ports that send or receive data one bit at a time, and *parallel* ports that send a stream of data eight bits at a time. Typically, you connect the cable from an external device (such as a printer or modem) directly into a port at the rear of the PC.

A serial port—also called a *communications port*—is used most often to connect a mouse, modem, or plotter to a PC. A few printers connect to a serial port, but serial ports generally are not used for printers. Although a computer can be configured with as many as four serial ports, one or two serial ports is more common. In DOS, the names for the serial ports are COM1, COM2, and so on. (The term "COM" stands for *Communication*.)

A parallel port—also called a *printer port*—is used almost exclusively to connect a printer to the computer. DOS names the parallel ports LPT1, LPT2, and so on. (*LPT* stands for Line Printer.)

The great majority of printers connect to a parallel port (and sometimes are referred to as *parallel printers*). A few printers connect only to a serial port, whereas some printers can be connected to either a parallel or serial port. When a single printer is connected to a PC, the most common configuration has the printer connected to the parallel port LPT1. If an additional printer is attached to the same PC, port LPT2 typically is used.

Nondescriptive names, such as PRINTER, do not help workstation users identify a particular printer. Clearly, if your network has only one shared printer, almost any name is fine.

A Typical LAN Configuration with a Shared Printer

The representative LAN described in the preceding chapter is used also for the examples in this chapter. The LAN contains two server machines: JUANITA and MAXWELL.

A laser printer, which will be offered for sharing throughout the network, is attached to the LPT1 port of JUANITA.

Creating a Network Printer

To create a shared network printer, follow these steps:

1. At the DOS prompt, type **net** and press [Enter] to activate the menu system and open the Main menu.

   When creating a network printer, you typically use NET on the server machine. You can create the network printer from any node that has supervisor privileges, however. (By default, all nodes have supervisor privileges.)

2. Move the highlight to Supervise the network, the bottom choice on the Main menu.

3. Press [Enter] to open the "Supervise the Network" menu.

4. Move the highlight to Network printers, as shown in Figure 8-1.

5. Press [Enter] to pop open the Network Printer box shown in Figure 8-2.

   If no network printers currently exist, as is the case in this example, the Network Printer box is empty.

6. Press [Ins] to inform NET that you want to add a new network printer.

   A box pops open, displaying the servers on the network: in this case, JUANITA and MAXWELL (see Figure 8-3).

7. Move the highlight to the name of the server to which the printer is attached. In this example, a laser printer is attached to the LPT1 port of the server JUANITA.

8. Press [Enter].

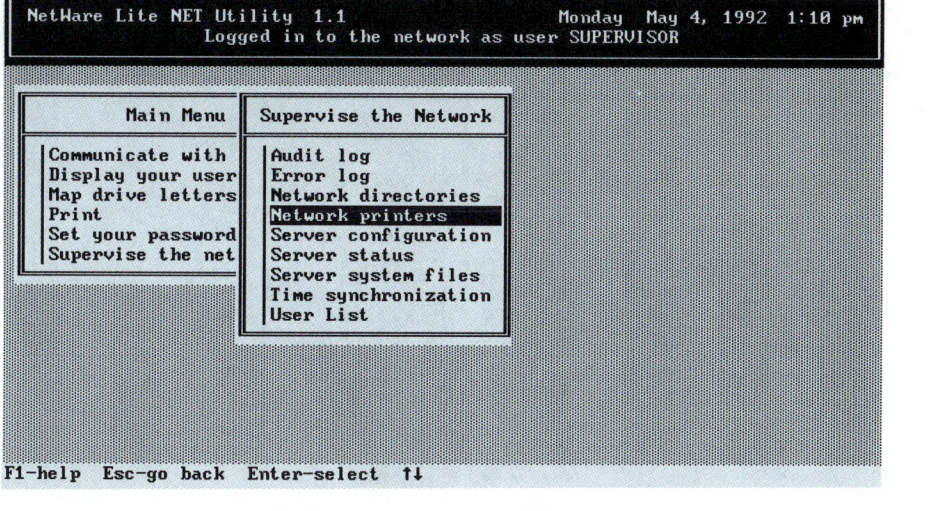

Sharing Printers

```
NetWare Lite NET Utility 1.1                    Monday   May 4, 1992  1:10 pm
              Logged in to the network as user SUPERVISOR

         ┌─────── Main Menu ───────┬─── Supervise the Network ───┐
         │ Communicate with        │ Audit log                   │
         │ Display your user       │ Error log                   │
         │ Map drive letters       │ Network directories         │
         │ Print                   │ Network printers            │
         │ Set your password       │ Server configuration        │
         │ Supervise the net       │ Server status               │
         │                         │ Server system files         │
         │                         │ Time synchronization        │
         │                         │ User List                   │
         └─────────────────────────┴─────────────────────────────┘

F1-help  Esc-go back  Enter-select  ↑↓
```

The "Network printers" option is selected
Figure 8-1.

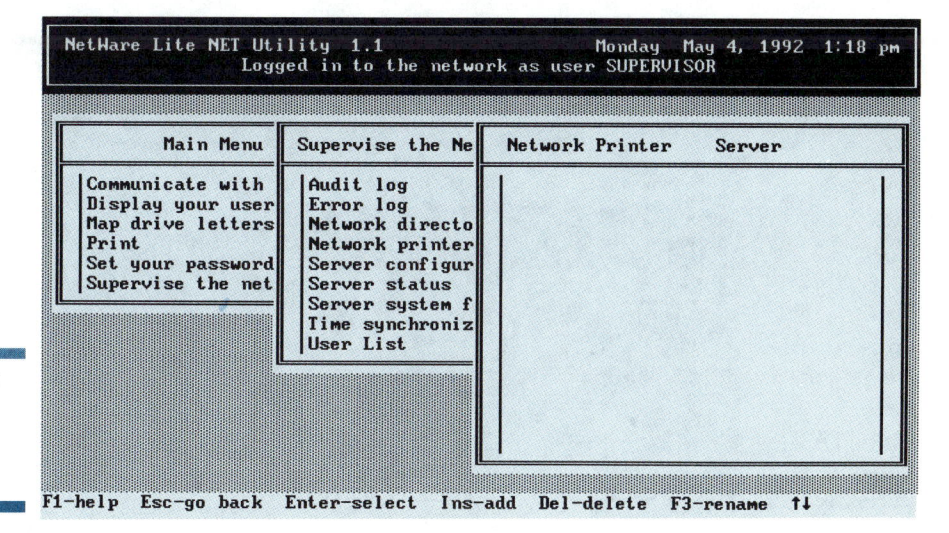

```
NetWare Lite NET Utility 1.1                    Monday   May 4, 1992  1:18 pm
              Logged in to the network as user SUPERVISOR

  ┌─── Main Menu ───┬─ Supervise the Ne ┬── Network Printer      Server ──┐
  │ Communicate with │ Audit log         │                                 │
  │ Display your user│ Error log         │                                 │
  │ Map drive letters│ Network directo   │                                 │
  │ Print            │ Network printer   │                                 │
  │ Set your password│ Server configur   │                                 │
  │ Supervise the net│ Server status     │                                 │
  │                  │ Server system f   │                                 │
  │                  │ Time synchroniz   │                                 │
  │                  │ User List         │                                 │
  └──────────────────┴───────────────────┴─────────────────────────────────┘

F1-help  Esc-go back  Enter-select  Ins-add  Del-delete  F3-rename  ↑↓
```

The Network Printer box opens
Figure 8-2.

9. NET prompts you for the server name. Type a descriptive name for your network printer. As Figure 8-4 shows, the name LASER is used in this example.
10. Press [Enter] to pop open a box showing the available server ports (see Figure 8-5).

NetWare Lite Made Easy

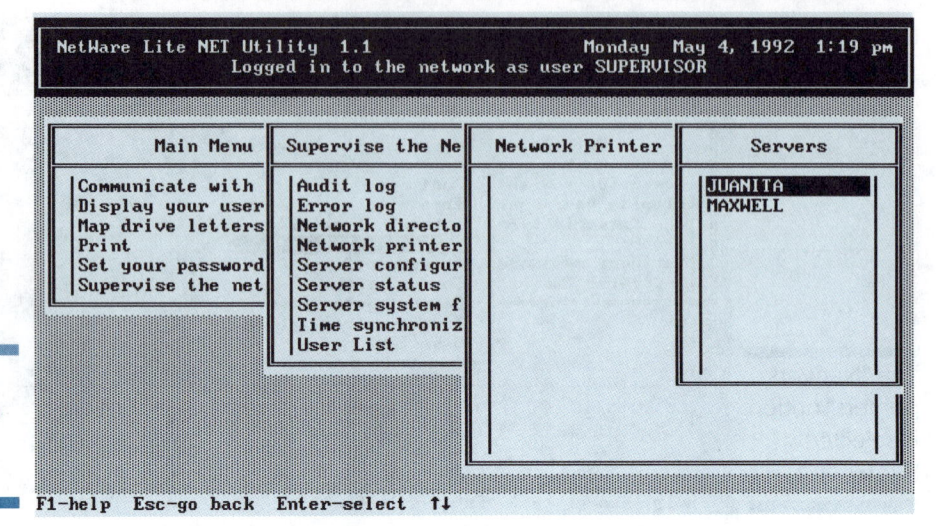

NET displays the servers on the network
Figure 8-3.

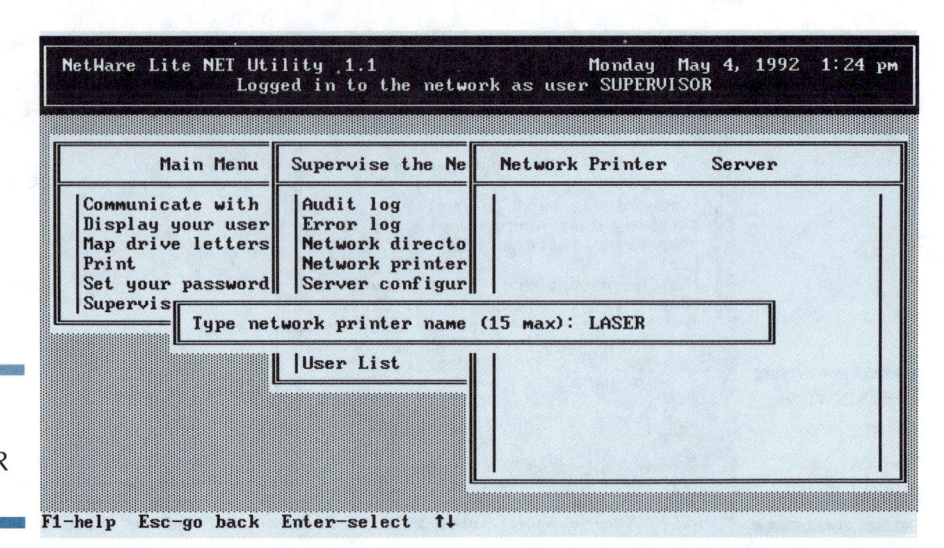

The network printer is named LASER
Figure 8-4.

11. Move the highlight to the port to which the network printer is attached (LPT1, in this example).

    Here you select the actual port on the server to which the printer is physically attached. For most LAN configurations, this port is the first parallel port: LPT1.

Sharing Printers

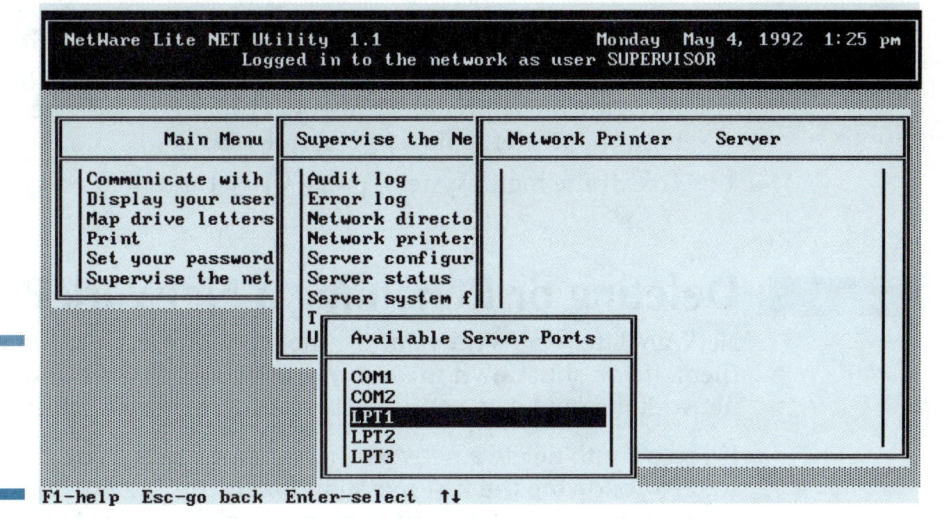

NET displays the available server ports
Figure 8-5.

12. Press Enter.

    NET displays a box (see Figure 8-6) showing default information for the new network printer. The different options are described later in this chapter, in the "Modifying the Capture Port Settings" section.

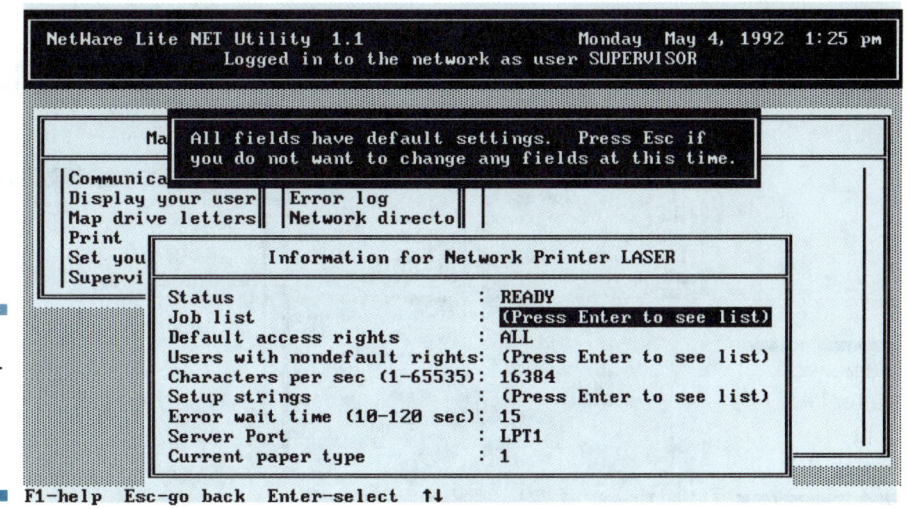

NET displays information for the network printer
Figure 8-6.

13. Press [Esc] to indicate that, for now, the default settings are acceptable.

    As Figure 8-7 shows, the Network Printer box indicates that the network printer named LASER now exists.

14. To exit the menu system, press [Alt]-[F10] and then press [Enter].

Deleting or Renaming a Network Printer

NetWare Lite retains the names of network printers after you define them. If you shut down the network after a day's work and start the network the next day, your network printers are still defined.

If you want to delete a network printer or rename an existing printer, start by following the first five steps for creating a network printer. Now, in the Network Printer box, move the highlight to the network printer you want to change.

To delete the printer, press [Del]. A confirmation box pops open. Press [Enter] to confirm the deletion.

To rename a printer instead of deleting it, press [F3] instead of [Del]. A box pops open that prompts you for the new name. Type the new name and press [Enter].

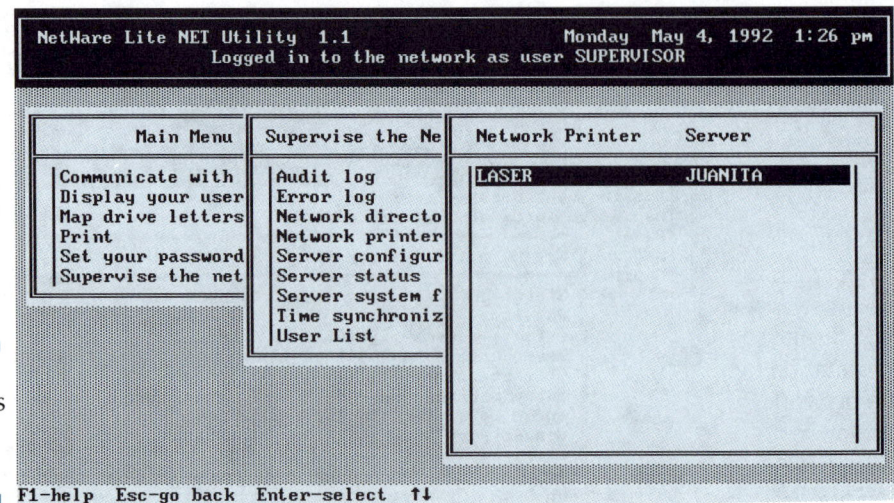

The network printer LASER is created
Figure 8-7.

Capturing a Printer Port

To exit the menu system, press [Alt]-[F10] and then press [Enter].

For you to send print jobs to a network printer from a workstation, the workstation must capture a port. This process assigns a local port name (on the workstation) to the network printer.

NetWare Lite allows the workstation to capture the LPT1, LPT2, or LPT3 port. The application software running on the workstation acts as though a printer were attached to that local port. NetWare Lite intercepts all jobs directed to the local port, however, and redirects the printed output to the network printer.

The workstation may capture LPT2 to the network printer, for example. Suppose that the workstation runs a word processor as a local application. (In this context, "local" means that the word processor is stored on the workstation's hard disk.) When the word processor was installed on the workstation, the default printer was assigned to LPT2, even though no actual printer was attached to that port on the workstation. (The installation process for most word processors includes a step in which you specify the port to which the printer is attached. Alternatively, with most word processors, you can select or change the printer port at any time.) When print jobs are created at the word processor, the word processor routes the jobs to LPT2. NetWare Lite however, redirects the job to the network printer attached to the server.

NOTE: A workstation may capture LPT1, LPT2, or LPT3 even if no such physical port exists on the workstation. The captured port is a virtual device, just as a mapped drive letter is a virtual disk drive.

Capturing Ports on Workstations with Local Printers

If an individual printer is physically attached to your workstation, it most likely is attached to your workstation's LPT1 port.

Suppose that you want to redirect printer jobs to the server's printer. If you want to retain access to your local printer, you must choose LPT2 or LPT3 when capturing a port.

Application software, such as a word processor or spreadsheet, typically expects to send output to LPT1. If this is the case with your application software, you can capture LPT1 to the network printer. Netware Lite will route your print jobs to the shared printer.

CAUTION: If you capture the LPT1 port when you have a local printer attached to LPT1, you lose the ability to print on your local printer while the port is captured. To regain access to your local printer, you must cancel the capture as explained later in this chapter.

How To Capture a Printer Port

To capture a printer port, follow these directions. In the example, the workstation captures LPT2 to the network printer, called LASER.

1. From the workstation, at the DOS prompt, activate the menu system by typing **net** and pressing [Enter].
2. Move the highlight to `Print` and press [Enter].

   As Figure 8-8 shows, the box that pops open lists the printer ports LPT1 through LPT3.

3. Move the highlight down to `LPT2` and press [Enter].

   A box pops open that lists all the defined network printers. Figure 8-9 shows that the network printer named LASER is defined on the server JUANITA.

4. Press [Enter] to select the network printer LASER.

   NetWare Lite pops open a box that displays the default capture settings (see Figure 8-10). As described later in this chapter (in the "Modifying the Capture Port Settings" section), you can customize the way NetWare Lite treats print jobs routed through this captured port by changing the values of these settings.

5. Press [Esc] to select the default capture settings.

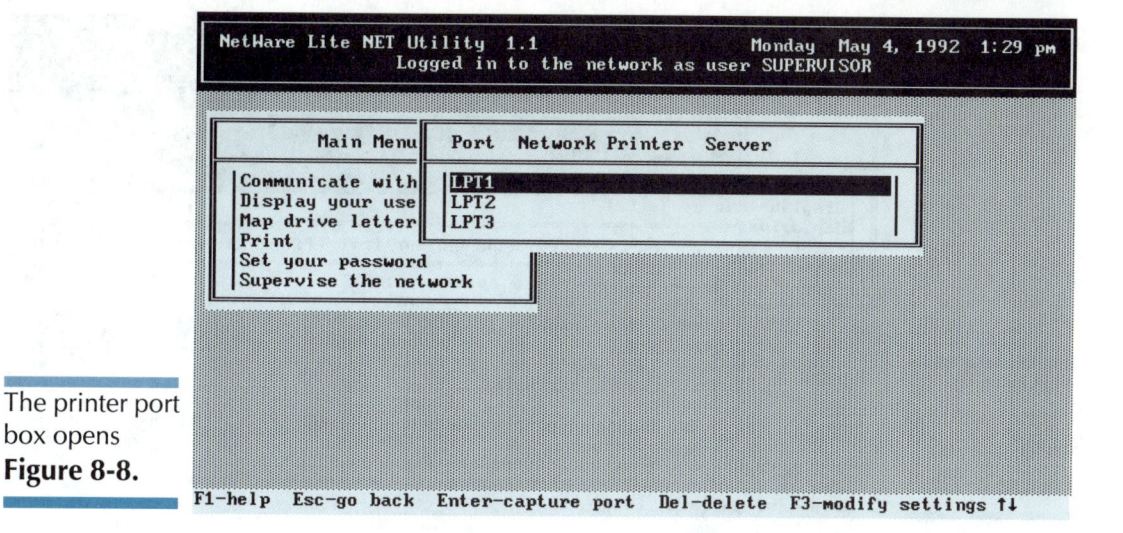

Sharing Printers

```
NetWare Lite NET Utility 1.1                Monday  May 4, 1992  1:29 pm
              Logged in to the network as user SUPERVISOR

         Main Menu    Port  Network Printer  Server
       Communicate with   LPT1
       Display your use   LPT2
       Map drive letter   LPT3
       Print
       Set your password
       Supervise the network


F1-help  Esc-go back  Enter-capture port  Del-delete  F3-modify settings ↑↓
```

The printer port box opens
Figure 8-8.

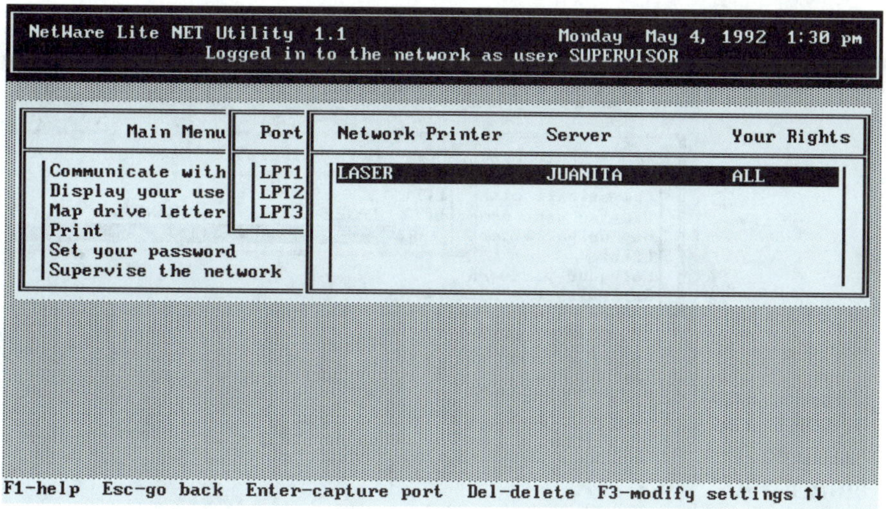

```
NetWare Lite NET Utility 1.1                Monday  May 4, 1992  1:30 pm
              Logged in to the network as user SUPERVISOR

         Main Menu    Port   Network Printer     Server         Your Rights
       Communicate with   LPT1   LASER            JUANITA           ALL
       Display your use   LPT2
       Map drive letter   LPT3
       Print
       Set your password
       Supervise the network


F1-help  Esc-go back  Enter-capture port  Del-delete  F3-modify settings ↑↓
```

The Network Printer box opens
Figure 8-9.

The printer port box now displays the newly captured port. As Figure 8-11 shows, port LPT2 has been captured to the network printer named LASER on the server JUANITA.

6. To exit the menu system and return to the DOS prompt, press [Esc] twice and then press [Enter].

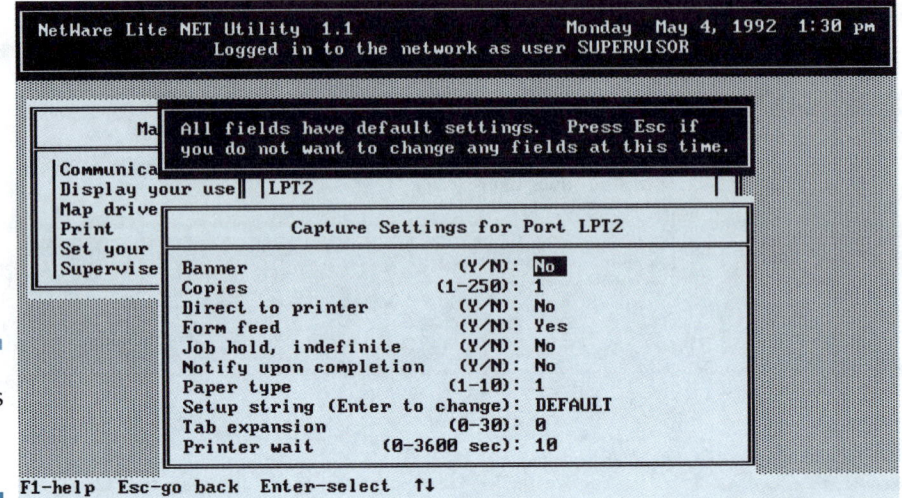

```
NetWare Lite NET Utility 1.1                  Monday  May 4, 1992  1:30 pm
            Logged in to the network as user SUPERVISOR

          Ma┌──All fields have default settings. Press Esc if──┐
    Communica│  you do not want to change any fields at this time.│
    Display your use│ │LPT2                                    │
    Map drive│                                                 │
    Print    │     Capture Settings for Port LPT2              │
    Set your │                                                 │
    Supervise│  Banner                      (Y/N): No          │
             │  Copies                    (1-250): 1           │
             │  Direct to printer           (Y/N): No          │
             │  Form feed                   (Y/N): Yes         │
             │  Job hold, indefinite        (Y/N): No          │
             │  Notify upon completion      (Y/N): No          │
             │  Paper type                 (1-10): 1           │
             │  Setup string (Enter to change): DEFAULT        │
             │  Tab expansion             (0-30): 0            │
             │  Printer wait      (0-3600 sec): 10             │

    F1-help  Esc-go back  Enter-select  ↑↓
```

The default capture settings are displayed
Figure 8-10.

```
NetWare Lite NET Utility 1.1                  Monday  May 4, 1992  1:31 pm
            Logged in to the network as user SUPERVISOR

         ┌────── Main Menu ──────┐┌── Port   Network Printer   Server ──┐
         │ Communicate with      ││   LPT1                               │
         │ Display your use      ││   LPT2   LASER             JUANITA   │
         │ Map drive letter      ││   LPT3                               │
         │ Print                 │└─────────────────────────────────────┘
         │ Set your password     │
         │ Supervise the network │
         └───────────────────────┘

    F1-help  Esc-go back  Enter-capture port  Del-delete  F3-modify settings  ↑↓
```

The port LPT2 is captured
Figure 8-11.

Testing the Network Printer

The workstation's LPT2 device name is now redirected to the printer named LASER on the server JUANITA. On the server, the actual laser printer is connected to port LPT1.

Any commands on the workstation that send output to LPT2 cause the data to be sent over the LAN to the server's printer. To test this connection, type the following command at the DOS prompt and press Enter:

copy c:\autoexec.bat lpt2

This command prints the contents of your workstation's AUTOEXEC.BAT file on the server's printer.

CAUTION: Before sending any job to a network printer, you must be sure that the printer is powered on and online.

Try redirecting a printed document to the server while running an application on the workstation. Load a document (or create a document) while working in a word processor on your workstation, for example. When you print the document, the job routes to the server's printer. For this redirection to work properly, your word processor must send printed output to the local port that you have captured (LPT2 in this example).

Printer Access from a Server

If you are working from a server's keyboard and want to access a printer attached to another server, you must capture a port as explained in this chapter's "How To Capture a Printer Port" section. Because you act as a workstation when you access another server's resources, the steps are the same. On your server, NetWare Lite should be installed as a server and client.

Accessing a server's shared printer from that same server is a little tricky. You may think that there's no need to do anything special. After all, this computer has a printer attached to LPT1 (for example), and it may seem that you can continue using this printer as if the computer were not on the LAN.

The problem is that other computers share the use of this server's printer over the LAN. After NetWare Lite establishes a redirection to a network printer, the printer can only be used over the LAN. Even the server to which the printer is attached must capture its own port to use the printer. You must use NET to tell the server to access its own shared printer through redirection. Only when shared printers are accessed exclusively through the LAN can the server software coordinate every computer's printer use.

If this server has a printer connected to LPT1, and you want to use the printer over the LAN, type **net** and press [Enter] at the server's keyboard to start the NET menu system. Move the highlight to Print on the Main menu and press [Enter] to open the list of ports. Then move the highlight to LPT1 and press [Enter]. From the list of network printers, select the server's own printer (LASER, in this example) and press [Enter]. When the list of capture settings appears, press [Esc] to select the default values. Then exit NET. From that point on, you can use the server's shared printer from that server without conflicting with other workstations that also use the printer.

Canceling Printer Redirection from the NET Menu

To cancel printer redirection at a workstation, you follow a process similar to the one you use to cancel redirection of a mapped drive letter. Type **net** and press [Enter] to activate the menu system. From the Main menu, select Print and press [Enter]. Move the cursor down to the LPT2 line or whichever redirected printer you want to cancel. Press [Del]. Then press [Enter] to confirm the cancellation. Finally, press [Esc] twice and press [Enter] to end NET.

Modifying the Capture Port Settings

When you capture a port, NetWare Lite assigns certain default attributes to print jobs redirected through that port. You can modify these attributes to customize the way Netware Lite processes redirected print jobs through that port.

To modify the settings, you enter the menu system and pop open the box that displays the port's capture settings. This box, shown in Figure 8-10, pops open as part of the process of capturing a port.

Sharing Printers

For an existing captured port, you can pop open this box by following these steps:

1. Type **net** and press [Enter] to open the menu system.
2. From the Main menu, select `Print` and press [Enter].
   NetWare Lite displays a list of the captured ports.
3. Move the highlight to the desired port and press [F3].

Table 8-1 shows the capture settings you can modify. The second column is the default value, whereas the third column shows the range of allowable values.

To modify a value, use the [↑] and [↓] keys to move the highlight to the value you want to modify. Then type the new value. When you have specified all the values, press [Esc]. To exit the menu system, press [Alt]-[F10] and press [Enter].

Each setting is explained in the following paragraphs.

Banner   A description of each print job, the banner prints on a single page just before the job itself. *Banner* information includes the date,

Table 8-1. Modifiable Capture Settings

Setting	Default Value	Possible Values
Banner	No	Yes/No
Copies	1	1-250
Direct to printer	No	Yes/No
Form feed	Yes	Yes/No
Job hold, indefinite	No	Yes/No
Notify upon completion	No	Yes/No
Paper type	1	1-10
Setup string	DEFAULT	(Any)
Tab expansion	0	0-32
Printer wait	10	0-3600 (sec)

time, client name, captured port, and file being printed.

Copies   By adjusting the value of *Copies*, you can print multiple copies of each document.

Direct to Printer   This parameter controls whether jobs are sent to the normal print queue. If you select Yes, the job is sent directly to the printer, bypassing the normal NetWare Lite queuing system.

Form Feed   When *Form feed* is Yes, NetWare Lite sends a form feed to the printer when each job completes. For some printers, especially various laser printers, when the last page of a print job is a partial page, you need to manually take the printer offline and press the printer's form-feed button to eject the partial page. For such printers, if *Form feed* is set to No, you still will have to manually eject the final page. If you set *Form feed* to Yes, NetWare Lite will send a final form feed. On some printers, however, the Yes setting results in an unnecessary blank page at the end of each document. Experiment with your printer to determine the proper setting.

Job Hold   Changing *Job hold* to Yes causes NetWare Lite to retain jobs indefinitely in the print queue. The jobs will not actually print until you change the value to No. You can hold jobs to allow higher-priority jobs from other workstations (or from your workstation) to print first.

Notify upon Completion   If you change *Notify upon completion* to Yes, NetWare Lite displays on the bottom line of your screen a message indicating when each of your print jobs completes. To clear the message from your screen, press [Ctrl]-[Enter].

NOTE: The Notify upon completion setting does not exist in version 1.0 of NetWare Lite.

Paper Type   When you modify the value of *Paper type*, a message appears on the server's screen indicating that the printer's paper should be changed to the specified type. You must establish your own network conventions for which paper type you associate with each of the numbers from 1 to 10. You can use this setting also to indicate that you want a laser printer's font cartridge to be changed.

Setup String A special message string sent to a printer to change the printer's operating mode. Consult your printer's documentation for information about setup strings. Setup strings are used in special situations; you normally do not have to adjust this value.

Tab Expansion Converts all tab characters in the print document to the specified number of blank spaces.

Printer Wait Sets the time the captured port will wait while receiving a print job from an application on the client. When the specified wait time elapses, the print job is sent across the network to the shared printer. For more on selecting a value for this parameter, see Chapter 14.

The Print Queue

When you redirect your workstation's printer port to a server's shared printer, something occurs that may not be obvious. Consider for a moment a situation in which two workstations are redirecting printer output to the same shared printer. Suppose that both workstations send output to the printer at the same time. The printer might produce a garbled mixture of both sets of output. The problem intensifies if more than two jobs are sent simultaneously to the shared printer.

NetWare Lite handles simultaneous print jobs by processing the jobs one at a time. Instead of sending a workstation's print job directly to the shared printer, NetWare Lite temporarily stores the printer output on the server's hard disk. Each workstation's output is printed in its entirety, one job at a time. (Because of this need for temporary disk storage, be sure that your server's hard disk has at least 1MB of unused disk space if a printer is attached.)

NetWare Lite keeps track of separate printer jobs by the use of a printer queue. A *queue* (pronounced like the letter Q) is simply a waiting line—the computer equivalent of what you stand in while waiting for a bank teller. NetWare Lite copies each workstation's printer output to a separate disk file and keeps track of which files are associated with each user. If several users send print jobs to the same shared printer when the printer is already busy printing, NetWare Lite organizes a waiting line (a queue) for those print files, which must wait until the printer is available.

The area on the server's disk where all this printer information is stored is called the *printer spool area*, or just the *print spool*. (The disk area is located in a subdirectory of the C:\NWLITE directory created during installation of NetWare Lite.) When your workstation sends printer output to the server's hard disk, the process is called *spooling*. Afterwards, when the server sends the data from its hard disk to the printer, the process is called *despooling*. Each printer file the server stores on disk is called a *print file* or a *print job*.

Viewing the Print Queue

Because the printer queue can build up (like a bank's teller line on Friday afternoon), and you may want to know what jobs are in the print queue, NetWare Lite has the capability to display the current status of all print jobs.

To view jobs in the print queue, enter the NET menu system and select Print from the Main menu. NetWare Lite displays the list of captured ports and network printers. Move the highlight to the network printer you want to view and press (Enter). A box pops open that shows a list of the jobs in the print queue.

The box displays four items of information: job number, user, job name, and job status. The *job number*, which starts at 0 and increases sequentially, is assigned by NetWare Lite for each job entering the queue. The *user* is the account name specified with the NET LOGIN command when the client logged into the network. *Job name* is the name NetWare Lite assigns to the job. For most jobs, this name is "LPT1 Capture" (or whatever port has been captured). The name may be the name of the file being printed. *Job status* indicates the current status of the print job. Table 8-2 explains the possible values of job status.

Figure 8-12 shows the status of a print queue containing two jobs. The first job, with status PRINTING, is currently printing while the second job, with status READY, waits to be printed.

Sharing Printers

Job Status	Description
PRINTING	The job is currently printing
READY	The job is in the print queue waiting to print
DIRECT	Direct to Printer is set to Yes for this job
ON HOLD	The job is in the queue but suspended from printing
FILLING	The job is being sent to the print queue

Possible values of a print job's status
Table 8-2.

Deleting a Print Job

You can delete a job from the print queue so that the job will not print. To do so, move the highlight to the desired job while viewing the box that displays the print queue. Then press [Del]. When the confirmation box appears, press [Enter] to indicate Yes. The print job will be removed from the queue.

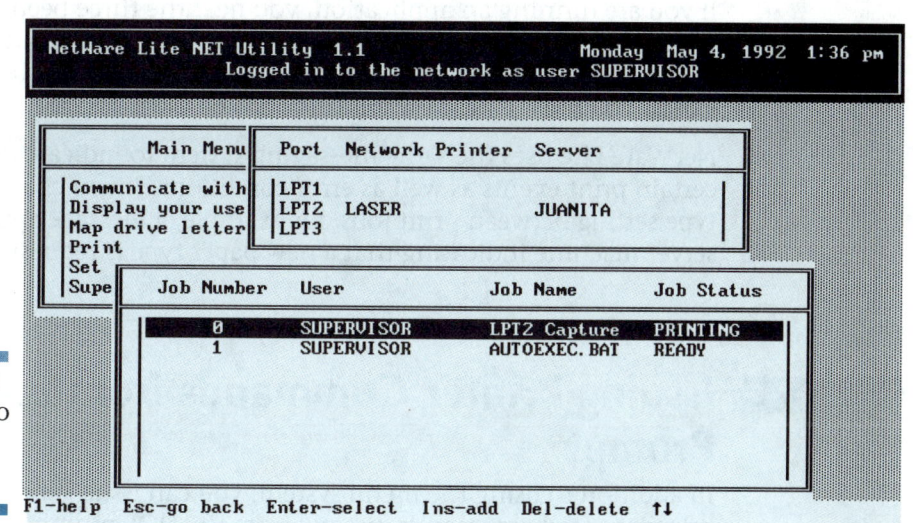

A sample print queue with two jobs pending
Figure 8-12.

> **NOTE:** You cannot delete a job currently printing but you can delete any job waiting to be printed.

Error Warnings and Status Messages

If NetWare Lite detects a problem with a network printer or a particular print job, a warning message is sent to the appropriate machine. If a network printer is offline when print jobs are in the queue, for example, NetWare Lite sends to the server machine a message indicating that the printer is offline.

A warning message is accompanied by three short beeps. A box pops open onscreen containing the message. To clear the warning box, you must press [Esc]. A warning message appears only when your computer is displaying a DOS prompt or you are working in the NetWare Lite menu system.

If you are running an application, you hear the three beeps but the message does not display. NetWare Lite periodically (about once a minute) sounds the three beeps to let you know that a problem still exists. You must exit the application to see the message.

NetWare Lite uses the same messaging system to indicate the status of certain print events as well as error conditions. If you change the paper type setting between print jobs, for example, a message appears on the server machine indicating that a new paper type is requested.

Issuing Printer Commands from the DOS Prompt

In addition to using the menu system, you can issue various printer-related commands directly from the DOS prompt.

Displaying a List of Network Printers

To see a list of the currently defined network printers, type **net nplist** at the DOS prompt and press Enter.

Capturing a Port

Use the NET CAPTURE command to capture a port.

To see which ports currently are captured, and the settings defined for those ports, type **net capture** and press Enter.

To capture a port, include the port name and the name of the network printer. The following command, for example, captures LPT2 to the network printer, LASER:

    net capture lpt2 laser

The port name is optional. The command **net capture laser** works. If you don't specify a port, NetWare Lite uses the first available port.

To delete an existing capture, type **del** and the port name after **net capture**. The following command, for example, deletes the capture of port LPT2:

    net capture del lpt2

Printing a File on a Network Printer

If a printer port is captured on a workstation, you can redirect the printing of a file to the network printer. Use the command **net print** followed by the name of the file to be printed. If the file is not in the current directory, specify the complete path to the file. The following command, for example, prints on the network printer the AUTOEXEC.BAT file from the workstations's hard disk:

    net print c:\autoexec.bat

You can print a file on a mapped directory. Suppose, for example, that the workstation's drive J is mapped into drive C on the server. The following command, issued at the workstation, prints the server's CONFIG.SYS file on the network printer:

> net print j:\config.sys

If more than one port is captured on a workstation, you must add the name of the network printer to the end of the command. The following command, for example, prints the workstation's AUTOEXEC.BAT file on the printer LASER:

> net print c:\autoexec.bat laser

Modifying the Capture Settings

To specify such capture settings as the banner, copies, and form-feed options, you use one or more optional parameters at the end of a **net capture** command. The following command, for example, redirects printer jobs for LPT2 to the printer LASER and specifies No for Banner, Yes for Form feed and a Wait time of 30 seconds:

> net capture lpt2 LASER b=n f=y w=30

You specify each setting with a parameter of the form *letter=value*, as shown in the following table:

Setting	Parameter	Possible Values
Banner	b=	y,n
Copies	c=	1-250
Direct	d=	y,n
Form feed	f=	y,n
Hold	h=	y,n
Notify	n=	y,n
Paper type	p=	1-10
Setup	s=	Any 15 characters
Tabs	t=	0-32
Wait	w=	0-3600

Using Postscript Printers

PostScript printers are a special class of printers that define printed output with the special PostScript language. If you use a PostScript printer as a shared resource over the LAN, make sure that Banner and Formfeed are both set to No, and Tabs is set to 0. These settings are necessary for the printer to operate properly. Note that because Banner and Formfeed are set to Yes (by default), you must modify these settings. The default value of Tabs (0) does not need modification, however.

Shared Printer Products

If you have worked with several PC printers, you undoubtedly have formed opinions about which products you do and don't like. A LAN environment puts special emphasis on printers and related products. This section briefly describes a few products worth considering for your LAN.

Hewlett-Packard Laser Printers

In today's PC world, the most desirable workhorse printer is a laser printer. And in today's marketplace, Hewlett-Packard is the market leader. Beginning with the original HP LaserJet printer, HP has established the standards against which other printer products are compared. HP's current product line is the LaserJet III series. The top of the line—the HP LaserJet IIISi, shown in Figure 8-13—has collected an impressive array of awards as a LAN printer. This model prints at a rate of 17 pages per minute (ppm). It has two 500-sheet input paper trays, an optional feeder for up to 100 envelopes, and can stack up to 500 pages of output. These capacities make it ideally suited for high-volume printing on a medium to large LAN. The list price of $5,495 is steep, however.

On a smaller LAN with lower-volume printing needs, the HP LaserJet III (see Figure 8-14) or IIID are more appropriate. Both print 8 pages per minute. The IIID has two 200-page input paper trays and the III has one. The IIID can perform *duplex printing* (printing on both sides of the paper). List price for the IIID is $3,495; the III lists for $2,495.

The baby of the family—the HP LaserJet IIIP—prints 4 pages per minute and holds only 70 input pages in a single tray. List price is $1,695. If

The
Hewlett-Packard
LaserJet IIISi
Figure 8-13.

The
Hewlett-Packard
LaserJet III
Figure 8-14.

your budget is small and your output volume is low, the IIIP may be an appropriate choice.

All these models are available from discount suppliers or mail order for about one-third off the list price. Sometimes you can get even lower prices.

Other Laser Printers

Many other companies make laser printers, some of which sell for less than the HP models. Most experienced computer users have discovered that skimping on a printer is not a good idea, however. Paying a little extra to ensure high quality and minimal problems is a worthwhile investment. Unless buying another printer can save you a great deal of money—compared to an HP printer—you are safest sticking with HP. If you need the speed of an HP IIISi but can't handle the price, consider alternatives such as the Texas Instruments microLaser XL PS35. It prints at 16 ppm, has built-in PostScript capability (an extra-cost option for the HP models), and lists for $3,149. Unfortunately, it doesn't accept HP-compatible font cartridges and has only a 250-page input paper tray. A second input paper tray that handles 500 pages costs an additional $345.

Laser Printer Font Cartridges

If you share a laser printer on a LAN, you may want a special font cartridge. Laser printers come with only a few built-in fonts (typefaces). If you need fonts other than the built-in ones, you have to use either a font cartridge or downloadable soft fonts. *Soft fonts* are disk files you copy to a laser printer to give the printer temporarily the capability to print other special fonts. For a printer connected to a single PC, this soft font approach is fine, but using soft fonts on a shared printer generally is not practical. Different users want to download different fonts, and the printer's memory has room for only so many. Each user would have to reset the printer with a special command and then download his or her own special fonts—a slow process. If, on the other hand, you install a multifont cartridge, a wide variety of fonts is always available.

Two varieties of font cartridges are available. One variety has a set of unchangeable fonts, and the other is "customizable" (you can install your own soft fonts into the cartridge). Some models are for early HP printers—typically the model II family and earlier—and others are for the HP III family, which supports scalable fonts. *Scalable* fonts are those that the printer can change to virtually any size. (The HP II family cannot scale fonts.)

The following two companies are the leaders in the field of multifont cartridges:

- ✦ Pacific Data Products, located in San Diego, California, sells (for the HP III family) the Complete Font Library Cartridge, which supports 51 typefaces, all of which are scalable by the HP III. For the HP II family and earlier they sell the 25 in One! cartridge. This cartridge, which contains 172 combinations of typestyle, size, symbol set, and orientation, also works on the HP III. The company's customizable cartridge, the FontBank Cartridge, works on both the HP II and III families.

- ✦ IQ Engineering, located in Sunnyvale, California, has a similar line of products. The Super Cartridge 3 Creative Collection has 66 scalable typefaces. For portrait orientation (longer dimension vertical), the Super Cartridge 2 competes with the Pacific Data Products 25 in One! cartridge. IQ also has a landscape (longer dimension horizontal) model. At this time, IQ has no customizable cartridge.

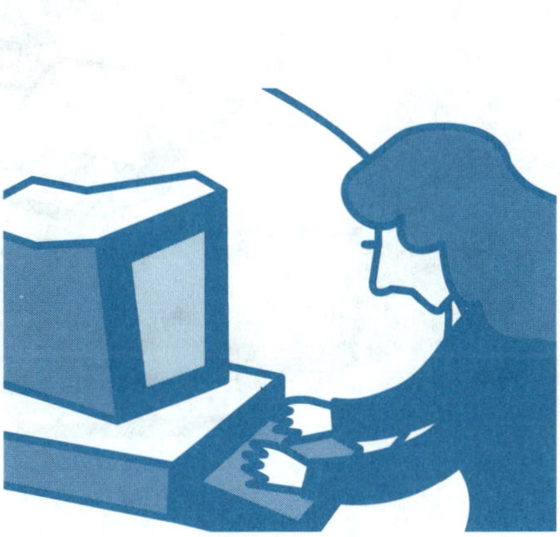

CHAPTER

9

SHARING OTHER RESOURCES

The sharing of hard disks and printers is the driving force behind most LANs. NetWare Lite, however, offers other capabilities that can make you and your workgroup more productive. This chapter discusses some NetWare Lite features that are less commonly implemented by LAN users, but nevertheless can be worthwhile, interesting, and even fun.

In this chapter, you learn how to use and share different non-printer resources.

In particular, you will learn about the following resources:

- Text messages sent from node to node
- CD-ROM disk drives
- Modems and two-way plotters
- Tape backup systems
- Portable computers attached to the LAN

Also, this chapter explains individual user accounts. By creating named user accounts and having users log into the network with individual names, you can send text messages to specific users.

Individual User Accounts

So far, each user has logged into the network with the name SUPERVISOR. Instead of using this method, you can create individually named user accounts and have everyone log into the network under his or her own account name. The benefits of individual accounts include the following:

- Text messages can be sent from user to user.
- NetWare Lite can maintain an audit log and an error log that monitor LAN usage and error conditions for each user account.
- For security purposes, various LAN privileges can be restricted for individual users.

Chapter 12 discusses user accounts in depth, with special emphasis on the security issues. For purposes of this chapter, user accounts provide a way to send messages to individual users. The following sections explain how to create a user account, log into the network with a user name, and send and receive messages.

Creating a User Account

Follow these steps to create a user account. You can create an account from any node logged into the network. In this example, the new

Sharing Other Resources

account is named DAVE. Accounts named CRYSTAL, ROY, and UDAY already exist.

1. At the DOS prompt, type **net** and press [Enter] to start NetWare Lite's menu system and pop open the Main menu.
2. Move the highlight to Supervise the network and press [Enter] to pop open the box labeled "Supervise the Network."
3. Move the highlight to User List and press [Enter] to pop open a list of all current user accounts.
4. Press [Ins] to indicate that you want to create a new user account.

   A box pops open, prompting you to supply the new user name.
5. Type the user name (**DAVE**, in this example) but don't press [Enter] yet. See Figure 9-1.

   The name is limited to 15 characters. All letters must be uppercase; NetWare Lite converts lowercase letters to uppercase. Any blank space you type becomes an underscore (_) character.

   Note that, in Figure 9-1, the users named CRYSTAL, ROY, and UDAY already exist. (NetWare Lite creates the SUPERVISOR account when you install the network.)
6. Press [Enter].

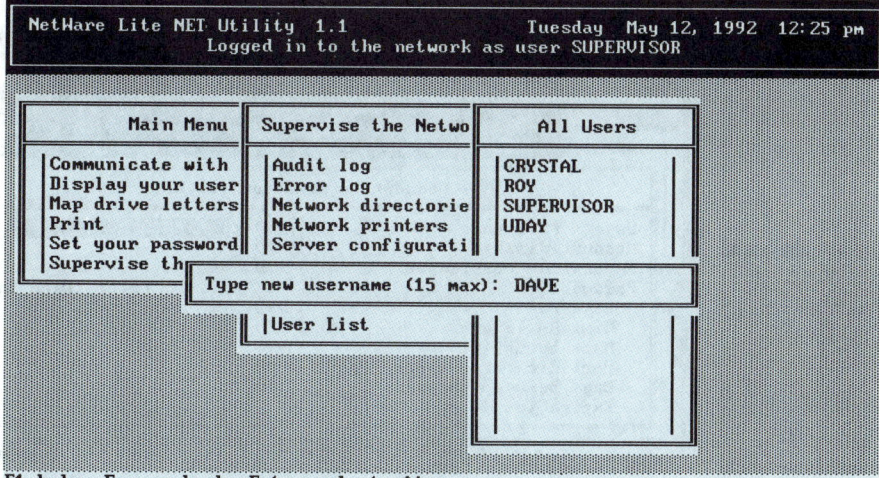

The user name DAVE is entered
Figure 9-1.

NetWare Lite prompts you to supply the account information for the new user DAVE (see Figure 9-2). Chapter 12 explains the different options and discusses user accounts in greater detail.

7. Press [Esc] to accept all the default values.

   As you can see from Figure 9-3, the list of users now shows the new account name (DAVE, in this example).

8. Press [Alt]-[F10] and then [Enter] to exit the menu system.

You don't have to take any special steps to have NetWare Lite save a record of each new account name. The new name is added automatically to the known accounts. When you start the network the following day, NetWare Lite will recognize the new account.

Logging into the Network with an Account Name

When you have an account name for everyone who uses the LAN, each user can log into the network under his or her own account name. Type the name as part of the NET LOGIN command. (Remember that you typically log into the network with NET LOGIN immediately after

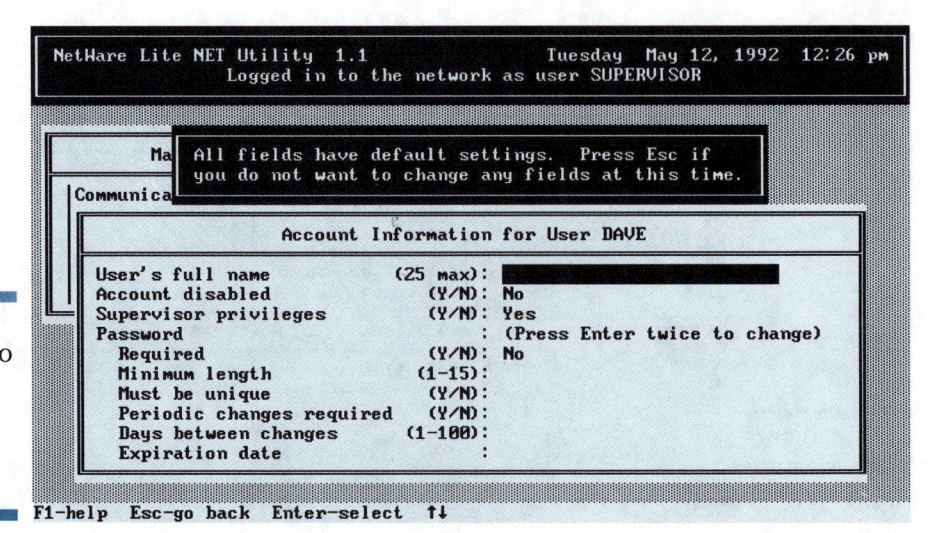

NetWare Lite prompts you to supply new account information
Figure 9-2.

Sharing Other Resources

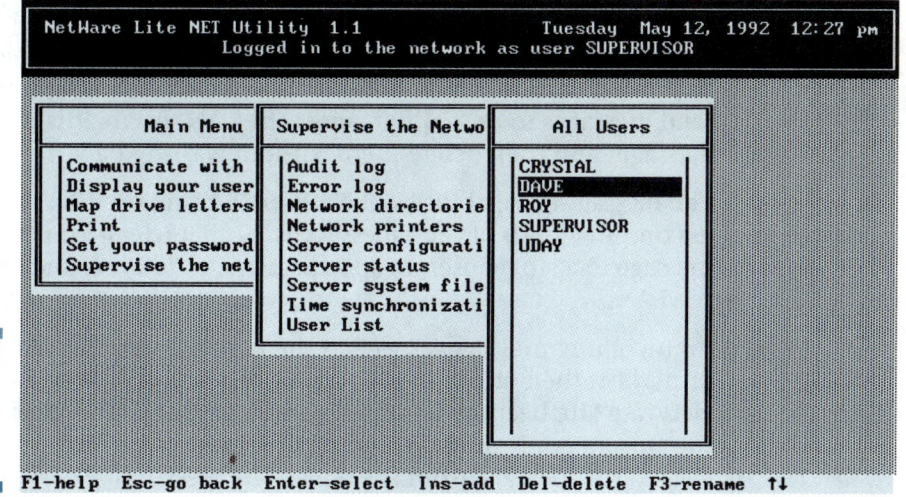

```
NetWare Lite NET Utility 1.1           Tuesday  May 12, 1992  12:27 pm
              Logged in to the network as user SUPERVISOR

        ┌──── Main Menu ────┬── Supervise the Netwo ──┬──── All Users ────┐
        │ Communicate with  │ Audit log               │ CRYSTAL           │
        │ Display your user │ Error log               │ DAVE              │
        │ Map drive letters │ Network directorie      │ ROY               │
        │ Print             │ Network printers        │ SUPERVISOR        │
        │ Set your password │ Server configurati      │ UDAY              │
        │ Supervise the net │ Server status           │                   │
        │                   │ Server system file      │                   │
        │                   │ Time synchronizati      │                   │
        │                   │ User List               │                   │
        └───────────────────┴─────────────────────────┴───────────────────┘

 F1-help  Esc-go back  Enter-select  Ins-add  Del-delete  F3-rename  ↑↓
```

DAVE is added to the list of users
Figure 9-3.

starting the network software with the STARTNET command.) To log into the network as DAVE, for example, type the following command:

   net login dave

Account names are linked to the user, not necessarily to the computer on which the user logs in. Each user—whether he or she always works on the same PC or works at different PCs from time to time—should log into the network with his or her own account name.

When each user logs into the LAN with a unique account name, you can use the NetWare Lite messaging system to send a message to any individual user. (The messaging system is described in the next section.) If two or more users log in with the same account name (usually SUPERVISOR), you won't have unique account names for each node.

NOTE: By default, NetWare Lite gives supervisor privileges to each user account. As a result, any user logged into the network under a private account name can supervise the network to the same extent as users logged in as SUPERVISOR. Chapter 12 explains how you can change the security defaults for any user account.

Communicating with Text Messages

NetWare Lite's built-in message system provides a convenient way to improve communication between members of a workgroup. Users can send messages to each other across the LAN. Recipients can read the messages and then delete them without wasting paper.

The messaging capabilities of NetWare Lite are useful but limited. The maximum length of each message is 30 characters. You can send a message to a single user, to specific users, or to everyone connected to the LAN.

An incoming message, as well as the name of the user who sent it, displays at the bottom of the screen. When you receive a message, NetWare Lite beeps your speaker and locks up your computer, pausing the current application. You cannot resume work until you have cleared the message from the screen (by pressing Ctrl-Enter). To avoid the possibility of unwelcome pauses during critical work, you can turn off message reception.

NOTE: Only client nodes can send or receive messages. Machines configured as clients and servers can utilize messaging, but dedicated servers cannot. (The reason dedicated servers cannot send or receive messages is that messaging is done with NET, and dedicated servers cannot log into the network or use NET.)

Any number of reasons exist to send a message across the LAN. Here are a few common situations in which electronic messaging may be useful:

✦ Inform attendees that a meeting is about to begin

✦ Announce that a new LAN resource (network directory or printer, for example) is ready for sharing

✦ Inform others that you will be out of the office for a while

✦ Ask users to watch for an upcoming memo

✦ Request that the person responsible for a shared laser printer change the paper or font cartridge before transmitting a print job

✦ Invite a group to lunch

Sharing Other Resources

In practice, most workgroups located in one small office area seldom use NetWare Lite's electronic messaging. The larger the workgroup and the greater the distance between users, the more useful messaging becomes. If everyone in your workgroup has a computer connected to the LAN and you all use your computers frequently, give electronic messaging a try.

NetWare Lite messages are adequate for the simple requirements of many workgroups. You can purchase add-on products that provide more extensive electronic mail (*e-mail*) features such as storing messages on disk so that you can view them later, delayed transmission, and text editors to compose and modify long messages. For a discussion of using e-mail packages with NetWare Lite, see Chapter 10.

Sending a Message

You can send a message from the menu system or by using NET from the DOS prompt. Messages can be sent only to users currently logged in to the network.

Using the Menu System To Send a Message

Follow these steps to send a message using the NET menu system:

1. At the DOS prompt, type **net** and press [Enter] to activate the NET menu system.
2. When the Main menu pops open, press [Enter] to select the option labeled Communicate with users. (This is the highlighted option when the Main menu appears.)
3. When the "Communicate with Users" menu pops open, move the highlight to Send messages. See Figure 9-4.
4. Press [Enter] to pop open a box labeled "Connected Users." See Figure 9-5.

   This box lists all users currently connected to the network. As the upcoming "Selecting Users to Receive Messages" section explains, you can send a message to one user, all users, or any combination of selected users.

5. Move the highlight to the name of the user who will receive your message.

   In this example, the message is sent to DAVE. The highlight is moved to the line that reads DAVE. (If you select ALL CONNECTED USERS, the message is sent to all users currently logged in to the network.)

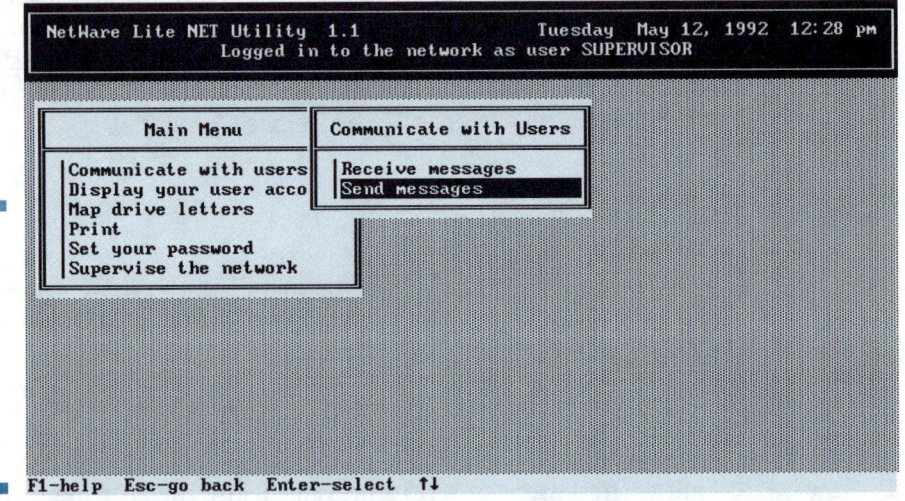

"Send messages" is highlighted on the Communicate with Users menu
Figure 9-4.

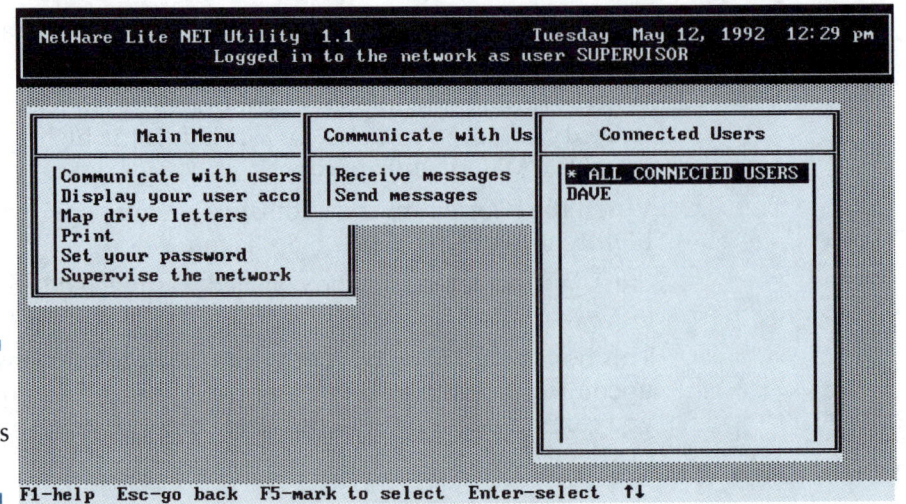

NetWare Lite displays the connected users
Figure 9-5.

Sharing Other Resources

6. Press [Enter] to pop open a box that prompts you to enter the message.
7. Type the message (up to 30 characters).

   As you type the message, you can use [Backspace] to delete unwanted characters. Also, you can move the cursor with the [←] and [→] keys. Figure 9-6 shows a message that has already been entered.
8. Press [Enter] to send the message.

   The screen again displays the box that lists the connected users. You can now send another message by repeating Steps 5 through 8.
9. Press [Alt]-[F10] and [Enter] to exit the menu system.

Selecting Users To Receive Messages

You can send the same message to several users by selecting more than one user when the "Connected Users" box appears (refer to Figure 9-5). To do so, move the highlight to each user you want to select and press [F5]. (A selected name blinks while the highlight is on the name and displays in a different color when the highlight is moved off the name.) To deselect a user, press [F5] when the highlight is on the name of a selected user. When you have selected the users you want, press [Enter] so that you can start typing the message.

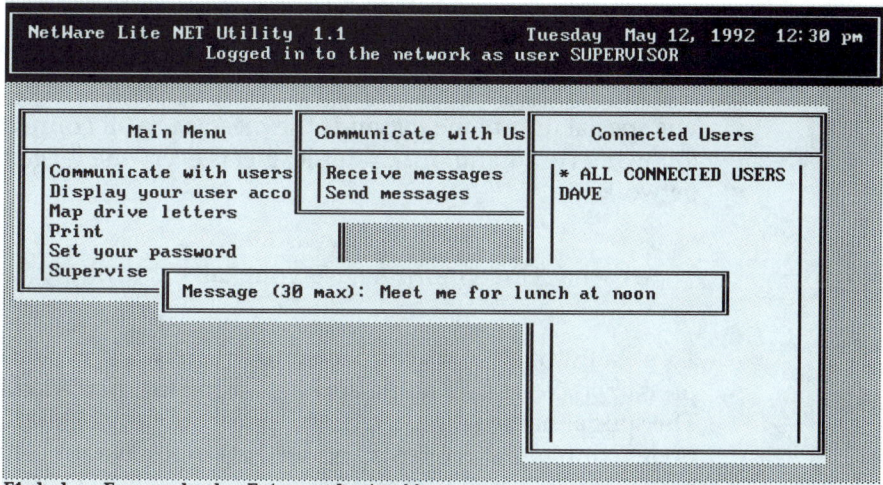

The message is entered
Figure 9-6.

```
NetWare Lite NET Utility 1.1          Tuesday  May 12, 1992  12:30 pm
              Logged in to the network as user SUPERVISOR

    Main Menu         Communicate with Us      Connected Users
 Communicate with users  Receive messages    * ALL CONNECTED USERS
 Display your user acco  Send messages         DAVE
 Map drive letters
 Print
 Set your password
 Supervise
              Message (30 max): Meet me for lunch at noon


 F1-help  Esc-go back  Enter-select  ↑↓
```

The list of users will contain the name SUPERVISOR for each user logged into the network as SUPERVISOR. Your own user name is not on the list because you cannot send a message to yourself.

Sending a Message from the DOS Prompt

You can bypass the menu system and send a message directly from the DOS prompt by using the NET SEND command, which takes several forms.

The following command sends the message "Afternoon meeting canceled" to a user named JODI:

> net send "Afternoon meeting canceled" jodi

You must enclose the message in quotation marks. If the message is longer than 30 characters, NetWare Lite asks whether you want to send the message truncated to the first 30 characters.

You can send a message to selected users by specifying more than one user at the end of the command, using a space to separate each user name from the others. The following command, for example, sends a message to users named CARMEN, JORGE, and KIMBALL:

> net send "Printer is now working" carmen jorge kimball

The special user name *all* sends the message to all connected users. The following command, for example, greets everyone logged into the network:

> net send "Good morning everyone" all

To see a list of all users connected to the network, type **net ulist** and press Enter. Your user name appears on the list, preceded by an asterisk. The special name NWLITE_CLIENT appears for any clients (including nodes configured as clients and servers) that have run STARTNET but have not yet logged into the network with a NET LOGIN command.

Sharing Other Resources

Receiving a Message

Messages appear only if your video screen is in text mode. You can see messages while you are working at the DOS prompt, while in the NetWare Lite menu system, or while you are running any application in text mode. In Figure 9-7, the message on the bottom line of the screen was received from the user named DAVE just after you entered the NET menu system.

Receiving Messages in Special Situations

If your video screen is in graphics mode when someone sends you a message, you do not see the message or hear a beep. Your machine does not pause and you can continue working without interruption. You have no way of knowing that a message was sent. If, for example, you are running a word processor (such as WordPerfect or Microsoft Word) in graphics mode, you will not see any incoming messages.

The message is not irretrievably lost, however. If someone sends you a message while your PC is in graphics mode, NetWare Lite stores the message on your hard disk. As soon as you return the screen to text mode, the message appears and the speaker beeps.

NetWare Lite can store one incoming message at each workstation. Suppose that two users send you a message, one right after the other.

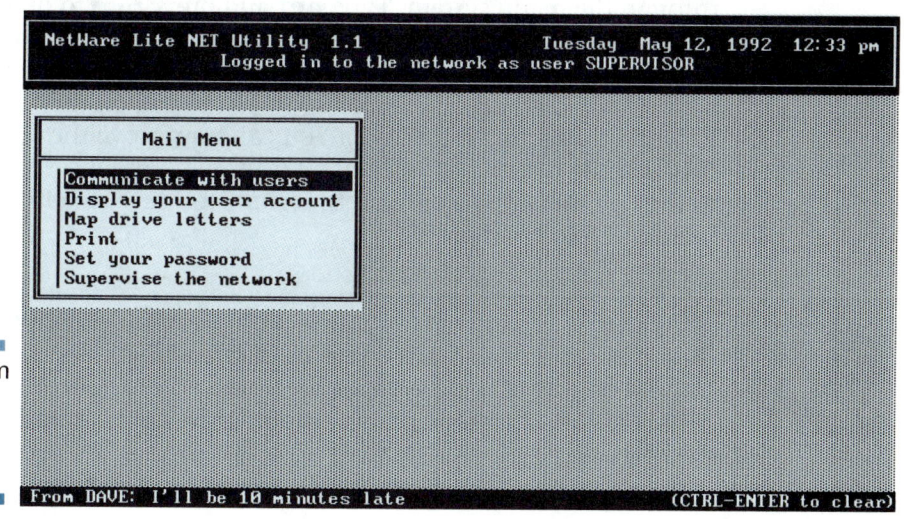

A message from DAVE is received
Figure 9-7.

Your screen displays the first message and then, when you press Ctrl-Enter to clear the message, the second message appears. Should a third message be sent before you clear the first message, however, you cannot recover that third message.

CAUTION: Because NetWare Lite messages are limited to 30 characters, you may be tempted to send one long message as a series of shorter messages. The danger is that each message after the second is lost if the recipient does not clear each message fast enough.

NOTE: When you send a message, you never know whether the message is lost because the recipient has not cleared two previously sent messages. If it is important that you know whether a message has been received, ask the recipient for a reply as part of the message.

Turning Message Reception On and Off

If you do not want incoming messages to interrupt your work by making your computer pause, you can turn off message reception through the menu system. Type **net** and press Enter to open the Main menu. With the highlight on Communicate with users, press Enter to pop open the "Communicate with Users" menu. With the highlight now on Receive messages, press Enter to pop open the "Turn Reception" box (see Figure 9-8). You can now move the highlight between the Off and On options. With the highlight on Off, press Enter to turn off message reception. To resume message reception, move the highlight to On and press Enter.

CAUTION: If you leave your machine unattended while a lengthy application (such as a complex database update) runs, be sure to turn messaging off before you leave. Otherwise, an incoming message will make your machine pause, stopping the application until you clear the message.

Sharing Other Resources

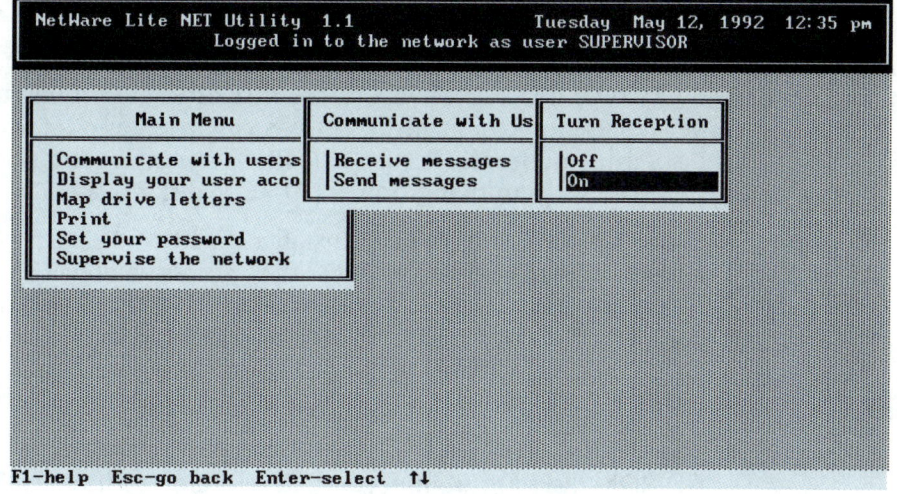

```
NetWare Lite NET Utility 1.1            Tuesday  May 12, 1992  12:35 pm
            Logged in to the network as user SUPERVISOR

        Main Menu            Communicate with Us   Turn Reception
   Communicate with users    Receive messages      Off
   Display your user acco    Send messages         On
   Map drive letters
   Print
   Set your password
   Supervise the network




 F1-help  Esc-go back  Enter-select  ↑↓
```

The "Turn Reception" box allows you to turn message reception off or on
Figure 9-8.

You can turn message reception off or on from the DOS prompt also. To turn message reception off, type **net receive off** and press Enter. To turn message reception back on, type **net receive on** and press Enter.

When you have message reception turned off, any messages sent to you are irretrievably lost. (Turning message reception back on does not display waiting messages.) The sender has no way of knowing that you are not receiving messages. Again, as a sender, request a reply if you need confirmation that a message was received.

NOTE: When message reception is off, you can still send messages.

Sharing CD-ROM Disk Drives

CD-ROM (Compact Disk, Read-Only Memory) is a relatively recent technology for data storage and retrieval. The popularity of CD-ROMs is growing exponentially. Think of a CD-ROM disk drive as an incredibly high-capacity floppy disk drive from which you can read data but to which you cannot write data. That is, you can copy data *from* a

CD-ROM disk to your hard disk, but you cannot copy data *to* the CD-ROM disk. That's why a CD-ROM disk is called a *read-only device*.

A CD-ROM disk drive and a floppy disk drive are similar in that both devices use removable media. Just as you insert and remove floppy disks into and from a floppy disk drive, you insert and remove CD-ROM disks into and from a CD-ROM disk drive.

CD-ROM technology puts a wealth of information at your disposal.

Using NetWare Lite, you can install a CD-ROM disk drive on a server and allow everyone on the network to access whatever CD-ROM disk is in the drive. Because a CD-ROM works a bit differently from a regular hard disk or floppy disk, you need to take a few extra steps to make a CD-ROM disk available to clients. These steps are explained later in this chapter, in the "Installing a CD-ROM Disk Drive" and "Accessing a CD-ROM Drive" sections.

CD-ROM disks are an important, developing technology. The following sections introduce CD-ROMs and the potential benefits they offer a workgroup.

Data Capacity of CD-ROM Disks

The familiar audio CD, which has virtually replaced vinyl record albums, can store more than 60 minutes of music. The computer CD-ROM disk is based on the same technology and looks exactly like an audio CD. The CD-ROM disk is a silvery platter about 4.7 inches in diameter and one-sixteenth of an inch thick. (Most CD-ROM drives can play audio CDs also.) But instead of music, a CD-ROM disk can hold more than 600MB of data.

Think for a second about just how much 600MB of data really is. The typical hard disk on a desktop computer has a capacity somewhere between 40 and 150MB.

Consider that this book contains approximately one million characters of text. Using standard computer storage techniques, each character occupies one byte, so the book contains approximately 1MB of text data. One CD-ROM disk could contain the text of 600 books the size of this one. By using some simple data-compression techniques, even more data can fit on a single CD-ROM disk. That's a tremendous amount of data in such a small package.

> **NOTE:** One megabyte (1MB) is not precisely 1 million bytes but rather 1,024 times 1,024, or 1,048,576 bytes. For this discussion, the numbers are approximations. It's simpler to think of a megabyte as 1 million bytes.

CD-ROM Indexes

Not all 600MB of a CD-ROM disk are available for storing data. Because so much data is stored on each disk, a CD-ROM drive needs to find data on a CD-ROM disk as quickly as possible. To speed up the data access time, the CD-ROM drives use elaborate indexing schemes. These indexes occupy space on each CD-ROM disk (more than 100MB, for some disks).

Consider the index used for library books. In a library, you may look in the card catalog to find books about a particular subject. Then you can go straight to the proper shelf, based on the subject's Dewey Decimal System number (or, in some libraries, the Library of Congress number). You don't have to search through every book on every shelf until you find the book you want.

CD-ROM indexes work much like the library's card catalog. You can purchase on a single CD-ROM disk, for example, all the articles printed in the *Los Angeles Times* newspaper during a six-month period. You can search this database in a number of ways. One type of search is to request all articles containing a single word that you provide. Suppose that you are interested in lawsuits about copyright infringement. If you enter the word "lawsuit," the search software quickly examines an index file and tells you within a second or two (the time varies depending on the CD-ROM disk drive model) that 1,636 articles from January through June of 1991 contain the word "lawsuit." If you ask how many of those articles also contain the word "copyright," you learn within another second that 31 do. Then you can read each article. Retrieving each article takes about one or two seconds.

Instead of searching for words, you can search by title, author, subject, and many other criteria or combinations. Without extensive indexes to speed up the search process, the software would have to read sequentially through all the data until your request was found.

Compared to indexed searches, sequential searches are extremely time consuming. You wouldn't put up with having to wait for a sequential search. Even though an index sometimes occupies more than 100MB of space on a CD-ROM disk, the disk still has space for plenty of data.

CD-ROM Costs

One important aspect of CD-ROM technology is that the manufacturing cost to produce a CD-ROM title is relatively low. An original master data disk costs several thousand dollars. Each disk copy, however, can be produced for about $2. The costs vary somewhat depending on the manufacturing techniques and the size of the production run, but these numbers give you a rough idea. Do a little arithmetic and you'll see that a manufacturer who produces a few thousand CD-ROMs of a particular title can produce the disks for $4 to $10 each.

The price of a CD-ROM product can vary widely.

Of course, that's just the manufacturing cost. The data that goes on the CD-ROM disk doesn't come free. Someone has to research, acquire, and prepare the data and indexes. An encyclopedia, atlas, newspaper, or other CD-ROM database doesn't write itself. Also, there are the typical business costs for advertising, distribution, sales commissions, profit, and so on. These other costs tend to dwarf the manufacturing cost. As a result, a CD-ROM disk can cost the consumer anywhere from $10 to over $1,000. Specialized databases for businesses or professionals generally cost the most. Mass-market databases, promotional materials, and data from the public domain (such as old literary works that no longer have copyright protection) cost the least.

The $10 to $1,000 price tag indicates what you can expect to pay for each CD-ROM disk. (People who produce and sell CD-ROM disks use the terms *CD-ROM title* or *CD-ROM software* when referring to the disk and the data stored on the disk. Sometimes "CD-ROM software" refers to the computer software you run to access the CD-ROM data. Such software is also called the *search engine* or *search software*.)

The next consideration is the cost of the CD-ROM drive itself. You cannot read the data on a CD-ROM disk unless you insert the disk into a CD-ROM drive.

In recent years, the increased popularity of CD-ROMs has led to a drop in prices for CD-ROM disk drives. Only a few years ago, you had to

Sharing Other Resources

spend at least $1,000 for a CD-ROM disk drive; today, the most popular models are priced in the $400 to $600 range. The lower-cost models access data more slowly than more expensive models. Many models are available in package deals that include several CD-ROM titles. These titles may be included free or may raise the price by perhaps $100 to $200. Some packages include two, three, or even six or more CD-ROM titles, which might cost $500, $1,000, or more if you bought the disks separately, rather than with the disk drive. If you shop for a CD-ROM drive, look carefully at the different package deals available.

Careful shopping can save you large amounts on a CD-ROM drive.

For about $500 (less, if you shop rigorously) you can buy a CD-ROM disk drive bundled with plenty of reference material, games, or other interesting titles. This price is steep enough to attract only buyers with a strong need or desire for CD-ROM.

Suppose that you could buy a CD-ROM disk drive for the attractive price of $100. In a way, that's just what you can do with your NetWare Lite LAN. Connect the CD-ROM disk drive to a server. If you have five PCs on the LAN, all five nodes can access the CD-ROM disk. In effect, each user pays one-fifth the cost. If you have 10 PCs, the cost is only $50 each.

Drawbacks to CD-ROM

Life is not perfect. Here are some precautions to consider before you run off and spend that $500 on a CD-ROM drive.

Disks may be single-user   Some CD-ROM titles are sold only for use by a single user. Such titles cannot be shared legally on a LAN. Other disks permit several users to access the data over a LAN but charge a higher price.

Possible incompatibility with NetWare Lite   The search software on a few CD-ROM titles may not work with NetWare Lite. Most popular software does work, however.

Changing CD-ROM disks may be inconvenient   The CD-ROM disk drive reads only one CD-ROM disk at a time. If one person wants to search a CD-ROM encyclopedia while another user wants to search a CD-ROM newspaper database, someone has to wait. Every time you switch to a different CD-ROM disk, you have to go to the server, manually remove one disk and insert another. Some special multidisk CD-ROM players are available to switch automatically between different CD-ROMs. But these units are expensive, priced at $1,000 and up. One model takes seven seconds to switch CD-ROM disks. That may seem fast, but computer users accustomed to instantaneous responses find the delay interminable. See the "CD-ROM Disk Drive Products" section later in this chapter for more information. Another alternative, of course, is to install more than one CD-ROM drive on your LAN so that you can have a different CD-ROM database in each drive.

Search time can be slow with shared use   A CD-ROM disk is much slower than a hard disk. If more than three or four users search the disk at once, everyone's response time slows down. Instead of waiting one or two seconds to find a dictionary entry or a magazine article, you might wait 10 or 20 seconds. Many users become impatient after about five seconds.

Installing a CD-ROM Disk Drive

CD-ROM disk drives are made by several manufacturers. Most models are fairly similar. The biggest difference is between external and internal disk drives. An *external* drive is housed in its own box, which you place next to the computer. A cable from the disk drive connects to a card or port on the back of the computer. External units have a power cord you must plug into an electrical outlet. An *internal* drive, much like a floppy disk drive, is installed inside a computer. Like a floppy drive, you can insert and remove disks through an opening in the front of the computer. Internal drives run off the computer's power supply.

To help you learn more about CD-ROM drives, here is a short description of the installation process for the Toshiba TXM3300 (shown to the right in Figure 9-9). The TXM3300 is an external CD-ROM drive. Toshiba's internal version of the TXM3300—called the XM-3300—is shown to the left in Figure 9-9.

An external CD-ROM drive kit typically consists of the drive itself, an interface card you install in the server, a connecting cable, a power cable, and a floppy disk with CD-ROM driver software.

Sharing Other Resources

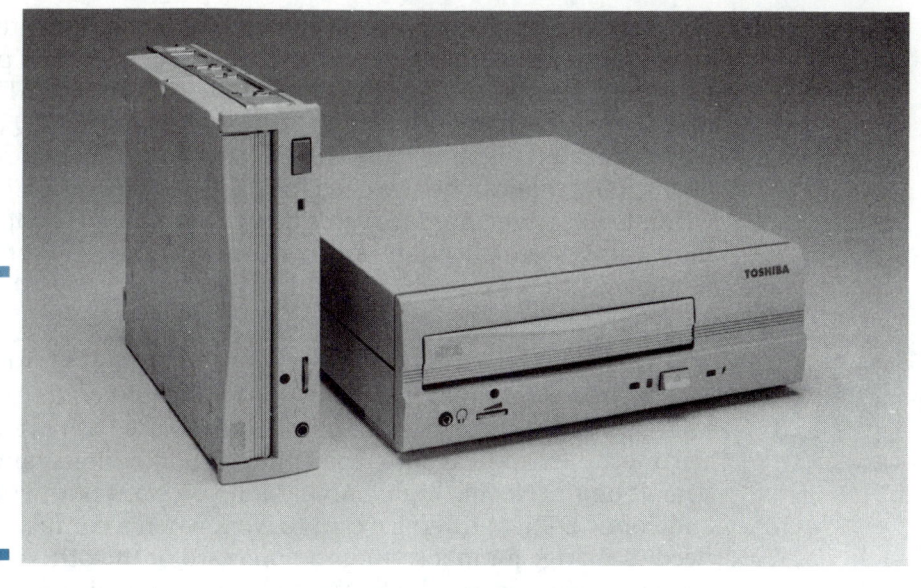

Toshiba CD-ROM drives: XM-3300 internal (left) and TXM3300 external (right)
Figure 9-9.

> **CAUTION:** When buying a CD-ROM drive, be sure the interface card is included. You may not need an interface card, however. If your computer's hard disk uses a SCSI (small computer system interface) controller card, you may be able to connect the CD-ROM drive to your existing card.

CD-ROM Hardware Installation

Step one of the hardware installation is to install the interface card, if you need one, on the server computer. The Toshiba comes with a SCSI interface card. A SCSI card installs in much the same way as any other add-on card, such as a LAN card. (The installation of LAN cards is described in Chapter 4.)

The only difficulty you may have when you install the interface card would occur if the CD-ROM card's settings for IRQ or I/O ports conflict with the LAN card or some other card in your computer. The Toshiba's interface card comes with default settings of 5 for the IRQ (which can be set instead to 3), and an 8K memory area, starting at hex address CA00:0000, that can be switched instead to C800:0000, CE00:0000, or DE00:0000. (Some interface cards do not use I/O port addresses. With these cards, there cannot be any conflict with the I/O port addresses used by your LAN card.)

CAUTION: Some interface cards are set by default to use I/O port addresses that may conflict with the I/O port addresses set on your LAN card. Some interface cards, for example, use I/O port addresses starting at hex address 300—the same I/O port address range used by default on the Novell/Eagle LAN card. If you want both your LAN card and your CD-ROM interface card to work when a conflict exists, you need to change jumper settings on one card or the other. (If you change the jumper on the LAN card, you should reinstall NetWare Lite to specify the new setting.)

After the interface card is installed, the next step is to install the cable between the interface card and the CD-ROM drive. For most brands (including the Toshiba), the cable connects easily and is secured by screws or clips.

Then, as is the case for any SCSI device, you must set the SCSI device number on the drive. Because you can daisy chain several SCSI devices on the same SCSI interface card, every SCSI device needs a unique number. The Toshiba drive has a default setting of 4. If the default device number on your drive conflicts with another SCSI device, you can change jumpers (or, for some drives, flip switches) on the drive to select a new number.

CAUTION: Hard disk drives on some PCs use a SCSI controller. If your hard disk drive is a SCSI device, you must verify that the device number, IRQ, and port addresses of your hard disk drive don't conflict with the settings for the CD-ROM drive's interface card. (The SCSI controllers for some hard disks don't use IRQs or port addresses. For such controllers, there cannot be conflicts in these settings.) If your

Sharing Other Resources

hard disk has a SCSI controller, check the documentation with your computer (or hard disk) to determine the device number and other settings for your SCSI controller.

The end of each SCSI daisy chain requires a terminator so that the electronic signal does not reflect back at the end of the chain and cause errors. The Toshiba drive requires attachment of a plug device, which is included with the drive.

Finally, you connect a power cable between the drive and a wall outlet or other power source to complete the hardware installation.

CD-ROM Software Installation

Like the LAN operating system software, CD-ROM software is designed in layers. A low-level CD-ROM driver controls the CD-ROM disk drive itself. A high-level CD-ROM driver, called Microsoft CD Extensions, or MSCDEX, interfaces between the low-level driver and DOS. On top of that layer is the application program for the particular CD-ROM database product you use. The application program contains the search software. Figure 9-10 shows these layers.

Because CD-ROM software has several layers, the software installation requires several steps. Each step is simple, but you must do each step to ensure that everything works together properly.

1. Install the CD-ROM driver software on your hard disk.

   The CD-ROM driver disk that comes with the CD-ROM drive typically includes a SETUP or INSTALL program which installs the driver software on your hard disk. At least two files—the low-level driver and the high-level driver—are necessary. For the Toshiba drive, the SETUP procedure creates on the hard disk a directory (called DEV) in which SETUP puts the low-level driver program (MDSCD_FD.SYS). SETUP creates another directory (called \bin) for the high-level driver (MSCDEX.EXE).

2. Modify your CONFIG.SYS file to include the low-level driver software.

   You can use EDLIN, EDIT, or another line editor to update CONFIG.SYS. (For more about EDLIN, EDIT, and modifying a

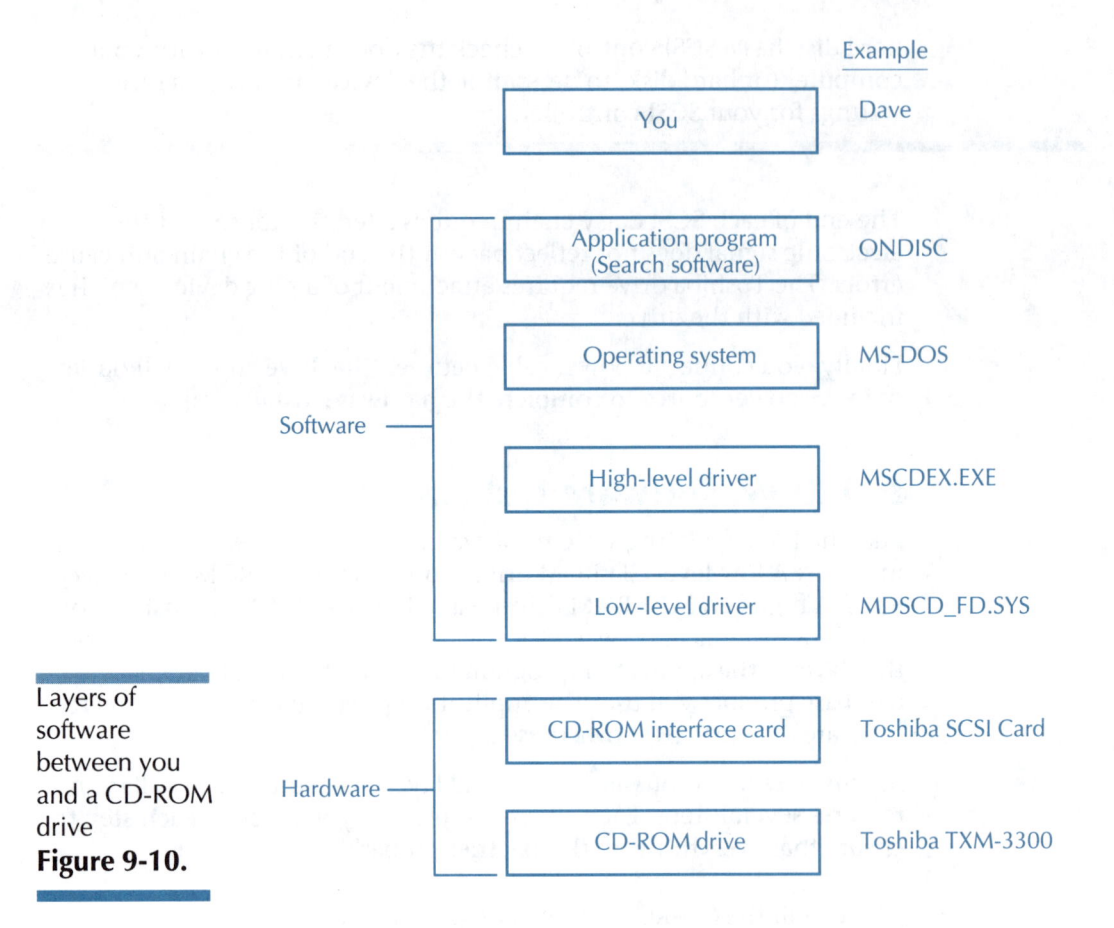

Figure 9-10. Layers of software between you and a CD-ROM drive

		Example
	You	Dave
Software	Application program (Search software)	ONDISC
	Operating system	MS-DOS
	High-level driver	MSCDEX.EXE
	Low-level driver	MDSCD_FD.SYS
Hardware	CD-ROM interface card	Toshiba SCSI Card
	CD-ROM drive	Toshiba TXM-3300

CONFIG.SYS file, see Appendix C. You must add to CONFIG.SYS a command that installs the low-level driver whenever you boot your computer. This is the command for the Toshiba drive:

device=\dev\mdscd_fd.sys /d:mscd000 /n:1

The command for the Toshiba drive specifies the location of the driver file, including the DEV subdirectory name. The parameter */d:mscd000* provides an internal name for the CD-ROM drive. This particular name was chosen by the SETUP program, but you can specify any DOS-type name (of up to eight characters). The last parameter, */n:1*, specifies the number of CD-ROM drives installed in this computer.

3. Install the application software on each client.

   Follow the instructions with the application software to install the search software on each client's hard disk.

4. Run NET and make the server's CD-ROM drive available.

   From NetWare Lite's point of view, the CD-ROM drive is just like any other disk drive offered for sharing. You make the CD-ROM drive available on a server as a network directory and then client machines can map a drive letter to the CD-ROM drive. The procedure for sharing hard disks is explained in Chapter 7.

   When you are creating a network directory for a CD-ROM drive, use the server's next available drive letter as the actual directory path. For example, if the server has a hard disk drive C, but no other hard disk drives, use drive D for the CD-ROM. Enter **D:** when prompted for the `Actual directory path`. (You can assign another drive letter name, if you like. If you do, you must specify that drive letter when you run the MSCDEX program as described in Step 4 of the following section.) Make the network directory name CDROM or some other easily recognized name.

Accessing a CD-ROM Drive

All the previous steps to install the hardware and software need to be done only once. With the CD-ROM installed and available over the network, follow these steps whenever you want a client to access the shared CD-ROM:

1. If the CD-ROM drive is external, turn on the CD-ROM disk drive power switch.

   This switch is typically on the back of the drive. Internal drives get power from the computer and don't need to be turned on separately.

2. Boot the server computer.

   The point here is that you may need to power on the CD-ROM drive before you turn on the power to the server. If the CD-ROM drive is not powered on first, the low-level driver software may not install. Some will, some won't. Experiment once by leaving the CD-ROM drive powered off when you boot the server. Look for an error message that says the driver software is not installed. If you see such a message, you know that the CD-ROM disk has to be turned on first.

3. Start NetWare Lite on the server.

4. Start MSCDEX on the server.

   For the Toshiba example, the MSCDEX program is in a subdirectory named \bin. The following command does the trick:

   ```
   c:\bin\mscdex /d:mscd000
   ```

   The /d parameter again provides the device name and must match the name you used in CONFIG.SYS to install the low-level driver program. You can also specify a disk drive name by adding an /l parameter, such as /l:M to make the CD-ROM drive your drive M. Otherwise, MSCDEX uses the next available name, usually D (unless you have a hard disk or a RAM disk configured as drive D). If you chose something other than the next available drive letter when creating the CD-ROM's network directory (in Step 4 of the preceding section), use the /l parameter to specify that drive letter.

5. Start NetWare Lite on the client, if you haven't already done so.

6. Run NET on the client to map a disk drive name to the server's CD-ROM disk.

   The name doesn't have to match the physical name you assigned on the server. For example, you can map the client's drive M, even if the actual directory path to the server's CD-ROM is drive D.

7. Run the CD-ROM application software on the client.

   You may need to specify the disk drive name you chose on the workstation, or the software may be "smart enough" to figure out the name. For example, Dialog Information Services provides a program called ONDISC to use with the L.A. Times and Standard & Poors databases. To use ONDISC with a CD-ROM disk mapped using drive name K, you type the following command and press `Enter`:

Sharing Other Resources

ondisc k:

to bring up ONDISC's opening screen.

CD-ROM Disk Drive Products

CD-ROM disk drives and CD-ROM disks are available from many sources. Popular CD-ROM disk drive brands, in addition to Toshiba, are Chinon, Sony, NEC, Hitachi, Philips, and Magnavox.

If you frequently need to change CD-ROM disks in your drive, you can buy a CD-ROM changer that works much like a CD-ROM jukebox. A typical product holds a certain number of CD-ROMs and, in response to a software command, exchanges the disk in the drive. For example, the Pioneer DRM-600 MiniChanger, which lists for approximately $1,200, stores six CD-ROM disks and can exchange a disk in seven seconds.

For users who need simultaneous access to more than one CD-ROM disk, several manufacturers make cabinets that house multiple drives and run the drives from a single controller card. One example is the Toshiba TXM-3301A4, which lists for $3,170 and includes four CD-ROM drives, stacked on top of each other. Before purchasing any CD-ROM changer or multiple-drive device, check with the manufacturer to be sure that the product is compatible with NetWare Lite.

CD-ROM titles are available from many vendors, most of whom also sell drives. A list of some vendors who offer large catalogs of CD-ROM titles follows:

- *Updata Publications, Inc., 1736 Westwood Blvd., Los Angeles, CA 90024* Excellent catalog, logically grouped and indexed, offers a variety of titles and hardware

- *Compact Disk Products (CDP), 272 Route 34, Aberdeen, NJ 07747* Offers a variety of titles and hardware

- *CD ROM, Inc., 1667 Cole Blvd., Suite 400, Golden, CO 80401* Excellent catalog offers a variety of titles and hardware

- *PhoneDisc U.S.A. Corp., 8 Doaks Lane, Marblehead, MA 01945* Specializes in phone directories on CD-ROM

Sharing Modems and Other Two-Way Serial Devices

A *modem* is a hardware device that translates a computer's electrical signals into the communication signals used over telephone lines, and vice versa. You install a modem in your computer and then connect a phone line to the modem. Computer modems can be internal (on a card you install in an empty computer slot) or external (in a separate box that connects to an interface card in your computer).

With a modem and appropriate software, your computer can communicate with other similarly equipped computers. You can send and receive files (and other information) between computers. Also, you can access electronic bulletin boards and information services such as CompuServe and Prodigy.

NetWare Lite does not allow you to share a modem unless you buy special modem-sharing software. One such software product—ArtiCom, from Artisoft of Tucson, Arizona—is discussed here in depth. Some other vendors of modem-sharing software are mentioned at the end of this section.

If you're thinking about modem sharing, consider the financial implications. Modems have become so inexpensive that modem sharing is not cost effective for most workgroups. If you can install a $50 internal 2400 bps (bits per second) modem in every PC, spending the money (typically $300 or more) to buy modem-sharing software doesn't make sense.

The two primary reasons you might want to share modems follow:

1. A 2400 bps modem may not be fast enough. If several group members need to use a 9600 bps modem, which costs substantially more than a 2400 bps modem, modem sharing may be appropriate.
2. Telephone line costs may overshadow other costs. If installing and using, say, eight individual phone lines for your eight-person workgroup is too expensive, and three shared lines would be enough, modem sharing makes sense.

Determine your modem and telephone line needs, for both shared and individual usage. Determine whether every individual in the workgroup

Sharing Other Resources

needs a modem, and what speed modem would suffice. Try to ascertain how many group members are likely to need modems simultaneously.

Check current prices for the types of modems you need and look into local telephone costs, both for installation and monthly use. Then compare the costs, benefits, and drawbacks for shared and unshared configurations and make your decision.

The next section shows how modem sharing works, using ArtiCom as an example. If modem sharing does not make sense for your workgroup, you can skip this section.

Introducing ArtiCom

ArtiCom enables modem sharing through NetWare Lite.

ArtiCom sets up a special communication process between the LAN nodes to support serial devices that require two-way communications. These serial devices usually are modems, but ArtiCom also supports certain plotters and other devices that use two-way communication. ArtiCom routes messages back and forth between a PC with a modem and another PC that needs to use the modem. The software uses only about 6K of RAM on each PC, but it also requires that you run the NetBIOS program, which uses about 30K more.

Without special hardware you can have as many as four serial devices on a PC, attached to ports COM1 through COM4. You can buy special devices called *multiport serial adapters*, which allow you to connect up to eight serial devices on one COM port (thus, as many as 32 serial devices on one computer). ArtiCom supports multiport serial adapters made by four companies: Stargate, Arnet, Quatech, and DigiBoard.

On a single PC, you can install a single modem or as many as 32. Because all LAN users can use these modems, everyone has access to outside computer facilities without a modem being installed in every computer. You can put these modems on any of your LAN nodes, not just on servers. If you like, you can install modems on one or two clients to avoid bogging down a server that has a heavy database (or other) workload. Also, a client is more likely to be able to absorb the RAM requirements of NetBIOS and ArtiCom than a server that already has several TSRs loaded.

ArtiCom works by capturing a port on a workstation. The process is similar to the port captures used by NetWare Lite to share printers. See Chapter 8 for more information on capturing ports.

After ArtiCom makes the connection between a modem PC and another user's PC, you can use ArtiCom to dial a remote computer, upload and download files, and capture the dialog to a disk file. If you prefer, you can use your own favorite communications program, as long as the program adheres to a standard called the *INT 14h standard* (interrupt 14 hexadecimal). This standard specifies the way the PC communicates with the modem. Many newer software communication products follow this standard, or at least have an option to let you configure the product to follow the standard. Some of these products are Procomm Plus Network, CrossTalk Mark IV, Mirror III, SmarTerm, Softerm, and BLAST PC.

Installing ArtiCom

ArtiCom is a software product. If you have a functioning NetWare Lite LAN (or any other LAN that conforms to NetBIOS standards) and at least one modem or other bidirectional serial device, you have all the hardware you need to use ArtiCom. Because you most likely will use ArtiCom to share a modem over the LAN, that usage is covered here. For simplicity, the explanation is for a LAN with one modem on one computer. Every node on the LAN can share this modem. The computer with the modem is called the *modem server*, even if the computer is not configured as a NetWare Lite server.

NOTE: Any NetWare Lite client or server can be set up as a modem server. A computer that makes use of the shared modem is called a *modem workstation*.

The ArtiCom software installs much like the NetWare Lite software, as discussed in Chapter 5. ArtiCom comes on both 5 1/4-inch and 3 1/2-inch floppy disks; use whichever size is appropriate for your computer. You can put the disk in either drive A or drive B (the example here assumes that you use drive A).

Modem Server Installation

Put the ArtiCom floppy disk in drive A of the computer that has the modem, type **a:ainstall**, and press Enter. Your screen should look like that shown in Figure 9-11.

The AINSTALL program expects you to press the cursor-movement keys to highlight different options and then press Enter to change the options. The first option, Type of Software Installation, has a default value of Workstation AND Server. This setting allows this computer not only to offer its modem to other computers that need access, but also to connect to other modem servers to use their modems. Because this computer has the only modem on the sample LAN, press Enter to change the setting to Server ONLY.

The default settings for the next three options do not need to be changed. With these default settings, AINSTALL will load the ArtiCom software from drive A into a disk directory named ARTICOM on drive C. To identify the server for users who want to access the modem, the modem server is named MODEM-SERVER.

Move the cursor to the option labeled Number of automatically selected ports, set by default to 2. Press Enter to see the screen shown in Figure 9-12.

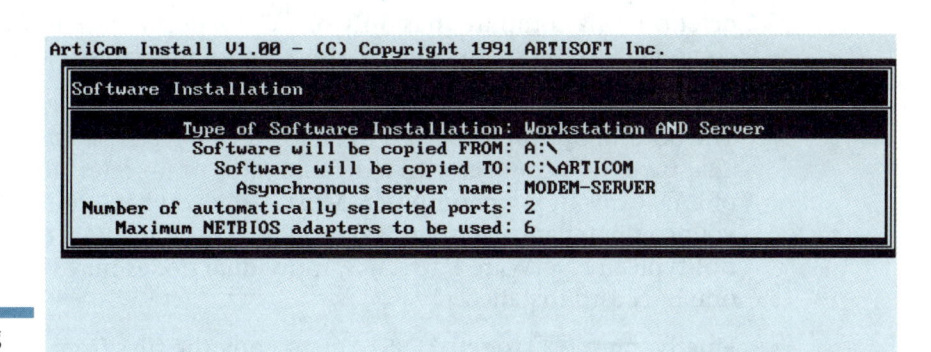

```
ArtiCom Install V1.00 - (C) Copyright 1991 ARTISOFT Inc.
Software Installation
              Type of Software Installation: Workstation AND Server
                   Software will be copied FROM: A:\
                     Software will be copied TO: C:\ARTICOM
                       Asynchronous server name: MODEM-SERVER
     Number of automatically selected ports: 2
           Maximum NETBIOS adapters to be used: 6




 Enter-Modify, F2-Start Install, ESC-Exit, F1-Help
```

The opening screen from ArtiCom's AINSTALL program
Figure 9-11.

```
ArtiCom Install V1.00 - (C) Copyright 1991 ARTISOFT Inc.
Software Installation
            Type of Software Installation: Server ONLY
    ┌─────────────────────────────────────────────────┐
    │ Shared Port Name    => Local COM device         │
    │ COM-PORT1           => COM1                     │
    │ COM-PORT2           => COM2                     │
    └─────────────────────────────────────────────────┘
Enter-Modify, Ins-Add port, Del-Delete port, Esc-Exit, F1-Help
```

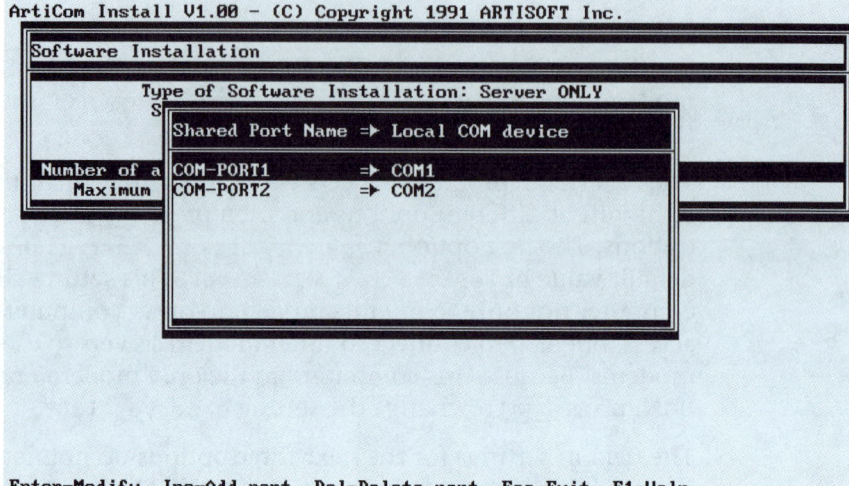

The serial ports that potentially can be shared
Figure 9-12.

Figure 9-12 shows the devices this modem server can make available to modem workstations. Rather than make all these devices available, delete the devices that are not modems. (Otherwise, users may try to share your mouse.) On this computer, the modem is configured by jumpers on the modem card to use the COM2 port. The COM1 port is connected to a mouse. To delete the COM1 port, highlight COM1, press [Del], and then (when prompted) press [Enter] to confirm the deletion. (If a computer has only one COM port and that port is connected to the shared device, this step isn't necessary.) Finally, press [Esc] to return to the Main menu box.

The bottom option displayed in Figure 9-11—Maximum NETBIOS adapters to be used, with a default value of 6—refers to the number of LAN cards in your computer. Most likely you have one LAN card in your computer and can set this option to 1. (In some LAN environments, not typically NetWare Lite LANs, individual nodes may have more than one LAN card installed.)

Finally, press [F2] to tell AINSTALL to copy the files from the floppy disk to the hard disk and activate your chosen settings. The installation of the modem server is now finished. The files are on the modem server's hard disk and ready for use. The next step is to start the ArtiCom software.

Sharing Other Resources

Workstation Software Installation

To install the software for a modem workstation, you begin as you did for the modem server. Type **a:ainstall** and press [Enter] to start the AINSTALL program. Then press [Enter] twice to change the `Type of Software Installation` to `Workstation ONLY`. The screen should now look like the one shown in Figure 9-13.

Only the first two options remain. The default values for the file paths should be appropriate; if not, you can change them. Then press [F2] to install the workstation software. The AINSTALL program displays the name of each file being installed and then a completion message. The workstation software installation is complete.

Running ArtiCom

To run ArtiCom, whether on a NetWare Lite server or client, you first must start NetWare Lite. If you have not already done so, type **cd \nwlite** and press [Enter] to switch to the NetWare Lite disk directory; then type **startnet** and press [Enter] to start the network software.

Next, you need to run the NETBIOS program. This program makes NetWare Lite respond properly to application software that uses

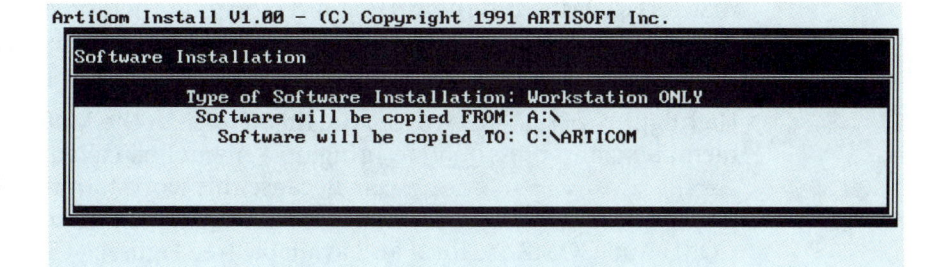

```
ArtiCom Install V1.00 - (C) Copyright 1991 ARTISOFT Inc.
Software Installation
            Type of Software Installation: Workstation ONLY
               Software will be copied FROM: A:\
                 Software will be copied TO: C:\ARTICOM



Enter-Modify, F2-Start Install, ESC-Exit, F1-Help
```

The AINSTALL screen for the installation of workstation software only
Figure 9-13.

standard NetBIOS commands for communication between LAN nodes. NetBIOS is discussed further in Chapter 15. To start the NETBIOS program, type **netbios** and press [Enter].

As soon as the Lite software is running, type the command **cd \articom** to make ArtiCom's directory the current directory. Then type either **a-server** (on the modem server computer) or **a-redir** (on a modem workstation) and press [Enter]. The modem server displays the following output:

```
Asynchronous Server (A-SERVER) V1.00 -
(C) Copyright 1991 ARTISOFT Inc.
          ---- A-SERVER installed ----
```

The modem workstation displays the following output:

```
Asynchronous Redirector (A-REDIR) V1.00 -
(C) Copyright 1991 ARTISOFT Inc.
          ---- A-REDIR installed ----
```

These A-REDIR and A-SERVER programs communicate with each other across the LAN, with A-REDIR running on a modem workstation and A-SERVER on the modem server.

Now you are ready to actually make contact between the workstation and the modem on the modem server. On the workstation, make sure that ARTICOM is still the current directory and then type the command **acom** and press [Enter]. The ACOM program displays the screen shown in Figure 9-14.

Highlight `Terminal Emulator`, the first choice in the Main Functions menu box, and press [Enter] to bring up a menu box called `Select COM Port for Terminal Emulation`. Because this workstation has two serial ports, neither with a device attached, the menu box indicates that COM1 and COM2 are local and available (see Figure 9-15). This means that the two ports are actual ports on the computer. A third choice, COM3, is shown as available. COM3—a nonexistent port—is available for assignment to the server's modem (just as a client can map a nonexistent disk drive name to a server's network directory).

Move the highlight line down to COM3 and press [Enter], bringing up (on the right) a menu box that lists modem servers available on the LAN. Press [Enter] to select MODEM-SERVER, the name of the only

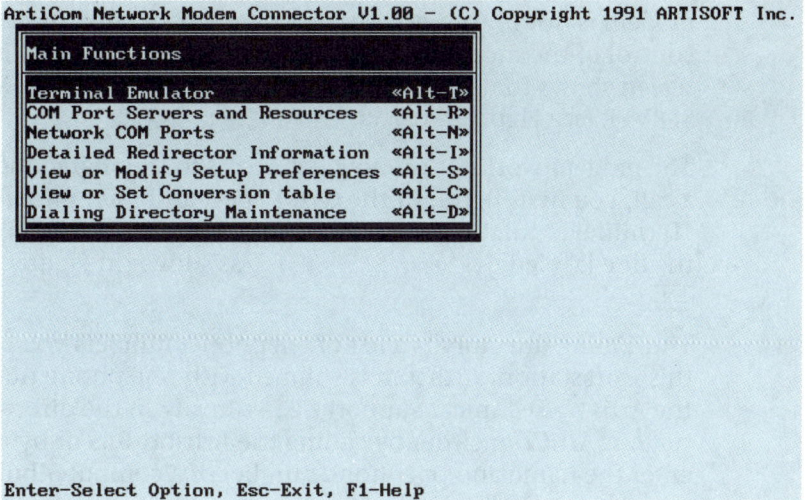

Sharing Other Resources

```
ArtiCom Network Modem Connector V1.00 - (C) Copyright 1991 ARTISOFT Inc.
┌Main Functions─────────────────────────────┐
│ Terminal Emulator                 «Alt-T» │
│ COM Port Servers and Resources    «Alt-R» │
│ Network COM Ports                 «Alt-N» │
│ Detailed Redirector Information   «Alt-I» │
│ View or Modify Setup Preferences  «Alt-S» │
│ View or Set Conversion table      «Alt-C» │
│ Dialing Directory Maintenance     «Alt-D» │
└───────────────────────────────────────────┘

Enter-Select Option, Esc-Exit, F1-Help
```

The ACOM program's opening menu
Figure 9-14.

modem server on this LAN. The result, the screen shown in Figure 9-15, lists the resources available on the modem server.

ArtiCom shows the available resource COM-PORT2 (the modem on the server's COM2 port). The column labeled `In use by` shows that the

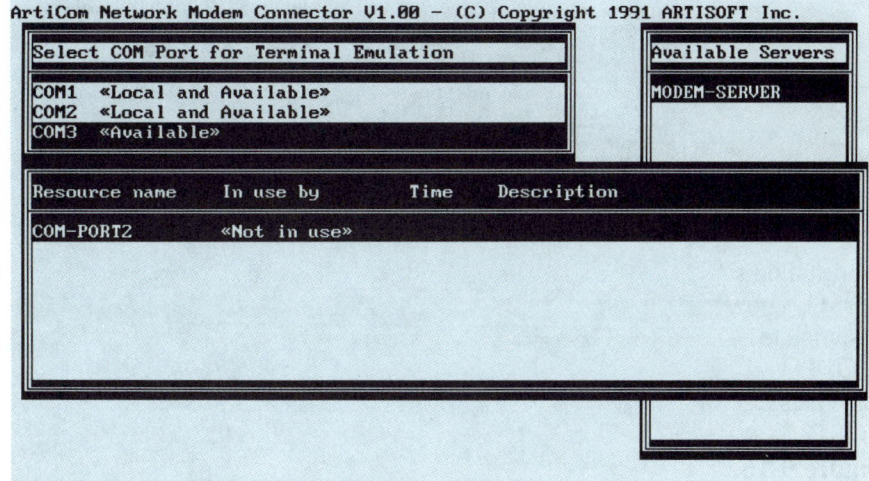

```
ArtiCom Network Modem Connector V1.00 - (C) Copyright 1991 ARTISOFT Inc.
┌Select COM Port for Terminal Emulation─────┐  ┌Available Servers┐
│ COM1  «Local and Available»               │  │ MODEM-SERVER    │
│ COM2  «Local and Available»               │  │                 │
│ COM3  «Available»                         │  │                 │
└───────────────────────────────────────────┘  └─────────────────┘
┌Resource name    In use by     Time    Description─────────────────┐
│ COM-PORT2       «Not in use»                                      │
│                                                                   │
└───────────────────────────────────────────────────────────────────┘

Enter-Redirect, Space-Update, Esc-Exit, F1-Help
```

The ACOM program shows the server's available serial devices
Figure 9-15.

modem is not in use (no other modem workstation has already taken control of the modem). The modem is available for use. Press [Enter]; the screen shows that COM3 is assigned to COM-PORT2 on MODEM-SERVER (see Figure 9-16).

The modem workstation now has access to the shared modem. To place a call, you first highlight the COM3 port and then press [Enter]. When a "Terminal Emulator" menu box appears, move the highlight down to the line labeled Dialing Directory (as shown in Figure 9-17) and press [Enter].

The dialing directory is a list of telephone numbers you can call from this workstation. ArtiCom is shipped with one phone number—that of the Artisoft Technical Support BBS—already in the directory. You can test out ArtiCom either by calling the Artisoft BBS or by pressing [Ins] to enter the name and telephone number of a computer bulletin board you choose. Highlight the number you want to call and press [Enter] to dial the number. If the modem has a speaker, hearing the modem server computer make the phone call while your modem workstation computer does the dialing may be a strange experience for you.

When the remote computer answers your call, press [Alt]-[T] to switch to terminal mode and start your dialog. When you have finished your call

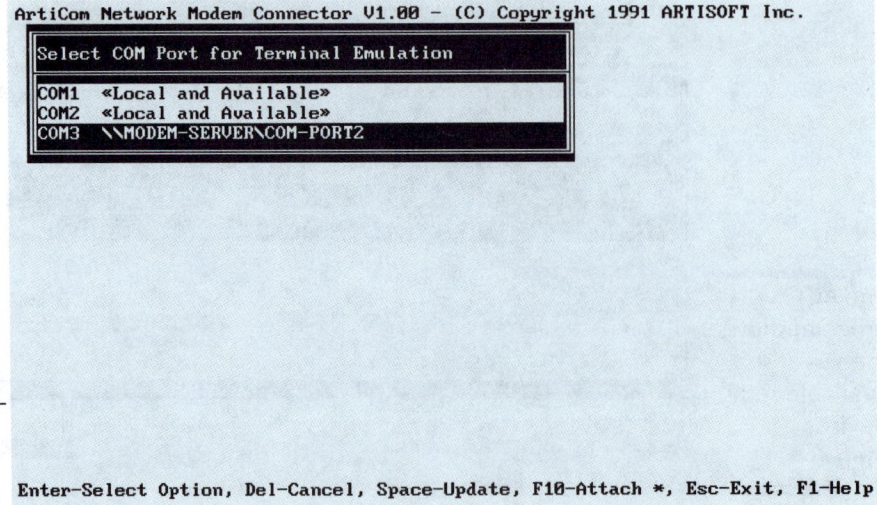

```
ArtiCom Network Modem Connector V1.00 - (C) Copyright 1991 ARTISOFT Inc.
┌─────────────────────────────────────────┐
│Select COM Port for Terminal Emulation   │
├─────────────────────────────────────────┤
│COM1   «Local and Available»             │
│COM2   «Local and Available»             │
│COM3   \\MODEM-SERVER\COM-PORT2          │
└─────────────────────────────────────────┘




Enter-Select Option, Del-Cancel, Space-Update, F10-Attach *, Esc-Exit, F1-Help
```

The workstation's COM3 is now assigned to MODEM-SERVER's COM-PORT2
Figure 9-16.

Sharing Other Resources

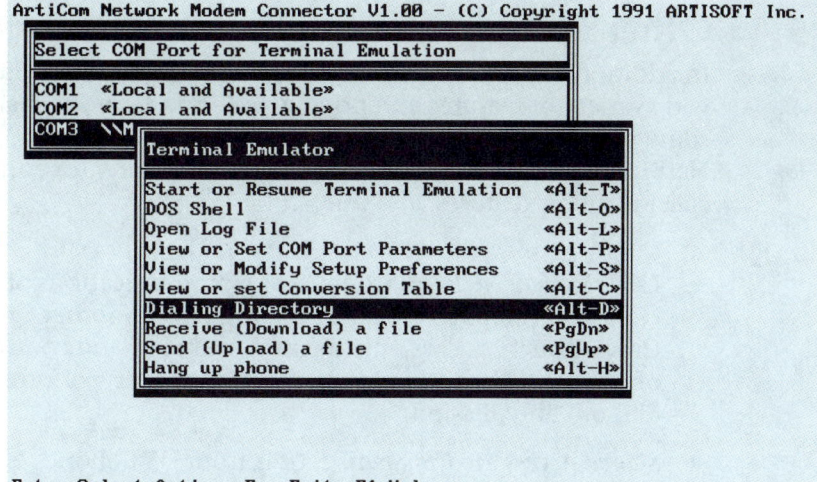

```
ArtiCom Network Modem Connector V1.00 - (C) Copyright 1991 ARTISOFT Inc.
Select COM Port for Terminal Emulation
COM1  «Local and Available»
COM2  «Local and Available»
COM3  \\M
      Terminal Emulator
      Start or Resume Terminal Emulation    «Alt-T»
      DOS Shell                             «Alt-O»
      Open Log File                         «Alt-L»
      View or Set COM Port Parameters       «Alt-P»
      View or Modify Setup Preferences      «Alt-S»
      View or set Conversion Table          «Alt-C»
      Dialing Directory                     «Alt-D»
      Receive (Download) a file             «PgDn»
      Send (Upload) a file                  «PgUp»
      Hang up phone                         «Alt-H»

Enter-Select Option, Esc-Exit, F1-Help
```

The highlight is on the Dialing Directory option of the Terminal Emulator menu
Figure 9-17.

to the remote computer, press Alt-T again to end terminal mode and return to the Terminal Emulator menu box. Press Esc to see the menu box labeled Select COM Port for Terminal Emulation (refer to Figure 9-16). Then, to free the modem so that someone else can use it, press Del to cancel COM3's redirection to the server's modem.

The Terminal Emulator menu box has options with which you can customize the terminal program. The View or Set COM Port Parameters option lets you select the baud rate (speed of the modem in bits per second), parity, word length, and number of stop bits to match the remote computer's requirements. Another option, View or Modify Setup Preferences, provides options for selecting the type of terminal emulation you want, choosing a download protocol (XMODEM, YMODEM, or YMODEM batch), and selecting other preferences.

NOTE: If you have no experience calling remote computers, the terminology in the preceding paragraph may be bewildering. You need to educate yourself about the language of data communications and the resources available by modem. For a wealth of information, see *Dvorak's Guide to PC Telecommunications*, Second edition, by John Dvorak and Nick Anis, (Berkeley, CA: Osborne/McGraw-Hill, 1992).

Other Modem-Sharing Products

In addition to ArtiCom, other modem-sharing software products with a wide variety of features and pricing options are on the market. Here are some products for which the manufacturers claim NetWare Lite or NetBIOS compatibility. (Contact the manufacturer for current specifications, features, and prices.)

- *LAN+Modem NetBIOS*, from Cross Communications of Boulder, Colorado, supports outgoing dialing only. Another Cross product, Cross+Touch, allows outside users to dial in and control a computer on the LAN. A third product, Cross+Connect, performs both dial-out and dial-in.

- *Shared Access Modem Sharing Kit* is from US Robotics of Skokie, Illinois. The kit is available in a *Single Port* version, which includes one 9600 bps modem, and a *Dual Port* version, with two 9600 bps modems. Both versions include software for dialing out and dialing in, and support for NetWare Lite (without the need to run NETBIOS). If you need to buy 9600 bps modems and want to save the RAM that NETBIOS uses, consider this product.

- *Modem Protocall NetBIOS*, a product from Protocall Communications of Toronto, Ontario, Canada, supports both dial-out and dial-in.

- *Norton pcANYWHERE/LAN* is a product from Symantec Corporation of Cupertino, California. In addition to other capabilities, this product performs dial-in to control a computer on the LAN.

- *Carbon Copy Plus* is from Microcom, Inc., of Norwood, Massachusetts. In addition to other capabilities, Carbon Copy Plus allows remote computers to dial in and control LAN computers.

Using a Tape Backup System

One of the most important duties of a LAN administrator is ensuring that all critical LAN files are sufficiently backed up. Chapter 11 discusses the duties of a LAN administrator. See that chapter for detailed explanations of the terminology, philosophy, and need for backups. For most LANs, the best way to create backup copies is to use a tape backup system.

Most tape backup systems consist of an interface card you install in a PC (although some models use your floppy disk controller card instead, and others even connect through a parallel port), plus a tape drive (installed internally or externally), a connecting cable, tape cartridges, and software. The tape drive looks a good deal like a floppy disk drive, except that you insert a tape cartridge where the floppy disk would go. A single cartridge can hold as much data as a large server disk. The size of most cartridges is about midway between that of an audio cassette and of a video cassette. Low-cost tape systems typically store from 40MB to 525MB on a cartridge and cost from $300 to $1,500. The interface card is sometimes priced separately. More expensive tape systems store even more data on a cartridge.

Using Tape Systems with NetWare Lite

Special software is needed to use most tape backup systems.

DOS doesn't communicate with most tape systems the same way it communicates with disk drives. You need special backup programs to read and write data to and from tape systems. Most tape systems come with backup programs customized to work with those tape systems, and use a menu from which you choose the actions you want to take. The simplest way to back up a server's disk is to install the tape system on a client computer and have the backup program copy all the files from drive L (or whatever drive letter you map to the server's network directory) to the tape cartridge.

Figure 9-18 shows the menu screen from the SY-TOS software that comes with a Tapemaster 250 tape backup system from CMS Enhancements. In this example the tape system and SY-TOS software are installed on a client. The client user ran the NET program before running SY-TOS and mapped the drive letter L to the server's hard disk. Then, for the purpose of a short example, the user requested that SY-TOS make a *selective backup* (certain files only) by copying to the tape cartridge all the .DOC (document) files from the WORD55 directory on drive L. The screen in Figure 9-18 shows the result of the backup operation.

SY-TOS, like other backup programs, has many features such as incremental backups, automatic timed backups, batch file control (so that you can automate the steps you want SY-TOS to take), and tape verification (for verifying that the files you just copied to tape are readable).

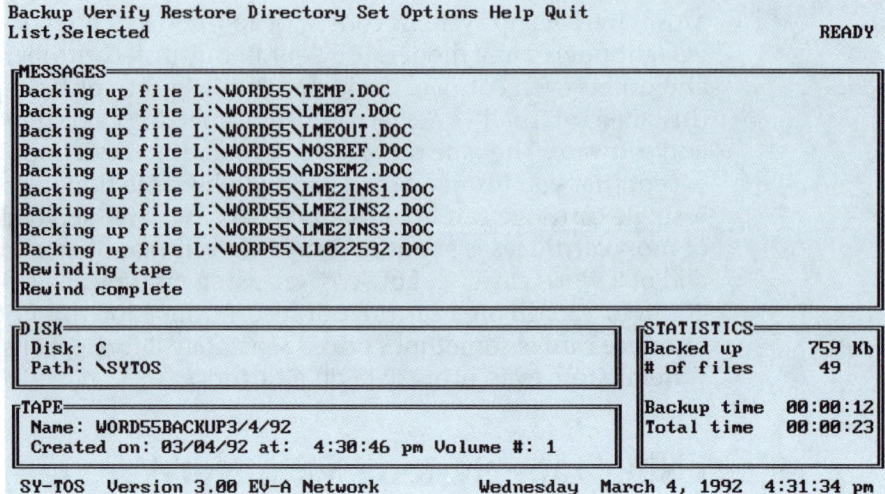

A menu screen from the SY-TOS backup program following completion of a backup to a tape cartridge
Figure 9-18.

```
Backup Verify Restore Directory Set Options Help Quit
List,Selected                                                    READY
┌MESSAGES─────────────────────────────────────────────────────────────┐
│Backing up file L:\WORD55\TEMP.DOC                                   │
│Backing up file L:\WORD55\LME07.DOC                                  │
│Backing up file L:\WORD55\LMEOUT.DOC                                 │
│Backing up file L:\WORD55\NOSREF.DOC                                 │
│Backing up file L:\WORD55\ADSEM2.DOC                                 │
│Backing up file L:\WORD55\LME2INS1.DOC                               │
│Backing up file L:\WORD55\LME2INS2.DOC                               │
│Backing up file L:\WORD55\LME2INS3.DOC                               │
│Backing up file L:\WORD55\LL022592.DOC                               │
│Rewinding tape                                                       │
│Rewind complete                                                      │
├─DISK─────────────────────────────┬─STATISTICS──────────────────────┤
│ Disk: C                          │ Backed up         759 Kb        │
│ Path: \SYTOS                     │ # of files         49           │
├─TAPE─────────────────────────────┤ Backup time    00:00:12         │
│ Name: WORD55BACKUP3/4/92         │ Total time     00:00:23         │
│ Created on: 03/04/92 at: 4:30:46 pm Volume #: 1                    │
│ SY-TOS  Version 3.00 EV-A Network      Wednesday March 4, 1992 4:31:34 pm
```

Most backup programs, including SY-TOS, will not back up a file that is open (in use). To be sure that you back up everything, you should make backup copies when no one is using the server. Chapter 11 explains how to plan your backups and rotate your backup cartridges.

Tape Backup Suppliers

Some of the leading manufacturers of tape backup systems in the low to medium price range are Cipher, CMS Enhancements, Colorado Memory Systems, Everex Systems, Mountain Computer, Tallgrass Technologies, and Tecmar. Nearly all models are compatible with NetWare Lite (provided that you avoid conflicts with IRQs and I/O port base addresses). To verify NetWare Lite compatibility, check with Novell or the tape drive manufacturer.

Software products for making backup copies with these tape systems are included with the tape system or can be purchased separately from independent companies. The following is a list of some of the independent software products:

Product	Company
Back-It 4 LAN	Gazelle Systems
CPBACKUP (part of PC Tools)	Central Point Software
SY-TOS, Sytos Plus	Sytron Corporation

In addition to the obvious consideration of whether you can afford a tape backup system, you need to decide whether buying a tape drive system satisfies two main criteria. First, make sure that you can copy all your backup data onto a single tape cartridge, both now and in the foreseeable future. One of the big advantages of a tape system (compared with floppy disks) is that backups can be unattended. You can automate the entire process by using batch files or script files, depending on the software product. All you have to do is insert a tape cartridge before the process starts and check the results to be sure that everything ran properly. A floppy disk backup, on the other hand, requires that the disks be changed manually. When you shop for a tape system, be sure that the storage capacity of a single cartridge is larger than the total amount of data you need to back up. Or, if that's not possible, make sure that the tape can hold at least the largest incremental backup you expect to make. An *incremental backup* copies only the files that have changed since the last backup. For more about the benefits of incremental backups and other backup strategies, see Chapter 11.

Second, you need to ensure that the backup process will complete in the time you have available. This is generally not a problem if you make automated backups overnight because—in most workgroups—you have about 14 hours to complete the job (from 6 P.M. until 8 A.M. the next morning). In some workgroups, however, people work the swing shift, which reduces the window of opportunity. Other groups work around the clock. You need to find a time slot during which no one needs the servers that must be backed up. If your available time slot is from 2 A.M. to 2:30 A.M., you need to verify that the tape system is fast enough to do the job in 30 minutes. Another time constraint may be that, for security and safety reasons, the network computers do not remain powered on all night. You must make the backup copies at the end of the day, after everyone else leaves. How late you stay depends on how fast the tape drive can copy data. Most tape drives copy data at a rate of between 2MB and 8MB per minute. Some low-cost models are slower.

Attaching Portable Computers

You can attach any IBM-compatible computer to a NetWare Lite LAN, but a portable computer is a special case. Most portable computers do not have standard expansion slots and therefore cannot accommodate standard LAN cards. But you may want to attach (probably temporarily) portable computers to your LAN.

The solution is a portable LAN adapter, which attaches the portable computer to the LAN cable using a small device that connects to the portable computer's printer port. Several companies make portable LAN adapters; Xircom, of Calabasas, California, is the market leader. This section briefly outlines the steps required for using a Xircom adapter to attach a portable PC to a Lite LAN.

Xircom makes two families of LAN adapter models of interest to NetWare Lite users. The Pocket Ethernet Adapter family includes a model called the PE10B2, which works with a thin Ethernet LAN, and the Pocket Ethernet Adapter model PE10BT which works with 10BASE-T. Other models in the Pocket Ethernet Adapter family are available for ARCnet and token ring. A more recent product line, called the Pocket Ethernet Adapter II, has a set of models similar to those of the Pocket Ethernet Adapter family.

A Pocket Ethernet Adapter is small enough to fit in a shirt pocket. The unit weighs five ounces and measures about 5 inches by 2 1/2 inches by 7/8 inch—roughly the size of an audio cassette box or a medium-size hand calculator. Because of its compact size, this adapter is easy to carry around with a portable computer. On one end of a Pocket Ethernet Adapter is a connector for the portable computer's parallel port. On the other end is a connector for the LAN—a BNC connector on the thin Ethernet model and an RJ45 socket on the 10BASE-T model. On the same end as the BNC connector is a connector for the supplied power cord.

Sharing Other Resources

Hardware installation is simple. You attach the Pocket Ethernet Adapter to a parallel port of the portable computer. LPT1 is the default port that the software assumes, but you can override the default and use LPT2 or LPT3 instead. Connect the appropriate type of LAN cable (not supplied) to the other end of the adapter. A BNC T-connector is supplied with the thin Ethernet model. Attach the power cord and plug it into a power source. The adapter has no power on/off switch; when the power cord is connected, the unit is powered on.

Along with the hardware, Xircom provides software drivers for various LANs. Because the early family (the Pocket Ethernet Adapter) does not include a driver for NetWare Lite, you must contact Xircom to get the appropriate driver. Xircom has a convenient computer bulletin-board system from which you can download the driver (named PE_ODI.EXE).

The newer family (the Pocket Ethernet Adapter II) includes, with the adapter, an appropriate driver for NetWare Lite. During NetWare Lite's INSTALL process, you should select *OTHER CARDS as your network adapter card and then provide the name of the appropriate software driver.

After you run STARTNET to start the LAN software on the portable computer, the portable should work like any other computer attached to the LAN. Because of the parallel port's limitations, throughput will be much slower than for a computer with a LAN card.

CHAPTER

10 USING APPLICATION SOFTWARE

A significant part of the productivity gained with NetWare Lite is the result of better use of application software. Without a network, members of your workgroup run applications on their individual PCs and share data files by exchanging floppy disks. With a network, workgroup members can simultaneously access shared data files from a server, and they also can share the application programs.

Chapter 2 briefly explained how to use application software with NetWare Lite. This chapter goes into more detail about how you can use Lite with popular application software products.

Using your LAN, you can share applications in two basic ways, as follows:

◆ Install the software application on each individual client and share the data files on a server. You might install a word processor on each client, for example, but store documents on a server.

◆ Install the software application on the server and have clients share the program.

This chapter is divided into two main sections. The first section explains the different ways application software products work on your NetWare Lite LAN. The second section provides tips and details about using specific major application products with NetWare Lite.

Various Application Software Designs

As you may recall from Chapter 2, you can use many types of software applications—ranging from major applications (word processors, databases, and spreadsheets) to specialized applications (accounting packages or programming languages, for example) to groupware (such as schedulers and electronic mail)—on a LAN.

Nearly all popular software applications are compatible with NetWare Lite. With rare exceptions, any software product sold for use on a stand-alone computer also works (to some degree) while you run the network. The issue of LAN compatibility, however, is not cut-and-dried. In many cases, you cannot simply declare a software application to be either 100 percent compatible or completely incompatible. A considerable gray area exists between the two extremes.

A product's degree of compatibility can be classified into one of the following four categories:

Using Application Software

Incompatible The product does not work at all with NetWare Lite.

Compatible without LAN support Although the product was not designed to work with a LAN, the application works with NetWare Lite's mapped drives and shared printers.

Compatible with LAN support The product was designed to take advantage of LAN features and/or to allow more than one user to access a file simultaneously.

LAN dependent The product not only works on a LAN but *requires* a LAN to work.

Each of the following sections examines a level of compatibility in greater detail.

Incompatible

A few application software products either do not work at all with NetWare Lite (or, often, with any LAN), or they work in such a limited way that they are effectively incompatible.

Several types of products can be incompatible with NetWare Lite.

Ill-behaved TSR programs A TSR program stays in memory after it is run, waiting for a special keystroke or some internal event before activating. Examples of commercial TSR programs are pop-up desktop utility programs such as SideKick and antivirus programs such as Central Point Anti-Virus. The NetWare Lite programs themselves are TSR programs. Sometimes TSR programs can conflict with each other; two separate TSR programs may try to activate themselves when a particular keystroke combination is pressed, for example. Some TSR programs (usually versions written before 1990) are designed to be the final program loaded into memory. These TSRs will not work in conjunction with any TSR loaded afterwards. Most TSR programs written in the last few years, however, will work with other TSRs.

Disk-management and disk-analysis programs   Some disk-management and disk-analysis programs expect to have direct physical access to the hard disk; they fail when used on a mapped disk. Most programs that use only the normal disk functions, such as copying data and deleting files, work fine. Typically, however, programs that perform nonstandard functions (such as recovering deleted files and defragmenting your hard disk) work only on a nonmapped hard disk and may not work properly on network machines configured as both client and server. For more information on disk defragmentation, see Chapter 14, "Optimizing LAN Performance."

Incompatible LAN programs   Remember—NetWare Lite is not NetWare. Most software developers who say their products are "NetWare compatible" are referring to NetWare 2.x and 3.x, Novell's high-end client/server network products. You cannot assume that a NetWare-compatible program works with NetWare Lite unless NetWare Lite compatibility is explicitly indicated. Also, some programs require NETBIOS and therefore will run with NetWare Lite only if you run the NETBIOS program also.

Memory-hungry programs   Application programs that require a great deal of RAM may not work with NetWare Lite. Some applications just barely fit in a 640K PC. Depending on the version of DOS you use and the parameters you specify in CONFIG.SYS, a 640K PC has from about 570K to 620K of RAM available for the application program after you boot the machine. NetWare Lite takes up about 30K more of this memory space on a client and about 60K on a server. Suppose that your PC has 570K available after you turn on your computer and load DOS. Then you start NetWare Lite as a client and only 540K is available. If you try to run an application that needs 550K of RAM, the application won't run with NetWare Lite (even though it would run without Lite). Usually you can overcome this problem by changing some DOS parameters, using third-party memory-managing software, or by upgrading to DOS 5, which gives you ways to reduce RAM usage on most PCs. See Chapter 14 for details.

Compatible Without LAN Support

The lion's share of application software falls in this category. As you may recall from Chapter 2, most software applications work with NetWare Lite even though the applications were not designed to work with a LAN. Because NetWare Lite maps a drive letter on the client to the server, the application software on the client "thinks" it is using a hard disk physically located on the client. Each client can use data files on the server; the server software takes care of keeping things straight between the clients and server. The application software can access files on a mapped drive (drive G or another mapped-drive letter) as easily as files on a local physical drive called A, B, or C.

Accesing files at the same time can cause problems.

The only problem arises when two or more clients try to access the same server data file simultaneously. If you try to read a file at the same time another user is updating the file, you may read garbled data that is partly old and partly new. Even worse, if two users try to update (save) a file simultaneously, one user's updates may overlay the other's. The new file can end up being unlike what either user wants.

Using SHARE To Avoid Simultaneous Access

By utilizing the SHARE program, NetWare Lite avoids the problem of clients simultaneously accessing a server file. SHARE, which NetWare Lite loads on each server, is a TSR supplied with DOS.

SHARE keeps track of which files currently are in use and prevents other clients from using the same files (unless the client uses software that follows certain rules). If the software was not designed to allow data files to be used simultaneously by several users, SHARE permits only one user at a time, thereby ensuring the integrity of files.

SHARE tracks the following to maintain order among users of shared files:

- *File names*, complete with directory paths, so that no two users will inadvertently update the same file at the same time
- *Locks*, which are a special way an application program can request permission to temporarily "lock out" other users from a file (or a portion of a file). If a program is not designed to ask explicitly for a lock, SHARE locks the entire file by default.

You need to run SHARE on a server, not a client computer, because only on a server will more than one computer try to access a file at the same time. NetWare Lite's installation program adds to each server's STARTNET batch file a line that runs SHARE when you initialize the network. As long as you don't need to modify SHARE's default values, NetWare Lite automatically loads SHARE for you.

By default, SHARE uses 2,048 bytes for filenames (SHARE's /F parameter) and 20 locks (SHARE's /L parameter). You probably need to increase these values if users on your LAN frequently try to access simultaneously the same files or applications. Database programs, in particular, typically use many files and locks. See your application software's documentation for recommendations.

Loading SHARE when you boot your computer is quick and easy.

You can modify SHARE's default values and load SHARE with an INSTALL statement in your PC's CONFIG.SYS file. The following statement, for example, increases filename space to 4,096 bytes and the number of locks to 50:

```
install=c:\dos\share.exe /f:4096 /l:150
```

This example assumes that you have the SHARE program in a subdirectory called DOS on drive C. You pay a price for increasing SHARE's default parameters. The larger the values you specify, the more RAM you use on the server. For more about SHARE, consult your DOS documentation and see Chapter 14, "Optimizing LAN Performance."

Running the Software

To run a software application that is NetWare Lite compatible but not designed for a LAN, you don't have to make any changes from stand-alone use. You can simply install the application on each client computer (if the application wasn't already installed when you installed NetWare Lite) and run the application normally, as if you had no LAN.

To share data files (such as word processor documents or spreadsheets) with this application, you have the following two options:

- ◆ Save your shared files directly on a mapped drive. (This is the preferred method.) If you have mapped drive G to a server directory, specify a filename (by typing *g:filename* for example) when saving the file in your application program.

Using Application Software

◆ Save your files on your local hard disk (drive C, in most cases). Then exit your application program and, using the DOS COPY command, copy any files you want to share to a mapped network directory.

Sharing Application Software

For most application software products, you have an option other than installing a separate copy on each client computer. You can install the application once on a server and let all clients access the product from there.

To properly set up a shared application program on a server, follow these steps:

1. On the server, create the directory in which the application will be installed.
2. Using NET, designate this directory as a network directory.
3. Decide on a standard drive letter (such as G, for example) to associate with the product across all potential clients.
4. On a client, map drive G to the server's network directory.
5. Following the manufacturer's installation instructions, install the application on the client's drive G.

Although you install the application on the client computer, the directory mapping causes the software to be installed on the server's hard disk. From then on, any client that maps the designated drive letter (G, in this example) to the network directory can run the application. For the product to run correctly, however, a client must map the associated drive letter, not any other drive letter.

NOTE: You must install the software from a client to a server, not directly on the server's drive C. By installing from the client, the application's installation program knows to set up file paths on the mapped drive (G, in this example) rather than on drive C. Otherwise, when you run the software on a client, the application looks on the client's local drive C for program files. The files are not there; they are on the server's drive, which is mapped as the G drive from the client's perspective.

License Restrictions

You still must comply with legal restrictions when running software from a server. If five people use a software product from five different machines, nearly all manufacturers require you to buy five copies of the software. If you buy only one copy of a software program, install the program on a server, and have everyone use the software from the server, you are just as guilty of pirating the software as if you buy one copy and install the copy on five computers. To stay legal and sleep well at night, buy five copies—even if you never unwrap four of them. (Typically, because everyone wants a set of manuals anyway, all five packages will be opened and used.)

One other legal note: When you "buy" application software, you don't really buy it. What you buy is a license to use a copy of the software on one computer. The manufacturer retains ownership of the software itself. That's why the manufacturer can demand (in varying forms of legalese) that you buy a license for each computer.

Configuration Setup Considerations

All users may have to share the same configuration setup for software they run from the server. Most software allows you to customize screen colors, disk path names, and other choices. Typically, the application saves the user's customized setup choices on a disk file. If everyone shares the same software from a server's disk, only one copy of the setup file is created. If one person changes colors, everyone else's colors change also. You can avoid this problem if, as is sometimes the case, your software lets you specify where you want to save the setup file; just save a local copy on each client's drive C.

Caution: If all users must share a single configuration setup, unsolvable incompatibilities can occur. For example, the setup file may specify a VGA video display if VGA was selected during the software installation. If a particular client does not have VGA video, however, the software may not work at all for that client.

Using Application Software

Sharing Violations

As some software applications run, they create temporary work files. If these files are created on the shared disk, you may encounter sharing violations when several users try simultaneously to update a temporary file. You can avoid the problem, however, by directing the work files to each client's local drive C.

Sharing violations may occur also when several users try to access the program files at the same time. DOS will deny a second user simultaneous access to a file unless the file is marked by DOS as read-only. The *read-only* attribute means that, from the point of view of DOS, users can read the file but cannot write to the file or resave the file.

You can use the ATTRIB command in DOS to designate a file as read-only. For each shared software application, you need to do this just once, after installing the software. (You don't have to issue ATTRIB commands each time you start the network.) To set the attribute of each program file to read-only, follow these steps:

1. Make the network directory the current directory on the client machine. Type **g:** (if drive G is the mapped drive) at the DOS prompt and press [Enter].
2. Type **cd** and press [Enter].
3. Now, type the following DOS commands, one-by-one, pressing [Enter] after each line:

    attrib +r *.exe
    attrib +r *.com
    attrib +r *.ovl
    attrib +r *.bat

These four commands usually do the trick. Just think of typing these ATTRIB commands as the final step in installing the software.

Compatible with LAN Support

An increasing percentage of application software is being designed for a LAN. As LANs become increasingly popular, many manufacturers are upgrading their products to be compatible with a LAN and to take advantage of a LAN's features. The upgraded applications typically include any or all of the following features:

- Logic to handle file sharing and locking on a server in an intelligent way

- Individual user configuration files to be placed on local drives rather than the server

- The capability to map drives and capture printer ports directly from within the application

- Instructions in the product's documentation to explain how best to use the product in a LAN environment

- Pricing and licensing alternatives for a LAN environment

Purchasing and Installation Precautions

LAN-compatible applications simplify your job of installing and using application software. The instructions tell you what to do, and the software knows how to work with a LAN. A few potential pitfalls exist, however.

Once again, remember that NetWare Lite is not NetWare. If the documentation or installation program tells you how to make the product work with NetWare, the documentation is not referring to NetWare Lite unless it specifically says so. Unlike regular Netware, NetWare Lite is a peer-to-peer LAN that runs in conjunction with DOS. The product may offer instructions or installation options for various types of LANs. If the product has no specific instructions for NetWare Lite, follow the instructions for "IBM-Compatible LAN" or "PC Network" or "Peer-To-Peer" or "Other LAN", *but not* "NetWare" or "Novell." When in doubt, contact the manufacturer directly and verify that the product works with NetWare Lite (be sure to stress that you mean Lite, not NetWare 2.x or 3.x). Then find out what product versions you need for your LAN configuration.

Pay careful attention to instructions about how to configure your nodes—both server and client—to run the product. Such instructions

Using Application Software

normally include recommendations for SHARE parameters and statements in CONFIG.SYS, on both the client and the server.

LAN software pricing and licencing has been source of confusion for many users.

No industry standards have yet evolved regarding pricing, licensing, and configuration options. Some products come in a regular, single-user version and a separate LAN version (sometimes called a *server edition* or a *network version*). Some products have a server version that you install on the server, and separate node editions or workstation versions that you install on each client. And some products have only the single-user version, which is designed to be "LAN-compliant" or "LAN-aware" or "LAN-compatible." As you saw in Chapter 2, pricing is similarly confused and constantly changing. If you are in doubt about which product versions you need for your LAN, contact the manufacturer directly.

In some cases, you still need to deal with the issues mentioned in the preceding "Compatible Without LAN Support" section. Either the product manufacturer or Novell (through the NetWare Lite Automated Fax System) has instructions about how to use the product successfully in a NetWare Lite environment.

LAN Dependent

Some software requires a LAN. As explained in Chapter 2, *groupware* is the name given to software that helps a group of people accomplish group goals. To run efficiently, some groupware products use special LAN software features. That's wonderful, provided that your LAN is compatible with the LAN for which the groupware is designed. Groupware designed to run with NetWare works with NetWare 2.x or 3.x, but not with NetWare Lite. Similarly, some special-purpose LAN utility programs run on NetWare, not NetWare Lite. Don't worry. These products, which are designed for large NetWare LANs, would be of little use on your NetWare Lite LAN.

Some other LAN-dependent software requires NETBIOS, a supplemental TSR program supplied with NetWare Lite. NETBIOS establishes a standard methodology for application programs to communicate between LAN nodes. You can use these NETBIOS-based products with NetWare Lite, but to do so you have to run the NETBIOS program on each node. The only drawback is that NETBIOS uses a little extra RAM (about 10K) on each computer.

Application software that requires another LAN operating system, such as Microsoft LAN Manager or Banyan VINES, will not run with NetWare Lite.

Major Application Software Products

Now that you have an understanding of the concepts behind running application software on NetWare Lite, it's time for a discussion of specific products. Although examining all of the many thousands of applications software products is not possible here, the following discussions are designed to help you understand how several major products work with NetWare Lite. The products covered here are the standard DOS versions; for Windows information, see Chapter 15, "Running on Various Software Platforms."

NOTE: The upcoming product discussions focus on installing the software directly on the server because special considerations often apply in that case. In many NetWare Lite LANs, however, separate copies of application software are installed on individual clients and shared data files are stored on the server's hard disk.

Word Processing

Word processing is undoubtedly the most popular application on PCs. Almost every PC user runs a word processor at least some of the time, and many users run no other application. Hundreds of word processors are on the market. This section examines the two most popular: WordPerfect and Microsoft Word.

WordPerfect

WordPerfect, the PC word processor with the largest market share, is manufactured by WordPerfect Corporation of Orem, Utah. The single-user version of WordPerfect 5.1 is LAN compatible and includes LAN installation instructions. You can install WordPerfect on each client computer or install a single copy on a server for everyone to use.

Using Application Software

To install a single shared copy on a server, install WordPerfect from a client computer and choose "Other" for the network type when you configure WordPerfect. Because you can have separate configuration and setup files for each user, you do not have to make the screen colors and other options the same for all users. These configuration files are stored on the server in a separate subdirectory. You can store and retrieve document files using either the server's hard disk or the client's hard or floppy disks.

Like most applications, WordPerfect requires a license for each computer on which the software runs. By breaking the seal on the package containing the installation disks, you agree to abide by this license. Even if you install WordPerfect on a server, you need to buy a separate copy for every computer that uses the application.

Microsoft Word

Microsoft Word comes from Microsoft Corporation of Redmond, Washington. Microsoft Word 5.5 runs with NetWare Lite in much the same way as WordPerfect. Like WordPerfect, the same stand-alone version of Word that people buy for a single computer can be installed on a server from a client. Microsoft also sells a "node edition" of Word for use in LAN environments. The node edition, which costs a few dollars less than the regular version, does not include manuals, however. You can buy one or more regular copies of Word, depending on how many sets of manuals you want in your group, then buy node editions for all other users.

The Microsoft Word node edition is designed to work on a LAN.

When you install Word, the SETUP program gives you the choice of installing on a hard drive, floppy disk, or network. You can select "network" to install a shared copy of Word on a server from a client. After the installation is complete on the server, you configure each client computer (do so directly from each client) by typing **setup user** and pressing [Enter]. The configuration files for each user can be saved on either the server or the client.

Spreadsheets

Spreadsheets are probably the second most popular PC application. Lotus 1-2-3 is the longtime market leader and Quattro Pro has a significant market share.

There are several different versions of 1-2-3 for networks.

Lotus 1-2-3

Lotus 1-2-3 is manufactured by Lotus Development Corporation of Cambridge, Massachusetts. The current versions are 2.3 and 3.1. Lotus sells three different editions of Lotus 1-2-3 version 2.3: the server edition, the node edition, and the single-user edition. The server edition (the box has a symbol showing two computers connected together and the words "Network Version") contains the software to install on either a server or a single computer. The node edition contains no software, just the 1-2-3 manuals and a license agreement. The single-user edition (a symbol on the box shows a single computer) includes the software for a single computer.

To install the server edition, run the 1-2-3 INSTALL program from a client computer. In this manner, you install the software on a server via a mapped drive. After installation, use the provided COUNT program to set the maximum number of simultaneous 1-2-3 users to the number of legal licensed users you have on the LAN.

You can install the single-user version of 1-2-3 on a server from a client, but only one user at a time can run the software.

Quattro Pro

Quattro Pro is from Borland International of Scotts Valley, California. Quattro Pro 3.0 is fully compatible with NetWare Lite and includes many networking features, such as file locking. You can install the spreadsheet as a stand-alone application or as a shared program on a network server. In the network configuration, individual clients can maintain local configuration files appropriate for the hardware on each workstation.

When you install Quattro Pro as a shared program, the installation program requests that you choose the network type from the list of options. Select "Other" for NetWare Lite. Individual clients can create customized configuration files, which are stored on the server in a subdirectory named \QPROPRIV.

Clients that use Quattro Pro should execute the DOS SHARE program at the beginning of each work session. The simplest way to execute SHARE is to place in one of the client's batch files (either AUTOEXEC.BAT or STARTNET.BAT) a statement that invokes SHARE.

Using Application Software

Quattro Pro is sold under several different licensing agreements. A single-user package permits only a single user to access Quattro Pro at any one time. A LAN package licenses the number of users specified at the time of purchase. (You can increase the number of authorized users by contacting Borland.)

Databases

In some workgroups, the primary reason to install a LAN is to run shared database applications. Dozens of application software products support shared databases, thus enabling all workgroup members to access the same information simultaneously. Three leading products—dBASE III Plus, Paradox, and Q&A—are discussed next.

dBASE III Plus

dBASE used to be published by Ashton-Tate, but is now owned by Borland.

dBASE III Plus is manufactured by Borland International of Scotts Valley, California. dBASE III Plus 1.1 comes in only one version, which you can install on an individual computer or on a server. To allow multiple users to access dBASE on a server, you can buy a "LAN Pack" that contains several manuals and a license for sharing the product on a LAN. For server installation, install dBASE from a client to a server using a mapped disk drive on the client. Because dBASE III Plus supports only one set of configuration files, all users that access the software from the server have to be able to use the same configuration file. Having to use a single configuration file creates a problem if, for example, some users have VGA video cards on their PCs but other users have monochrome cards.

After you install dBASE III Plus on a server to provide simultaneous access for several users, you have to use the DOS ATTRIB command to set the read-only attribute on all files in the dBASE directory. dBASE III Plus supports file and record locking. (*Record locking* locks only a portion of a file, enabling other users to access different parts of a database file while one user updates a single record.)

Paradox

Paradox is another product from Borland International. Paradox 3.5 is a fully compliant LAN product that works either as a stand-alone application or as a shared program on a NetWare Lite server. Paradox supports full file locking. The Paradox simultaneous-access feature, called *coediting* by Borland, works with NetWare Lite LANs.

When you set up Paradox as a shared program, you install the software from a client machine onto the server's mapped network directory (usually called \PDOX). When you run the Paradox program that configures the database for networks (a program called NUPDATE.EXE) you must choose the network type from a menu of choices. Select "Other" for installation under NetWare Lite.

Make sure the Paradox files are set to "read-only" status.

After Paradox is installed in the server's network directory, you should set the program files on the server to read-only. To do so, use the DOS ATTRIB command from a workstation. Map the client's drive to the network directory containing the Paradox program files. Suppose that the mapped drive letter is H. At the client's DOS prompt, type **h:** and press Enter to make the mapped drive active. Then type **attr +r *.*** to set the program files on the server to read-only.

Borland licenses Paradox in several configurations. A single-user version permits only one user at a time to access Paradox. Multiuser LAN packages permit a specified number of users to access Paradox simultaneously.

Q&A

Q&A is from Symantec Corporation of Cupertino, California. Q&A 4.0 is more than a database; the product also includes a word processor module. The software is fully LAN compatible and features full file locking. You can create individual configuration and setup files on client nodes.

You install a shared version of Q&A from a client onto the server's mapped drive. You don't have to specify a network type, however. Each client's customized configuration and data files can be stored in a private directory on the server or on the client's hard drive.

Symantec licenses Q&A as a single-user application that is network compliant. To use multiple copies of Q&A simultaneously, you need to purchase network packages.

Using Application Software

Graphics Software

For many workgroups, graphics are an important part of the normal workload. Whether they are used for creating diagrams, charts or sales graphs for internal reports, or transparencies for full-scale presentations, graphics packages are an important part of the software market. Simultaneously sharing graphics files is trickier than sharing text-based files (such as word-processed documents) because graphics files, unlike text files, typically cannot be updated in sections. If two users simultaneously try to modify a "part" of a graphics file, the result is likely to be that the last update overwrites the previous update. Two leading graphics software products are Harvard Graphics and Freelance.

Harvard Graphics

Harvard Graphics does not perform file locking on charts.

Harvard Graphics is from Software Publishing Corporation of Mountain View, California. Harvard Graphics 3.0 supports network use with individual clients able to create customized setup and configuration files. Harvard Graphics does not lock the graphics chart files, however. Two users simultaneously working on the same file may find that the work of one user overwrites that of the other user. Harvard Graphics does issue a warning message when one user tries to save a file that has been modified by another user.

You can install Harvard Graphics on individual client machines or as a shared program on a server. The program installs from a client onto the server's mapped drive. You do not need to specify a network type during installation.

Software Publishing licenses Harvard Graphics as a single-user product that is network compatible. To enable clients to share a server's copy simultaneously, you must purchase a Node License package. These packages come in 5- or 20-user versions.

Freelance

Freelance is from Lotus Development Corporation of Cambridge, Massachusetts. As with Harvard Graphics, Freelance 4.0 can be run on individual clients or as a shared application on a server. In a server configuration, individual workstations can have customized configuration files which may be stored on the server or on the workstations. Because Freelance does not support file locking, two users working at the same time cannot update a shared graphics file and have both updates take effect. Two users working simultaneously should not share data charts because the most recent update overwrites the preceding one.

When you make Freelance a shared program, you install the software from a client to the server. The installation program does not ask you to specify the network type.

Printing Freelance graphics may be slow and troublesome.

Printing Freelance graphics on network printers tends to be slow. If Freelance (or any application) does not send output to the printer within NetWare Lite's prescribed waiting time (15 seconds, by default), NetWare Lite cancels the print job in the mistaken assumption that the application is finished transmitting. To guard against such printer interruptions, you can use NetWare Lite's NET CAPTURE W= command to tell NetWare Lite to wait longer before canceling a print job. On the client, set the W= parameter to a high value (200 is a reasonable value for a 386 server machine). Here is an example of a command you might issue at the DOS prompt on a workstation:

net capture Laser w=200

You may need to experiment with different w= values to determine a satisfactory value for the servers and printers on your network. For more information about the NET CAPTURE command, see Chapter 14.

Lotus sells the network version of Freelance in server and node editions. The server edition contains all the software and a set of manuals; a node edition, which also contains a set of manuals, licenses one client to access Freelance from the server. You must buy a separate node copy for each client requiring access to Freelance on the server.

Groupware and Electronic Mail

Groupware—the name of a relatively new category of application software—refers to products designed to make an entire LAN workgroup more productive. The classic workgroup application—if one

Using Application Software

can be a classic in so short a time—is electronic mail (often referred to as *e-mail*), which enables group members to send typed messages back and forth.

There are numerous benefits to e-mail packages.

In Chapter 9, "Sharing Other Resources," you learned about NetWare Lite's limited message-sending capability. E-mail products do much more. They contain a simple word processor so that you can compose and edit messages. They support address lists, enabling you to create a list of names and electronic addresses, and then send the same message to any subgroup of people in your list. They allow you to attach files (word processing documents, spreadsheets, or whatever) to your messages. You can even forward messages you receive from other group members, and save the messages you receive for future reference.

An extremely small workgroup located in a single office may have no need for e-mail. The larger the group and the more often individual group members write notes to each other, the greater the benefits of e-mail. Many workgroups find that e-mail becomes their fundamental method of communication when face-to-face communication is not feasible.

Other groupware capabilities include group calendaring (coordinating everyone's appointment calendars), resource scheduling (coordinating the use of such shared resources as company cars and conference rooms), and utility functions, such as a desktop calculator and a simple database program for maintaining telephone lists.

Most groupware products support a combination of these functions. Almost all products support e-mail, and most products also support some combination of other features.

WordPerfect Office LAN and cc:Mail, two of the leading products, are presented here. Many other groupware products also work with NetWare Lite. Some products may require you to run the NetWare Lite NETBIOS program on each PC.

WordPerfect Office LAN

WordPerfect Office LAN, from WordPerfect Corporation of Orem, Utah, is the groupware market leader. Counting both the LAN and non-LAN versions, the product has more than 300,000 users. (WordPerfect Office is also sold in a non-LAN version. This version, designed to run on an individual PC, includes many utility functions but does not provide e-mail.) WordPerfect Office LAN is not just for users of the WordPerfect word processor, but WordPerfect users typically learn WordPerfect Office easily because the commands are similar. The current version of WordPerfect Office LAN is 3.01.

WordPerfect Office LAN (called "Office," for short) includes e-mail, group calendaring, resource scheduling, and several utilities. The product supports up to 5 users. (A 20-user version is available for about three times the cost.) WordPerfect also sells a product, called WordPerfect Connections, for linking your LAN e-mail to outside users.

WordPerfect Office LAN runs as a shared application from the server's hard disk. To install Office, you run its INSTALL program directly on the server where it is being installed. INSTALL decompresses and copies the Office files into several directories on the server. Then you run the GENOFF (generate office) program, which sets up Office for your LAN and its users. For NetWare Lite, specify "Other" for the network type when you run GENOFF. In other respects, the installation follows the Office manuals and onscreen menu prompts.

cc:Mail

cc:Mail is the largest selling e-mail software.

cc:Mail is from Lotus Development Corporation of Cambridge, Massachusetts. cc:Mail 3.2 is strictly an electronic-mail product. It supports a wealth of options to facilitate communication, such as bulletin boards for open group communications about specific topics, file folders to help you organize your saved messages, and mailing lists to simplify the process of communicating with a variety of subgroups.

The cc:Mail Platform Pack for DOS contains the cc:Mail programs. You install the product on a server, thereby creating a "post office" on the server. Then you use one or more cc:Mail User Packs (each Pack supporting 8 to 25 additional users) to set up access for the number of users you need to support on your LAN. Other cc:Mail products are available for remote dial-in access to your LAN, or to link to such external e-mail systems as MCI Mail or such mainframe-supported mail systems as PROFS or UnixMail. One reason cc:Mail is the e-mail market leader is that Lotus provides add-on products that make cc:Mail capable of linking to just about any other electronic communication system you can find.

Using Application Software

The cc:Mail installation procedure uses an INSTALL program to set up the server. The process—both to install the software and to add users—is easy to follow. It is explained in detail in the *cc:Mail Administrator Reference Manual*.

Other Application Software

The marketplace boasts a staggering array of other software applications. Instead of trying to explain in any detail how to use all of them, the following lists include many popular products that have been tested and verified to be compatible with NetWare Lite. Check with the manufacturers for current version numbers and usage notes.

Accounting

Every business must do accounting, at least to some degree. LAN accounting packages keep track of financial records on the server's hard disk so that everyone with a need can access the information. Here is a list of accounting packages:

Product	Manufacturer
ACCPAC Plus	Computer Associates
Champion Accounting	Champion
DacEasy Network Accounting	DacEasy
Great Plains Accounting	Great Plains
Managing Your Money	MECA
Open Systems Accounting	Open Systems
Quicken	Intuit

Other Application Software Products

The assorted products on this list work with NetWare Lite. Don't assume that a product not listed here is incompatible with NetWare Lite. Although some of these products may not work if they are installed on and shared from a server, they all work with NetWare Lite when installed on a client.

Product	Manufacturer
AutoCAD	Autodesk Inc.
Automenu	Magee Enterprises
Back-It 4 LAN	Gazelle
Borland C++	Borland International
Carbon Copy Plus	Microcom
Central Point Anti-Virus	Central Point
Clarion Professional Developer	Clarion
Clipper	Nantucket
Collage Plus	Inner Media
Crosstalk XVI and Mark IV	DCA
Da Vinci eMAIL	Da Vinci Systems
DrawPerfect	WordPerfect
EasyCAD	Evolution Computing
Fastback Plus	Fifth Generation Systems
GEM Desktop Publisher	Digital Research
Generic CADD	Autodesk Retail Products
GrandView	Symantec
Harvard Project Manager	Software Publishing
Hijaak	Inset Systems
LapLink	Traveling Software
Lotus Agenda	Lotus Development
Lotus Magellan	Lotus Development
Lotus Symphony	Lotus Development
Lotus Works	Lotus Development
Microsoft Bookshelf	Microsoft

Using Application Software

Product	Manufacturer
Microsoft C	Microsoft
Microsoft Chart	Microsoft
Microsoft QuickBASIC	Microsoft
Microsoft Works	Microsoft
Norton AntiVirus	Symantec
PCBoard	Clark Development
PFS First Choice	Spinnaker
PFS First Publisher	Software Publishing
PFS Professional File LAN	Software Publishing
PKZIP	PKWare
Procomm Plus	DataStorm Technologies
Q-DOS	Gazelle
RightWriter	Que
Right Hand Man II	Futurus
SpinRite II	Gibson Research
Stacker	Stac Electronics
Turbo Pascal	Borland International
Ventura Publisher Network Edition	Ventura/Xerox
Volkswriter	Volkswriter
WordPerfect	WordPerfect Corp.
WordPerfect Library	WordPerfect Corp.
WordStar	WordStar International
XTreePro Gold	Xtree Company

CHAPTER

11
THE ROLE OF THE LAN ADMINISTRATOR

Every LAN needs a manager—someone responsible for the overall well-being of the LAN and its users. For a small LAN (two to five nodes), administration usually is simple and not at all time-consuming whereas, for a large or extremely active LAN, administrative work is a bigger job. In either case, the critical point is that someone has to take the role of LAN administrator and be responsible for a few regular maintenance and management duties. If not, you face the same fate as when you neglect going to the dentist: big problems that could have been avoided by regular, routine examinations.

If you have a small LAN, appointing a full-fledged LAN administrator may seem ridiculous. Fine. Don't make a big deal out of it. Just be sure that someone thinks of himself or herself as the one responsible for keeping the LAN running properly. If not, everyone assumes that someone else has that responsibility.

As a workgroup and LAN grow, administration becomes more critical and more time-consuming. The administrator's responsibilities increase, because extra effort is required to coordinate the additional LAN resources and new users. If your LAN is expanding, make sure that you budget additional time for the LAN administrator's duties.

Selecting the LAN Administrator

In many workgroups, the best candidate for LAN administrator is the person who has already displayed the most interest in the workgroup's computers. If that person is also a meticulous, reliable person who likes to keep things organized, you've got your LAN administrator.

Sometimes the office computer guru is not the best choice for LAN administrator. Perhaps your most qualified computer expert is not well-organized or reliable, or cannot devote as much time to performing LAN duties as the job requires. In such cases, deciding on a LAN administrator is more difficult. Computer knowledge, or at least a willingness to learn, is important in a LAN administrator, but other personal traits such as trustworthiness, organizational skills, and reliability (including a good attendance record) are even more important. You may want to choose the second- or third-best computer person if that person's personal traits rank way ahead of those of the computer guru.

The Primary LAN Administrator

In most small offices, one person usually can handle the responsibilities of LAN administrator. Larger organizations may need to spread the job's duties among several people.

The Role of the LAN Administrator

Using several people to administer a LAN poses several potential dangers: LAN users may not know who to see about a particular LAN problem, the administrators may lose sight of who has which responsibilities, and the administrators may have to spend more time in unproductive coordination meetings than in doing meaningful work.

With a single LAN administrator, one person is in charge but that one person does not *do* all the LAN administration work. Undoubtedly, the primary administrator will delegate specific responsibilities to members of the workgroup. The important thing is that the LAN administrator oversees the LAN and is the focal point for problems and policy.

The Secondary LAN Administrator

In addition to the primary LAN administrator, you should officially or unofficially name a secondary LAN administrator. Even in a small office in which the LAN connects only two or three computers, the primary LAN administrator will occasionally be sick, on vacation, traveling, or busy with a high-priority project. Also, the primary LAN administrator may leave the organization or be disabled for a long time. At least one other person should be in a position to fill in temporarily and take over permanently if necessary. Don't put all your eggs in one basket.

Duties of the LAN Administrator

Learning what a LAN administrator does will help you understand why the job is so important. The duties can be grouped into seven categories, each of which is described in detail in this chapter.

Data Integrity   Shared data and programs must always be available and uncorrupted. In general, the LAN administrator must ensure the integrity of shared resources. Two important responsibilities are backing up disk files and guarding against computer viruses.

LAN Security   The security of the LAN primarily involves determining which users can access which LAN resources. Using various NetWare Lite features such as user accounts and passwords, the administrator can take appropriate action to restrict access. For a complete discussion of LAN security, see Chapter 12, "Securing the Network."

User Support   The LAN administrator must provide user support by troubleshooting, informing users of such LAN developments as new equipment or procedures, answering questions, and training new users.

Hardware Maintenance and Checking   The LAN hardware must be maintained and serviced. The administrator should establish periodic checks to verify that the computers are working properly and that the cable connections are sound. Disk space on the servers must be monitored to ensure that sufficient free space is available and that shared disks are not cluttered with needless data. Also, routine maintenance chores must be performed on the peripheral devices. Someone must check regularly, for example, that printers have enough paper and that the proper font cartridges are installed.

Configuration Management   Managing the LAN configuration includes initially setting up the LAN, setting up new users' hardware and software, upgrading NetWare Lite software, installing new applications, upgrading existing applications, and implementing new procedures.

Budgeting   Keeping expenses down is always important. The LAN administrator must monitor the LAN's operating costs and make sure that expenditures are within the established budget. New financial plans must be formulated as required.

LAN Optimization   Opportunities for optimization cover many facets of LAN performance. The administrator can, for example, look for ways to improve server response time, reduce the amount of RAM used on servers and clients, reduce the amount of disk space used, make parameter changes to improve performance, and determine the need for upgrades and new products.

As you read the rest of this chapter, assume that you are the LAN administrator for your NetWare Lite LAN. Each of these seven categories of duties is explained so that you can understand the administrator's job.

Data Integrity

Your first priority as LAN administrator is to protect the LAN's data and your group's ability to access that data. The basic techniques involved include making regular backup copies and protecting against computer viruses. Two other techniques—implementing physical security measures and verifying that the servers have plenty of available disk space—also are related to protecting data. These techniques are discussed later in this chapter in the "LAN Security" and "Server Disk Space" sections, respectively.

> **NOTE:** Computers and printers are not the most valuable resources on a LAN. For most workgroups, the most valuable resource is the data. As a LAN administrator, you must take steps to ensure that critical data is protected from perils such as computer viruses and from being inadvertently erased. You can always replace a computer or application software, but unprotected data can be lost forever.

Data Backup

Because of the value of your data, your most important duty as LAN administrator is to make sure that current backup copies of all critical disk files are available at all times. Most computer users don't appreciate the value of backups until their first loss of important data—and by then, of course, it's too late. If a LAN administrator must be fanatic about anything, it is making and protecting backup copies.

No matter what else may go wrong, you can recover if you have a backup copy of all your important data files and system files. Backup copies are a form of insurance for your workgroup. As LAN administrator you, in effect, make sure that the insurance premiums are paid and that the policy has sufficient coverage.

The Perils of Losing Data

An amazing number of things can go wrong when you depend on computers. If a problem occurs, you need an extra copy of your data. Otherwise, the documents that took you such a long time to write and the spreadsheets you so meticulously created may be gone forever.

If you are asking yourself what can happen, here is a short horror list of potential catastrophes. Imagine facing one of the following calamities without a backup copy of your valuable data.

Hard Disk Failure After about three years of use, chances increase that a hard disk will fail because of wear and aging.

Theft Increasingly, burglars are targeting computer equipment because computers are valuable and relatively easy to sell. When a computer disappears, so does the data on its hard disk.

Viruses The number and sophistication of computer viruses continue to increase. Whenever you use a computer program you loaded from floppy disks (even a program purchased from a reputable manufacturer), you run the risk of losing data because of a virus.

Software Failures A computer program may malfunction without notice and create corrupt disk files. When you discover the problem, you need to retrieve backup files created before the problem cropped up.

Disasters Fire, flood, lightning, spilled coffee, or any natural or human-made disaster can destroy both hard and floppy disks.

Sabotage A disgruntled coworker or ruthless competitor may destroy or modify critical data.

Your Own Mistakes By accidentally using the name of an old file when you save a new file, you may wipe out the old one. Or you may delete a group of supposedly obsolete files, only to discover later that you need one of them. Human errors like these undoubtedly cause more lost data than any other kind of error.

NOTE: The list of possible mishaps is endless. They all lead to the same conclusion: your best protection against data loss is to have a backup copy.

Creating Backups

When a data loss occurs, you can use the backup copy to restore the lost data to its previous form. Then you can continue as if the problem had never happened. To be useful, the backup copy must be current

The Role of the LAN Administrator

and complete. Neither a year-old copy of your inventory nor a floppy disk that contains only one quarter of your client-history information will be of much help.

Everything said so far about backup applies to stand-alone computers as well as to computers connected to a LAN. After you put the critical data from your entire workgroup on a server so that everyone has access to the data, however, any data loss affects the entire group rather than just one user.

Of course, if your workgroup consists of only two or three people who create only a few word processing documents and spreadsheets (or other data files) each week, backup methods can be uncomplicated. You must convince everyone to copy any new or changed file to a floppy disk regularly. "Regularly" can mean immediately after saving a file or at the end of each day. If people develop this habit, backing up data is painless. Human nature often leads to less than 100 percent consistency, however. Even the smallest group may not back up important files perfectly.

In addition, the more data a group collects and the more everyone in the group uses the data, the more critical the need for making regular, frequent, complete backup copies of the data.

You can make backup copies in several ways.

Use Floppy Disks   Copying data to floppies is the time-honored way to make backup copies. The process is awkward if your server's hard disk stores 40MB or more of data whereas each floppy disk can hold a maximum of only 1.4MB of data.

Use Other Computers   If two computers are connected on a LAN, one of them can copy all the data from its hard disk to the other computer's hard disk, and vice versa. Then if either computer loses data, the other has a copy ready for immediate use. This is better than nothing, but far from ideal. To hold the data from both computers, each hard disk has to be twice the size of the hard disk used by a single user before the LAN. If you have five or ten computers, the disks need to be even bigger and, of course, more expensive. And if the copy you make is already corrupt, you need to go back to an earlier version of a backup copy—but all you have is the copy you just made.

Use a Tape Backup System To avoid the problems inherent in the preceding two methods, use a tape backup system. Most tape backup systems consist of an interface card you install in a PC (although some models use the floppy disk controller card instead, and some even connect through a parallel port), a tape drive (either internally or externally installed), a connecting cable, tape cartridges, and software. The tape drive looks much like a floppy disk drive, but you insert a tape cartridge where the floppy disk would go. A single cartridge can hold as much data as even a large server disk. The size of most cartridges is about midway between that of an audio cassette and of a video cassette. Low-cost tape systems typically store from 40 to 525MB on a cartridge and cost from $300 to $5,000. The interface card is sometimes priced separately. More expensive tape systems store even more data on a cartridge.

Chapter 9, "Sharing Other Resources," explains how to use a tape backup system, which in most LAN environments is the best device for creating backup copies. If your workgroup creates such a small amount of updated data that backups on floppy disks are practical, however, you may not need a tape backup system.

Backup Strategies

Before you start making backup copies of your data, you need to decide on a methodology or strategy for backups. Here are some ideas.

Ask yourself how long it will take to recover your data, and at what cost.

To help determine which backup strategy makes the most sense for your workgroup, first ask yourself how long recovering your data will take, if you lose it, and at what cost. Also, if for some reason you cannot recover the data, how much does never again having access to the data hurt the workgroup? Be aware that the answers to these questions change over time. When you first install the LAN you may not immediately put much valuable data on a server. Several months later, however, the server may hold a great deal of irreplaceable data. If your data is costly to replace and your organization would suffer without it, backup copies are critical. A few hundred dollars for equipment, plus a few minutes work each day or two, can save your company from a disastrous loss.

The Role of the LAN Administrator

> **NOTE:** A backup typically occupies a single tape cartridge, a set of floppy disks, or a subdirectory on another computer's hard disk. For the moment, assume that you make backups on a tape cartridge; you can substitute the phrase "set of floppy disks" or "another hard disk" for "tape cartridge" in the following discussion if you choose.

Rotating Backups

To safely make backups, you need several tape cartridges (each typically costs $20 to $50) so that you can rotate the backups and have more than the most recent copy available. Never make a backup copy on a tape cartridge that already contains your most recent backup—if something goes wrong, you lose your best backup copy.

A daily backup will minimize the chance of losing data.

An example of one way to minimize the chance of losing your current backup is to make a complete backup copy of your server's hard disk daily, using one of three tape cartridges. On Monday use #1, on Tuesday use #2, and on Wednesday use #3. Then on Thursday use #1 again. On Friday, if you need to restore a file from the backup tape, you can use Thursday's tape. If Thursday's tape is damaged or missing, you can use either Wednesday's or Tuesday's. This method of rotating backup tapes is called the *grandparent-parent-child method*, or just the *rotation method*.

A variation on the rotation method is to designate a tape cartridge for each day of the week. Every Monday you make a backup copy on the tape cartridge labeled "Monday," thereby replacing last Monday's copy. On Tuesday you use the "Tuesday" tape cartridge, and so on.

If you use data files over long periods of time, you may want to keep monthly (or even yearly) backups. Just designate a tape cartridge for each month of the year and then, once a month, say on the first of each month, make a backup to the monthly cartridge.

Maintaining Off-Site Backups

Another important backup technique is to maintain an *off-site backup*, keeping a copy of your critical data somewhere away from your computer (ideally, in another building). An off-site backup copy reduces your risk in case of fire, flood, theft, or other disaster. In a small office, the easiest way to guarantee that you have an off-site backup may be to take the next-most-recent backup copy home with you each night. Then if the most recent backup is damaged, you can go home and get the previous backup.

In a larger company, you can arrange to ship backup copies back and forth between your office and a different building with storage facilities. Also, you can hire a service company that takes backups on site and then stores them somewhere else.

Making Incremental Backups

Many backup software products give you the capability to make an incremental backup as well as a complete backup copy. In an *incremental backup*, the only files copied are those that have changed since the last time you made a backup. Suppose that your 200MB hard disk is nearly filled with data files. To copy the entire disk to a tape cartridge may take an hour or more (even longer on floppy disks), depending on your tape drive and LAN. If users typically change only a few files each day with a total size of about 5MB, why not copy just the changed files? That would take only a couple of minutes. You may want to make a full backup copy every Friday, with only incremental backups on other days. The backup software keeps track of which files are on each tape cartridge (or set of floppy disks) so that you can retrieve the most current backup copy of any file.

Locating the Tape Backup on the LAN

Usually, the best place to install a tape backup system is on a client computer. If your LAN has more than one server, the tape backup software can access all servers from the client. Some people like to define all PCs on their NetWare Lite LANs to be server/client combinations so that the tape system can back up everyone's hard disk, not just one shared server's hard disk.

Ideally, you should back up a server when no one is using it. If anyone is using a file on the server, the backup software cannot make a copy because an update of the data may be under way. Most workgroups handle this situation by making backups at the end of the day, just before going home. Another approach is to schedule the backup process

The Role of the LAN Administrator

during the night when no one is around. Many backup software products provide the capability to perform a tape backup automatically at a preset time. This approach is fine provided that you leave the computers turned on overnight. Be sure to monitor the first few automatic backups to verify that everything works correctly. Later, you can simply review the report generated by the backup software to be sure that all is well.

Choosing a Backup Strategy

The manual that accompanies a backup software product usually provides tips and recommendations for making backups based on the features of the product. Read the manual, evaluate your situation, and decide on a backup strategy.

As LAN administrator, you must evaluate your workgroup's backup needs and set up procedures to make regular backups of all important files. Ask your users, "Which files would you need to recover if you came to work tomorrow and discovered that all our computers had been stolen or burned?" For complete peace of mind, make sure that your backup plans include off-site backups to guard against a large-scale disaster affecting your entire office.

Computer Viruses

New strains of computer viruses are released almost daily.

Destructive computer viruses have become big news items in recent years. Hardly a month seems to go by without dire warnings of a new virus that may destroy some or all of your computer's data.

The computer virus threat is real. Computer vandals release new strains upon an unsuspecting public almost daily, and most experts agree that problems caused by computer viruses will continue to increase in the foreseeable future. Every computer user should understand certain fundamental concepts about computer viruses. LAN administrators, especially, should be educated and alert to computer viruses.

A *computer virus* is a program that spreads from one computer to another and causes damage or mischief to your computer's data and software. Typically, the damage is the destruction of the data on your hard disk. The disk itself is not damaged physically, but the data on the disk is altered or erased.

Some viruses do not cause much damage but are designed to be annoying. Such a virus may simply display a message periodically, or otherwise make itself known by altering your screen display in some way.

Writing an effective virus program requires a fair amount of computer programming knowledge. Speculation varies, but many people think that most virus authors are stereotypical "computer nerds" between the ages of 15 and 25 who create viruses for the challenge and ego gratification.

Whenever you execute a computer program that you received from an outside source, you run the risk of contracting a computer virus that can destroy your data. Because everyone on a LAN shares the same hard disk, one user can expose everyone else by unknowingly running a virus-infested program. That is why the LAN administrator has to be on guard.

How a Virus Spreads

A virus works in two stages, which you might call the contagious stage and the destructive stage. During the contagious stage, the virus attaches itself to programs on your computer's hard disk or floppy disks. The most common targets are the three basic MS-DOS boot programs: COMMAND.COM, IO.SYS, and MSDOS.SYS. (If you run PC DOS, IBM's version of DOS, the latter two programs are named IBMBIO.COM and IBMDOS.COM, respectively.) The two programs with the .SYS extension are "hidden" files you cannot see when you use the DIR command; they reside in your disk's root directory and cause your system to boot when you turn on the power. COMMAND.COM is the DOS program that processes the commands you type from the keyboard. Some viruses attack other programs, but virus authors usually concentrate on these three programs because they are on every DOS computer and they are executed every day.

The virus program attaches itself to one of these DOS programs, altering the DOS program by adding new programming instructions or modifying existing instructions. From that point on, the DOS program works slightly differently. Instead of performing only its normal work, the modified program also follows the virus program's instructions. These new instructions may cause the virus program to attach to additional programs, such as any program you copy onto a floppy disk.

Then when you give the floppy disk to another user, that user runs the program you supplied and another computer becomes infected. A computer virus epidemic can spread very quickly.

In addition to programs on floppy disks, other possible sources of infected programs are those you download from a computer bulletin board system or those you get or run from a server's hard disk.

> **NOTE:** You must run an infected computer program to infect your computer with the virus. You cannot infect your computer by simply copying an infected program from a floppy disk, BBS, or server to your own hard disk. The infection occurs when you run the program and the virus attaches itself to a host DOS program or some other program.

How a Virus Works

Now you know how a virus spreads, but you need to learn how it does damage or mischief. A virus is programmed with some sort of "trigger" logic. Sometimes the trigger is based on the computer's internal date. The virus may examine the computer's internal date (kept on the computer's clock/calendar chip) and do no damage except on a particular day of each year. With this kind of trigger, a virus may spread to other computers for as long as 364 days before damage suddenly occurs. Other viruses keep count of the number of floppy disks they infect and, having spread to a certain number, destroy the data on the hard disk of the computer they infect. These trigger mechanisms are effective because both of them ensure that the virus spreads to other computers before it is detected. Typically, you do not detect the virus until destruction of the data actually occurs or you see messages displayed by the virus program.

For a computer virus to spread, a delayed trigger mechanism is necessary because a virus that destroyed hard disk data immediately upon infecting a computer would not have time to spread to other computers. In addition to viruses, other destructive programs exist; when these programs (usually called *bombs* or *Trojans*) are run, they inflict damage immediately without going through a contagious phase.

Virus Treatment

You have three courses of action to protect against computer viruses: prevention, frequent checkups, and treatment. Certain products also are available to help combat computer viruses.

Prevention   The best way to avoid virus damage is to never become infected. Before running any new program on your computer, use a *virus-checker program*. Such a program (sometimes called a *virus-detection program*), scans other programs and can detect known viruses. If the virus-checker shows that the new program is infected, do not run the infected program.

Other products, called *antivirus programs*, do not check for specific viruses. Rather, they monitor your PC, checking for actions viruses typically take to spread infection or do damage. By checking for the proper actions, an antivirus program can detect that a virus is present and prevent damage even when you unknowingly run an infected program. If a programmer designs a virus that causes damage in a new way, however, the antivirus program will not help.

> *Antivirus programs check for the spread of infection.*

Frequent Checkups   Suppose that one of your LAN users runs an infected program without first checking the program for virus infection. Because most viruses stay in their contagious state for some time before they cause destruction, you usually can detect a virus on your hard disks or in your computers' memory by running a virus checker. Then you can take steps to eliminate the virus before harm occurs. Many LAN administrators run virus-checker programs daily to verify that server hard disks are free of viruses. For a group with active users, especially users who frequently bring in programs from outside the workgroup, daily virus-checking is a good idea. Less frequent checking may be adequate for a small group in which new programs are seldom used.

Treatment   As soon as you discover that a computer has contracted a virus, you need to act to eliminate the virus before it does damage. Use a *virus-cleanup program*, a program that in most cases can remove the virus portions of infected programs. For some viruses, cleanup programs cannot fix the infected programs; you have to delete the infected programs and reinstall them from your original floppy disks or backup copies. If you don't detect the virus before it destroys data, you may

The Role of the LAN Administrator

have to restore all your programs and data from backup copies. If you have no current backup copies, you learn the valuable and painful lesson of why you need backups.

Virus-Protection Products

A staggering array of virus-protection products has recently appeared. Some of these products are antivirus programs, some are virus-checkers, and some are virus-cleanup programs. Most leading products now are capable of performing all three functions.

Because virus authors constantly develop new viruses that old protection products cannot detect, you must use a recent version of any virus-protection product to have any confidence that it will prevent, detect, or clean up new viruses.

When you buy a virus-protection product, you put your trust in the company that created the product. You should check to see how thorough their testing was, what viruses the product protects against, how much of an effort the company makes to release updated versions which provide protection from newly-detected viruses, and what their policy is for providing you with upgrades to new versions of the product.

Investigate the products available and find out which suits you best. Be sure to follow the manufacturer's directions carefully. Here are some of the leading products:

- The VIRUSCAN series (VIRUSCAN, VSHIELD, CLEAN-UP) from McAfee Associates. McAfee distributes these products as shareware for home use, but you must license the products for business use. VIRUSCAN (also called SCAN) is a virus checker, CLEAN-UP does virus cleanup, and VSHIELD is an antivirus program. Revised versions of VIRUSCAN usually are developed every two or three months. If you use CompuServe, type **go virusforum** to gain access to McAfee-led discussions about viruses.

- ViruSafe/LAN, a product from Xtree Company, performs antivirus, virus-checker, and virus-cleanup functions.

- Virex-PC, a product from Microcom, performs antivirus, virus-checker, and virus-cleanup functions.

- Central Point Anti-Virus, Central Point Software's product, performs antivirus, virus-checker, and virus-cleanup functions. Another Central Point Software product, PC Tools, includes a virus-checker capability among its utility programs.

- Norton AntiVirus, from Symantec, performs antivirus, virus-checker, and virus-cleanup functions.

CAUTION: The products are listed for your information. Neither the authors nor the publishers of this book represent that any of the products guarantee your protection from damage caused by viruses. The products work on stand-alone computers and are not necessarily designed to be shared over a network. Upgrades are frequent, however, and it is your responsibility to verify that any version you purchase is compatible with NetWare Lite.

LAN Security

NetWare Lite's built-in security features are covered in depth in Chapter 12, which shows you how to set up user accounts, passwords, and supervisory privileges. You also learn how to oversee LAN activity with built-in auditing procedures.

LAN security also involves the physical integrity of the LAN. Your company should implement some physical security measures. As LAN administrator, you may be the only person who keeps an eye on overall office security. You are in the best position to remind management of the value of the group's computer data; if you find that physical security is inadequate, make sure that your company takes appropriate steps to address the problem.

If you don't succeed in improving door locks, fire prevention, and other measures, be sure to arrange for regular rotation of off-site tape backup copies. Your chances of needing a backup one day increase if physical security factors are weak and necessary improvements are not made.

User Support

Even though NetWare Lite is easy to learn and use, members of your workgroup will need your occasional support. A new user needs training, even if all you do is spend 10 minutes demonstrating how to

The Role of the LAN Administrator

map a disk drive and printer. Even long-time Lite users may occasionally need a question answered or an error message explained. If someone accidentally deletes an important disk file on the server, you may be called on to help restore the file from your most recent backup copy.

Even if you don't feel comfortable as the office LAN expert, you are the closest thing the workgroup has available. If you cannot figure out answers to questions yourself, you are the best choice to call Novell Technical Support to explain the problem's symptoms and your LAN configuration.

In addition, you are the person who will develop new or simplified procedures for users. Your workgroup may benefit from having customized STARTNET.BAT files or other batch files, or from having the NetWare Lite start-up commands included in each user's AUTOEXEC.BAT file. For example, you may want all users—upon logging into the network—to map drive L to the group's shared directory and LPT2 to a shared laser printer. You can also customize everyone's word processing program to use these shared resources. For more information on customized batch files, see Appendix D, "Sample Batch Files." Evaluate your workgroup's needs and NetWare Lite's capabilities. Then design and test batch files or written procedures that simplify everyone's LAN usage.

Communicating with Users

As LAN administrator, you are responsible for communicating LAN developments and policy changes to all users. Most LANs are vital, dynamic entities. Let everyone know when new users are added to the workgroup, when new computers and printers are added to the network, and when server software applications are added or updated. Make sure also that all users know about important changes, such as changes in backup policy.

You have many ways to communicate with your users. You can call meetings, write memos, or post notices on company bulletin boards, for example. And you can always take advantage of the LAN. Why not create a text file in which recent developments are announced? Then save the file on a server's disk for all users to access and read. Using the NetWare Lite message feature, you can send a message to all users indicating that a new LAN update file is available.

Hardware Maintenance and Checking

The LAN hardware requires maintenance. The tasks can be divided into two main categories: routine maintenance and checking server disk space.

Routine Hardware Maintenance

For any LAN to run smoothly, certain chores need to be done regularly. If all the computers in a company are connected with a network, the LAN administrator usually has the job of making sure that enough computer supplies such as printer paper and floppy disks are always at hand. If you shut down the LAN at night, each evening someone has to check that all computers have been turned off.

Printers always require attention. Someone must ensure that the paper is loaded and, if your printer uses font cartridges, that the proper cartridge is in place for any particular print job. For impact printers, ribbons and carbons must be changed as required. In general, sufficient supplies must be kept on hand.

Maintenance also includes periodic checking of the hardware to make sure that the computers are working properly, the LAN cables are firmly connected, and that no cables have "wandered" into dangerous positions where they may cause someone to trip or equipment to be damaged. If your LAN uses a tape backup unit, it also requires occasional cleaning and perhaps other maintenance. You should tour the LAN periodically, checking all the hardware and asking users about any problems.

Maintenance is one of those jobs that never ends (and for which no one seems to appreciate your efforts). As a LAN administrator, you are responsible for maintenance across the LAN. For a small LAN with only a few nodes, you are likely to do the maintenance chores yourself. For a larger or extremely active LAN, you probably will delegate maintenance chores to several individuals. The user physically closest to a printer, for example, may be responsible for all maintenance of that printer. Whether or not you delegate chores, however, you must assume ultimate responsibility for maintenance of the entire LAN.

Server Disk Space

Because everyone in the workgroup shares a server's disk space, the shared disk can become a cluttered jumble of files. Disk space is like closet space: no matter how much you have, you usually want more, and an occasional cleanup is necessary to make room for new things. A shared disk can quickly become a repository for everyone's junk. You, the LAN administrator, have to ask how a server disk that had 40MB of space available yesterday has only 2MB today. Then you have to figure out who put the new data there and what to do about it.

Users sometimes get into the bad habit of casually and unnecessarily copying their files to the server. Instead of sending only critical files to the server, for example, a user may simply copy everything on his or her hard disk. Perhaps pressed for time, the user does a global copy instead of taking the time to copy only the necessary individual files. This user probably thinks, "Tomorrow, when I have time, I'll delete the extraneous files from the server." But when tomorrow comes, the cleanup somehow never occurs. If this scenario plays only a few times, the server's disk quickly becomes cluttered with useless data.

You cannot allow your server's hard disk to become full. To have room for printer spool jobs and new data files, plenty of space must be available at all times. Sometimes, as a last resort, your only choice is to back up an unidentifiable big new file onto a tape cartridge (or a stack of floppy disks) and then delete it from the server's disk. The owner will come screaming to you about the missing file, at which time you can ask whether he or she has any idea how large the file is. If you then decide that the file should stay on the server, you can restore the file from your backup copy.

You (the LAN administrator) may already have one or more favorite software tools to help you manage your hard disk. Because NetWare Lite is DOS based, the same products should work on server disks. Some disk-management products are finicky, however, and work only on a physical (not a mapped) disk. Ask the manufacturer of your disk-management product about NetWare Lite compatibility, to be sure.

Configuration Management

If you were the first to be named as LAN administrator, you probably coordinated the original installation of the LAN hardware and software. Even if you became LAN administrator later, you are the logical choice to install hardware and software for new users. An inexperienced computer user may make mistakes installing either the LAN card or the Lite software, whereas you most likely have installed them before and can do it again quickly and accurately. Also, you can coordinate the LAN downtime necessary to cable a new user's computer to the LAN.

Novell will periodically release new versions of NetWare Lite. You should watch for these new versions and decide whether your workgroup will upgrade. If you decide to upgrade, you are the person who needs to make the plans and perform the new software installation. In general, you should avoid falling too far behind the current version. As with most software products, the new versions will fix bugs in past versions and also include new features and performance improvements.

After a new version is released, waiting a month or two before you install it is usually a good idea. That cushion of time gives you (and Novell) a chance to see whether any major problems exist with the new version. Check the NetWare Lite forum on CompuServe to find out whether users are complaining about unresolved problems. (Most such problems are caused by user mistakes, such as using nonstandard cables, setting LAN-card jumpers inaccurately, or incorrectly installing application software.)

CAUTION: No matter how thoroughly a software company like Novell tests new software, sometimes bugs show up only after real-world users begin running a new version. If you have a pioneering spirit, you can upgrade immediately. Just be aware of the hardships pioneers often face.

If your managers want to implement new functions (such as new application software or new shared hardware devices) using the LAN, you should get involved as soon as possible to evaluate alternative products, plan the installation, and install the software and/or hardware.

The Role of the LAN Administrator

After your workgroup becomes dependent on the LAN, your role as LAN administrator becomes more important. Because the LAN is a shared resource, it needs a central control point to be sure that configuration changes don't cause problems. You are that control point. You have to be sure that the LAN is available whenever group members need it, and that configuration changes (hardware or software) don't cause problems for group members who are trying to get work done.

Budgeting

In any organization, money is an important issue. If you are the administrator of a very small LAN for a small company, you may deal with budget issues on a case-by-case basis. Many companies, however, have specific budgets for the operation of the LAN as well as for other company needs and resources.

Perhaps you prepared the budget for the acquisition of your LAN hardware and software, installation costs, and periodic maintenance. Now that company management has approved your budget, you must try to hold costs to the funds available.

Generally, after a LAN is installed and operational, the costs of operating the LAN remain fairly constant. Each situation is different, however. You must monitor the costs of operating your LAN. If you see cost fluctuations, analyze why these variations occur and be sure that your budget accommodates typical fluctuations.

If you anticipate adding nodes to your LAN, budget the costs of such growth. To do so, you must keep abreast of current prices for computers and peripherals. In today's market, prices tend to fall while features and capability tend to rise and, as time passes, you typically can get more and more for your hardware and software dollar. As a result, a budget may need revision as often as every few months. You may find that you can afford faster, larger, or better hardware and software than you thought when the budget was created.

LAN Optimization

Chapter 14, "Optimizing LAN Performance," discusses NetWare Lite optimization in depth. *Optimization* (sometimes called *performance improvement* or *tuning*) refers to any efforts that result in the more efficient use of resources. On a LAN, optimization falls into three areas: improved speed, using less RAM, and conserving disk space. There are many ways to accomplish these results. As part of the effort, you may run *benchmark tests*—timed tests of controlled workloads. By comparing the timings before and after you make changes, you can determine whether the changes are beneficial.

As another part of optimization, you should perform *capacity planning*, in which you track the workgroup's LAN usage in order to anticipate the need for hardware upgrades because of an increasing workload. You need to decide whether upgrades (such as larger disk drives or faster servers) are really necessary to increase capacity or whether you can handle the increasing workload by optimizing. See Chapter 14 for details about such optimization.

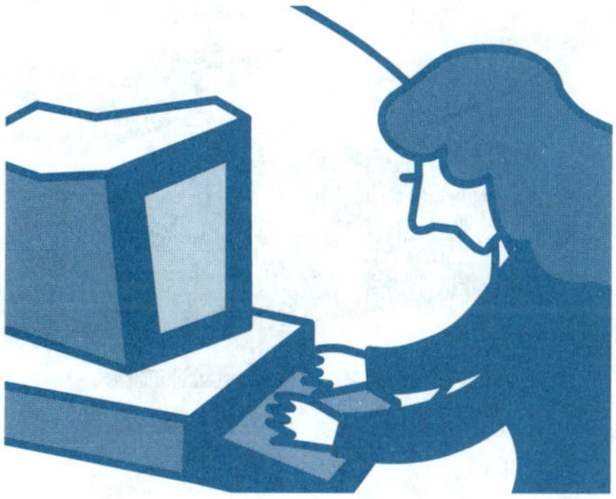

CHAPTER

12

SECURING THE LAN

In a LAN environment, security refers to making LAN resources available to the appropriate users. Your LAN contains valuable assets—not only the PCs and peripheral devices, but especially the data and program files stored on the hard disks. You want those assets safeguarded against damage or loss.

With NetWare Lite, you achieve security by restricting the freedoms granted to the LAN users. Most NetWare Lite LANs occur in small companies with a few employees who enjoy mutual trust. If you see no need to restrict access to your network servers in any way, fine. It's your choice. (A survey of dealers and users indicates that in over 90 percent of NetWare Lite installations, no security restrictions are implemented.) You may find reading this chapter worthwhile, however, so that you can decide whether security will help you control your LAN and protect your data.

The NetWare Lite software provides the following four methods for securing a LAN:

- Controlling who can log in to the network
- Controlling the access rights to a server's shared resources
- Limiting the files and directories a server offers
- Maintaining audit logs and error logs

The remainder of this chapter discusses each of these four security methods in turn. To implement most of the NetWare Lite security features, you use options available from the NET menu system.

The LAN administrator is responsible for controlling account names, passwords, resources offered, expiration dates, and other security-related constraints. If you are a LAN administrator and you

Physical Security

All of the security measures discussed in this chapter are software security measures. You are responsible for providing whatever physical security you believe appropriate, such as limiting physical access to your servers and workstations. The software security methods don't prevent someone from walking up to one of your servers, turning on the machine or rebooting it (from a floppy disk, if necessary), and viewing or deleting any files on the hard disk. The best way to prevent this type of security breach is to put your server in a locked room.

plan to implement security now or in the future, you need to know the material in this chapter. Even if you're not a LAN administrator, you should understand just what you can and cannot do when network security is in force.

Controlling Who Can Log in to the Network

If you select all the default options when you install NetWare Lite with the INSTALL program, you establish virtually no security restrictions. Anyone can access any resource available on any server.

The installation program sets up a network account named SUPERVISOR. This account has full supervisory privileges, which means that anyone logged in to the network under this account can create, modify, or delete network resources. These resources include the network directories, network printers, and the list of user accounts.

In Chapter 9, you learned how to create additional user accounts with individual names. By default, an individual user account has full supervisory privileges. Thus, a user logged in to the network under an individual account can manipulate the network resources as fully as a user logged in as SUPERVISOR. You can, however, also restrict what a user logged in with a particular account name can do.

Here's a brief list of the kinds of restrictions you can place on LAN users by implementing the NetWare Lite security features that control log-ins and account names:

- Restrict access to some of the server's resources, on a user-by-user basis
- Require anyone logging in to the network to enter a valid account name and password
- Force users to change passwords periodically, to minimize problems if an unauthorized user discovers someone's password
- Make a user account expire on a preset date so that the user (a temporary employee, for example) can no longer log in to the network after that date

You don't have to establish all these restrictions. You can use as many or as few as you like.

Creating Passwords

You can associate a *password* with each user account as a mechanism to prevent unauthorized users from gaining access to the network. If password security is in force, a user must type the proper password when logging in to the network.

In many LANs, the LAN administrator creates each new account and assigns the password for each account. For some LANs, individual users create their own accounts and passwords. This section explains the process of creating passwords for new and existing user accounts.

Choosing a Password

Choosing a good password is important. Password names follow the same rules as user names. You can use a maximum of 15 characters—letters, digits, or blank spaces. (NetWare Lite converts each blank space into an underscore character.)

> **NOTE:** For best security, make sure that the password is not too short. For convenience, however, the name should not be too long. Usually, five to eight characters is a good compromise.

Make sure that the password is not a word anyone else can easily associate with the name of the account or the name of the primary user. Suppose that the user's name is Elizabeth. Examples of bad password choices are LIZ, BETH, ZIL (Liz spelled backwards), her middle or last name, her husband's name, her children's names, the name of her dog, one of her hobbies, her birthday, or any other personal information. These passwords are too easily guessed by others.

One good password choice is a random word (of reasonable length). You might get a such a word by opening the dictionary to any page, closing your eyes, and pointing a finger. Also, including random digits or blank spaces in a password makes the password hard to guess.

Securing the LAN

Avoid any password the user might take as a compliment or as an insult (FUNNY, NASTY, HEADACHE). If users find a password amusing or outrageous, they may talk about it with others—and the whole point of a password is to keep it secret.

Each user on the LAN should understand these basics of password construction. As explained later in this chapter, users can change their own passwords at will. Picking an unguessable random password for Elizabeth is a waste of your time if she changes her password to LIZ the next day.

CAUTION: NetWare Lite will not display the password associated with any account. If, as a LAN administrator, you keep a written record of the passwords for each account, be sure to keep that record in a secure place, such as a locked desk drawer. If users change their passwords, make sure that you know about the changes. As a user, remembering your password without writing it down is usually a good idea. If you forget your password, you can ask the LAN administrator to refresh your memory, or you can change the password as described later in this chapter.

Creating a Password on a New Account

The following example assumes that you are working at a node from which you have logged in to the network as SUPERVISOR. You will create a new account named SHOWME, with the password MISSOURI.

To create a new account with an associated password, follow these steps:

1. At the DOS prompt, type **net** and press [Enter] to activate the menu system and open the Main menu.
2. Move the highlight to Supervise the network, and press [Enter].

   The "Supervise the Network" menu pops open.
3. Move the highlight to User List (the bottom option), and press [Enter].

   A box labeled "All Users" pops open. This box lists every user account recognized by the network.
4. Press [Ins] to create a new user account.

NetWare Lite pops open a box that prompts you to supply the user name for this new account.

5. Type a user name for this new account (**SHOWME**, in this example) and press Enter.

   Account names are limited to 15 characters. NetWare Lite does not distinguish between upper- and lowercase letters.

   As shown in Figure 12-1, a box labeled "Account Information for User SHOWME" pops open.

6. Move the highlight down to the fourth option, labeled "Password."

7. Press Enter twice to indicate that you want to change the password (in this case, the password is being created for the first time).

   As shown in Figure 12-2, a box that prompts you to supply the new password pops open.

8. Type the password (**MISSOURI**, in this case).

   To maximize security, NetWare Lite does not display the characters you type for the password. As with user names, NetWare Lite does not distinguish between upper- and lowercase letters in passwords.

9. Press Enter after you type the password.

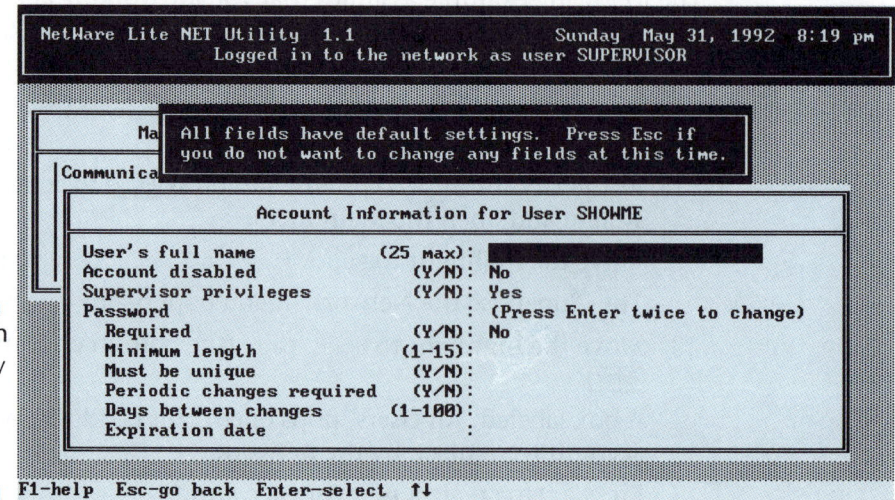

The Information box for the new account, SHOWME
Figure 12-1.

```
NetWare Lite NET Utility 1.1                    Sunday  May 31, 1992  8:19 pm
                   Logged in to the network as user SUPERVISOR

        Ma┌─────────────────────────────────────────────────────────┐
          │ All fields have default settings.  Press Esc if         │
   Communica│ you do not want to change any fields at this time.    │
          │                                                         │
          │         Account Information for User SHOWME             │
          │                                                         │
          │   User's full name          (25 max):                   │
          │   Account disabled          (Y/N): No                   │
          │   Supervisor privileges     (Y/N): Yes                  │
          │   Password                        : (Press Enter twice to change) │
          │     Required                (Y/N): No                   │
          │     Minimum length          (1-15):                     │
          │     Must be unique          (Y/N):                      │
          │     Periodic changes required (Y/N):                    │
          │     Days between changes    (1-100):                    │
          │     Expiration date               :                     │
          └─────────────────────────────────────────────────────────┘
  F1-help  Esc-go back  Enter-select  ↑↓
```

Securing the LAN

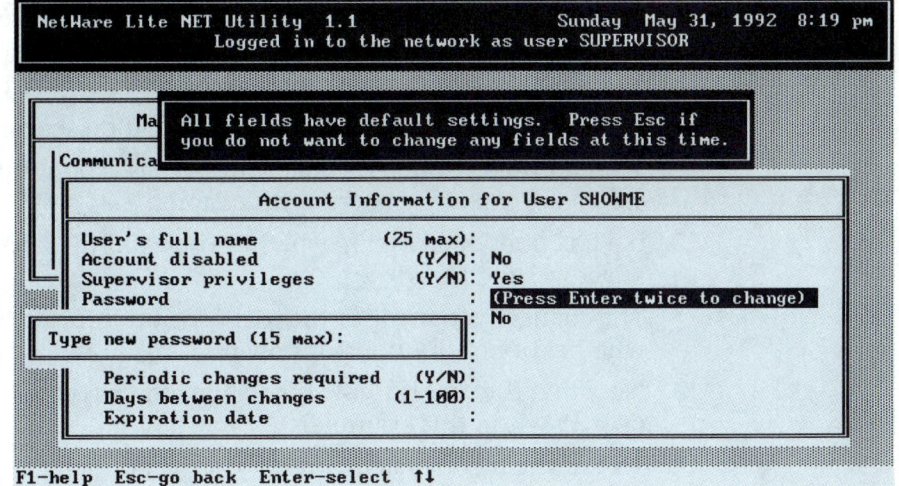

```
NetWare Lite NET Utility 1.1                Sunday  May 31, 1992  8:19 pm
                Logged in to the network as user SUPERVISOR

        Ma┌─ All fields have default settings.  Press Esc if ─┐
          │  you do not want to change any fields at this time.│
   Communica└───────────────────────────────────────────────────┘

                      Account Information for User SHOWME

           User's full name            (25 max):
           Account disabled               (Y/N): No
           Supervisor privileges          (Y/N): Yes
           Password                            : (Press Enter twice to change)
                                               : No
           Type new password (15 max):

             Periodic changes required   (Y/N):
             Days between changes       (1-100):
             Expiration date                  :

   F1-help  Esc-go back  Enter-select  ↑↓
```

NetWare Lite waits for you to type the new password
Figure 12-2.

As shown in Figure 12-3, a box that prompts you to retype the password pops opens. This box lets you confirm that you typed your intended password correctly the first time. (Remember—you can't see the password as you type.)

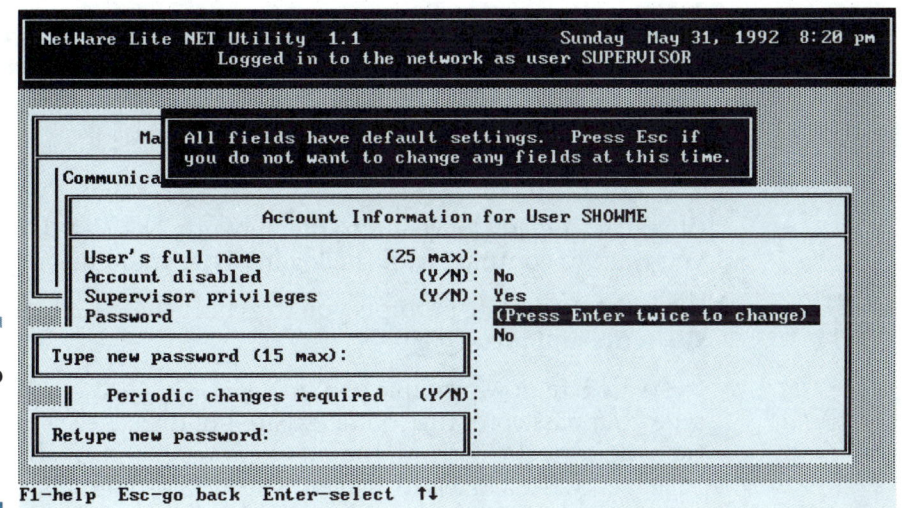

```
NetWare Lite NET Utility 1.1                Sunday  May 31, 1992  8:20 pm
                Logged in to the network as user SUPERVISOR

        Ma┌─ All fields have default settings.  Press Esc if ─┐
          │  you do not want to change any fields at this time.│
   Communica└───────────────────────────────────────────────────┘

                      Account Information for User SHOWME

           User's full name            (25 max):
           Account disabled               (Y/N): No
           Supervisor privileges          (Y/N): Yes
           Password                            : (Press Enter twice to change)
                                               : No
           Type new password (15 max):

             Periodic changes required   (Y/N):
           Retype new password:

   F1-help  Esc-go back  Enter-select  ↑↓
```

NetWare Lite waits for you to retype the new password
Figure 12-3.

10. Retype the password and press [Enter].

    If the retyped password does not match the initial password, NetWare Lite prompts you to type the new password all over again.

11. Press [Esc] to exit the new account information screen.

    The additional options available from the account information screen are explained later in this chapter.

12. If a box pops open asking whether you want to "Save Changes," select Yes and press [Enter].

    The changes you made to the user account information determine whether or not this box pops open.

13. Note that the user list now shows the new account name (SHOWME, in this example).

14. To exit the menu system, press [Alt]-[F10] and then press [Enter].

Logging in to the Network with a Password

If a password is established for an account name, you must type that password whenever you log in to the network under that account name. In that way, unauthorized users who know your account name but not your password cannot log in to the network.

To log in to the network under the SHOWME account, for example, type the following command at the DOS prompt and press [Enter]:

    net login showme

(If you are already logged in to the network, NetWare Lite asks whether you want to continue with the log in. Type **y** and press [Enter].)

When NetWare Lite prompts you to Type your username:, type **showme** and press [Enter].

NetWare Lite now prompts you to Type your password:. When you type your password, the characters are not displayed onscreen. If you type the correct password, the message You are logged in to the network as SHOWME. is displayed. The DOS prompt appears, and you are logged in.

Securing the LAN

If you don't type the correct password, however, you see the message `Invalid password and username combination`. Then the DOS prompt appears and you can try again to log in.

Using the Menu System To Change Your Password

As an individual user, you can change the password on your own account either by using the menu system or directly from the DOS prompt. If you want to use the menus, move the highlight to the option `Set your password` (on the Main menu) and press [Enter].

A box pops open, prompting you to type the old password. As a measure of security, NetWare Lite requires you to type the old password before you can create a new one. Type your old password and press [Enter]. A new box pops open, prompting you to `Type new password (15 max):`. Now type your new password and press [Enter]. As shown in Figure 12-4, a third box pops open, asking you to `Retype new password:`. Do so, press [Enter], and you have changed the password on your account. To exit the menu system, press [Esc] and then [Enter].

Just as when you typed your old password, the new password does not appear onscreen as you type it. You are prompted to retype the new password as a safeguard against typing mistakes.

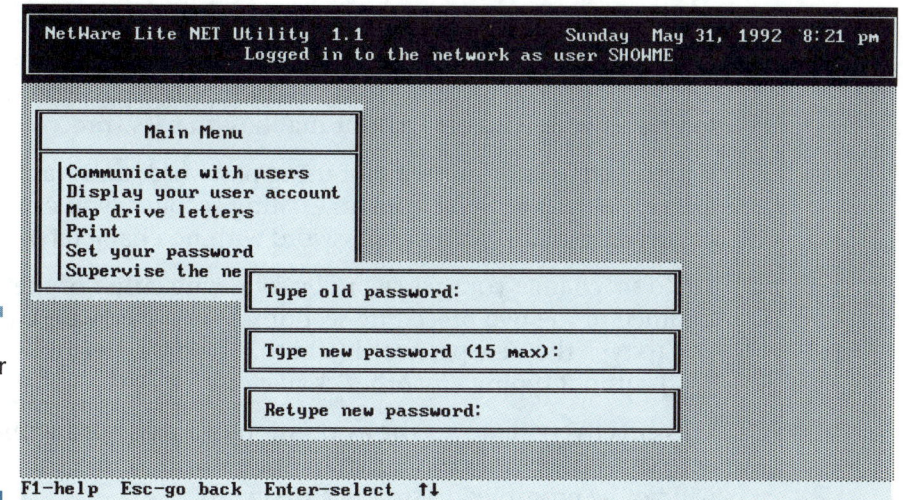

NetWare Lite prompts you for the old and new passwords
Figure 12-4.

> **NOTE:** Periodically changing your password is a good idea. That way, you tighten LAN security by limiting how long an unauthorized user who discovers a password can access the LAN.

Changing Your Password from the DOS Prompt

To change your password without using the menus, type the following command at the DOS prompt and press Enter :

    net setpass

As with the menu system, you are prompted to type your old password, then to type and retype the new password. When you finish the process, NetWare Lite displays the message `Your password has been changed`.

Removing Passwords from an Account

By default, NetWare Lite does not associate a password with each new user account. You are not prompted to supply a password if you log in to the network with an account that has no password.

If you change your mind about using passwords and want to disassociate a password from an existing account, you can change the password to a null string (a password with no characters).

To do so, change your password by following either of the techniques outlined in the two preceding sections. When NetWare Lite prompts you to type the new password (and to retype the new password), press Enter without typing any other characters.

This effectively removes the association of a password with your account. When you next log in to the network under that account, you will not be prompted to supply a password.

Changing a Password on Another User's Account

If you have supervisor privileges on the LAN, you can change not only the password on your account but also the password on any other user's account. To do so, you must be logged in to the LAN as SUPERVISOR, or as a user with supervisor privileges.

Enter the menu system. Select `Supervise the network` and then `User List`. When the list of users appears, move the highlight to the user whose password you want to change and press Enter. The Account Information box (similar to Figure 12-1) for that account appears. As you did when creating a new account, move the highlight to `Password` and press Enter twice. Then type (and retype) the new password. Press Esc to close the information box. To exit the menu system, press Alt-F10 and then Enter.

Creating and Changing the Password on the SUPERVISOR Account

If security issues are paramount on your LAN, you may want to create a password for the SUPERVISOR account. After all, the first thing an unauthorized user who wants to access a NetWare Lite LAN will do is try to log in as SUPERVISOR. If the SUPERVISOR account has a password, you can thwart such would be intruders.

To change the password on the SUPERVISOR account, use any of the techniques explained earlier in this chapter for changing the password on an individual user's account. If you create a password for SUPERVISOR, each user who logs in under that name must know the password.

CAUTION: Creating a password for SUPERVISOR is a two-edged sword, especially for very small LANs with no other user accounts, or for a LAN of any size in which SUPERVISOR is the only account with supervisor privileges. On the one hand, you need a password so that unauthorized users cannot easily access the LAN. On the other hand, if you forget the password, you cannot access the LAN. If no one can remember the password, you may have to reinstall NetWare Lite (losing your defined network directories and network printers in the process).

If you use a password with SUPERVISOR, be sure to write down the password and store it in a secure place under lock and key.

Setting Password Attributes

You can set various controls over how and when users can change their account's password. These controls include specifying a minimum password length and requiring the user to change the password within a specified time period.

To change the password attributes of a user's account, you must log in to the LAN as SUPERVISOR, or as a user with supervisor privileges. The modifications are made on the Account Information screen for the user's account, the same screen on which you changed the password.

To reach the Account Information screen, follow the same steps you took to change the password. Enter the menu system. Select `Supervise the network` and then `User List`. When the list of users appears, move the highlight to the user whose password attributes you want to change and press (Enter). The Account Information box for that account (similar to the one shown in Figure 12-1) appears.

Five password attributes are listed below the line labeled `Password`. Table 12-1 lists those attributes, along with the permissible settings and their default values.

To change an attribute, you move the highlight to that attribute and type a new value. As is explained in the following discussion of each attribute, you can move the highlight only to particular attributes, according to the values you set for other attributes.

Password Attributes
Table 12-1.

Attribute	Possible values	Default value
Required	Y, N	N
Minimum length	1-15	4
Must be unique	Y, N	N
Periodic changes required	Y, N	N
Days between changes	1-100	40

Securing the LAN

Required   The default value of N (no) means that you choose not to set any other attributes. To modify the value of any of the other attributes, change the value to Y (yes). Note that even if the value of this attribute is N (the default), a user logging in to the network under this account name must still enter the proper password (assuming, of course, that a password has been created for this account).

Minimum length   This attribute sets the minimum password length (in characters) a user can type for a new password. Making this value as small as 1 or 2 is not a good idea because unauthorized users may be able to stumble onto the correct password by just trying several short guesses.

Must be unique   If set to Y, the user of this account cannot specify a new password that already is being used on another account.

Periodic changes required   If set to Y, the user must change the password within the time period specified in the next attribute. If set to N, the default value, you cannot move the highlight to the next attribute (Days between changes).

Days between changes   This attribute defines the time period (in days) within which the password must be changed. NetWare Lite displays the date at the end of the time period in the next line, which reads `Expiration date`.

Figure 12-5 shows each of the password attributes for the SHOWME account set to a nondefault value. After you have set the attributes, press [Esc]. A box pops open asking you to confirm that you want to save the changes. Select `Yes` and press [Enter]. You can then press [Alt]-[F10], followed by [Enter], to exit the menu system.

Disabling a User Account

You can disable a user account so that no one can log in to the network using that account name, regardless of whether a password is established on that account. Log-in privileges can later be restored to a disabled account.

Disabling an account is helpful in situations in which you want someone to have intermittent access to the LAN. Suppose, for example,

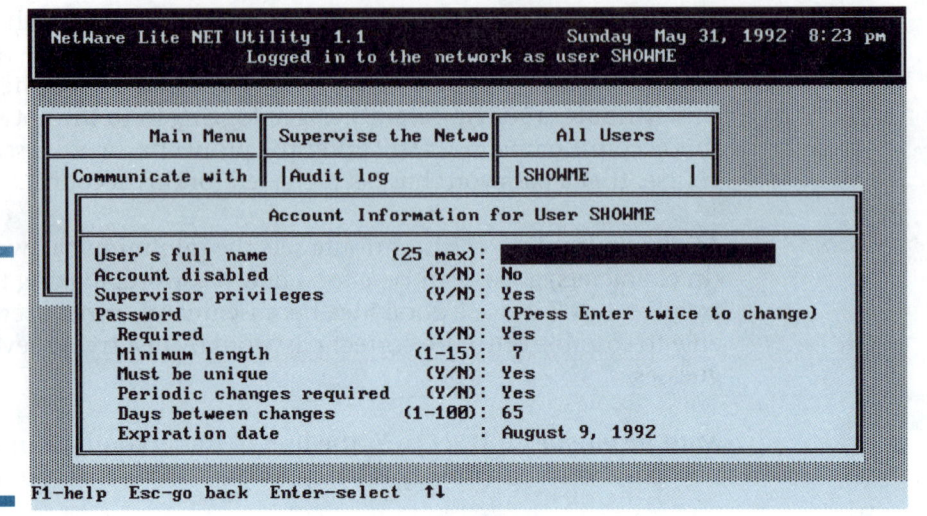

NetWare Lite Made Easy

```
┌─────────────────────────────────────────────────────────────────────┐
│ NetWare Lite NET Utility  1.1           Sunday  May 31, 1992 8:23 pm│
│              Logged in to the network as user SHOWME                │
├─────────────────────────────────────────────────────────────────────┤
│                                                                     │
│      ┌──────────────┬──────────────────┬──────────────┐             │
│      │  Main Menu   │ Supervise the Netwo│  All Users │             │
│      │Communicate with││Audit log       ││SHOWME      │             │
│      │        Account Information for User SHOWME                   │
│      │ User's full name        (25 max):                            │
│      │ Account disabled           (Y/N): No                         │
│      │ Supervisor privileges      (Y/N): Yes                        │
│      │ Password                        : (Press Enter twice to change)│
│      │   Required                 (Y/N): Yes                        │
│      │   Minimum length          (1-15): 7                          │
│      │   Must be unique           (Y/N): Yes                        │
│      │   Periodic changes required(Y/N): Yes                        │
│      │   Days between changes   (1-100): 65                         │
│      │   Expiration date              : August 9, 1992              │
│                                                                     │
│  F1-help  Esc-go back  Enter-select  ↑↓                             │
└─────────────────────────────────────────────────────────────────────┘
```

Password attributes for SHOWME are set to nondefault values
Figure 12-5.

that you have an accountant who comes once a week on Thursday mornings to work with your financial files. You can set up an account for the accountant (and enjoy a certain kind of poetic harmony in doing so). Generally, you leave the account disabled, but one of your first tasks each Thursday morning is to enable it. Just before lunch, after the accountant finishes working, you can disable the account again. In that way, the accountant can access the LAN only during the prescribed time periods.

To disable an account, use the menu system to pop open the Account Information screen for the desired account. (Refer to Figure 12-1, which shows that screen for the SHOWME account.)

Move the cursor to the line labeled `Account disabled`. The default value (No) means that the account is not disabled and users can log in with this account name. To disable the account, press **Y** and then press Enter. Similarly, if the account is already disabled, you can press **N** followed by Enter to restore the default value.

Disabling an account is not the same as deleting the account name. When you disable an account, NetWare Lite retains a record of the account information, including the password. When you delete an account, you lose all information pertaining to the account.

Securing the LAN

Denying Supervisor Privileges

As you have seen, NetWare Lite grants, by default, full supervisor privileges to each new account. With supervisor privileges, you can do anything from the menu system—while logged in with an individual account name—that you can do while logged in as SUPERVISOR. For increased LAN security, however, you can deny network privileges to any particular account.

To deny supervisor privileges, you again use an option on the Account Information screen for the desired account. Refer again to Figure 12-1, which shows that screen for the SHOWME account.

Move the cursor to the line labeled `Supervisor privileges`. The default value (Yes) means that the account has full supervisor privileges. To deny these privileges, press **N**, followed by [Enter]. You can then exit the menu system and users can log in with this account name. Similarly, if the account is already disabled, you can press **N** followed by [Enter] to restore the default value.

With the account disabled, you can change the password for the account but you cannot change the password attributes (the menu options such as `Minimum length` and `Days between changes`).

NOTE: You cannot remove supervisor privileges from the SUPERVISOR account. NetWare Lite treats the SUPERVISOR account as a special case.

Supervisor Privileges

By denying supervisor privileges, you limit what a user can do after he or she logs in to the LAN. The restrictions apply to the `Supervise the network` option on the Main menu. Figure 12-6 shows the "Supervise the Network" box that pops open when you select that option from the Main menu.

The following discussion examines each of the "Supervise the Network" options in terms of the restrictions imposed if you do not have supervisor privileges.

```
NetWare Lite NET Utility 1.1              Sunday  May 31, 1992  8:24 pm
              Logged in to the network as user SHOWME

         Main Menu          Supervise the Network
     Communicate with      Audit log
     Display your user     Error log
     Map drive letters     Network directories
     Print                 Network printers
     Set your password     Server configuration
     Supervise the net     Server status
                           Server system files
                           Time synchronization
                           User List

F1-help  Esc-go back  Enter-select  ↑↓
```

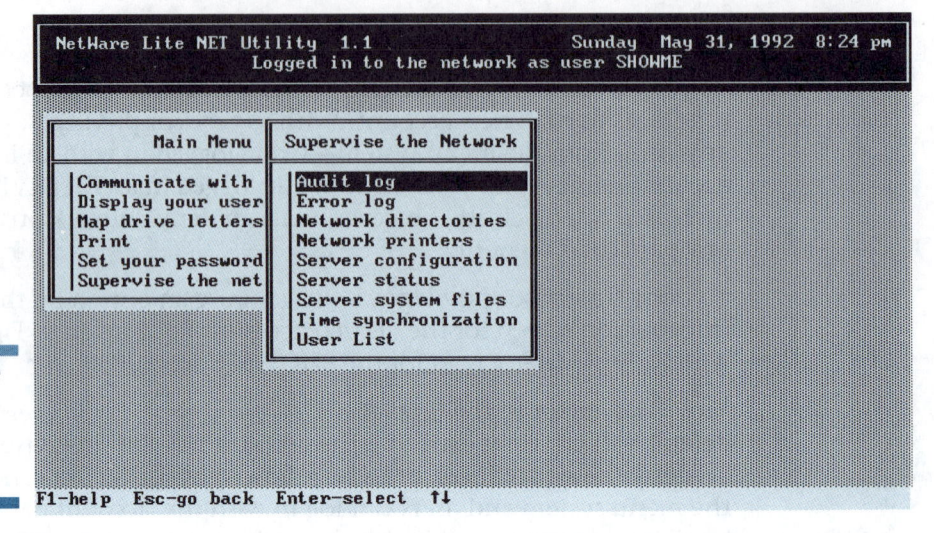

The Supervise the Network menu
Figure 12-6.

Audit log and Error log   These options, which are explained later in this chapter, cannot be used by an account without supervisor privileges.

Network directories   You cannot delete, rename, or modify any network directories except those residing on the server with which you are working. If you are working at a dedicated workstation (with no server capability), you cannot modify any network directories. If you are working at a server, you retain full rights to manipulate only the network directories on that server.

Network printers   The restrictions are similar to those for network directories. You can modify the network printers only on the server with which you are working.

Server configuration, Server status, and Server system files   You can execute these options only for the server with which you are working.

Time synchronization   This option, explained in Chapter 15, is available only to users with supervisor privileges.

User List   You can use this option only if you have supervisor privileges. If you do not have supervisor privileges, you cannot delete, add, modify, or view any user accounts.

Securing the LAN

Determining the Status of a User Account

You can have NetWare Lite display information about the status of your user account. To do so, activate the menu system and select `Display your user account` from the Main menu.

NetWare Lite displays a screen that shows the account information for your user account (the account name you used when you logged in to the network). This screen shows whether the account has supervisor privileges, whether the account is disabled, and the various attributes assigned to the password (such as the minimum length, whether the password is required, and the expiration date).

Controlling Access Rights

By default, each user has full access rights to any network directory or network printer. In the case of a network directory, full rights means the freedom to read, modify, delete, and save any files in a network directory. For a network printer, full rights simply means the ability to capture a port to the printer.

NetWare Lite provides the capability to restrict these rights on selected user accounts. You can change the default rights for every user or grant particular rights to specific users, thereby allowing only selected users to access files containing personal or sensitive data (such as salaries or legal correspondence).

Network Directory Rights

For a network directory, you can set the access rights for each user account on an account-by-account basis. The following table explains the three access rights:

Right	Meaning
ALL	Grants full access to read, modify, delete, and save files
NONE	Denies any access
READ	Grants only the privilege of reading files

By default, NetWare Lite grants the ALL right to each account for every network directory. You frequently may want to restrict those rights.

Suppose, for example, that you have developed an important spreadsheet. To view the results of your spreadsheet, you want each user to be able to load it into a spreadsheet program, but you don't want anyone to be able to modify the file. Or perhaps you have a word processed document containing information you want others to see but not edit. The solution in both instances is to restrict the access rights of a particular network directory and then place these files in that directory.

Restricting the Network Directory Rights for All Users

In the following example, the access rights are modified to the network directory named TEXT_DOCUMENTS on the server JUANITA. The rights are changed to READ for all users. The example assumes that you are logged in to the network with SUPERVISOR or another account that enjoys supervisor privileges. Follow these steps:

1. At the DOS prompt, type **net** and press (Enter) to start the menu system.
2. Select Supervise the network and press (Enter).
3. Move the highlight to Network directories and press (Enter).

    A box displaying the list of network directories pops open.
4. Move the highlight to TEXT_DOCUMENTS and press (Enter).

    A box similar to the one at the bottom of Figure 12-7 pops open, showing current information about the network directory TEXT_DOCUMENTS.
5. Move the highlight to the Default access rights line.

    The current rights are ALL, which means that, by default, each user can access any file in this directory with full privileges.
6. Press (Enter) to pop open the "Rights" box shown in Figure 12-8.
7. Move the highlight to READ and press (Enter).

    With the default access rights changed to READ, the "Rights" box closes.
8. Press (Esc) to close the Network Directory Information box.
9. Press (Alt)-(F10), followed by (Enter), to exit the menu system.

Securing the LAN

```
NetWare Lite NET Utility 1.1              Sunday  May 31, 1992  8:28 pm
              Logged in to the network as user SHOWME

     Main Menu      Supervise the Ne   Network Directory    Server
  Communicate with  Audit log          CDRIVE               JUANITA
  Display your user Error log          CDRIVE               MAXWELL
  Map drive letters Network directo    TEXT_DOCUMENTS       JUANITA
  Print             Network printer
  Set your password Server configur
  Supervise the net Server status
                    Server system f
                    Time synchroniz
                    User List

      Information for Network Directory TEXT_DOCUMENTS on Server JUANITA
  Actual directory path  (40 max):  C:\SALES\REPORTS
  Default access rights           :  ALL
  Users with nondefault rights    :  (Press Enter to see list)

F1-help  Esc-go back  Enter-select  ↑↓
```

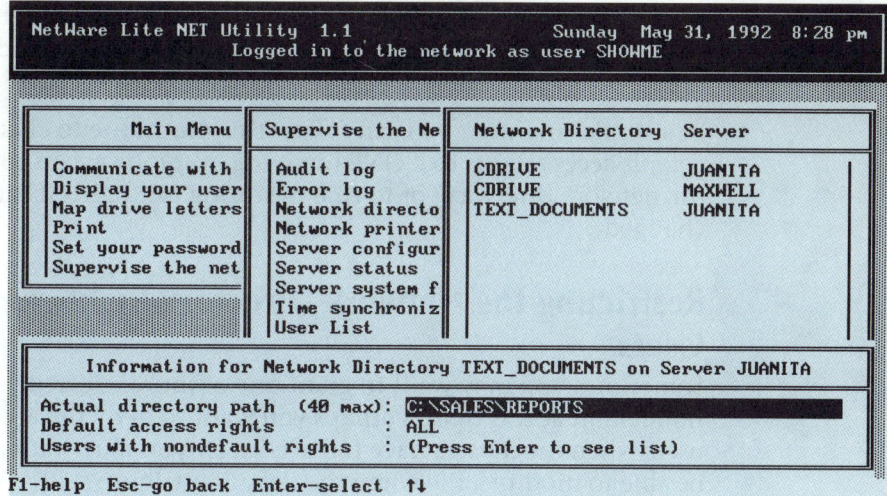

The Network Directory information box
Figure 12-7.

```
NetWare Lite NET Utility 1.1              Sunday  May 31, 1992  8:28 pm
              Logged in to the network as user SHOWME

     Main Menu      Supervise the Ne   Network Directory    Server
  Communicate with  Audit log          CDRIVE               JUANITA
  Display your user Error log          CDRIVE               MAXWELL
  Map drive letters Network directo    TEXT_DOCUMENTS       JUANITA
  Print             Network printer
  Set your password Server configur
  Supervise the net Server status
                    Server system f
                    Time synchroniz
                    User List            Rights

      Information for Network Directory TEX  ALL        Server JUANITA
  Actual directory path  (40 max):  C:\SALES NONE
  Default access rights           :  ALL     READ
  Users with nondefault rights    :  (Press Enter to see list)

F1-help  Esc-go back  Enter-select  ↑↓
```

The Rights box pops open
Figure 12-8.

With this modification, any user who maps a drive letter to the TEXT_DOCUMENTS network directory will be able to read the files in the directory but will not be able to edit and resave any files.

In a similar manner, you can follow this procedure to change the default access rights to NONE (denying everyone access to the files in the network directory) or to ALL (restoring full rights if the rights were changed).

Restricting the Network Directory Rights for Selected Users

Sometimes you may want to grant one or more selected users a nondefault access right. Perhaps you want to deny file access to a few users when most users have full access. Or you may want a few users to be able to modify a file when the default attribute is READ.

You can grant users selected rights, what NetWare Lite calls *nondefault* rights. Look again at Figure 12-7. The bottom option in the information box, Users with nondefault rights, is the one you use to grant selected rights. Here's how:

Activate the Information box screen for a selected network directory (follow Steps 1 through 4 in the preceding section). Move the highlight down to Users with nondefault rights and press [Enter] to see the list.

To specify special rights for a particular user, press [Ins]. NetWare Lite pops open a box that lists all the user accounts. Move the highlight to the desired account name and press [Enter]. A box pops open, displaying the three options (ALL, NONE, and READ). Select the option you want and press [Enter]. The selected user is now added to the list of users with nondefault rights. This list also displays the access right (ALL, NONE, or READ) granted to that user.

From this screen, you can also modify the nondefault rights granted to a particular user or delete the user from the list of users with nondefault rights. To modify the rights, move the highlight to the user name and press [Enter]. Then select the desired rights and press [Enter]. To delete the user from the list, move the highlight to the user name and press [Del]. A screen pops open asking to confirm that you really want to delete the user name. Select Yes and press [Enter].

Securing the LAN

When your nondefault rights are set correctly, press `Esc` to return to the screen displaying the Information for Network Directory. To exit the menu system, press `Esc`, `Alt`-`F10`, and then `Enter`.

Network Printer Rights

You can restrict access to the network printers in the same way you can restrict access to the network directories. For network printers, the only access rights are ALL and NONE. Access is either granted or denied.

The steps to restrict access to network printers parallel those used to restrict access to network directories. From the Supervise the Network menu (refer to Figure 12-6), move the highlight to `Network printers` and press `Enter`. A box pops open, listing the network printers.

When you move the highlight to the desired network printer and press `Enter`, the Information for Network Printer box pops open (see Figure 12-9). This example assumes a network printer named LASER on the server JUANITA.

The two options of interest here are `Default access rights` and `Users with nondefault rights`. Use the former to change the default

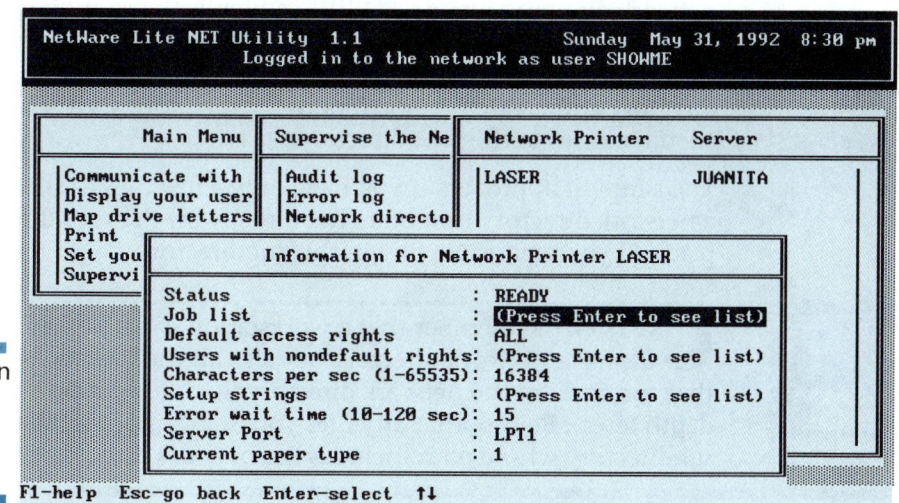

The Information for Network Printer box
Figure 12-9.

access right for all users, and the latter to set special rights for specific users.

You implement these options by using the same techniques you used to implement the options for network directories. Begin by moving the highlight to the desired option and pressing [Enter]. Then follow the same set of pop-open boxes you used for network directories.

Limiting the Scope of a Network Directory

Another type of security restriction is to limit the files a server makes available to the workstations on a LAN. You can do this by placing the files to be shared in specific network directories. Do not make your entire disk drive a network directory. If you do, you permit others to access any file on your hard disk. (As Chapter 7 explains, the scope of a network directory includes all the subdirectories in the path chain below the network directory.) You probably don't want others to have access to every file in your root directory.

Replacing CDRIVE with Your Network Directories

When you install NetWare Lite on a server (or on a node configured as a client and server), the installation program automatically creates a network directory named CDRIVE, which is the root directory on drive C. If you retain this network directory, you permit users to access any file on drive C. To better secure your files, delete the CDRIVE network directory and create your own network directories, which are subdirectories of the root directory.

The simplest approach, if you have only a few files to share, is to create a network directory that branches directly off the root directory and place all your shareable files in this subdirectory.

CAUTION: Remember that a workstation can access not only the files in a network directory but also all the files in subdirectories that spring from the network directory (including subdirectories to any depth level). Be sure that any files you do not want to share are not in a subdirectory whose path includes the network directory.

Securing the LAN

The following sequence of DOS commands makes drive C the current drive, makes the C drive's root directory the current directory, and then creates a subdirectory called GROUP (you can use another name if you like, of course). The complete path to this subdirectory is C:\GROUP. Type each command, pressing [Enter] after you type each one:

```
c:
cd\
md group
```

Now you can use the menu system to make GROUP a network directory. Place all the files you want to share in this directory.

Using Audit Logs and Error Logs

The fourth way to implement NetWare Lite security is to use an audit log and/or an error log. An *audit log* is a saved record of evidence that shows what users have done on the LAN. You can have NetWare Lite automatically track major LAN events such as users logging in and out, and can send your own messages to the audit log. An *error log* is a saved record of evidence that shows which errors have occurred on the LAN.

NetWare Lite's implementation of audit logs and error logs is relatively modest. The remainder of this chapter discusses both types of logs.

Audit Logs

You may want to keep an audit log for three main reasons:

- As part of security, you may want to know who has logged in to the network, and for how long.
- In some work environments, you may need to bill users for their LAN usage time.
- You want to monitor LAN activity in general, to get an idea of the workload of each server so that you can look for ways to improve LAN performance.

The audit log capability of NetWare Lite carries two costs you may not want to pay: disk space and performance degradation. The audit data has to be recorded somewhere, and NetWare Lite places the information on a disk file in the server's NWLITE directory. Depending on how active the LAN is, the amount of disk space used up can be substantial. One-quarter megabyte or more per day is not out of the question.

Recording all this data also puts an additional workload on the servers. Some users on larger NetWare Lite LANs report a noticeable slowdown in server performance when the audit log feature is enabled. If you decide to use an audit log, test carefully to determine whether you can tolerate the server disk space usage and performance loss that come along with it.

NetWare Lite keeps one audit trail for the entire LAN. The audit log feature can be turned on and off on a server-by-server basis, however. Each server can keep a separate copy of the audit log.

NOTE: Unfortunately, because NetWare Lite records only the most fundamental LAN events in the audit log, events such as users logging in and out, and servers going down, the NetWare Lite auditing feature is not as useful as it could be. The auditing feature would be more useful if events such as mapping network directories and unsuccessful log-in attempts were noted. Look for these features to be added in future releases of NetWare Lite.

Turning the Audit Log On and Off

To use the audit log features, you select the `Audit log` option on the "Supervise the Network" menu. Press [Enter] to pop open the "Audit Log" menu shown in Figure 12-10.

Here is a brief explanation of this menu's three options.

Display audit log   Displays the current audit log. You can scroll through the log by using the [Pg Up] and [Pg Dn] keys. When you finish viewing the log, press [Esc]. You then have the option of deleting the audit log file.

Save to a file   Permits you to save the audit log to a file on your hard disk. You can view or edit the file (a text file) later with any word processor or text editor. If you select this option, NetWare Lite prompts you to supply the path to the directory in which the file should be saved. The file is saved automatically with the name AUDIT.LOG.

Securing the LAN

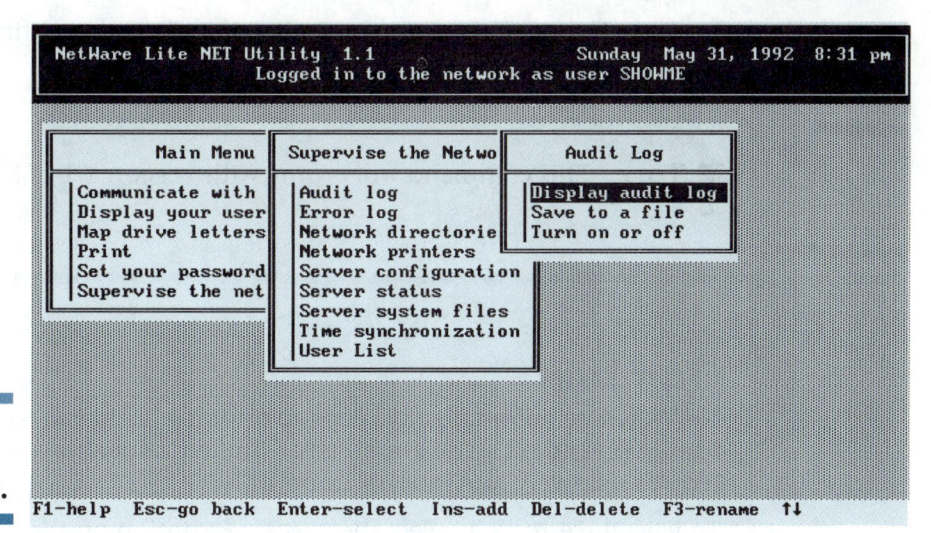

```
NetWare Lite NET Utility 1.1              Sunday  May 31, 1992  8:31 pm
              Logged in to the network as user SHOWME

        ┌──── Main Menu ────┐┌─ Supervise the Netwo ─┐┌──── Audit Log ────┐
        │ Communicate with  ││ Audit log             ││ Display audit log │
        │ Display your user ││ Error log             ││ Save to a file    │
        │ Map drive letters ││ Network directorie    ││ Turn on or off    │
        │ Print             ││ Network printers      │└───────────────────┘
        │ Set your password ││ Server configuration  │
        │ Supervise the net ││ Server status         │
        └───────────────────┘│ Server system files   │
                             │ Time synchronization  │
                             │ User List             │
                             └───────────────────────┘

  F1-help  Esc-go back  Enter-select  Ins-add  Del-delete  F3-rename  ↑↓
```

The Audit Log menu
Figure 12-10.

Turn on or off   Use this option to turn auditing on and off. Note that the status of auditing is maintained even when you shut down the network. If you don't turn auditing off before stopping work one day, auditing is still on when you bring the network back up the next day.

Writing a Message to the Audit Log

You can insert your own message into the audit log. To do so, you use the net audit command at the DOS prompt. The following command, for example, places in the audit log a message indicating that a tape backup was completed:

   net audit "Tape backup completed."

The text message must be enclosed in quotation marks and is limited to 80 characters. The date and time the message was sent are also written to the audit log. Auditing must be activated for this command to work.

Determining Whether Auditing is On or Off

You can determine whether auditing is on or off by typing the following command at the DOS prompt:

   net audit

NetWare Lite displays a message indicating whether auditing is currently on or off.

NOTE: This command works only with version 1.1 of NetWare Lite.

Error Logs

NetWare Lite automatically keeps an error log. (You cannot turn this feature on and off.) The error log has limited value, however, because it records relatively rare internal errors only.

To view the error log, select the `Error log` option on the "Supervise the Network" menu. The box that pops open gives you the options of displaying the error log or saving the error log to a file. These features work like their counterparts in the audit log.

Saving and Restoring a Server's System Files

NetWare Lite includes a built-in capability to back up and restore the system files on each server. The system files include a record of the network directories and network printers offered by the server as well as the server configuration information (such as buffer sizes and maximum number of connected clients).

With the current system files backed up, you can temporarily change the server's configuration and later restore the previous configuration. You can back up the system files, for example, and then change the server configuration by adding or deleting network directories. When you want to restore the server to the earlier configuration, you can do so with the backup.

Backing up and restoring system files provides a measure of security for your servers when configurations change frequently.

Securing the LAN

To back up a server's system files, follow these steps:

1. From the DOS prompt, type **net** and press [Enter] to activate the menu system.
2. Move the highlight to Supervise the network and press [Enter].
3. Move the highlight to Server system files and press [Enter].

    A box pops open, showing the servers connected to the network.

4. Move the highlight to the name of the server whose system files you want to back up, and press [Enter].

    A box labeled "System Files" pops open.

5. With the highlight on Back up, press [Enter].

    A box pops open, prompting you to supply the path to the directory where the backup copy is to be stored.

6. Type the path (not the file name). For example, type the path \NWLITE to save the files in the default NetWare Lite directory.
7. Press [Enter] to create the backup copy.

NetWare Lite saves the backup copy in the directory indicated by the path you specified. NetWare Lite creates a subdirectory with the name of the server to hold the backup files.

To restore a server's system files, start by following the first four steps you used to back up the "system files." When the System Files box pops open, move the highlight to Restore and press [Enter]. NetWare Lite prompts you to supply the path to the backup files. Type the path and press [Enter]. Then, to reinitialize the server's resources, you must reboot the server and restart the network.

CHAPTER

13 TROUBLE-SHOOTING

After a LAN is installed and working, it tends to continue working unless something obvious—like a cable accidentally ripped off a LAN card, or a user mistakenly deleting some critical files—causes a problem.

The problems mentioned in this chapter are not everyday occurrences. With a LAN, many things can go wrong—but most of the time, they don't. If you are moderately careful, everything mentioned in this chapter is either unlikely to happen or easily diagnosed and fixed.

Nevertheless, problems occasionally do occur. In many cases, an informative error message points you directly to the solution. Sometimes, however, the answer is not obvious and you must troubleshoot.

Troubleshooting is not an exact science—intuition is part of the mix. The more experience you have, the better your troubleshooting skills will be. You probably are a relative newcomer to networking and, therefore, your experience is necessarily limited. That's why this chapter discusses a methodology to troubleshooting as well as solutions to specific problems. By learning a general approach, you in effect increase your experience.

NOTE: You may think that if you have a specific problem, there must be a specific answer and you should be able to solve the problem straightforwardly. Often, of course, that is exactly the case. If the solution to a problem is not readily apparent, however, the more broad-based your troubleshooting approach is, the better are your chances of finding the answer. When troubleshooting, think "large scale" (in general terms).

If you have a problem this chapter does not solve, other resources are available. One source is the dealer who sold you NetWare Lite. If you purchased the product by mail order, however, or through someone who cannot provide assistance, don't hesitate to get help from a nearby Novell dealer. You will have to pay for the consultation, but remember that the dealers are professionals who should be able to get you up and running quickly.

Before the discussion gets into specifics, consider some general guidelines that apply to many potential problems.

Start with the Obvious

Some people assume that any problem has a tricky, hidden cause and cannot believe that something obvious would be the culprit. They assume that if the cause is obvious, they'll see it immediately. This reasoning is fallacious, a common trap. Failing to see the forest because

Troubleshooting

of all the trees is part of human nature. Check for simple, seemingly obvious things before you start tearing your computers and cables apart in search of obscure gremlins.

Check for Human Error

You shouldn't blame problems on the LAN hardware or NetWare Lite software until you rule out your own mistakes (or mistakes of your coworkers). Although software always has bugs and hardware can fail, the overwhelming majority of problems are caused by human error. Pressing the wrong key or misinterpreting an instruction is easy. Don't blame NetWare Lite when the real problem is that you specified the wrong LAN card during NetWare Lite installation, or you forgot to reboot your computer after running INSTALL, or you misspelled a parameter when you edited STARTNET.BAT.

Look First for the Most Obvious

A common joke on television comedies is about a do-it-yourselfer who works for hours to fix an appliance, only to discover that the power cord is not plugged into the wall socket. Many LAN problems have equally obvious causes. Here is a checklist of questions to ask:

- Is the computer plugged in? The monitor? The keyboard?
- Are all LAN cables firmly connected to the LAN cards?
- Do all LAN cables meet specifications? Is the maximum cable length exceeded?
- Are all the DOS and NetWare Lite files still on the hard disk? Has the NWLITE subdirectory been deleted?
- Does everything besides NetWare Lite work on the computer? Or is it just when you start the network that something goes wrong?
- Are you entering the appropriate commands in the proper sequence and are you spelling each command correctly?
- Did you overlook an onscreen error message when you powered on the machine or when you ran STARTNET to initialize the network?

♦ For thin Ethernet hardware, do you have terminators at the ends of the daisy chain of cables?

♦ For 10BASE-T, is the hub powered on?

♦ Is every computer running MS-DOS version 3.1 or higher (or DR DOS)?

To find out which DOS version is running on a PC, you can use the VER command in DOS. From the DOS prompt, type **ver** and press Enter.

Examine Recent Changes

If your LAN worked yesterday but doesn't work today, focus on determining whether any change or unusual event occurred in the interim. Something that was done during such a change or unusual event is the most likely cause of things working differently or not working at all. Become a detective and find out what anyone in the workgroup might have done. Here are some questions to consider:

Did someone move a PC from one location to another? This could damage the LAN cable or connection to the LAN card.

Did someone change or delete CONFIG.SYS? For NetWare Lite to work correctly, CONFIG.SYS must contain the right settings on both a server and a workstation. (INSTALL, the NetWare Lite installation program, creates or updates CONFIG.SYS for each computer. You shouldn't have any problems unless you modify CONFIG.SYS some time after installation.)

Did someone install new application software on a server or workstation? During the installation process, critical files may have been changed, replaced, or deleted. Sometimes the CONFIG.SYS file is modified without your knowledge. Another possibility is that the application software may not be compatible with NetWare Lite. Remember that "NetWare-compatible" generally refers to compatibility with NetWare 2.x and 3.x, not with NetWare Lite.

Did someone reformat the hard disk or wipe out a critical directory? Accidents can happen. Maybe someone inadvertently reformatted a hard disk (perhaps while trying to format a floppy disk). Or, in a similar

Troubleshooting

accident, maybe someone wiped out all the files in a directory (perhaps the \NWLITE directory). Such an accident can happen when you use the DOS wildcard characters (* and ?) while erasing selected files, for example.

Did someone modify the STARTNET.BAT file to "improve" it, "update" parameters, or eliminate "unnecessary" portions? Verify that the STARTNET.BAT file still runs the NetWare Lite programs in the proper sequence and uses the correct parameters.

Did someone install special software—such as a RAM disk, disk cache program, or TSR utility program? Some of these products are either incompatible with NetWare Lite or need to be installed in a particular way to coexist.

Did someone reconnect a cable that "fell off?" The cable may have fallen off because it was accidentally kicked and damaged.

Did someone run a "harmless" game or utility program borrowed from a friend or downloaded from a computer bulletin board? Such a program may have infected the LAN with a computer virus, which could destroy critical files or cause any number of other problems. See Chapter 11 for more information on computer viruses.

Did someone install a new expansion card in a computer that no longer works correctly? The card may use conflicting IRQs, I/O port base addresses, or memory addresses. The LAN card or cable may have been damaged during the installation of the new card. Or the cable to the hard drive or floppy drive may have been loosened or pulled off during installation of a new card. Another possible (but unlikely) problem is damage to the PC's chips and circuits because of excessive static electricity discharged from your fingers while you were working inside the computer.

The events just mentioned are only representative of the possible occurrences that may lead to LAN problems. Many other causes are also possible.

People often cannot recognize that a change may cause a seemingly unrelated LAN problem. Communication is important here. Encourage your workgroup members to tell you of *any* change since the last successful use of the LAN (or the PC, printer, or whatever is having problems). Stress that coworkers should inform you of any change, even one they feel *could not possibly* cause a problem. You may identify a cause-and-effect relationship that others miss. Although a failure sometimes occurs when nothing has changed—hard disks fail, memory chips go bad, and so on—many problems are the result of seemingly innocuous and unrelated actions and changes.

NOTE: As a troubleshooter, you must determine whether something changed recently and try to figure out how the change or new activity might cause a problem.

Look Up Error Messages

The NetWare Lite software displays specific error messages (called *status reports*) when certain problems and conditions are detected. (Some of these status-report messages are merely informative; they don't indicate error situations.)

When you see an error message, read it carefully and write it down. Note the status-report number displayed with the message. Then look for explanations in Appendix A (which lists these status reports in numerical order), in the Troubleshooting chapter of the NetWare Lite manual, or (for version 1.1 of NetWare Lite) in the README.TXT file. To avoid taking up too much space in the NetWare Lite software (which would cause NetWare Lite to use additional RAM), the messages are brief. The explanations in the manual, however, have much more information; they usually point you to the precise cause of the problem.

NOTE: If several error messages display in quick succession, pay special attention to the first one. Consider STARTNET, for example, which invokes several TSR programs (such as CLIENT.EXE and SERVER.EXE). If one of STARTNET's TSR programs detects an error, that program displays a message and ends. Because STARTNET is a batch file, STARTNET tries to run the subsequent programs, even though the earlier program did not run successfully. The later programs will undoubtedly display error messages, too. Those later error messages are not your concern, however; they occur only because the first program failed. When you see several error messages, concentrate on the first.

Also, you may get an error message produced by DOS. Examples of such messages are `Insufficient memory`, `Bad command or file name`, or `Bad or Missing Command Interpreter`. A DOS message, which may be caused by a problem with the NetWare Lite software or your LAN hardware, also may be caused by a problem that has nothing to do with your network. If you cannot find help in this chapter, consult your DOS manuals for additional information about the error message and potential causes.

Run INSTALL's Network Connection Verification

If you want to verify that your LAN hardware is properly connected and that NetWare Lite works, INSTALL is your best friend. (As you probably recall, you run INSTALL to install the NetWare Lite software.) Chapter 5 tells you how to run INSTALL's `Verify network connections` option and perform other fundamental tests. If the INSTALL verification shows that some of the computers are not communicating with others, look for a bad cable or terminator (for thin Ethernet) or a bad hub (for 10BASE-T), or a problem with the software setup for all the computers. If INSTALL indicates that one computer cannot communicate but the others can, look for a problem with that one computer's hardware or software.

Isolate the Problem

A LAN is harder to troubleshoot than a stand-alone computer for one simple reason: A LAN consists of many different computers and software components connected together. Because of the many components and connections, a problem can exist anywhere on the LAN's chain of hardware and software components. If a client cannot communicate with a server because of a hardware problem, the problem may be in the client PC, the client's LAN card, the server, the server's LAN card, or the cable connecting the client and server.

Similarly, a software problem may be in any of the software components on either computer: drivers, system software, application software, or parameters that you specify for any of the software. If any one piece of the hardware or software chain has a problem, communication doesn't work. The trick is to find that piece.

The basic troubleshooting technique is to isolate the problem. Divide and conquer. A number of simple techniques are helpful to track down problems. Unfortunately, you cannot always tell up front whether a problem is caused by hardware or software. Sometimes you have to try isolating both hardware and software problems. The following discussion presents appropriate isolation techniques.

Isolating Hardware Problems

Hardware failures may occur not only because of faulty equipment but also because components are not installed properly or adjustable configuration settings are not set to proper values. The two best approaches to pinning down hardware problems are part swapping and conflict elimination. These techniques are discussed in the following two sections.

Part Swapping

If one computer is not communicating with the others, swap (exchange) a cable connected to that computer with another cable. The other cable can be a spare unused cable or a cable you already are using in another part of the LAN. After the swap, determine whether the problem moved with the cable. If so, you've found the problem—the cable is bad. If not, the cable isn't the problem.

With thin Ethernet, one bad cable can prevent *all* computers from communicating. You need a spare cable to test for a bad cable. Swap the spare cable with one of your installed cables and then test your LAN with INSTALL's verification option. If the problem persists, swap a different cable and test again. If you replace every cable and the problem remains, your problem is not due to a bad cable (unless you have two bad cables).

If one computer cannot communicate, you can swap LAN cards between two computers to determine whether the problem follows the LAN card. If you have a spare terminator, replace each terminator, one

Troubleshooting

by one, to see whether the problem goes away. A bad or missing terminator, like a bad thin Ethernet cable, can prevent the *entire* LAN from communicating.

> **NOTE:** If possible, keep available one spare cable and, for thin Ethernet, one spare terminator and one spare BNC T-connector. These components are not expensive and can help you isolate problems quickly.

Conflict Elimination

If one computer won't work on the LAN, the problem may be a hardware conflict inside that computer. Remove all possible conflicting cards, such as a CD-ROM controller, a backup tape controller, a bus mouse, and every I/O card except the hard disk controller, floppy disk controller, and the LAN card. Test the computer with these cards removed. If the computer now works with the LAN, the problem is a conflict between the LAN card and one of the removed cards. Reinstall the removed cards one at a time, testing the LAN after each addition. When the problem returns, you know that the cause is a conflict with the card you just added. You can then try (either on the conflicting card or on the LAN card) a different IRQ, I/O port base address, or other setting, or get a replacement in the case of a faulty card.

Isolating Software Problems

A LAN that runs application programs has many more software components than hardware components. If a single computer won't work on the LAN, and you cannot isolate a hardware problem, the next step is to search for a software problem.

The best way to isolate a potential software problem is to start with the simplest possible software configuration and build it up until something fails. First, make a backup copy of your CONFIG.SYS, AUTOEXEC.BAT, and STARTNET.BAT files. (To make backups, you can copy the files to a floppy disk. Another way is to create, on the hard disk, a second version of each file. Give the second version a modified extension, such as .BAK or .OLD. You can use the COPY command in DOS to create backup copies. For example, the command

copy config.sys config.bak, for example, creates the file CONFIG.BAK as a backup to CONFIG.SYS.)

After creating the backups, modify AUTOEXEC.BAT as follows:

✦ Delete all statements except PROMPT and PATH statements.

✦ Modify the PROMPT statement to be PROMPT PG.

Now erase the CONFIG.SYS and STARTNET.BAT files. You can do so by using the ERASE command in DOS. Just type the following two commands, pressing Enter after each command:

    erase c:\config.sys
    erase c:\nwlite\startnet.bat

Reinstall NetWare Lite. Accept the option to add the NWLITE directory to the PATH in AUTOEXEC.BAT. Decline the options to add STARTNET.BAT to AUTOEXEC.BAT and to use the disk cache software (NLCACHE). Accept the default modifications to CONFIG.SYS. The installation process creates STARTNET.BAT.

Now reboot the computer and test the LAN. If your LAN works with this minimal configuration, you know that a problem existed with your original AUTOEXEC.BAT, CONFIG.SYS, or STARTNET.BAT files. To the new versions of these files, start adding—one by one—the statements you previously had in the original versions. Test the computer on the LAN after each change. Depending on the problem you are trying to solve, the test might be to run INSTALL's verification test, to run a software application that creates the problem, or both. When you run a test that won't work, you know that the cause of your problem is the statement you just added to one of the three files. After a test fails, try the test again to repeat the results and thereby verify that you have isolated the problem.

In general, if you run TSR utilities such as SideKick or ProKey, you should start them *after* you start the NetWare Lite software, not before. In other words, you should load any TSR after you run STARTNET.BAT.

Check whether you are using statements in your AUTOEXEC.BAT file to start the TSRs. If so—and if you run STARTNET after AUTOEXEC.BAT executes, or startnet is the last statement in your AUTOEXEC.BAT file—you are loading the TSRs before loading NetWare Lite.

Troubleshooting

This problem has two solutions. First, you can remove from AUTOEXEC.BAT the statements that load the TSRs. Then create a new batch file containing those statements. Now you can run the new batch file after running STARTNET.BAT. The second way is to copy the contents from your STARTNET.BAT file into AUTOEXEC.BAT. Be sure to add the STARTNET.BAT statements before the statements that start the TSR programs. If you invoked STARTNET.BAT from the AUTOEXEC.BAT file, remove the `startnet` line from the AUTOEXEC.BAT file. Now, whenever you boot your computer, the AUTOEXEC.BAT file will start the network and load TSRs in the proper order. For more information about batch files, including how to modify them, see Appendix C.

If you run Windows, see Chapter 15. If you run optimization utilities such as a disk cache (including NLCACHE*x* in NetWare Lite 1.1) or a memory manager such as QEMM or 386MAX, see Chapter 14. Any of these products, used incorrectly, can cause problems.

Specific Problems

If you follow the methods suggested so far, you should find the cause of most problems. You may run into some specific problems for which there are specific solutions, however. The remainder of this chapter discusses the most common specific problems.

Single Computer Lockup

A *locked-up computer* is an unresponsive computer. You can press keys until doomsday but you never get a response except maybe a beep. A lockup indicates some kind of internal error that prevents DOS from responding to your keystrokes. The only solution is to reboot the computer, either by using the three-key [Ctrl]-[Alt]-[Del] combination (which sometimes gets no response either), by pressing the hardware reset button (if your computer has one), or by powering off the computer, waiting a few seconds, and then powering it back on again. In any event, you lose any work you have done since you last saved your files.

A lockup has an assortment of colorful names, some of which are not acceptable in polite company. The acceptable names include a hung computer, a dead computer, a keyboard lockout, a system loop, and a system crash. Whatever you call it, a lockup is a pain you want to avoid.

Many types of internal conflicts can cause a lockup. Some lockups occur when you first run STARTNET. Others occur when you run an application program. The following sections focus on some things you should check if you have a lockup problem.

IRQ or I/O Port Base Address Conflicts

The conflict can be between the LAN card and the LAN software, or between the LAN card and another add-on card. Verify that the LAN card's jumper settings match the settings you specified during NetWare Lite's INSTALL process. For details on setting the jumpers and installing NetWare Lite, review Chapters 4 and 5. Although you are not likely to do so, be sure not to use an XT-type hard disk controller in an AT-type (286, 386, or 486) computer. The XT controller uses IRQ 5, whereas a disk controller on an AT is supposed to use IRQ 14. Some LAN cards use IRQ 5 as a default setting because IRQ 5 is usually available in an AT. Note that IRQ values above 7 do not even exist in XT computers. Table 13-1 shows possible IRQ conflicts. Table 13-2 shows possible I/O address conflicts. (Addresses are in hexadecimal notation.)

IRQ	AT (286 or higher)	XT
0	Internal timer	
1	Keyboard	
2	VGA/EGA video	VGA/EGA video
3	COM2, COM4	COM2, COM4
4	COM1, COM3	COM1, COM3
5	LPT2	Hard disk controller
6	Floppy disk controller	
7	LPT1	LPT1
8	Internal clock	
9		

Possible IRQ Conflicts
Table 13-1.

Troubleshooting

Possible IRQ Conflicts (continued) Table 13-1.

IRQ	AT (286 or higher)	XT
10		
11		
12		
13	Math coprocessor	
14	Hard disk controller	

Possible I/O Address Conflicts Table 13-2.

I/O Address(hex)	Device
200	Joystick, game controller
220	
240	
260	LPT2
280	LCD display (some portables)
2A0	
2C0	
2E0	COM4
300	COM2
320	Hard disk (XT)
340	
360	LPT1
378	LPT3
380	Bisynchronous interface
3A0	Bisynchronous interface
3BC	LPT1
3C0	EGA, CGA video
3E0	COM1, COM3, floppy disk controller

RAM Base Address Conflicts

Some LAN cards use a block of memory in the address range from 640K to 1024K. (This address range is often specified as hexadecimal segment addresses A000 to FFFF.) Other hardware and software can conflict with the LAN card's selected memory block. Possible problems come from expanded memory (EMS) hardware, memory-management programs such as QEMM and 386MAX, and VGA video cards in 16-bit mode while displaying certain graphics modes. Be sure that these products don't conflict with your LAN card. Specify to the memory-manager program that the LAN card's RAM address range is reserved. To verify whether the VGA card is the problem, put the VGA card in an 8-bit slot (and/or set a switch on the card to specify 8-bit mode).

Dealing with potential high-memory conflicts can be tricky. If you suspect such a problem, you may want to hire a consultant or contact a computer dealer for professional help. For some additional information on using NetWare Lite with high memory, see Chapter 14.

TSR Program Conflicts

TSR programs occupy memory. In most cases, a TSR waits for you to press a certain keystroke (or keystrokes) before it "pops up" and becomes active. Other TSRs are activated by internal computer events. Some TSRs are not compatible with NetWare Lite. In general, you should load TSR programs after you run STARTNET.BAT.

If you experience lockup (or other) problems, try running your network without loading any TSRs (other than the NetWare Lite TSRs that STARTNET.BAT loads). If your problem disappears, the cause is one of the non-NetWare Lite TSRs you are no longer loading. One at a time, load each TSR and run NetWare Lite until the problem reappears. In that way, you can isolate the TSR at fault. Contact the TSR's manufacturer or Novell to see whether there are known incompatibilities and ways for the TSR to coexist with NetWare Lite.

Sometimes a lockup occurs only because of a rare combination of events—several programs all do a certain unusual thing simultaneously. An environmental irregularity, although uncommon, might be the problem—overheating, static electricity buildup, power surges, for example. You might be able to reboot your computer and never see the problem again, but if the problem is frequent you need to find a solution.

Troubleshooting

Insufficient Memory

As you have seen, the NetWare Lite software consists of several TSR programs. As a result, with the network running, you have less RAM available on any PC than you have without the network. With the network loaded, application programs that fit in memory without the network may no longer fit. If you get the DOS error message `Insufficient memory`, the problem is likely to be that various TSR programs have taken up too much memory. For tips on conserving RAM with NetWare Lite, see Chapter 14.

Computer Viruses

If a computer virus wiped out critical DOS files or corrupted important system information on your hard disk, you may not even be able to boot your computer. Try to boot from a virus-free write-protected floppy disk and then run a virus-checking program. See Chapter 11 for more information about computer viruses.

Communication Breakdowns

Another type of problem is a computer that cannot communicate with other LAN computers. In some cases, none of the computers can communicate with each other. Sometimes this problem is consistent, other times it's intermittent. As discussed earlier in this chapter, your best tool for diagnosing connection problems is the verification test in INSTALL. Use the test to pin down the scope and consistency of the problem. You might look for one of the causes described in the following sections.

Computer Lockup Problems

The same things that can cause a lockup can cause an intermittent inability to communicate by one computer (or all computers if you set them all up the same). Check the troubleshooting advice in the "Single Computer Lockup" section earlier in this chapter.

Bad Cable

On a thin Ethernet LAN, one bad cable can prevent all computers from communicating. Substitute a good spare cable for each LAN cable in turn, as explained earlier in this chapter's "Isolating Hardware Problems" section. If any cables are exposed to view, the exposed area is the most likely location for damage. If you are handy with electronics, use an ohmmeter to test each cable for continuity and shorts.

Bad Connector

A bad connector is a variation on a bad cable. Sometimes a cable itself is fine, but the connector on the end of a cable is damaged. If the connector itself isn't damaged, the cable may have been pulled so hard that proper contact between the cable and connector is lost. Either install a new connector or replace the entire cable-connector combination. Another possibility is a bad BNC T-connector. Especially if you frequently pull hard on cables or disconnect and reconnect cables, the T-connector can become cracked or otherwise damaged. One by one, try replacing each T-connector with a spare to determine whether the problem goes away.

Nonstandard Cable Type or Length

Chapter 4 stressed the need for proper cables. For thin Ethernet, use RG58 A/U (the most readily available cable that meets specifications) or RG58 C/U. Do not use plain RG58 or RG58/U which, because they have slightly different electrical characteristics, may cause erratic problems or even damage to your LAN cards. Sometimes these nonstandard cables work in small configurations but fail when you either expand the LAN or begin using the LAN heavily. Don't take chances. Upgrade any nonstandard cable and use the same kind of cable (from the same manufacturer) throughout the LAN. Make sure that the total length of the cables does not exceed the 185-meter (607-foot) specification for thin Ethernet. For 10BASE-T, be sure each cable meets specifications and does not exceed the 100-meter (328-foot) length limit.

Environmental Hazards

Especially for 10BASE-T cable, be sure to avoid electrical interference from motors, power supplies, electromagnets, and light fixtures. Thin Ethernet is less susceptible to such hazards, but some installers claim that even a fluorescent light can sometimes cause problems.

Missing or Faulty Terminator

A missing or faulty terminator can prevent all or part of a thin Ethernet LAN from being able to communicate. Have spares on hand and check the terminators at both ends.

Bad LAN Card

If one computer cannot communicate but all others can, you may have a bad LAN card. Swap the card with another computer's LAN card and see whether the problem moves to the other computer. If so, either the LAN card is bad or its jumper settings are wrong (for both computers). If the problem stays with the computer, you probably have a hardware conflict (IRQ or other) or a bad card slot. Try moving the LAN card to another slot.

Bad Hub

For 10BASE-T, the hub/concentrator may be powered off, faulty, or configured incorrectly.

Corrupt Disk Files

Mysteriously damaged data files are a frustrating problem. In such a case, even though everything seems to work properly with your LAN, some of the disk files that you save or copy are corrupt. Data that seems to be successfully saved on disk is all gibberish or partly wrong when you later view or use it in an application program. Some possible causes for corrupt files are detailed here.

User Error

You may simply have made a mistake and not saved what you thought you saved. If the problem happens only once or extremely rarely, user error is the most likely cause. Try to reconstruct your exact steps to determine whether you entered a wrong command at some point.

Disk Cache Conflicts

A disk cache speeds up disk access by temporarily storing certain disk data in RAM. A computer can process data in RAM much faster than on disk. Although Version 1.1 of NetWare Lite comes with its own special disk cache programs, NetWare Lite will load its own disk cache only if you explicitly select the option to do so when you run INSTALL (or if you run NCLINST.EXE, a separate program that installs a NetWare Lite cache). Some third-party disk cache programs are either incompatible with NetWare Lite or require careful setup to work properly. See Chapter 14 for more information on disk caches.

Incompatible Application Software

If an application program is incompatible with NetWare Lite or any other network, the program may corrupt data files when two users run the program in the LAN environment. Make sure that your program is LAN compatible if two users may try to use the same file at the same time.

Failure To Use SHARE on a Server

The SHARE program in DOS prevents two users from simultaneously updating the same file on a server. You must run SHARE on a server to avoid file-corruption problems. (You don't need to run SHARE on a workstation, except that DOS 4 requires SHARE to support a hard disk over 32MB.) SHARE starts automatically when you run STARTNET, unless someone modified STARTNET.

CAUTION: Some people stop running SHARE on a server after encountering a `Share violation` error message. The message occurs when two people simultaneously access a file. Don't stop running SHARE! You must always run SHARE on any server. The only way to solve the SHARE violation problem safely is to use software designed for sharing files on a LAN or to set the attributes of shared files to read-only.

Using FASTOPEN

Some users (whether or not they are running NetWare Lite) report problems with the DOS FASTOPEN statement in CONFIG.SYS when running DOS 5.0. To be safe, remove FASTOPEN. See your DOS manual for details about FASTOPEN.

Troubleshooting

Failure To Bring Down the Server Gracefully

Don't just turn off a server's power. The server may be processing output data for a disk file. By powering off the server (or pressing a hardware reset button) you may prevent the server from leaving data files in good condition. Instead, make sure that no clients are actively using the server. Then press Ctrl-Alt-Del. When the NetWare Lite Server Shut Down box appears, press 1 to disable the server software. Then you can power off the server computer.

Power Problems

If your server or client occasionally loses power, two bad things can happen. First—because a power failure does not bring down the server gracefully—you can corrupt disk files. Second—your LAN card or other computer components can be damaged by the power surges and spikes that often accompany power failures. Use a surge protector as minimum protection. If you have frequent power failures, consider using a *UPS* (uninterruptible power supply) system.

Computer Lockup Problems

The same causes that lead to computer lockups can also cause corrupt disk files. To troubleshoot this problem, read the "Single Computer Lockup" section earlier in this chapter.

Other Problems

Other LAN problems usually are more localized than the problems already covered. Local problems may involve the inability of a certain client to access a certain server, for example, or they may be problems linked to printing output under certain circumstances, or many other specific things.

NOTE: If your problem is accompanied by a Status Report message, by far the number one tip for solving the problem is to read the message explanation in Appendix A and in the NetWare Lite manual's Troubleshooting chapter. For version 1.1, the README.TXT file in your NWLITE directory documents additional Status Reports.

UPS Systems

Chapter 3 briefly mentioned the advantages of using a UPS system if your office is susceptible to power failures or your applications are especially critical. The following paragraphs explain UPS systems and tell you where to obtain additional information.

Many varieties of UPS systems are on the market. A common kind, called a *switching UPS*, works as follows. You connect the computer's power cord to the UPS system, and the UPS system to the commercial power source. The commercial power passes through the UPS. Under normal circumstances, the UPS draws a little power to recharge its own internal batteries but most of the power passes through to the computer. If the UPS system detects a power loss or brownout, it provides power from its batteries so that the computer is unaffected by the power problem. Inexpensive UPS systems can sustain a computer for between 5 and 30 minutes. Thus, if the power outage is short, you can continue using your computers without interruption. If you become aware of the problem while the UPS system is providing emergency power, you have the opportunity to save your files, make backups, and bring down the server gracefully.

Some UPS models have a cable that connects to a computer's serial port to send a signal when commercial power fails. To take advantage of this feature, the computer's software must know how to process the signal—by sending warning messages to client computers, for example, or automatically shutting down a server. Because NetWare Lite does not yet have this capability, you have to take actions yourself.

Prices for low-capacity UPS systems (to support from one to five typical PCs) range from $200 to $1,000. Such UPS systems are available from several manufacturers, including the following:

- American Power Conversion of West Kingston, Rhode Island
- PARA Systems of Carrollton, Texas
- SOLA Electric of Elk Grove, Illinois
- Tripp Lite of Chicago, Illinois

Troubleshooting

The following sections describe some common problems and solutions.

An Application Program Does Not Work

Review the program's documentation for information about installing the program in a LAN environment. Follow the directions for a "Peer-to-peer LAN," a "PC LAN," or "Other network"—*not* for a "NetWare LAN" or "Novell LAN." (Remember—NetWare Lite is not NetWare.) If the documentation has no such instructions, the program may not work on a LAN. Call the manufacturer to find out. You may have to buy a special LAN version of the product. If the product requires NetBIOS to run, you need to run Lite's NETBIOS program after you run STARTNET. If the application doesn't run with NetWare Lite, but does work when the network is not installed, the problem may be caused by NetWare Lite's TSRs needing some of the computer's RAM. The application may not have enough RAM available. See Chapter 14 for information on making more RAM available to application programs.

Only Four Users Can Access a Server Simultaneously

By default, no more than four users can access a server simultaneously. If you need to have more than this default maximum, log into the network as SUPERVISOR and run NET. Select `Supervise the Network` from the Main menu and then select `Server configuration` for that server. Change the `Connections` number from four to whatever you need. Because a larger number uses additional RAM on the server, arbitrarily setting a large number is not without penalty. For more about optimizing server configurations, see Chapter 14.

A Client Cannot Access a Server's Resources

Be sure that the computer you think is a server is running SERVER.EXE, NetWare Lite's TSR program for each server. Check that the server's STARTNET.BAT file contains a line to load SERVER.EXE.

A Client Can Access the Server's Hard Disk but Not its Local Drive C

Don't map the client's drive C to a server's network directory. If you do, you are instructing NetWare Lite that drive C refers to the server's hard disk, not to the client's disk. Pick another letter (such as G or L) that doesn't correspond to one of the client's own hard disks.

A Sharing Violation Occurs When You Try To Run a Program on a Server

Use the ATTRIB command in DOS to set all the server's shared executable files to "read-only" status. Executable files are files with a filename extension of EXE, COM, BAT, and OVL.

Sometimes Clients Cannot Access Server Disk Files

Increase the number of FILES specified in the server's CONFIG.SYS file. Also try increasing the values for the /f and /l parameters for the SHARE program (on the server). SHARE may be started in CONFIG.SYS, AUTOEXEC.BAT, or STARTNET.BAT; look at these three files in the sequence shown here and modify the /f and /l parameters on the first case of SHARE you find.

Unacceptably Slow Server Response

You may find that your LAN works correctly, except that one or more servers are very slow when responding to clients' requests to share data or other resources. Chapter 14 presents several techniques to improve server performance.

Unacceptably Slow Printing

Occasionally, when sending output to a network printer, you may find that your print job takes an interminable time to complete. If printing is slow on your LAN, see Chapter 14 for tips on improving printer performance.

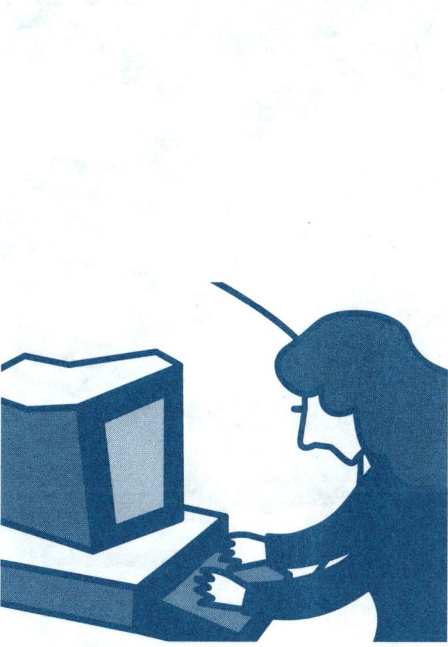

CHAPTER

14 OPTIMIZING LAN PERFORMANCE

Making NetWare Lite run is one thing; making it run well is another. In a LAN environment, optimization refers to improving the performance of the LAN. Generally, optimization efforts focus on accomplishing one or more of the following objectives:

- Realizing faster response time when a workstation interacts with a server
- Increasing the overall throughput on the LAN, which means that the entire group processes more work in a given time period, even if any one individual's response time is slower
- Increasing the amount of RAM available for applications that run on servers or clients (in other words, reducing the amount of RAM used by the NetWare Lite operating system components)
- Increasing the amount of available disk space on servers or clients

Determining What To Optimize

When considering how to optimize a LAN or improve server performance, most people think of gaining faster response time. An effort that results in better use of *any* resource is a form of optimization, however. Because many people think of time as the most valuable resource, speed usually is the focus of optimization efforts. In some environments, however, an improvement that keeps you from having to add another big, expensive hard disk to a server might be even more important than improving response time. For reasons like these, different observers can look at the same two LANs and draw different conclusions about which LAN runs better.

This chapter examines a number of optimization topics and provides recommendations for improving the performance of your LAN. You must judge which improvements mean the most in your environment. An improvement in one area often comes at a cost in another area. In particular, you often can gain speed by using more of a server's RAM. Whether such a trade-off is worthwhile is something you must decide for yourself.

Optimization Methodology

If you are an amateur scientist at heart, optimization will appeal to you. Optimization consists of a series of experiments. You measure how well your LAN runs, make a modification, and then measure again. If the measurements show that the modification improved performance, you make the modification permanent. If not, you step back and try again.

Optimization by Any Other Name

In addition to the term "optimization," other terms often are used to describe the improvement of LAN performance. These terms include system tuning, network tuning, performance analysis, performance tuning, resource optimization, and response time improvement. Some people just call it tweaking the LAN.

Benchmark Tests

To run optimization experiments, you need some way to measure how well your LAN runs. To measure speed, the classic method is to run benchmark tests. A *benchmark test* is a controlled, repeatable chunk of work you can measure to compare results. You may run a benchmark program and time how long it takes to complete, for example. You then make a LAN modification and rerun the benchmark program to compare completion times.

Most benchmarks are measured either in terms of time (answering the question, "How long did the benchmark take?") or else in the amount of work performed per some time unit ("How many bytes of data were transferred per second?" or "How many responses occurred per minute?").

To know whether your optimization efforts are working, you need to have some sort of benchmark test. Having several benchmarks is even better if you want to see whether your modifications improve only some kinds of work but not others.

Benchmarks are available from many sources. Utility software products, such as the Norton Utilities and PC Tools, include benchmark programs. Popular computer magazines, such as *PC Magazine* and *Byte*, construct benchmark workloads for their comparative tests. You can obtain these benchmarks and use them if you like. A set of benchmark tests is sometimes called a *benchmark suite*.

The best benchmark for you, however, is one that reflects your particular workload. If your workgroup uses Paradox databases heavily, for example, you should not test with a benchmark that runs dBASE IV because the results may not apply to your situation. If you find a Paradox benchmark, verify that the benchmark uses Paradox the same way you do. Maybe the benchmark includes equal amounts of database reads and database writes, whereas your workgroup performs database reads 98 percent of the time.

> **NOTE:** Although no benchmark is a perfect representation of your real workload, you should try to use a relatively simple set of tests that at least roughly approximates the work your group does most. If, for example, people mainly use your server's shared disk to copy files (using the DOS COPY command) between their hard disks and the shared disk, a good benchmark for your LAN would have many COPY commands similar to those used on the LAN. Without such COPY commands, your benchmark is not appropriate.

One concern with running a benchmark test on a LAN is that a real-world LAN has many things going on simultaneously. Your LAN may have eight computers connected, with all eight sometimes active and doing different things. Setting up a test that runs eight things at once can be difficult. A few possible benchmarks are suggested here, but you may find the suggestions too complex, too simple, or too artificial for your needs. In most cases, well-selected benchmarks are valuable in optimization efforts. Just be aware of their limitations.

Possible Benchmarks

Benchmark programs and the real work people do on a LAN fall into two broad categories—the transfer of large and small blocks of data.

Transfers of large data blocks Programs that read or write entire files of data at one time transfer large blocks of data across the LAN. Examples are the DOS COPY and XCOPY commands for medium or large files, file-management programs that copy files, and startup programs that reside on a shared hard disk.

Transfers of small data blocks Some programs and DOS commands send only small chunks of data across the LAN at one time. Examples

Optimizing LAN Performance

are most random reads and writes by database programs, the DOS DIR command on a server's disk, and the DOS COPY command for very small files.

Any single benchmark test you choose probably will transfer either large or small data blocks almost exclusively. Many of the optimization changes you make will improve performance for one type of processing but not the other. If your real workload consists of both types of work, use both types of benchmarks. If your workload is primarily one of the two types, use benchmarks of that type.

Large Block Benchmarks

Here are a few suggestions for benchmark tests you can run to test the speed of large data block transfers:

+ Execute a series of DOS COPY or XCOPY commands that copy large files from a workstation to a server and vice versa

+ Start up a large application program that resides on a server's hard disk, such as WordPerfect, Microsoft Word, Lotus 1-2-3, dBASE (any version), or Paradox

+ Run an artificial benchmark program, such as the Norton Utilities SYSINFO program, that reads and writes data from hard disk files and times the results

Small Block Benchmarks

Benchmarks that test transfers of small data blocks are more difficult to construct and measure. Here are some possibilities:

+ A word processing spell-check in which the dictionary file is on the server's shared disk

+ A batch file that executes a series of DOS COPY commands of very small files (no more than 2,000 bytes each—most of them smaller) to and from a server

+ A database program that searches and updates a known database file (that you restore before each test) using a fixed script of commands

+ An artificial benchmark program that transfers small blocks of data

Benchmark Tips

Here are some general tips and guidelines to follow whenever you run benchmarks. If you overlook these methods, your results may be false or misleading.

Make Sure Your Results Are Repeatable

Run your tests only on a LAN that no one else is using at the time. Otherwise, your results will vary depending on what other users happen to be doing during your tests. Do not use tests that rely on humans at each keyboard to "enter commands as usual" to simulate a real workload. People will not do the same thing each time (and will judge the LAN's responsiveness inconsistently) and your results will be worthless. Run each test at least twice, to be sure the times are consistent. If the times vary, either your benchmark has a problem or some variable factor is at work. If the benchmark consists of copying or querying files, make sure that the files are identical before each test. Be aware of the varying results you can get because of disk fragmentation (discussed later in this chapter).

Run Tests that Last Long Enough To Overcome Measurement Errors

Do not use a stopwatch to time a DOS COPY command that takes less than three seconds. Your reaction time can vary so much that you will not be able to tell whether two measurements of, say, 1.5 seconds and 1.8 seconds are really different. Be sure that any timed test runs at least five seconds, and preferably more than ten seconds. If you use the computer's standard internal clock, be aware that because its resolution is .0549255 seconds (about 18.2 timer clicks per second), you should assume only one decimal place of accuracy, even if two are displayed.

Avoid Tests that May Become Boring

If you run a database inquiry test that takes 15 or 20 minutes, you may get bored after a few runs (or even after one). If you do get bored, you will not monitor the test as carefully as you would a shorter test and you will be less likely to run a large number of tests to investigate various optimization changes. Keep each test under five minutes. Two minutes is better, depending on your attention span. After you make

Optimizing LAN Performance

optimization changes, of course, a two minute test may take only one minute.

Carefully Record All Your Results

Do not rely on your memory. Write down the timing (or other) results of each test, along with the optimization changes you made. Record the specific values you used for each parameter you tested. These results are useful not only to see which changes work best today, but also to compare with future tests.

Optimizing for Speed

Speed is what computers are all about. The primary reason computers are useful is that you can do certain things faster with computers than you can without them. To achieve better LAN performance, the classic improvement is to speed up response time on a server many users access simultaneously.

The fundamental type of LAN modification that does the most good is to put some data in RAM instead of on disk. A computer can access data in RAM much faster than on even the fastest disk.

You can try a dizzying array of things to improve the speed with which your server responds, including the following:

- Use a disk cache, such as one of the NLCACHEx programs that come with version 1.1 of NetWare Lite.
- Alter the number and size of buffers your servers use to hold data in RAM.
- Use the DEDICATE.COM program to temporarily configure your servers as dedicated servers.
- Optimize your hard disks for faster response.
- Upgrade your hardware with more RAM or faster adapter cards, processors, and disk drives.

This chapter covers each of these alternatives in detail. If your LAN isn't running fast enough to suit you, don't despair. This chapter lists many ways you can try to improve performance.

NOTE: Keep in mind that no single change or set of changes works best for everyone. Every LAN is different—the hardware, the software, and the workload all vary. Therefore, you have to test changes in your LAN environment to see what works best for you.

Disk Cache

In most NetWare Lite configurations, the best way to improve server performance is clear-cut: use a disk cache. A *disk cache* (pronounced like cash) is a piece of software that acts as an interface between DOS and your hard disk. The cache software sets up and manages an area of your RAM where disk data is stored, whether the data is being read from disk or written to disk. A disk cache improves your computer's speed in accessing disk data, for the following two main reasons:

1. Your computer can transfer large chunks of data to or from the disk instead of making many more transfers of smaller chunks.

   Because a great deal of overhead time is associated with each transfer, reducing the number of them improves performance.

2. When your program accesses data, the next data you need is probably close to the last data you accessed.

By putting a large amount of adjacent disk data in RAM, your computer frequently can avoid having to search the disk drive for requested data. The data is quickly accessible in RAM instead.

NOTE: If you want to improve the speed of server performance, the first optimization change you should try is to use a disk cache program.

Disk cache programs are complicated to create, especially for use with LAN software. Beginning with version 1.1 of NetWare Lite, Novell provides three disk cache programs: NLCACHEC.EXE, NLCACHEM.EXE, and NLCACHEX.EXE. As is explained later in this chapter, the memory configuration of your server determines which of these programs you use.

Optimizing LAN Performance

The NLCACHEx programs, developed specifically for use with NetWare Lite, are provided with NetWare Lite at no extra cost. When you run INSTALL, the installation program places the cache programs on your hard disk. The INSTALL procedure does *not*, however, automatically add to STARTNET.BAT the statements that activate the disk cache. You may have to add a statement to STARTNET.BAT yourself, as explained shortly. You can run one of these cache programs on a workstation, but the critical LAN benefit comes from running a disk cache on a server.

Because a disk cache program uses your computer's RAM to store disk data, you need to be clear on the different types of RAM in a computer. If you don't understand clearly the differences between conventional, expanded, extended, and XMS memory, the next section should help.

Different Types of Memory

To run a disk cache (and use other optimization techniques), you need to know how much and what kind of memory your computer has. Although an explanation of different memory types can be confusing, here's a simplified tutorial. (For more information, consult your DOS documentation or a book about computer memory, such as *Managing Memory with DOS 5* by Dan Gookin, published by Microsoft Press.)

To begin with, the type of memory under discussion is random-access memory, usually called *RAM*. RAM, which is inside the system unit of a PC, is made up of a series of integrated circuit chips. The information in RAM stays there as long as the computer's power stays on (and you don't reboot the machine). Turning off the computer causes the loss of any data stored in RAM. Before turning off your computer, be sure to save on disk any of the information (stored in RAM) you will need later.

The original IBM PC had only one kind of RAM—what is now called *conventional memory*. As Figure 14-1 shows, conventional memory is the first 640K of RAM. All PCs have conventional memory, usually at least 512K and most often the maximum possible 640K. Most application programs are designed to use only conventional memory. (The most recent versions of major application packages, especially database programs, often are designed to use memory other than conventional, as well as conventional memory.)

As the 640K memory barrier became limiting for newer and ever more grandiose software, manufacturers invented expanded memory.

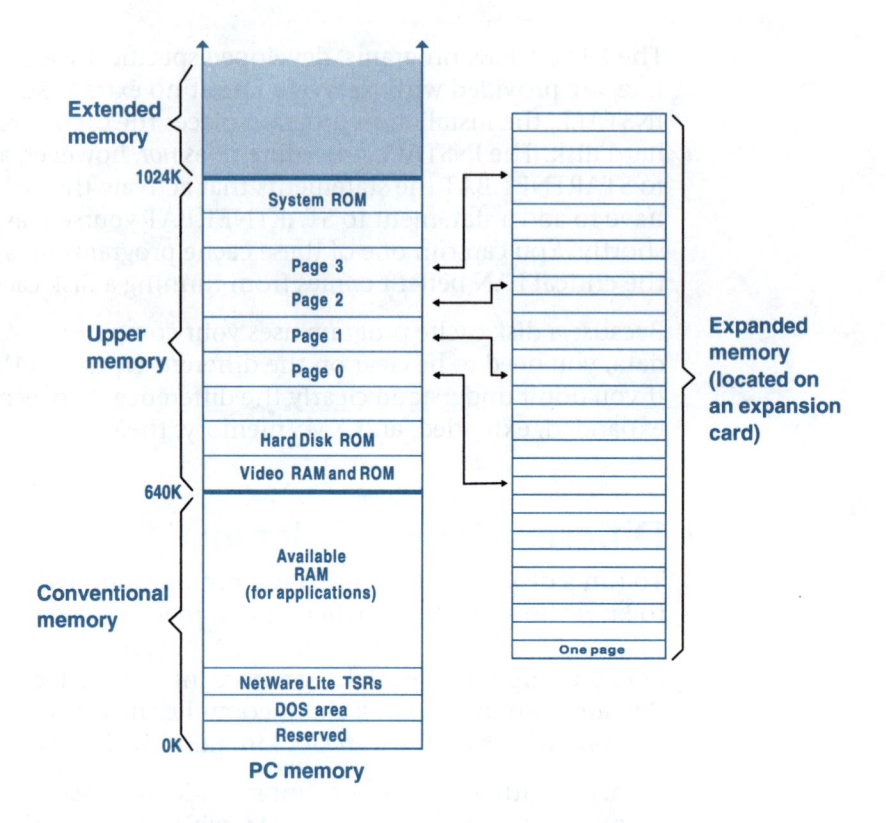

Types of PC Memory
Figure 14-1.

Expanded memory requires a special expanded memory card in your computer, with RAM chips installed on the card, as well as some software (called an expanded memory manager). As you can see from Figure 14-1, expanded memory uses a tricky scheme to flip-flop 16K chunks of memory (called *pages*) back and forth between the expanded memory card and part of a special memory area—between the 640K and 1024K marks—called the *upper memory* area. Normally the upper memory area is reserved for RAM and ROM (read-only memory) used by hardware devices (such as the computer's video and hard disk). Expanded memory represents the first type of extra memory available. It is still used on many computers and by many software products. Expanded memory is often abbreviated as EMS (expanded memory specification) or, because it was developed jointly by Lotus, Intel, and Microsoft, as LIM EMS.

Optimizing LAN Performance

A newer type of extra RAM, called *extended memory*, exists only on computers that use the 80286, 386, or 486 processors. As Figure 14-1 shows, extended memory references address locations above the 1024K mark. Many of these computers come with one, two, or four megabytes of memory. A one-megabyte (1024K) machine is typically configured as 640K of conventional memory and 384K of memory, starting at address locations above the 1024K mark. To use extended memory, a software application requires a special memory program called an extended memory manager.

> **NOTE:** On 386 and 486 computers equipped with extended memory, you can simulate expanded memory without having to use an expanded memory card. Special software known as an expanded memory emulator can make the extended memory act as though it were expanded memory.

Several standards exist for extended memory manager programs. The dominant standard is known as XMS (extended memory specification). Extended memory accessed by using XMS standard software is called *XMS memory*. DOS 5 includes a program, HIMEM.SYS, that conforms to the XMS standard. (A similar program in DOS 4 is XMAEM.SYS.)

To use a software application that requires extended memory, you must include in your CONFIG.SYS file a DEVICE statement that loads the extended memory manager when you boot the computer. The extended memory manager uses a small amount of the computer's conventional memory and makes the extra memory (XMS or expanded) available. The following is an example of a DEVICE statement in CONFIG.SYS:

```
device=c:\dos\himem.sys
```

(CONFIG.SYS is a text file you can modify with any text editor or word processor. For instructions on using EDIT to modify text files, see Appendix C.)

That completes a whirlwind explanation of the different types of memory. The important point is that your PC has conventional memory (0 to 640K), upper memory (640K to 1024K) and may have three other kinds of memory: expanded (EMS), extended without XMS, and extended with XMS.

Because NetWare Lite includes three disk cache programs, the cache you pick is determined by the type of memory in your machine. You may have to check with your computer vendor to find out how your machine's memory is configured. If you view your CONFIG.SYS file, however, and note the DEVICE statements (some of which have nothing to do with extra memory), you probably can figure out your memory configuration. See your DOS manual for an explanation of each DEVICE statement pertaining to memory management. For another clue to your memory configuration, watch the screen display when you boot the computer. Normally, you will see messages indicating how much expanded, extended, or XMS memory has been set aside in your computer. Another approach is to use a system information program such as SI or SYSINFO, available with PC Tools and Norton Utilities, respectively. These programs examine your machine's memory and display how much of each memory type you have. The NLCINST program, covered next, also shows how much memory of each type you have available.

Preparing To Run NLCACHE

The INSTALL program (which installs NetWare Lite) puts all three NLCACHE programs in your NWLITE directory but does not automatically put commands in STARTNET.BAT or other control files to start running the disk cache. Your three choices for starting the disk cache are described next.

Use the INSTALL option During the INSTALL process, you can specify that you want to install the disk cache. The default choice is Yes if your computer has at least 2MB of extra RAM (extended or expanded). You can see and modify this choice if you specify Yes when the INSTALL programs asks whether you want to preview changes to DOS system files.

Run the NLCINST program This is the easiest choice if you didn't use INSTALL to set up the disk cache. The NLCINST program, which is explained shortly, installs the disk cache. Even if you did use INSTALL to set up the cache, you can later use NLCINST to verify or change cache settings.

Enter your own startup instructions   This is the manual approach, which is not recommended because of the likelihood of errors caused by your not understanding the proper commands or by typing mistakes.

Using NLCINST To Install the Disk Cache

NetWare Lite includes a program called NLCINST (for "NetWare Lite cache installation") designed to simplify the process of starting the disk cache on your computer.

There are several ways to start the disk cache. You can modify any of three files: STARTNET.BAT, AUTOEXEC.BAT, or CONFIG.SYS. Most people choose to modify STARTNET.BAT, because doing so results in the disk cache running when you start the NetWare Lite software. Should you want to start the cache even when not running NetWare Lite, however, modify AUTOEXEC.BAT; the cache will start whenever you boot your computer. The option of using CONFIG.SYS to install the cache is usually not the best choice. CONFIG.SYS automatically loads the cache every time you boot your computer and you cannot remove the disk cache (to recover needed RAM) during a work session. If you use CONFIG.SYS, you install the cache as a special kind of software called a device driver, which you can remove from RAM only by removing the NLCACHE statement from CONFIG.SYS and then rebooting.

NOTE: For information about modifying AUTOEXEC.BAT, STARTNET.BAT, and other batch files, see Appendix C.

To run the NLCINST program, type **nlcinst** and press Enter. The program displays menus and lets you choose which of the NLCACHE programs you want, which parameters you may want to change, and into which control file the startup statement should go.

> **NOTE:** The file CACHE.TXT in your \NWLITE directory explains the NLCINST program options and contains general information about the NetWare Lite disk cache.

Select one of the following disk cache programs according to the type of memory available in your PC:

- ◆ NLCACHEC.EXE (Conventional memory)
- ◆ NLCACHEM.EXE (Expanded, EMS memory)
- ◆ NLCACHEX.EXE (Extended, XMS memory)

You can use only one of the programs at a time. Each of the three cache programs uses at least some conventional memory, even when the cache area is in expanded or extended memory. Be sure that you can spare the amount of conventional memory used. If you run large application programs on the server, you may have insufficient RAM if you try to run a cache program. See the "Optimizing the Use of RAM" section later in this chapter for details.

Using NLCACHE

You can use one of the NLCACHE programs whether or not you run NetWare Lite. There is no need to run STARTNET first. You can start the cache program before or after you start the Lite software.

The most important factor in determining how much benefit you derive from NLCACHE is the cache size. If your computer has at least 1MB (1024K) of free memory (extended or expanded) when you run INSTALL, the default value is Yes for the `Use NLCACHE and load it from STARTNET.BAT` option. INSTALL sets up a cache half the size of the free memory. If you have 3MB of free extended memory, for example, INSTALL inserts in your STARTNET.BAT file a statement that starts a 1500K cache using NLCACHEX.

As the preceding section explained, you can use NLCINST to set up your disk cache. NLCINST displays the amount of free memory

Optimizing LAN Performance

available for the memory type you specify. You can then choose to use any amount of available memory for the cache—from all the free memory down to any smaller amount.

> **CAUTION:** If you use NLCINST to set up a cache in conventional memory, the type of server makes a difference. For a server that also acts as a workstation, be sure not to use all the available memory for the cache. You need to leave some conventional memory to run your application programs. Keep at least 256K of conventional memory available (more if required by your application programs). For a dedicated server, however, you can use all the available conventional memory for a disk cache.

Instead of using NLCINST, you can simply enter the NLCACHE command from the DOS prompt. For example, if you want to start an extended memory cache of 512K, type **nlcachex 512** and press Enter.

Experiment with different cache sizes to see which size produces the best performance in your LAN environment. Give NLCACHE all the RAM you can spare. At least half a megabyte (512K) is a good size, and one or two megabytes (1024K or 2048K) is even better, especially on a busy LAN.

Another option is to buy additional memory. For most computers, you can purchase RAM chips for less than $50 per megabyte—a good investment to improve performance when you use the memory for a disk cache. If you have never installed memory, keep in mind that installation can be tricky. Get professional help to avoid problems.

How NLCACHE Disk Caching Works

When your application software writes data on a server disk controlled by NLCACHE, the data is not necessarily transferred immediately to the disk. By default, the deferred write delay (sometimes called *write caching*) feature of NLCACHE delays for two seconds the physical data transfer to disk. This delay in writing data to disk gives you another reason to power down (or reboot) a network node gracefully. If you simply turn off your computer's power, the data in the cache may not yet have been written out to disk and will be lost. You have three options: wait until the data is written to your hard disk, use NLCINST to set deferred write delay to zero (which disables delayed writes), or enter any one of the following commands to tell NLCACHEX (or whichever version you use) to write its data to disk:

```
nlcachex +
nlcachex –
nlcachex /q
```

To shut down a server, you can instead press Ctrl-Alt-Del and then press **1** or **2** (or Ctrl-Alt-Del again).

One more NLCACHE capability is important to note. While NLCACHEX (or NLCACHEM or NLCACHEC) is running, type **nlcachex** and press Enter to check periodically the cache performance. The program responds by displaying how much disk I/O has been saved with your use of the cache program. This information gives you an idea of how effective the cache is in your environment. If you see that you typically avoid 80 percent of your disk reads and 30 percent of your writes, you know that you are avoiding a great many slow disk accesses. By varying the size of the disk cache and running benchmarks after each variation, you can check these statistics to determine whether increasing the cache size significantly reduces the physical I/O performed.

Other Disk Caches

In addition to NLCACHE, other third-party disk cache products are available. As a rule, you should use NLCACHE because of its tight integration with NetWare Lite. You may prefer to use another disk cache product with which you are already familiar, however.

Most other disk cache products that support write caching will work reliably only if you disable the write-caching feature. Find out what parameter disables write caching before you use another disk cache. If you try write caching, test it very carefully. Sometimes failures occur only under a heavy I/O load.

Of the independent disk cache products on the market, Super PC-Kwik from Multisoft Corporation in Beaverton, Oregon, seems to have the largest body of satisfied users.

A disk cache program called SMARTDRV.SYS comes with DOS 5 (and other recent versions of MS-DOS) and Windows, but users report that its performance improvement generally does not match that of other disk cache products. Utility products such as Norton Utilities and PC Tools are another source of disk cache programs. Be sure not to use write caching with any of these products unless you verify in advance that write caching is compatible with NetWare Lite.

Some hard disks have a built-in disk cache in the hardware, either in the disk drive circuitry or the disk controller card. These disk drives and controllers provide some of the benefits of a software disk cache without any of the complexity caused by installation or setting parameters. But because most hardware disk caches are smaller than the RAM you would make available with a software disk cache, less data can reside in the cache at one time and performance improves less.

Tips on Using Disk Caches

When you use NLCACHE (or most other disk cache programs), you should lower the BUFFERS parameter in CONFIG.SYS. (See Appendix C for information on how to edit text files such as CONFIG.SYS, AUTOEXEC.BAT, and STARTNET.BAT.) The DOS buffers area is the RAM into which DOS puts disk data you read or write. By default, the NetWare Lite INSTALL program sets the number of buffers to 30 on a server. That's usually a good number if you don't run a disk cache. If you do run a disk cache, however, the DOS buffers area and the LAN cache both serve similar purposes. Too large a value for BUFFERS can actually slow down disk I/O because DOS wastes time searching through its buffers area for data the disk cache will find in its cache area. Try a BUFFERS value of no more that 8 or 10 if you run a disk cache. This reduction in BUFFERS will also reduce RAM use on the computer. Every 20 buffers you eliminate saves you about 11K of conventional memory.

NOTE: If the server doesn't have enough RAM to use at least 256K for the disk cache program, add RAM to the computer. On a heavily used server, allot at least 2MB (2048K) of extended or expanded memory for the disk cache. At some point, giving more RAM to a disk cache does little or no good. Unfortunately, you have to install the RAM and run tests to find out where that point is.

Disk Cache Benchmark Results

The benchmark results in this chapter should give you an idea of how optimization changes affect performance. The tests conducted in this chapter use a program called BENCH, created by the authors and available to you (see Appendix D). The BENCH program writes a disk file to the disk drive you select, which can be a client's local disk or a mapped disk on a server, and then reads the file back, while keeping track of how long each step takes. BENCH displays the elapsed time of each step and calculates the data transfer rate (thousands of bytes per second). The write-read cycle is repeated as often as you like. The tests reported in this chapter run five cycles. By specifying parameters, you can change the I/O *blocksize* (the size of each chunk of data written at one time). By default, BENCH writes and reads 10,000 bytes at a time in a 1MB file to simulate large block transfers.

For comparison, tests are shown also with 1K (small block) transfers. The tests were run on a Teltron 386/33 server computer with a 120MB IDE hard disk and the default parameters in CONFIG.SYS from both the DOS 5 and NetWare Lite 1.1 installation programs. The cache used was

Disk Cache versus a Processor Cache

Some 386 and 486 computers are advertised as including a 64K cache or a 256K cache as part of the system. The cache referred to is a *processor cache*, which allows the processor to execute instructions faster by accessing instructions and data from this processor cache area instead of from conventional RAM. The processor cache does not serve the same function as a disk cache.

Optimizing LAN Performance

NLCACHEX, with default parameters and XMS memory, using the DOS 5 HIMEM.SYS driver. (Results using XMS memory and regular extended memory were virtually the same.) The client computer is a CMS Enhancements 386/33 running DOS 4.01 with default installation parameters.

Table 14-1 compares running BENCH with no cache, with a 1024K (1MB) cache, and a 2048K (2MB) cache. The numbers show the average data-transfer rate in kilobytes per second (KB/second), where *KB* means 1000 bytes, not 1024. Higher numbers—indicating that more data is transferred each second—are better than low ones. As you can see, a significant increase in speed occurs when a 1MB cache is used, but a 2MB cache does not yield much additional improvement.

This benchmark uses a single client accessing the server. If several clients accessed the server at once, the larger cache would make a big difference. Normally, benchmark results can vary by 5 or 10 percent from one run to another, depending on the degree of disk fragmentation. Be sure to make several benchmark runs before you draw conclusions.

The DEDICATE Program

Another method provided by Novell to improve server performance is the DEDICATE.COM program. DEDICATE turns a nondedicated server into a dedicated server. A *dedicated* server is one that cannot function as a workstation while acting as a server. A dedicated server, because it can devote all its resources to being a server, can handle a bigger workload than a nondedicated server. The improvement often is only a small increase in speed, but in some environments even a modest gain can be significant.

Transfer rates (KB/second) of BENCH tests without and with NLCACHEX
Table 14-1.

Workload Type	Without NLCACHEX	With 1MB NLCACHEX	With 2MB NLCACHEX
10K writes	84	117	119
10K reads	181	291	294
1K writes	28	118	119
1K reads	115	227	235

The decision to run DEDICATE is not irreversible. Suppose that you are working on a machine configured as a client and a server. If you don't want to do any personal computing for a while, you can run DEDICATE. When you once again need to use the PC as a client, you can stop DEDICATE and resume your work.

To run DEDICATE on a computer already functioning as a server, simply type **dedicate** and press Enter. If you always want a server to run as a dedicated server, you should add DEDICATE to STARTNET.BAT (as the final statement in the batch file). Figure 14-2 shows the messages displayed when DEDICATE starts. To stop DEDICATE, simply press any key.

DEDICATE Benchmark Results

The tests reflected in Table 14-1 were rerun using DEDICATE and no other parameter changes. In most cases, DEDICATE made only a minor improvement in speed—usually about 1 to 8 percent. In one surprising case, reading 1K blocks without a disk cache, DEDICATE was about 6 percent slower.

```
C:\NWLITE>dedicate

NetWare Lite Server Performance Boost Program

Improves network performance of SERVER when
running on server machine.

To exit hit any key...
```

The screen display from DEDICATE
Figure 14-2.

Optimizing LAN Performance

DOS Parameters

MS-DOS provides a bewildering choice of parameters you can set to optimize your computer's operation. This section briefly explains the most significant options for improving LAN performance. See your DOS manuals for more information.

Disk Buffers

Note: The most important DOS parameter that can affect performance on either a server or client is the DOS BUFFERS setting in CONFIG.SYS.

If you run a disk cache program such as NLCACHE, set the number of DOS buffers as explained earlier in this chapter. If you do not use a disk cache, experiment with the number of buffers you use. On a server with a fast processor (such as a 386 that runs at 20MHz or faster), try using as many as 60 buffers. On slower processors, more than 30 buffers is unlikely to help. Too many buffers can slow down disk I/O because DOS wastes too much time searching through all of them.

Caution: Do not set the number of buffers to 99 (the maximum), erroneously figuring that more is better.

Too few buffers will definitely hurt performance if you don't run a disk cache program. Be sure to use at least 12 or 15 buffers. The INSTALL program's default value of 30 for a server is a good choice for most computers. But because the best number for each of your computers depends on the type of processor, the clock speed, the type of disk drive, the amount of RAM available, the type of work the computer does, and the version of DOS, you have to experiment to find the best value. As a rule, you are better off spending your optimization time experimenting with disk cache parameters instead, unless your computer has too little RAM (including extended or expanded) to support a disk cache.

FASTOPEN

FASTOPEN is a DOS program that keeps track of the files and directories you open (begin to use). The program speeds up your access to each file and directory. Its biggest benefit comes if you run programs (database programs are the best example) that repeatedly open and close files.

Unfortunately, many users (whether running NetWare Lite or not) have reported problems using FASTOPEN with DOS 5.0. The major problem seems to be that FASTOPEN can corrupt disk files. To be safe, don't use FASTOPEN with DOS 5.0. (It seems to work fine with DOS 4.0 and 3.3.) The easiest way to start FASTOPEN is by adding a statement to your CONFIG.SYS file. For details, see the manual for your version of DOS.

CAUTION: If you encounter disk-file corruption problems (disk files that are improperly updated), the problem may be caused by FASTOPEN. Stop using FASTOPEN until you can verify that it isn't the cause of your corrupted files.

RAM Disks

A RAM disk is another way to use RAM (instead of a disk drive) to improve speed. A RAM disk (sometimes called a virtual disk, to the confusion of those who call a mapped disk over a LAN a virtual disk) is software that uses a chunk of RAM to simulate a floppy disk. If your computer has two floppy disks (A and B) and a hard disk drive C, for example, you can create a RAM disk called drive D. Your software can read from and write to the RAM disk just like any other real disk, except much faster.

The disadvantages of a RAM disk are that it uses up RAM (although most versions can use expanded or extended memory, as well as conventional), and that the data you put in a RAM disk is temporary. In the RAM disk, unlike a real disk, the data disappears when you power off your computer. Thus, a RAM disk is best used for temporary files (ones your program writes out to disk and then reads back in, for

Optimizing LAN Performance

example), or read-only files that you can copy from a real disk to the RAM disk for temporary access. If you update any files on a RAM disk, you have to copy them to a real disk before you turn off the power. Otherwise, you lose the data.

DOS includes a RAM disk program called RAMDRIVE.SYS, which (for DOS 5.0) can use conventional, expanded, or extended memory. The RAMDRIVE program itself uses a small amount of conventional memory, but the disk drive space can use whatever type of extra memory you have. Other companies also sell RAM disk software, which may have different features and capabilities.

Usually a RAM disk does not improve overall computer or LAN performance as much as a disk cache. The typical situation in which a RAM disk is better is when your application software creates many small files and accesses them frequently. If you think your situation may be right for a RAM disk and you have some RAM to spare, experiment and compare the results with the results you get from a disk cache.

Other DOS Tips

The following are a few more "quickies" about DOS parameters and their potential effects on NetWare Lite performance.

SHARE

SHARE, which NetWare Lite loads on each server, is a TSR supplied with DOS. SHARE keeps track of which files are currently in use and prevents several clients from using the same files simultaneously (unless the software application allows multiple users at once). As explained in Chapter 10, SHARE tracks file names and file locks—the mechanisms with which an application program temporarily gains exclusive use of a file (or portion of a file) so that no other user can update the data at the same time. As explained in Chapter 15, you can modify SHARE parameters to improve the performance of your LAN servers.

Disk Partitions

If you have a large hard disk configured as one logical drive, consider separating the disk into several smaller partitions. If you have a 200MB hard disk that you use as your drive C (permissible under DOS 4.0 or

5.0), for example, use FDISK to repartition the drive into several 32MB logical hard disks called drive C, D, E, and so on.

DOS uses a file allocation table (FAT) to keep track of the disk space on each logical hard disk. The *FAT* is a separate area on your disk, which contains entries for all the used and unused disk areas. For a huge hard disk, the FAT can be extremely large; DOS must spend considerable time searching and updating it. A smaller disk partition has a smaller FAT; DOS can search it faster. Clearly, if your workgroup needs to share a 50MB disk file, you need a disk partition at least that big—plus room for growth. Also, if you set up six or seven logical drives (C through H, say), you have a tougher management job keeping track of which files are on each drive and what to do if a logical drive gets full. Those are the tradeoffs of this optimization technique.

Unfortunately, if you use FDISK to repartition a hard disk, you lose all the data on the disk. You have to back up all your data first and then restore the data after you complete the FDISK process. See your DOS manual for details about FDISK. If your 200MB hard disk is already partitioned into two logical disks of 32MB and 168MB, try putting your most heavily accessed disk files on the 32MB disk.

Server Parameters

The NetWare Lite SERVER.EXE program is the center of activity on a server computer. When you start the SERVER program (using the STARTNET.BAT file), you use a series of default parameters. For many servers, these parameters are adequate. If you want to improve performance, however, and especially if your server has a heavier than average workload, changes to some of these parameters can make a big difference.

To change these parameters for a server, use the NET program. Log in as SUPERVISOR, select `Supervise the network` from the Main menu, then select `Server configuration` from the submenu. After you select the server you want to reconfigure, NET displays a Configuration Information menu box for that server (see Figure 14-3). You can change the values of parameters, one at a time, by moving the cursor to each parameter whose value you want to change, and then typing a new

Optimizing LAN Performance

value. For each parameter, the numbers in parentheses show the permissible range of settings, the CFG column shows the settings in the current configuration, and the FUTURE column is where you make changes. After making your changes, press Esc and confirm that you want to save the changes. Then activate the changes by rebooting the server.

The optimization changes you may be considering (to change your server's configuration) point up the eternal confrontation between speed and memory. When you increase most of these server parameters, the server uses more RAM and either gains increased capacity or can execute work faster (until you reach a point of diminishing returns). You have to decide, based on your needs and experimentation, how much RAM you can sacrifice to increase speed. If you use too much RAM you may not be able to use the server as a client to run your application programs. Clearly, RAM use won't be a problem if you use the server as a dedicated server.

Although each of the parameters shown in Figure 14-3 may need to be changed in particular circumstances, the parameters discussed in the next two sections do the best job of improving server performance.

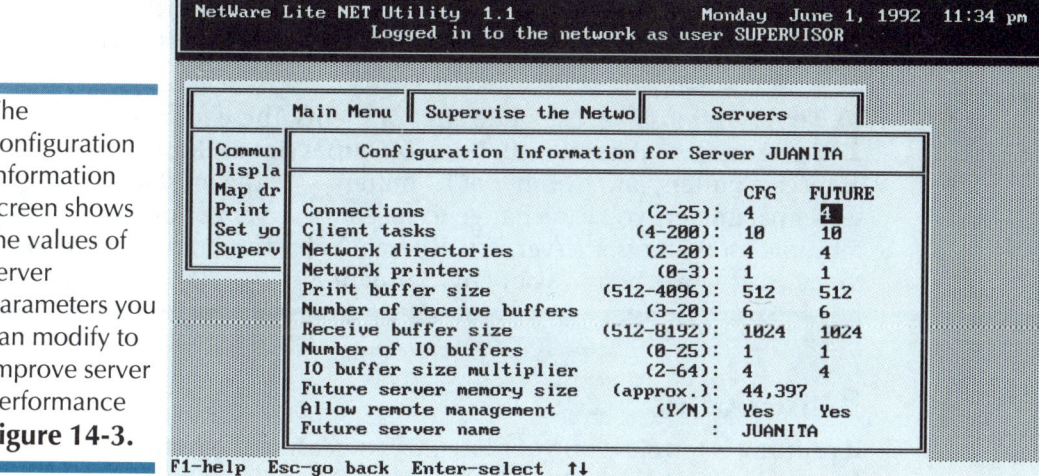

The configuration information screen shows the values of server parameters you can modify to improve server performance
Figure 14-3.

```
NetWare Lite NET Utility  1.1              Monday  June 1, 1992  11:34 pm
            Logged in to the network as user SUPERVISOR

         Main Menu  | Supervise the Netwo |     Servers
 Commun |     Configuration Information for Server JUANITA
 Displa |                                              CFG    FUTURE
 Map dr |
 Print  | Connections                    (2-25):      4      4
 Set yo | Client tasks                   (4-200):     10     10
 Superv | Network directories            (2-20):      4      4
         | Network printers               (0-3):       1      1
         | Print buffer size              (512-4096):  512    512
         | Number of receive buffers      (3-20):      6      6
         | Receive buffer size            (512-8192):  1024   1024
         | Number of IO buffers           (0-25):      1      1
         | IO buffer size multiplier      (2-64):      4      4
         | Future server memory size      (approx.):   44,397
         | Allow remote management        (Y/N):       Yes    Yes
         | Future server name             :            JUANITA

 F1-help   Esc-go back   Enter-select   ↑↓
```

Receive Buffer Size and IO Buffer Size Multiplier

To store the data the server processes for clients, the server sets up areas in RAM called a receive buffer and an I/O buffer. The I/O buffer size is a multiple of the receive buffer size. For a lightly loaded server, the default values are acceptable. A server that processes a heavy volume of sequential file requests (reads, writes, copies, and program starts from the server), should use a larger value for the receive buffer size. The receive buffer size is limited by the characteristics of your LAN cards and driver software, however. For the receive buffer size, try larger values that are multiples of 512 bytes (1536, 2048, 2560, and so on). Try various values from 2 through 8 for the I/O buffer size multiplier.

Number of Receive Buffers and Number of IO Buffers

For a small LAN that seldom has more than one person at a time reading or writing on the server's disk, leave these parameters set to their default values, or reduce the number of receive buffers to 3. If you often have two, three, or more active clients accessing a server, however, increase the number of receive parameters to the number of simultaneous users, or slightly more. The key is the number of *active* users, not just users who have a disk drive mapped to the server.

NOTE: In most NetWare Lite environments, these four parameters—Receive buffer size, IO buffer size multiplier, Number of receive buffers, and Number of IO buffers—are the most important server parameters you can change to speed up server performance when multiple users access a server. Try different values and run benchmarks to see what works best in your environment.

Print Buffer Size

If printing is too slow on your LAN, try increasing the print buffer size from the default value of 512 bytes. Try 1024 or 2048 (or more) and time the results. The printer buffer is a RAM storage area used by NetWare Lite to store data destined for one of the server's printers.

Another way to improve printer performance is to adjust the characters-per-second parameter when you create a network printer. This parameter controls how fast DOS drives the printer and therefore how often DOS is interrupted when sending information to the printer. You can adjust the value of this parameter when creating a network printer or after a network printer is defined. (Use the NET menu system to modify the characters-per-second parameter. Select `Supervise the network` from the Main menu. Then select `Network printers`. Now either move the highlight to an existing network printer or press Ins to create a new network printer.)

You can set the value of "Characters per sec" within the range of 1 to 65,535. The default value is 16,384. Try modifying this parameter when you modify the "Print buffer size" parameter. As you increase "Characters per sec," the printer is driven faster. By experimenting with different numbers, try to tune the values so that they match the speed of the printer. Although making "Characters per sec" higher than the printer can accommodate does not affect the printing speed, you may see a degradation in the performance of application software. For serial printers, a reasonable value for the characters-per-second parameter is the printer baud rate divided by 10. If the baud rate is 9600, for example, the "Characters per sec" value should be about 960.

NOTE: If you use version 1.0 of NetWare Lite, some "patches" are available from Novell to improve printer performance when you run certain applications, such as WordPerfect. Get these patches, which are modifications to your NetWare Lite software, from your Novell dealer or from CompuServe. If you use version 1.1 of NetWare Lite, these patches are included in your software. From time to time, other patches may be developed to fix newly discovered printer (or other) problems, however.

Benchmark Results

Table 14-2 shows the results of running the BENCH program with differing parameters for the receive buffer size. Notice that a large buffer means a big improvement when large block reads and writes are performed, but virtually no change for small blocks. (Actually,

Adjusting Printer Wait Time

If you find that print jobs do not complete or are split into two or more sections, you may need to adjust the printer wait time. The *wait time* specifies how long a captured printer port waits for the next portion of a print job before assuming that the entire job is finished. If an application is slow sending a print job to the captured port, and the wait time runs out, whatever part of the print job is at the captured port is sent to the print queue as though it were the entire job.

You specify the wait time in seconds with a value of from 0 to 3600 (1 hour). The default value is 10. As explained in Chapter 8, you can modify the value of the wait time either through the menu system or from the DOS prompt. To adjust the value from the menu system, select Print from the Main menu and press Enter. Move the highlight to the name of the captured port and press F3. Then move the highlight to Printer wait and type a new value. To set a nondefault value from the DOS prompt when capturing a port, use the w= parameter with the NET CAPTURE command. The command **net capture laser w=100**, for example, sets the wait time to 100 seconds.

If your print jobs are incomplete because your application sends jobs slowly to the printer port, increase the value of wait time. A value of 100 is reasonable for a 286 server machine. Try a value of 200 on a 386 or 486 machine. By lowering the wait time, you can improve turnaround in the print queue. You must be careful not to set the wait time so low that applications cannot send jobs quickly enough to the captured port, however. By setting the wait time to 0 (not a recommended procedure), you can keep the print job open until the application explicitly closes the job. Most applications do close print jobs, but some applications do not.

You may need to experiment with different w= values to determine a satisfactory value for the servers and printers on your network.

performance decreases slightly for small-block reads.) The negligible difference for small-block transfers occurs because the 1K blocks used in

Optimizing LAN Performance

Transfer rates (KB/second) of BENCH tests with different values for a server's receive buffer size
Table 14-2.

Workload Type	1024	4096	2MB NLCACHEX and 4096
10K writes	84	178	165
10K reads	181	213	348
1K writes	28	28	120
1K reads	115	107	239

the small block benchmark fit in the 1024-byte buffers. For large block tests, however, the 10K blocks benefit from having larger server buffers.

Notice also the huge difference in performance—about twice the speed—between the default NetWare Lite settings (1024-byte receive buffer size and no disk cache) and two simple changes (4096-byte receive buffer size with 2MB disk cache). The lesson here is to change your default settings and use a disk cache if you want better performance.

One footnote: Because of the limitations of the LAN card used, the receive buffer size was truncated to 1449 bytes, not 4096. The I/O buffer size increased in spite of this truncation, however, contributing to improved performance.

Other Speed Tips

This section lists an assortment of other speed tips you can try. Some of these tips apply to any computer, not just a NetWare Lite server or client. Clearly, computers optimized to run their fastest are apt to produce improved performance regardless of whether a network is running.

Check Your Interleave Factor

Check that your server's hard disk uses its optimal interleave factor. An *interleave factor* describes the number of revolutions a hard disk must perform to transfer an entire disk track of data into RAM. Most newer hard disks have an interleave factor of one, which means that only one revolution is necessary. Older hard disks often alternate their disk sectors in such a way that two, three, or more revolutions are required. Depending on the hard disk and its controller, you may be able to reduce the interleave factor and improve disk performance.

> **CAUTION**: Reducing the interleave factor can also make performance much worse if the controller cannot keep up with the disk revolution speed. Use a utility program to check and, if appropriate, change your disk interleave factor. Look at PC Tools, Norton Utilities, and SpinRite II. You cannot run these products on a server's disk while other users access the disk. You have to stop the server and run the products directly on the server computer while the server software is not active. Before adjusting the interleave factor, be sure to back up all critical server files.

Fix Disk Fragmentation

As you add, delete, and update files on a disk, the space used by each file tends to become fragmented, or noncontiguous. This situation, in which different portions of a file are scattered on a disk, is called *disk fragmentation*. You can purchase special utility programs that can put these pieces together again (something all the king's horses and all the king's men can't always do).

When a disk's files are fragmented, the disk takes longer to read or update each file because the disk head has to move farther to access all the fragments. A file stored in one contiguous area on disk is quickly accessed. Unless your server's hard disk frequently becomes nearly full, disk fragmentation probably is not a severe performance problem for you. To be safe, you should occasionally run a "defrag" program to defragment your server's hard disk. Some people go overboard and run these programs weekly or even daily. In most environments, once a month is plenty. You can gauge how often you need to defragment by the degree of fragmentation you see when you run the defragmentation software. Before running a disk defragmenter, you may want to back up critical files for extra protection. Some products that perform defragmentation are OPTune from Gazelle Systems, PC Tools, and Norton Utilities. You cannot run these products on an active server.

Have Plenty of Server Disk Space Available

As a disk becomes nearly full, performance suffers for two reasons. First, DOS has more trouble finding available space for updated disk files, which leads to more fragmentation problems. Second, each disk directory contains more files and DOS must perform longer searches to find a particular file. Eliminate unneeded disk files from your server's hard disk, especially from the drives that contain shared files.

Upgrade Your NetWare Lite Software

Each new version of NetWare Lite has internal performance improvements as well as new parameters you can change to enhance performance. Version 1.1 has major improvements from version 1.0, and future versions are certain to have even more. If you are running an old version of NetWare Lite, upgrade. If for some reason you can't upgrade, at least look into getting any patches that exist for the version of NetWare Lite you use from CompuServe. See Appendix D for details.

Upgrade Your Hardware

Sometimes there's no substitute for raw power. Your best performance improvement may come from upgrading your hardware, especially processors, disk drives, RAM, and LAN cards and cable (if you don't use Ethernet). If your server computer uses an 80286 processor or less, or a slow disk drive, an upgrade to a 386 or 486 with a faster disk drive can work wonders. If your server has only 640K of RAM, adding RAM and running a disk cache should help greatly (as you've seen from this chapter's benchmark tests). If your LAN cards are ARCnet, a switch to Ethernet can make a big difference.

Try to determine which hardware component is the cause of your slowdown. If the bottleneck is a slow disk drive and controller on your server, you don't need to upgrade your processor. Upgrading an 8-bit LAN card to a 16-bit LAN card on a server may improve performance, but don't expect a doubling of throughput.

Eliminate Cable and LAN Card Problems

Faulty LAN cables or a faulty LAN card may degrade your LAN's performance by causing the LAN software to spend considerable time recovering from collisions or CRC errors. To be sure that you maintain consistent connections between all LAN nodes, use the INSTALL program's `Verify network connections` option. You can also start the NETBIOS program and then monitor network errors by running analysis programs available from this book's authors (see Appendix D). Normally, you should see an error percentage under 1 percent. Collisions may occasionally be slightly higher on an extremely active LAN with many simultaneous users. If errors are too high, follow the steps outlined in Chapter 13 to isolate and fix bad cables, connectors, or LAN cards.

You can monitor LAN activity on a server by using the status screen available from the menu system. To do so, type **net** at the DOS prompt and press [Enter]. From the Main menu, select `Supervise the network`. Then, from the next menu, select `Server status`. Next, move the highlight to the desired server and press [Enter]. NetWare Lite responds with a screen (see Figure 14-4) that shows the current configuration of the server as well as the active events on the server.

```
NetWare Lite NET Utility 1.1                    Monday  June 1, 1992  8:13 pm
              Logged in to the network as user SUPERVISOR

                         Status for Server JUANITA

 Server up-time    0 Days  2 Hours 56 Minutes  2 Seconds

 Server version                v1.1
 Server address          00001B1D97F7                      CFG   PEAK  CURR
 Network auditing                  On   Connections         4     1     1
 SHARE running                    Yes   Client tasks       10     1     0
 Server memory size            43,872   Open files         30     1     0
                                        Num net directories 4           2
                                  CUM   Num net printers    1           0
 Server-busy packets                2   Print buffer size 512
 Server cache hits                 0%   Receive buffers     6
 Packets received               9,812   Receive buffer size 1,024
 Bad packets received               0   IO buffers          1
 Watchdog terminations              0   IO buffer size  4,096


 F1-help   Esc-go back
```

A typical server status screen
Figure 14-4.

The screen conveys a wealth of information. Note, for example, that it shows the number of bad packets received (which, if greater than 1 or 2, may indicate a faulty cable or LAN card). Additional information includes buffer sizes and the number of open files and connected users. Values for several parameters are displayed on the right: The CFG column indicates the maximum parameter value set with INSTALL; the PEAK column represents the largest value achieved in this session since the server was initialized; the CURR column indicates the number currently being used.

Separate Your Workload

If a server handles heavy loads of file sharing and of printer sharing, separate the two workloads. Put the shared printers on one server and the shared files on another to reduce contention between the two workloads. Similarly, if you run two different database applications on the same server, move one of them to another server. This simple step of separating workloads can, in some workgroups, make a far greater difference than any other optimization action.

Don't Use Windows

Microsoft Windows 3.0 puts a great deal of overhead on a server. Remove Windows and see whether performance improves. Also, if a particular workstation has performance problems and runs Windows, and if your applications do not require Windows, try running the applications without Windows. Windows 3.1 offers some improvements in performance but falls well short of the performance possible when you run DOS without Windows. Keep an eye on future releases of Windows to see whether performance improves. For more about using NetWare Lite with Windows, see Chapter 15.

Optimizing the Use of RAM

The speed optimization techniques covered so far in this chapter often come at the expense of conventional RAM. If you make a buffer bigger, the server runs faster. The bigger buffer takes some of the server's RAM, however, leaving less RAM available for the application programs a user at the server's keyboard wants to run. Some applications need 500K,

550K, or more of conventional RAM. They won't run if DOS and NetWare Lite take up so much RAM that the necessary memory isn't available. Generally, you have two courses of action to free more RAM on your servers or clients:

✦ Reduce NetWare Lite and DOS buffer sizes and other settings, at the possible cost of reduced speed

✦ Use upper memory and extended memory whenever possible to reduce use of the 640K conventional memory area (see the explanation in the "Different Types of Memory" section earlier in this chapter)

To measure the results of your changes, you can use a utility program or DOS command that shows how much RAM of each type is being used at any time. If you have DOS 5, type **mem/c** and press [Enter] to see a summary of memory use. (With DOS 4, you can type the command **mem/program|more** and press [Enter] to see similar but less concise information which, unfortunately, shows numbers in hexadecimal.) For DOS 3.3 and earlier, you need an independent utility program such as PC Tools SI, Norton Utilities SYSINFO, or the freeware PMAP from The Cove Software Group (available on CompuServe in the IBM Utilities forum).

Your goal in reducing RAM is (almost always) to decrease use of the precious 640K of conventional memory. That's the memory most programs use. If you try to run an application program and it fails because of insufficient memory, the problem almost always is a shortage of conventional memory. You need to reduce the space used by NetWare Lite or DOS or, if possible, move some TSRs or drivers to upper or extended memory.

NetWare Lite Parameters and DOS Parameters

The first way to reduce RAM use is to be sure not to waste RAM by specifying uselessly large parameters for a server or for DOS. By specifying unnecessarily large parameters, you set up memory areas that take up RAM space but don't improve performance (or improve performance by only miniscule amounts). The next two sections cover the most likely offenders.

Optimizing LAN Performance

Server Parameters

RAM use is most often a concern on a computer that acts as both a server and client. You need to increase the values of some parameters to make the server perform well, but you also want as much conventional RAM as possible for running application programs. If the server does not also act as a client, you can use all the RAM you like.

Almost all the parameters listed in the NET configuration information screen (shown in Figure 14-3) and in the server status screen (shown in Figure 14-4) use more conventional RAM when you specify larger numbers. Use values no larger than necessary. If no more than two people will ever make connection to the server at the same time, for example, set `Connections` to 2 and the `Number of receive buffers` to 3 or 4. As you change numbers, the `Future server memory size` line shown in Figure 14-3 indicates the effect on the server RAM. The number shown is the amount (approximately) of RAM the server software will use. Lowering this number increases the amount of RAM available for application programs on the server. To minimize RAM use, use the lowest numbers that provide tolerable performance.

The NLCACHE programs (such as NLCACHEX) use conventional memory in proportion to the size of the disk cache you specify. If you instruct NLCACHEX to set up a 1024K extended disk cache, for example, the program uses 31,632 bytes of conventional RAM in addition to the 1024K bytes of extended RAM. But if you instruct NLCACHEX to set up a 2048K extended disk cache, NLCACHEX uses 43,920 bytes of conventional RAM from your precious 640K total. Because each megabyte (1024K) of cache uses an additional 12,000 bytes (approximately) of conventional RAM, make your disk cache no larger than you need. If a 1024K disk cache gives you about the same performance as a 2048K cache, stick with the smaller one and save 12K of conventional RAM. In fact, try a 512K cache and see whether you can save another 6K.

DOS Parameters

Several DOS parameters in CONFIG.SYS use RAM. Of particular concern are BUFFERS and SHARE, discussed earlier in this chapter. If you use a disk cache on the server, reduce BUFFERS and save about 11K of RAM for every 20 BUFFERS you eliminate. FILES, LASTDRIVE, and FCBS also use a small amount of memory each. By reducing their settings to only the minimum you need, you can recover a little RAM. Use LASTDRIVE=F instead of LASTDRIVE=M, for example, and specify STACKS=0,0 in CONFIG.SYS (if you don't run Windows) to save about 7K of memory on most computers. Finally, look at every DEVICE and INSTALL statement in CONFIG.SYS. You may not need all of them. (You may have to consult a DOS expert to determine which statements are necessary with your configuration.) Each DEVICE and INSTALL statement uses RAM; the size of the device driver or program determines how much. See your DOS documentation for more details. (For details about how to edit CONFIG.SYS and other files, see Appendix C of this book.)

Using Upper Memory

On a 386 or 486 computer, extended memory is your savior, the key to gaining more conventional memory. You can use the DOS 5 LOADHIGH capability in conjunction with the EMM386 memory manager that comes with DOS (or run a memory-manager program such as QEMM, 386MAX, or NetRoom) to move many of your software components from conventional memory to upper memory. The key facts are that you must have extended memory on your computer, and the processor must be a 386 or higher.

See Appendix C for sample CONFIG.SYS and STARTNET.BAT files that use upper-memory management to reduce the use of conventional memory.

Optimizing the Use of Disk Space

The key to optimizing disk space use is simple human vigilance. Someone has to monitor the server's hard disk to be sure that plenty of space is available. The techniques are simple: Remember to check every day and use file-management utility programs to help you do the work. Use DOS commands or programs such as Q-DOS from Gazelle Systems, XTree Pro Gold from XTree Company, or PC Tools from Central Point Software. These programs help you quickly search files by date created, size, or directory to determine which files are eating up disk space.

If you have a tape backup system, you can archive programs regularly. (This has the side benefit of enabling you to more easily convince people that some files do not have to stay on the server's hard disk

Optimizing LAN Performance

forever.) Often, the only reason someone keeps a file on the server is the vague notion that the file may be needed some day. If you save a copy on tape, you can remove the file from the server's disk and keep other users happy. (You can save a copy on floppy disks, but doing so takes more work if the files are large.)

If your server's hard disk is too small and your budget cannot tolerate a bigger hard disk, one product you should consider is Stacker, from Stac Electronics of Carlsbad, California. Stacker doubles (approximately) the amount of disk space on the existing hard disk drives. A hardware version, which includes a coprocessor card for the ISA bus, can be purchased for less than $200. Stacker reportedly gives you access to twice as much disk data with no significant speed penalty. A software-only version is even less expensive but doesn't run as fast. Stac has drawn rave reviews for developing data-compression techniques and PC-integration methods that allow their products to work, problem-free, on a wide variety of computer systems running virtually any software.

Highlights

This chapter has covered many optimization techniques. Here's a quick list of the techniques that make the biggest difference for most people:

✦ Use a disk cache such as NLCACHEX. If you need more RAM to create a large enough cache to improve performance, get the additional RAM.

✦ Experiment with SERVER's startup parameters, especially the receive buffer size, to improve performance without using more RAM than necessary.

✦ Be sure that each server's hard disk uses an optimal disk interleave factor.

✦ Be sure that each server's hard disk always has plenty of space available and doesn't suffer from severe fragmentation.

✦ Separate your workload between two servers if contention is a problem.

- Do not use DOS and NetWare Lite parameters so large that you waste RAM space. Use extended memory and LOADHIGH, if necessary. If RAM use is a severe problem, use a memory-management product such as QEMM, 386MAX, or NetRoom.
- Sometimes there is no substitute for faster hardware or more RAM.

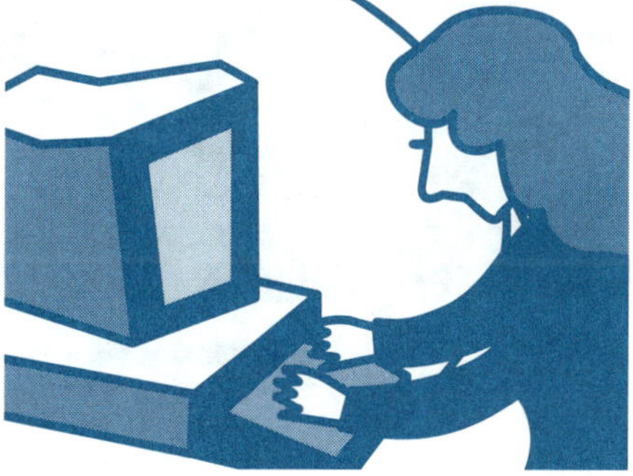

CHAPTER

15 RUNNING ON VARIOUS SOFTWARE PLATFORMS

This chapter examines the following software environments, or software platforms:

✦ *Windows 3.1 (and 3.0)*

✦ *NetBIOS*

✦ *NetWare 2.X, 3.X*

✦ *SHARE*

These environments are all compatible with NetWare Lite and offer your LAN extended capability.

Using Windows

Microsoft Windows extends DOS with a graphical user interface (optionally manipulated with a mouse) and an enriched operating system environment. Many software developers have created applications (such as word processors and spreadsheets) that take advantage of the Windows interface. With the release of version 3.1 in the spring of 1992, Windows' popularity is at an all-time high.

There are several reasons for the success of Windows:

- ◆ It is a consistent, graphical user interface that many people find easier to use than the DOS prompt interface.
- ◆ It offers more automatic installation and execution of applications written to run under Windows.
- ◆ It has the ability to share data between applications.
- ◆ It can run multiple applications simultaneously.

These are attractive advantages. There is a downside, however. Here are some of the shortcomings of Windows:

- ◆ It has high RAM requirements (10K or more) compared to the use of DOS without Windows.
- ◆ It requires quite a bit of disk space (about 8 MB).
- ◆ It suffers from slow performance, especially on AT-class machines or 386 PCs running at less than 33 MHz.
- ◆ There are some reliability problems, although version 3.1 shows an improvement in this area.
- ◆ The cost of purchasing Windows-specific versions of software applications is high, especially if you have already paid for DOS versions of the applications.

Running on Various Software Platforms

Methods of Running Windows With NetWare Lite
If you have Microsoft Windows version 3.0 or 3.1, you can run NetWare Lite and Windows together in two fundamental ways:

The Single-User Windows Configuration In this configuration, you install a separate copy of Windows on each node of the LAN. Then, each computer runs a private copy of Windows from its own hard disk and can access shared resources over the LAN.

The Multiple-User Windows Configuration For this configuration, you install Windows in a multi-user configuration on a server instead of installing a copy of Windows on each workstation. Then, each workstation accesses a shared copy of Windows from the server. This approach saves disk space on each workstation, but it usually results in slower performance, plus greater setup complexity and bigger workloads on both the server and LAN.

For More Information About Windows...
This book makes no attempt to teach Windows terminology or the fundamentals of using Windows. That's a big job better addressed by books devoted to Windows, such as *Windows 3.1 Made Easy* by Tom Sheldon, published by Osborne/McGraw-Hill, or the *Microsoft Windows User's Guide* that comes with Windows. The focus of this chapter is how to install NetWare Lite and Windows so they work together.

NOTE: The Windows instructions in the remainder of this chapter concentrate on Windows 3.1.

Single-User Windows Configuration
The most common way to run NetWare Lite and Windows together is to install a separate copy of Windows on each LAN node, whether the node is a workstation or server. With this method, each computer runs its private copy of Windows rather than having every computer share a common copy from a server. In fact, when you run a separate single-user Windows copy on each workstation, you probably do not

> ### Upgrade to Windows Version 3.1
>
> If you are currently running version 3.0 of Windows and you wish to use Windows in conjunction with NetWare Lite, you should upgrade to Windows 3.1. Version 3.1 improves Windows' "LAN awareness." In addition, version 3.1 is more stable, producing less computer lockups and other inconveniences while networking.
>
> When upgrading, erase from your hard disk the old version of Windows before you install version 3.1. That way, the Windows initialization files are completely rewritten (rather than merely updated). This ensures maximum compatibility with NetWare Lite.

want to run Windows on a server unless the server is used by someone who needs to run Windows. A server provides the workstations with better performance if it is not encumbered with the overhead of running Windows.

This section shows you how to install and run a single-user version of Windows on any network node.

Installing Windows in a Single-User Configuration

To install NetWare Lite and Windows together on either a workstation or server, follow these steps. These instructions are based on installing Windows 3.1 on a node where NetWare Lite 1.1 is already installed but *not* currently running.

1. Install Windows on your computer's hard disk. Follow the instructions in Chapter 1 of *Getting Started with Microsoft Windows*, supplied with the Windows software. You may use either the express setup or custom setup options. Accept whatever choice SETUP detects for the Network option (either "No network" or "Microsoft Network"). Complete the Windows installation.

2. Run Windows SETUP once again to make sure that Windows is configured for NetWare Lite. Assuming you installed Windows on your drive C and used the default disk directory name, type **c:** and press [Enter], then type **cd \windows** and press [Enter]. Finally, type **setup** and press [Enter]. SETUP displays a screen that looks like the one in Figure 15-1.

3. Check whether the Network: line shows "No Network Installed." If it does, press [Enter] or [F3] to exit from SETUP and skip to step 5. If it does not, move the highlight up to the Network: line and press [Enter] to open a selection box which lets you select a network.

4. Move the cursor downward by continuously pressing [↓] until you highlight the option "No Network Installed" as Figure 15-2 shows. (Do not select any of the options that refer to Novell NetWare. These options are for regular NetWare, not NetWare Lite.) Then press [Enter]. Press [Enter] again to accept the current configuration. Press [F3] to exit from the SETUP program. SETUP updates your Windows configuration and returns you to the DOS prompt.

The SETUP screen when run after installing Windows 3.1
Figure 15-1.

```
Windows Setup

    If your computer or network appears on the Hardware Compatibility List
    with an asterisk next to it, press F1 before continuing.

    System Information
        Computer:           MS-DOS System
        Display:            VGA
        Mouse:              Microsoft, or IBM PS/2
        Keyboard:           Enhanced 101 or 102 key US and Non US keyboards
        Keyboard Layout:    US
        Language:           English (American)
        Codepage:           English (437)
        Network:            No Network Installed

        Complete Changes:   Accept the configuration shown above.

    To change a system setting, press the UP or DOWN ARROW key to
    move the highlight to the setting you want to change. Then press
    ENTER to see alternatives for that item. When you have finished
    changing your settings, select the "Complete Changes" option
    to quit Setup.

ENTER=Continue   F1=Help   F3=Exit
```

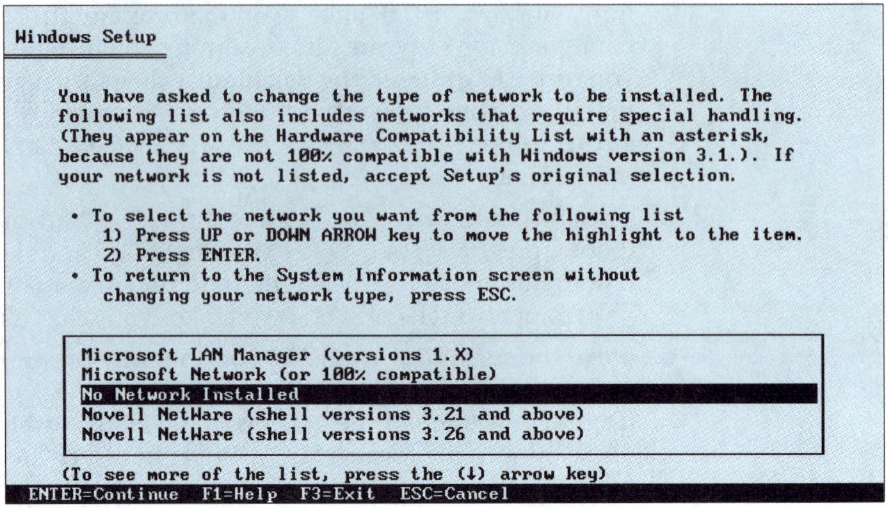

```
Windows Setup

You have asked to change the type of network to be installed. The
following list also includes networks that require special handling.
(They appear on the Hardware Compatibility List with an asterisk,
because they are not 100% compatible with Windows version 3.1.). If
your network is not listed, accept Setup's original selection.

  • To select the network you want from the following list
    1) Press UP or DOWN ARROW key to move the highlight to the item.
    2) Press ENTER.
  • To return to the System Information screen without
    changing your network type, press ESC.

    ┌─────────────────────────────────────────────────────────┐
    │ Microsoft LAN Manager (versions 1.X)                    │
    │ Microsoft Network (or 100% compatible)                  │
    │ No Network Installed                                    │
    │ Novell NetWare (shell versions 3.21 and above)          │
    │ Novell NetWare (shell versions 3.26 and above)          │
    └─────────────────────────────────────────────────────────┘
    (To see more of the list, press the (↓) arrow key)
 ENTER=Continue   F1=Help   F3=Exit   ESC=Cancel
```

Select the "No Network Installed" option
Figure 15-2.

5. Edit the file SYSTEM.INI in the WINDOWS directory. (You can use a line editor such as EDLIN or EDIT in DOS 5.) Find the section of the SYSTEM.INI file labeled [386Enh] at the left margin. (This section controls the Windows configuration when running 386 Enhanced mode.) The last line of this section reads PSPIncrement=5. Add the following two lines to the end of this section:

   ReflectDOSInt2A=TRUE
   OverlappedIO=OFF

   Find the line in the same section of SYSTEM.INI that begins network=*. Modify this line to include VIPX.386 as follows:

   network=*dosnet, *vnetbios, VIPX.386

6. If your LAN card maps a RAM address range onto the card's RAM, you need to tell Windows to exclude that address range in 386 enhanced mode. (Such cards are often ARCnet cards. The Novell/Eagle NE1000 and NE2000 series do not require this step.) This requires another insertion into the SYSTEM.INI file. You must add an EMMExclude directive that excludes the mapped address ranges from the EMM386 device drivers. Consult the documentation for your LAN card, or call the card manufacturer, to determine if your card maps addresses and, if so, which

addresses. For example, the following line specifies a typical address range:

EMMExclude=D800-D9FF

7. Resave the SYSTEM.INI file and return to the DOS prompt.
8. Copy the four files TASKID.COM, TBMI.COM, TBMI2.COM, and VIPX.386 from the C:\NWLITE directory to the C:\WINDOWS\SYSTEM directory. To do so, type **cd\windows\system**, press (Enter) to change the current directory, and type the following four DOS commands:

```
copy \nwlite\taskid.com
copy \nwlite\tbmi.com
copy \nwlite\tbmi2.com
copy \nwlite\vipx.386
```

9. You now need to run Windows to change one of the options that affects printing. Type **win** and press (Enter). From the Main program group in the Program Manager, choose (double-click) the Control Panel icon, and then choose the Printers icon.
10. Double-click on the Connect button. Click on the box labeled "Fast Printing to Direct Port" until the box does *not* contain an X. Figure 15-3 shows the resultant screen.

    The reason to deselect the "Fast Printing" option is that, by default, Windows controls printers with its own drivers that bypass DOS. By deselecting this option, you instruct Windows to let the normal DOS drivers control printing. Because NetWare Lite uses the DOS drivers, this step enables NetWare Lite, rather than Windows, to control the print queue when you send print jobs to network printers from a Windows application.
13. Exit from Windows.

You have now completed the installation process that enables you to use Windows and NetWare Lite together. Follow the same process on each workstation and server on which you want to run Windows.

Using the Single-User Configuration

Once you complete installation, NetWare Lite and Windows are compatible as long as you run things in the right sequence.

Removing the "Fast Printing Direct to Port" option
Figure 15-3.

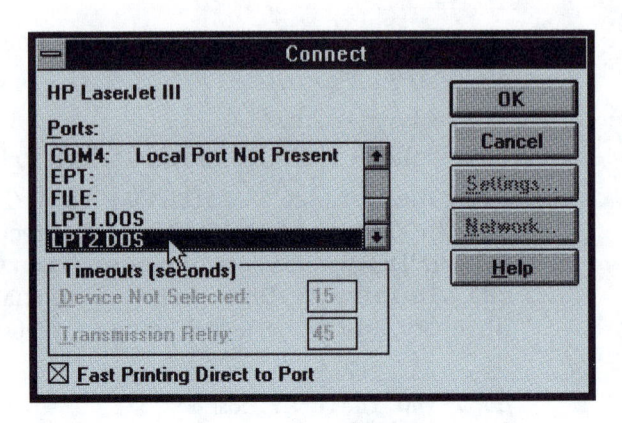

Always start NetWare Lite and redirect disk drives and printers *before* you start Windows—this means that you should run STARTNET.BAT and NET before you run WIN. The simplest way to be sure you do everything in the right sequence is to put all your commands into one batch file. Either AUTOEXEC.BAT or STARTNET.BAT will do, or make your own new batch file. See Appendix C for instructions on modifying batch files.

To access subdirectories on a local hard disk drive using a drive letter, the SUBST command in DOS is more efficient than using NetWare Lite to map a drive letter. For more information on SUBST, consult your DOS documentation.

As long as you have all your disk drives and printers redirected before you start Windows, your Windows applications can use them just like locally attached devices. Mapped drive letters will appear for use in Windows. For example, as Figure 15-4 shows, the mapped drive F is available in the Windows File Manager.

CAUTION: Be sure not to redirect a workstation's local hard disk drive name to a server's hard disk. For example, don't use NET to redirect your drive C to the server's drive C. If you do, your computer can no longer access your own drive C (because the C drive name points to the server) and Windows no longer has access to necessary files on your hard disk. The result is a lockup, forcing you to reboot your workstation.

Running on Various Software Platforms

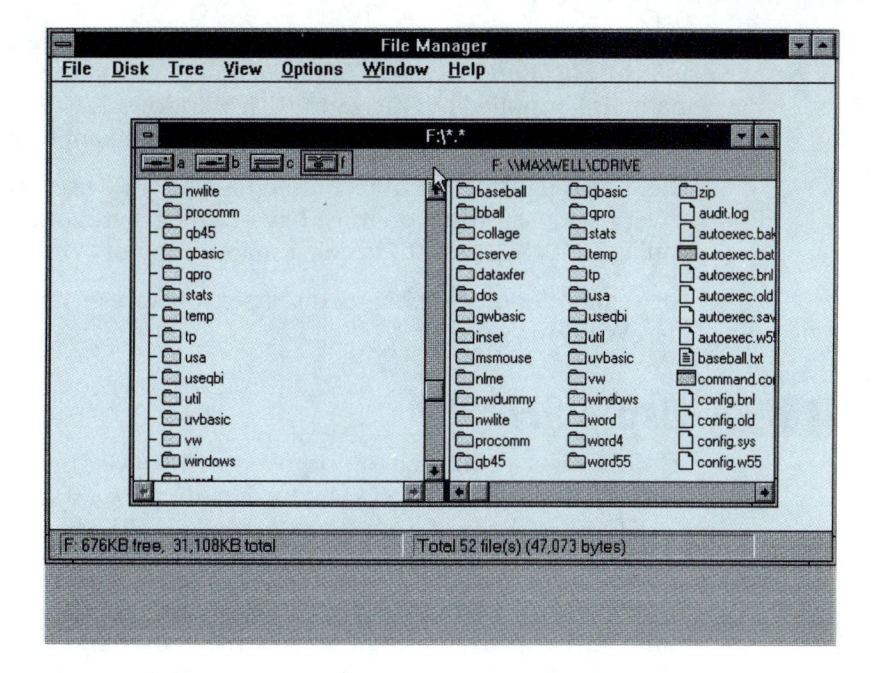

Drive F is available with the Windows File Manager **Figure 15-4.**

When beginning a DOS compatibility box in Windows' real or standard mode, load TASKID.COM when the DOS prompt appears. To do so, type **taskid** and press [Enter]. Just before exiting from the DOS box, unload TASKID.COM. To do so, type **taskid u** and press [Enter].

CAUTION: The NetWare Lite messaging system does not work under Windows. If you send a NetWare Lite message to a user running Windows, the message is not received and becomes irretrievably lost.

Running Windows as a Shared Application

Installation of Windows on a server for sharing across the LAN is similar to, but more complicated than, the single-user configuration. When running Windows SETUP, type **setup/a** and press [Enter] to use the "administrative mode," the mode for creating a server copy. For instructions, see pages 6-12 of *Getting Started with Microsoft Windows*, and the *Microsoft Windows User's Guide*, especially Appendix A. These manuals—supplied by Microsoft with Windows 3.1—explain many of the concepts and techniques pertinent to shared application.

The shared method is not recommended because users can expect slow server response. Also, you must have 16 megabytes of hard disk space available on the server to install a shared copy of Windows.

The remainder of this chapter discusses software environments other than Windows.

Using SHARE

SHARE.EXE is a TSR program supplied with DOS. The NetWare Lite installation program (INSTALL), by default, puts a statement in the STARTNET.BAT file of each server to load SHARE. As a result, SHARE is loaded each time you initialize the server by running STARTNET.BAT.

SHARE keeps track of the server files currently in use and prevents multiple clients from using the same files simultaneously (unless the software application allows simultaneous users). As explained in Chapter 10, SHARE tracks file names and file locks, which are the mechanisms for an application program to temporarily gain exclusive use of a file. You need to run SHARE on a server, not a client computer, because only on a server will more than one computer try to access a file at the same time.

If you don't specify any parameters on the SHARE statement in STARTNET.BAT (the default created by INSTALL), DOS 5.0 allocates space for 20 locks and a file name space of 2048 bytes. If your network supports database applications or has more than a handful of active users, 20 locks may be insufficient. Some applications will fail because of insufficient locks, but others may run very slowly as a result of constant waiting for locks to become available. For average file and path name lengths, 2048 bytes is enough for only 50 or 60 files open at once.

If you suffer from occasional slow response while running a network application, try changing your SHARE statement in STARTNET.BAT to the following:

```
SHARE /F:4096 /L:200
```

This statement sets the amount of memory space used for file sharing to 4,096 bytes (double the default value) and the maximum number of file locks to 200 (ten times the default). You do pay a price to enlarge the /F and /L parameters: a reduction in the RAM available for applications.

> **CAUTION:** Your computer may already start SHARE in either the CONFIG.SYS or AUTOEXEC.BAT file. If either of these files has a SHARE statement, make the recommended modification to that SHARE statement, or else modify the SHARE statement in STARTNET.BAT and remove the SHARE statements from CONFIG.SYS or AUTOEXEC.BAT. In some cases, SHARE must be in CONFIG.SYS (such as to support a large disk partition under DOS 4.0). The first SHARE that DOS encounters is the one that remains in use. DOS encounters possible SHARE statements in the following file sequence: CONFIG.SYS, AUTOEXEC.BAT, and then STARTNET.BAT (or any other batch file you execute).

Using NetBIOS

NetBIOS (Network Basic Input/Output System) is a software layer designed to let application programs communicate with a LAN operating system. NetWare Lite does not normally use NetBIOS. However, regular NetWare and many other networks do use NetBIOS.

NetBIOS provides a set of program specifications that enable a software developer to design an application to run in the NetBIOS environment. As such, the software application works on LANs that support NetBIOS, regardless of the LAN's physical topology, individual hardware, or operating system.

Many LAN software packages are written for NetBIOS because NetBIOS provides a common denominator that most LANs support. Software packages that run under NetBIOS include groupware packages, modem sharing software, and other applications.

NetWare Lite includes a TSR program (NETBIOS.EXE) that adds NetBIOS functionality to NetWare Lite. To activate NETBIOS.EXE, type **netbios** at the DOS prompt and press Enter.

When you activate NetBIOS, you reduce your available RAM by approximately 30K. To unload NetBIOS and recover the 30K of RAM, type **netbios u** at the DOS prompt and press ⏎.

NOTE: To successfully unload NetBIOS, you must not have loaded any other TSRs after you loaded NetBIOS. If so, you must unload the other TSRs before you can unload NetBIOS.

Running Regular NetWare

NetWare 2.X and 3.X are Novell's high-end networking software products. These products, often called "regular" NetWare, are designed for high-performance client/server LANs. NetWare LANs, unlike NetWare Lite LANs, are not DOS-based, peer-to-peer LANs. Servers on a regular NetWare LAN do not run DOS, but instead run Novell's proprietary LAN operating system, known as NetWare. Workstations on a NetWare LAN run NETx.COM, known as the NetWare Shell.

NetWare and NetWare Lite Compatibility

It is possible to run NetWare Lite and regular NetWare on the same LAN. You can load NetWare Lite on NetWare workstations. The ramifications of doing so depend on the configurations of the NetWare LAN and the NetWare Lite LAN. Consult your NetWare LAN administrator. A detailed explanation of the techniques is beyond the scope of this book. Of necessity, the discussion here is a short treatment of a complex subject.

To load NetWare Lite on NetWare workstations, you must modify the STARTNET.BAT file that is run on each workstation. The typical STARTNET.BAT file for a NetWare Lite node configured as both a client and server looks as follows:

```
SHARE
LSL
NE2000.COM
IPXODI A
SERVER
CLIENT
```

The third line is the LAN card driver, NE2000.COM in this example. Your LAN card driver may be different.

Modify STARTNET.BAT to appear as follows:

```
SHARE
SERVER
CLIENT
NETx.COM
```

If you want this node to be a client or server (but not both) when running NetWare Lite, remove the SERVER or CLIENT line from STARTNET.BAT as appropriate. The line NETx.COM loads the NetWare shell.

With NetWare already loaded on this computer (IPX.COM loaded), but without the NetWare shell yet loaded, you can execute the modified STARTNET.BAT. This loads the NetWare Lite files and the NetWare shell in the proper order.

CAUTION: Running NetWare and NetWare Lite simultaneously can cause drive mappings (and other network resources) to conflict. Be careful if you map a drive letter with NetWare Lite and then log into a NetWare server. If your NetWare login script maps a drive letter already in use by NetWare Lite, the NetWare mapping becomes active. In NetWare Lite, you may see the same drive letter mapped twice. The NetWare Lite mapping becomes inactive and cannot be accessed. To regain access to the NetWare Lite mapping, you must first cancel the regular NetWare mapping.

Upgrading NetWare Lite to NetWare

NetWare Lite and regular NetWare are distinct software products that provide separate LAN operating systems. However, NetWare Lite and NetWare can utilize the same LAN hardware—computers, LAN cards, and cables.

At the present time, Novell has no policy for upgrading NetWare Lite software to regular NetWare. To convert a NetWare Lite LAN to NetWare, you must purchase the NetWare software and install the software on your existing computers.

Synchronizing Time on Servers and Clients

In many working environments, while various software applications are running, it's important that the system date and time are synchronized on the various network nodes. There are many reasons for this synchronicity requirement. For example, groupware communication packages may record the date and time when sending messages. And some applications may trigger an event at a certain time, such as updating a spreadsheet or calling a remote bulletin board to receive a file.

The built-in clocks on many PCs have a tendency to drift away from the correct time. With NetWare Lite, you can synchronize the times on the network nodes to make sure that all necessary PCs have the same date and time.

Synchronizing the Times On Network Servers

To synchronize the times on each NetWare Lite server, follow these steps:

1. At the DOS prompt, type **net** and press [Enter] to activate the menu system.
2. Move the highlight to Supervise the network and press [Enter].
3. Move the highlight to Time synchronization.
4. Press [Enter] to pop open the box labeled "Synchronize Date and Time on Servers," as shown in Figure 15-5.
5. Modify the date and time to desired values. To do so, press [Enter] to move the highlight between the date and time fields. Type in the correct value for each field.
6. Press [Esc] when the date and time are set correctly. A box labeled "Synchronize Date and Time on Servers" pops open.
7. Move the highlight to Yes.
8. Press [Enter] to synchronize the date and time.
9. Press [Alt]-[F10] followed by [Enter] to exit from the menu system.

Running on Various Software Platforms

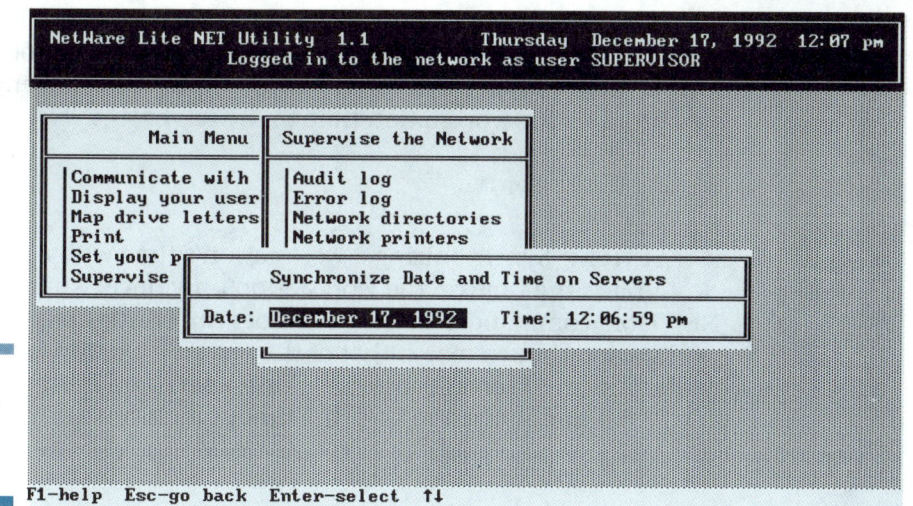

The date and time fields are displayed
Figure 15-5.

Synchronizing the Time on a Workstation with the Network Servers

To synchronize the time on a workstation with the network servers, use the NET TIME command from the DOS prompt. From a workstation, type the following command and press Enter.

```
net time
```

This command changes the time kept on the workstation to the time on the server to which the workstation's default drive is mapped.

If the current drive letter is not mapped to any network server, the workstation's time is synchronized with the first server that responds to the synchronization request. If your network has only one server, or if you have synchronized the time on all servers, the workstation time is synchronized to that known time.

You can optionally include a server name as part of the NET TIME command. If you do that, the workstation time is synchronized to the time kept on the specified server. For example, the following command synchronizes the workstation time to the server JUANITA.

```
net time juanita
```

CAUTION: Synchronizing a workstation's time with a server's time adjusts the time on the workstation only once, when you issue the NET TIME command. NetWare Lite does not continuously adjust the workstation time to match that of the server. If the times kept on your workstation and server continually drift apart, you must reissue NET TIME commands often to keep the times synchronized.

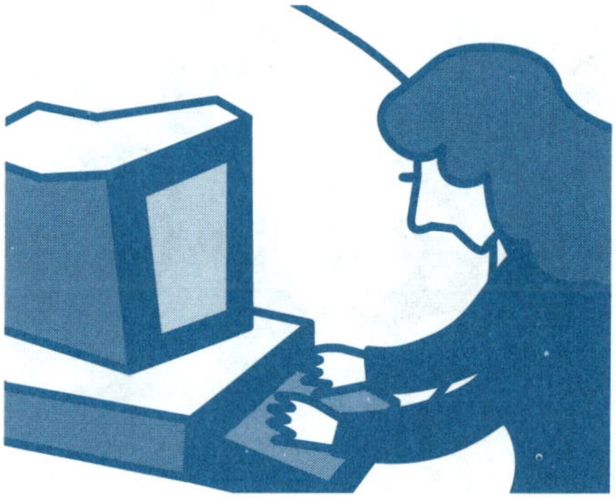

APPENDIX

A NETWARE LITE STATUS REPORTS (ERROR MESSAGES)

NetWare Lite messages indicate error conditions, successful completion of certain operations, and other information regarding network status. Each message, called a status report, is numbered.

When displaying an error-message status report, NetWare Lite displays the number of the report along with the message. When displaying a purely informative status report, however, NetWare Lite displays the text of the message but not the status report number.

This appendix lists the status reports in numerical order, along with brief explanatory comments. Special emphasis is paid to indicating the cause of errors and the likely solutions.

The status-report messages in this appendix are for version 1.1 of NetWare Lite. Although status reports for version 1.0 of NetWare Lite are similar, the text of some of the messages was changed between versions. The numbering is consistent, however; each status-report number and message from version 1.0 is retained with the same number and meaning in version 1.1. Version 1.1, however, adds several status reports not included with version 1.0.

Status Reports

1. `Version 1.1 Copyright (c) 1991, 1992  Novell, Inc. All Rights Reserved.`
2. `SERVER.EXE was already loaded in memory; it was not loaded again.`

   SERVER.EXE, the TSR program that provides server functionality to a network node, can be loaded only once. This message indicates that you attempted to load SERVER.EXE after it had already been loaded. The most likely cause is rerunning the STARTNET.BAT file or running a custom batch file that attempts to load SERVER.EXE, after it had already been loaded.
3. `SERVER.EXE was loaded successfully.`
4. `SERVER.EXE was not loaded because DOS version 3.0 (or above) was not in memory.`

   NetWare Lite requires DOS version 3.x, 4.x, 5.x, or DR DOS. This message indicates that NetWare Lite cannot detect the presence of an acceptable version of DOS.
5. `DOS SHARE was not executed before an attempt to load SERVER.EXE; SERVER.EXE will be loaded anyway.`

   SHARE.EXE is the TSR program supplied with DOS that resolves potential file-sharing conflicts with networks. Typically, SHARE is loaded into memory as one of the commands in the

NetWare Lite Status Reports (Error Messages)

STARTNET.BAT file. NetWare Lite's INSTALL program places the SHARE command in STARTNET.BAT. This message indicates that SHARE.EXE was not loaded when you attempted to load SERVER.EXE. If you get this error message, check that SHARE appears before SERVER in your STARTNET.BAT file.

6. `SERVER.EXE was not loaded because IPXODI.COM had not been executed.`

    IPXODI.COM is a TSR program that controls the communication between network nodes. Typically, STARTNET.BAT loads IPXODI.COM after LSL.COM and the LAN card driver are loaded but before SERVER.EXE and CLIENT.EXE are loaded. IPXODI must be loaded before either SERVER.EXE or CLIENT.EXE can be loaded. The INSTALL program creates STARTNET.BAT with the proper loading sequence. If you get this error message, check that IPXODI appears before SERVER in your STARTNET.BAT file. If necessary, reinstall NetWare Lite by running the INSTALL program.

7. `SERVER.EXE was not loaded because the NetWare Lite configuration file could not be found.`

    NetWare Lite maintains special system and configuration files in a hidden directory (created by INSTALL) with the path C:\NWLITE\NLCNTL. Files in this directory are created and maintained as you use NetWare Lite. If you get this error message, a special file named SERVER (not to be confused with SERVER.EXE) in the hidden directory has been deleted or corrupted. The simplest solution is to rerun INSTALL.

8. `NetWare Lite Client - Version 1.1 Copyright (C) 1991, 1992  Novell, Inc. All rights reserved.`

9. `SERVER.EXE was not loaded because its version and the version of NET.EXE are incompatible.`

    This error message indicates that a conflict in version numbers exists between SERVER.EXE and the NET program. The error can arise after upgrading improperly to a new version of NetWare Lite. Perhaps some files from the old version were not correctly upgraded to the new version. Rerun your most recent version of INSTALL.

10. `SERVER.EXE will be loaded even though the FILES= parameter in CONFIG.SYS is lower than 30, the minimum suggested.`

The minimum recommended value for FILES= in CONFIG.SYS is 30. If FILES is less than 30, the performance of the network can be degraded. By default, the INSTALL program modifies the value of FILES for you. If you choose not to modify CONFIG.SYS while running INSTALL, you may end up with FILES= set to a value less than 30. This message is a warning that you should modify the value of FILES= in CONFIG.SYS. You can also rerun INSTALL.

11. `The print area control file for a defined printer was not found. SERVER.EXE created one with default values.`

    NetWare Lite maintains, in the hidden C:\NWLITE\NLCNTL directory, a special file used to configure and control network printers. This message indicates that the file is missing and, therefore, the configuration of any previously defined network printers has been lost. NetWare Lite creates a default file with default printer settings. If you get this error message, use the NET menu system to redefine the settings on your network printers. Select the `Network printers` option from the "Supervise the network" menu.

12. `CLIENT.EXE was loaded successfully.`

13. `CLIENT.EXE is already in memory; it was not loaded again.`

    Similar to Status Report 2, but for CLIENT.EXE rather than SERVER.EXE.

14. `CLIENT.EXE was not loaded because DOS version 3.0 (or above) was not in memory.`

    Similar to Status Report 4, but for CLIENT.EXE rather than SERVER.EXE.

15. `CLIENT.EXE was not loaded because the appropriate IPX file had not been executed. Load IPX before loading CLIENT.EXE.`

    Similar to Status Report 6, but for CLIENT.EXE rather than SERVER.EXE.

16. `NetWare IPX Protocol Vx.x (date) (C) Copyright 1990, 1991 Novell, Inc. All Rights Reserved.`

    This message, which indicates the version and date of IPX, displays when you load the IPXODI.COM program.

NetWare Lite Status Reports (Error Messages)

17. `Print jobs were found in printer area. All jobs were placed on HOLD.`

    This message arises when you unload SERVER.EXE while print jobs are pending and then load SERVER.EXE a second time. With the pending print jobs placed on hold, you can enter the NET menu system and delete the print jobs or release the hold to print the jobs.

18. `FATAL: IPX already loaded.`

    This messages arises when you attempt to load IPXODI.COM after the program has already been loaded. The usual cause is the mistaken belief that IPXODI was previously unloaded when you tried to load the program a second time. Despite the "FATAL" designation, network operations can continue normally.

19. `The print area control file for a defined printer was not found. SERVER.EXE created one with default values.`

    This status report carries the same message as Status Report 11. When a print control file error occurs, Report 11 is displayed while Report 19 is recorded in the network error log.

20. `NetWare Link Support Layer Vx.x (date) (C) Copyright 1990, 1992 Novell, Inc. All Rights Reserved.`

    This message indicates the version and date of the Link Support Layer, one of NetWare Lite's low-level TSR programs required for the network to run. The message displays when you load the IPXODI.COM program (normally done by STARTNET.BAT).

21. `The user database file is corrupt or missing.`

    NetWare Lite maintains, in the hidden C:\NWLITE\NLCNTL directory, a special file used to identify the users recognized by the network. This error message indicates that the file is either missing or damaged. To correct the problem, you can either log in to the network on another server (by logging in, you update the special file on all servers) or, for networks with only one server, rerun INSTALL.

22. `FATAL: LSL already loaded.`

    This message, which arises when you attempt to load LSL.COM while the program is already loaded, usually is caused by inadvertently running STARTNET.BAT (or a customized batch file) a second time. Despite the "FATAL" designation, network operations can continue normally.

23. `CLIENT.EXE was not loaded because an IPX socket could not be opened. Please configure IPX with more sockets before loading CLIENT.EXE.`

    A *socket* is an internal address used by IPXODI.COM to facilitate data transfers across the network. This error message indicates a problem with IPXODI.COM. Try rerunning IPXODI.COM. Also, using a word processor or text editor, you can modify the NET.CFG text file (created by the INSTALL program and placed in the C:\NWLITE directory) to allocate additional sockets. Contact Novell Technical Support for information about how to do this.

24. `SERVER.EXE cannot initialize network printer.`

    NetWare Lite maintains, in the hidden C:\NWLITE\NLCNTL directory, a special file used to control network print jobs. This error message indicates that the file is missing. To correct the problem, use NET to delete and then redefine the network printer.

25. `More network directories and printers have been defined than are allowed by the configuration of SERVER.EXE.`

    NetWare Lite defines the maximum number of network directories and network printers permitted on each server. This message indicates that the prescribed maximum has been exceeded. To adjust the maximum values, using the NET menu system, select the `Server configuration` option from the "Supervise the network" menu.

26. `The file that defines network directories and printers is corrupt or missing.`

    This error message indicates a problem with the file (in the C:\NWLITE\NLCNTL directory) that maintains a list of the network printers and network directories. To correct the problem, either delete and redefine the offending directory or printer, or reinstall the network by running INSTALL.

27. `SERVER.EXE was loaded but is not operational.`

    Depending on the severity of the problem, NetWare Lite may load SERVER.EXE even when an error occurs. This message indicates that a problem was found but that SERVER.EXE was loaded

NetWare Lite Status Reports (Error Messages)

anyway. Server status is not functional, however. This message usually is accompanied by another message indicating the specific error.

28. `SERVER.EXE could not update printer control information. The printer may need to be restarted for printer attributes to take effect.`

    This error message is recorded in the network error log when a network printer problem occurs. To fix the problem, first try unloading and reloading SERVER.EXE. If the problem persists, delete and redefine the offending network printer.

29. `The user database file is corrupt or missing.`

    This status report carries the same message as Status Report 21. When the user file is invalid, Report 21 is displayed onscreen, whereas Report 29 is recorded in the network error log.

30. `Error opening IPX socket.`

    The message carried by this status report is similar to that of Status Report 23. The difference is that Report 23 pertains to loading CLIENT.EXE, whereas this report pertains to loading SERVER.EXE. In each case, the TSR could not load because the three required sockets are unavailable. The solution for this error is the same as that recommended for message 23. Status Report 30 is recorded in the network error log.

31. `Print jobs were found in printer area. All jobs were placed on HOLD.`

    This status report carries the same message as Status Report 17. When the user file is invalid, Report 17 is displayed onscreen, whereas Report 31 is recorded in the network error log.

32. `The size of receive buffers specified in the server configuration is too big for the LAN card being used. The receive buffer size was changed to the maximum packet size allowed by the LAN card.`

    This report is informative. NetWare Lite detected and corrected a problem with the buffer sizes.

33. `The size of read buffers specified in the server configuration is too big for the LAN card being used. The read buffer size was changed to the maximum packet size allowed by the LAN card.`

This report is informative. NetWare Lite detected and corrected a problem with the buffer sizes.

34. `SERVER.EXE cannot initialize network printer because the number of configured printers is too small.`

    NetWare Lite defines the maximum number of network printers permitted on each server. This message indicates that the prescribed maximum has been exceeded. To adjust the maximum value using the NET menu system, select the `Server configuration` option from the "Supervise the network" menu.

35. `SERVER.EXE cannot initialize network printer because the number of configured printers is too small.`

    This status report is identical to Report 34.

36. `Selected configuration of SERVER.EXE exceeds 64k of data memory. Use NET.EXE to reduce configuration parameters. Reboot computer now; then reconfigure server with NET.EXE, while SERVER.EXE is not loaded.`

    This message generally occurs when you attempt to load SERVER.EXE into upper memory and the available upper-memory blocks are not large enough. To reduce the size of the SERVER.EXE configuration, select the `Server configuration` option from the "Supervise the network" menu. Decrease the number of buffers, the size of the buffers, and other configuration parameters.

37. `CLIENT.EXE was loaded before SERVER.EXE. SERVER.EXE should be loaded first if a Network Printer is, or will be, attached to this machine.`

    If a network node is configured as a server and a client, SERVER.EXE should be loaded before CLIENT.EXE. The INSTALL program specifies the correct order in the STARTNET.BAT file. If you have inadvertently modified STARTNET.BAT to load the programs in the incorrect order, either remodify STARTNET.BAT to reestablish the correct order, or rerun INSTALL.

38. `Not enough memory to load.`

    This message indicates that insufficient RAM is available to load one of NetWare Lite's TSR programs. To fix the problem you must increase the amount of available RAM. You may solve this problem in several ways, which include purchasing additional RAM,

NetWare Lite Status Reports (Error Messages)

unloading unnecessary (nonnetwork) TSR programs, or, if possible, loading DOS or other programs into high or extended memory.

39. `The IO buffer size specified in the server configuration is not a multiple of 16. The IO buffer size was changed to a multiple of 16.`

    This message indicates an internal inconsistency in the size of the IO buffers used by the network to exchange information. This message is informative, as NetWare Lite can detect and fix the problem.

40. `The IO buffer size multiplier specified by the server configuration is not a valid multiplier of the receive buffer size. The IO buffer size was changed to 2 times the receive buffer size.`

    This message indicates an internal inconsistency in the size of the IO buffers used by the network to exchange information. This message is informative, as NetWare Lite can detect and fix the problem.

41. `The number of IO buffers specified in the server configuration is greater than the number of connections. The number of IO buffers was changed to the number of connections.`

    This message indicates an internal inconsistency in the size of the IO buffers used by the network to exchange information. This message is informative, as NetWare Lite can detect and fix the problem.

42. `Byte value greater than 255 in configuration file was truncated.`

    This message is informative. The error is corrected automatically by NetWare Lite.

43. `CLIENT.EXE was not unloaded because it is not currently loaded.`

    You can unload CLIENT.EXE by typing the command **client u** at the DOS prompt. This message indicates an attempt to unload CLIENT.EXE when it is not currently loaded.

44. `CLIENT.EXE was not unloaded because the version of CLIENT.EXE in memory is not the same as this one. You`

must run the same version of `CLIENT.EXE` in order to unload it.

This message indicates that the version of CLIENT.EXE used with the client u command is not the same version of CLIENT.EXE used to load the client software.

45. `CLIENT.EXE was not unloaded because another program was loaded after it. You must unload this other program first before unloading CLIENT.EXE.`

   When you unload NetWare Lite TSRs, each TSR must be unloaded in the opposite order of the loading sequence.

46. `CLIENT.EXE was unloaded from memory.`

47. `Byte value greater than 255 in NET.CFG configuration file was truncated.`

   This status report carries the same message as Status Report 42. When an offending byte value is detected and corrected, Report 42 is displayed onscreen, whereas Report 47 is recorded in the network error log.

48. `Bad route address syntax in NET.CFG configuration file.`

   A directive in the NET.CFG file was specified incorrectly. To solve the problem, you must modify the NET.CFG file as required or rerun the INSTALL program.

49. `SERVER.EXE was not unloaded because it is not currently loaded.`

   This is the companion message to Status Report 43, except that this report is for SERVER.EXE rather than CLIENT.EXE.

50. `SERVER.EXE was not unloaded because the version of SERVER.EXE in memory is not the same as this one. You must run the same version of SERVER.EXE in order to unload it.`

   This is the companion message to Status Report 44, except that this report is for SERVER.EXE rather than CLIENT.EXE.

51. `SERVER.EXE was not unloaded because another program was loaded after it. You must unload this other program first before unloading SERVER.EXE.`

   This is the companion message to Status Report 45, except that this report is for SERVER.EXE rather than CLIENT.EXE.

NetWare Lite Status Reports (Error Messages)

52. `SERVER.EXE was unloaded from memory.`
53. `This copy of SERVER.EXE is for update use only. SERVER.EXE did not load.`

    An incorrect version of SERVER.EXE was run. If necessary, rerun INSTALL.

54. `This copy of CLIENT.EXE is for update use only. CLIENT.EXE did not load.`

    An incorrect version of CLIENT.EXE was run. If necessary, rerun INSTALL.

55. `SERVER.EXE was not loaded because an IPX socket could not be opened. Please configure IPX with more sockets before loading SERVER.EXE.`

    This is the companion message to Status Report 23, except that this report is for SERVER.EXE rather than CLIENT.EXE.

56. `SERVER.EXE was not loaded because NETx.COM has been loaded. Please load SERVER.EXE before loading NETx.COM.`

APPENDIX

B

CHECKLISTS FOR PLANNING A LAN

The following checklists summarize the planning issues discussed in Chapter 3. Use these lists as the backbone of your network plan.

Inappropriate Situations for NetWare Lite

If any of the following situations apply to your workgroup, NetWare Lite is probably not your best choice:

+ You need to use PCs other than DOS-based IBM compatibles
+ You need to use an incompatible hardware or software product
+ You need to connect more than 15 computers
+ You plan to do any of these things in the near future

Clarify Objectives

List the objectives for your workgroup's LAN. Your list probably will include entries such as the following:

Shared disk space

Shared printers

Shared applications

    Database

    Word processor

    Spreadsheet

    Presentation graphics

    Other _____

Workgroup productivity applications

    Electronic mail

    Resource scheduling

    Calendaring

    Other _____

Shared modems

Checklists for Planning a LAN

Shared plotters

Shared CD-ROM drives

Other _____

Determine Workgroup Needs and Wants

The following list provides a step-by-step guide for preparing and selecting a NetWare Lite LAN:

1. List all desktop PCs, noting each machine's specifications and who uses each PC.
2. List portable PCs that have LAN connectivity needs.
3. Determine local and remote connectivity methods to use for portable PCs.
4. Check that all PCs use DOS 3.1 (or higher) or DR DOS 6.0.
5. Check that all PCs use ROM BIOS dated 1986 or later.
6. Check that all PCs have an available card slot for the LAN card.
7. Determine whether a Macintosh connection is needed and, if so, what to do.
8. Determine the total number of PCs to connect to the LAN. If more than 25, NetWare Lite cannot support the LAN. If more than 15 (thin Ethernet or 10BASE-T), determine how to configure.
9. List each peripheral device attached to any of the PCs.

    - Printers
    - Modems
    - Plotters
    - CD-ROM drive
    - Other _____

10. Determine whether additional software is needed for modems, printers, or plotters.
11. Obtain or sketch a floor plan.
12. Identify locations of all PCs.

13. Determine locations of shared printers and plotters.
14. Update the floor plan by sketching tentative cable positions between PCs, for both thin Ethernet and 10BASE-T.
15. Verify that cables can run in the sketched locations. Revise floor plan, if necessary.
16. Determine cable lengths and verify that the lengths comply with limitations.
17. Choose between thin Ethernet, 10BASE-T, or possibly ARCnet or Token Ring LAN cards and cables.
18. Evaluate the office environment for needed changes, paying particular attention to the following potential problems:

    ◆ Need for electrical surge suppressors and filters
    ◆ Need for UPS
    ◆ Dust, water, building security, and other hazards

19. Determine the source for obtaining LAN equipment and decide who will install and test the LAN.
20. Determine which application software is needed.
21. Verify that the LAN configuration will adequately support the application software and expected usage.
22. Choose and train a LAN administrator; get the administrator started in the planning process.
23. Begin plans to train users on LAN usage and policies.
24. Verify that the available budget can accommodate the purchases needed. Revise plans if necessary.
25. If necessary, get approval to spend the money.
26. Order the needed hardware and software.
27. Install the hardware and software.
28. Test the hardware and software.
29. Begin using NetWare Lite.
30. Throw a post-installation party.

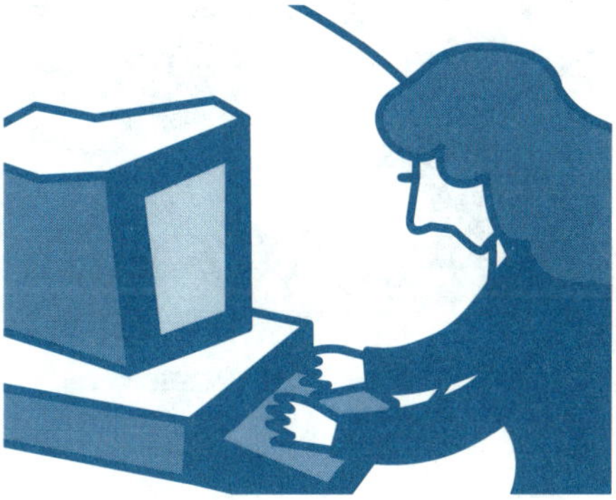

APPENDIX

SAMPLE BATCH FILES

This appendix discusses batch files and system files (particularly the AUTOEXEC.BAT, STARTNET.BAT, and CONFIG.SYS files) used on the PCs of a NetWare Lite LAN. Included are explanations of the different files, descriptions of how to modify the files, and sample files for various LAN configurations.

Although you don't have to use files exactly like the ones in this appendix, these files should give you some examples to work from and some ideas of parameters and options to try. If not otherwise stated, the files apply to an 80286 or higher PC with at least 640K of RAM. The files are constructed with the assumption that all the DOS files are in a directory called \DOS on drive C. In all cases, a hardware configuration using thin Ethernet LAN cards (such as the Novell/Eagle NE2000) is assumed. NetWare Lite version 1.1 is assumed also, but most files work with version 1.0 of NetWare Lite as well. (The biggest difference is that the NetWare Lite disk cache programs are new to version 1.1 and not available with version 1.0.)

The statements in the files are shown in all uppercase letters to reflect the way NetWare Lite and DOS create the files. (All uppercase letters also helps avoid confusion between the letter *L* and the number *1*, but you still have to be careful about the letter *O* versus the number *0*.) If you prefer, you can use lowercase letters; DOS and NetWare Lite accept upper- and lowercase interchangeably.

Clearly, this appendix cannot attempt to explain all the possible parameters and statements DOS permits in the system files AUTOEXEC.BAT and CONFIG.SYS. For more information about these files and what they can include, consult your DOS documentation.

Batch Files

A *batch file* is a text file that contains a series of DOS commands. When you execute a batch file, DOS executes the file's commands one at a time. It's as if you typed the first command in the file at the DOS prompt, waited for the command to execute, typed the second command when the DOS prompt reappeared, and continued to type the next command in the file whenever the DOS prompt reappeared.

The name of a batch file always ends with the .BAT extension (DOIT.BAT, for example). To execute a batch file, you simply type the name of the file at the DOS prompt (you don't have to include the .BAT extension). To execute a hypothetical batch file named DOIT.BAT, for example, you type **doit** and press [Enter].

The commands in a batch file frequently include the names of programs—DOS programs such as COPY or CLS, perhaps, or application programs, such as a spreadsheet or database program—that DOS should execute. You can place NetWare Lite NET commands in batch files to capture ports, map drives, or use other NetWare Lite features.

Sample Batch Files

To create batch files, you can use a word processor or text editor. (Remember that batch files are simple text files.) You can also modify existing batch files.

Two particular batch files—AUTOEXEC.BAT and STARTNET.BAT—have special meaning for NetWare Lite environments. These files are discussed in the following two sections.

AUTOEXEC.BAT

DOS recognizes a special batch file named AUTOEXEC.BAT. When DOS *initializes* (when you turn on your PC, or reboot), DOS looks for a file named AUTOEXEC.BAT in the root directory of drive C (on systems with a hard disk) or in drive A (on systems without a hard disk). If AUTOEXEC.BAT exists, DOS automatically executes the commands found in that file. You can place in AUTOEXEC.BAT any commands you want DOS to carry out at the beginning of each computing session. The installation of DOS creates an AUTOEXEC.BAT file for you.

When you install NetWare Lite with the default parameters, the installation program modifies your PC's AUTOEXEC.BAT file to include a PATH command to the \NWLITE directory (the directory containing the NetWare Lite files).

Here is a sample AUTOEXEC.BAT file:

```
PROMPT $P$G
PATH C:\;C:\DOS;C:\NWLITE
```

> **NOTE:** The PATH command provides DOS with a list of directories to search when you try to execute a program, batch file, or DOS command that is not in the current directory. The PROMPT command specifies what the DOS prompt should look like. For more about PATH and PROMPT, consult your DOS documentation.

To view the AUTOEXEC.BAT file on your PC, follow these two steps:

1. At the DOS prompt, type **cd** and press ⎣Enter⎦ to make the root directory the current directory.
2. Type **type autoexec.bat** and press ⎣Enter⎦.

STARTNET.BAT

STARTNET.BAT is a batch file created by the NetWare Lite installation program and stored in the \NWLITE directory. On each PC, this file contains the commands that initialize NetWare Lite. As explained later in this appendix, you can modify STARTNET.BAT to include NET and other commands that customize the way NetWare Lite is initialized.

For a node configured as a server and a client, here is a typical STARTNET.BAT file:

```
SHARE
LSL
NE2000.COM
IPXODI A
SERVER
CLIENT
```

CONFIG.SYS

Like AUTOEXEC.BAT, CONFIG.SYS is a special file used by DOS. When you turn on (or reboot) your computer, DOS looks for a file named CONFIG.SYS in the root directory of drive C (on systems with a hard disk). The file contains directives that specify how DOS should be configured.

The CONFIG.SYS directives may specify the number of buffers DOS should use, how many files can be opened simultaneously, device drivers to load, or other configuration information. (See your DOS documentation for information about various CONFIG.SYS directives.) Only after the directives in CONFIG.SYS are processed does DOS execute the commands in the AUTOEXEC.BAT file.

If you accept the default options when installing NetWare Lite, the installation program modifies (or creates) CONFIG.SYS to contain FILES, BUFFERS, and LASTDRIVE directives. Here is a typical CONFIG.SYS file:

Sample Batch Files

```
FILES=30
BUFFERS=30
LASTDRIVE=M
```

Editing Batch Files and CONFIG.SYS

You can modify (or create) batch files or CONFIG.SYS in a number of ways. Because these files are text files (also known as *ASCII files*), you can process them as text documents. The following sections discuss various ways to edit these files.

Use A Word Processor

You can modify or create a text file with a word processor, such as WordPerfect or Microsoft Word. You work with the file as you would with any text document. You must be sure, however, to treat the file as pure text, and not include any formatting characters or other special styles used by the word processor. Be sure to save the file in plain ASCII text format.

Use A Line-oriented Text Editor

Text editors are basically simplified word processors designed to work with text files. One type of text editor, called a *line editor*, works with files one line at a time. All versions of DOS include a line editor named EDLIN. You can use this program to create and modify text files. For information on using EDLIN, consult your DOS documentation.

Use COPY CON To Create A Text File

You can use the DOS command COPY CON to create a text file. To create a file named MYFILE.BAT, for example, follow these steps:

1. At the DOS prompt, type **copy con myfile.bat** and press [Enter].
2. Type the lines of the file, one at a time, pressing [Enter] after you type each line.
3. To save the file, press [F6] (which is equivalent to pressing [Ctrl]-[Z]) and then press [Enter].

Use A Full-screen Text Editor

A *full-screen* text editor enables you to work with the entire file onscreen (as opposed to a *line editor*, which works with one line at a time). You can move the cursor to any line of the file and make additions or corrections straightforwardly.

DOS 5 includes a full-screen editor named EDIT. (The program name is EDIT.COM.) With EDIT, you can easily modify (and create) batch files and other text files.

The following example shows you how to modify CONFIG.SYS, using EDIT. The example only touches on the features and capabilities of EDIT. Consult your DOS documentation for more information.

To use EDIT to modify the LASTDRIVE directive in CONFIG.SYS, follow these steps:

1. At the DOS prompt, type **cd** and press [Enter] to make the root directory the current directory.

2. Type **edit config.sys** and press [Enter].

   The editor screen opens to display the current CONFIG.SYS file (see Figure D-1). Note that the contents of your CONFIG.SYS file may not be identical to those shown in this figure.

3. Using the cursor keys, move the cursor to the "M" in the directive LASTDRIVE=M.

4. Press [T].

   The line now reads LASTDRIVE=TM. The cursor is under the "M".

5. Press [Del] to delete the "M" character.

   The line should now read LASTDRIVE=T.

   To add a new line, move the cursor to the location at which you want the new line to appear, type the new line, and then press [Enter].

   To delete a line, move the cursor to the beginning of the line and repeatedly press [Del] until the line is deleted.

6. Press [Alt]-[F] to activate the File menu.

7. To save the new version of the file, move the cursor down to Save and press [Enter].

8. To exit the editor, press [Alt]-[F] and then press [X].

Sample Batch Files

The EDIT program displays CONFIG.SYS
Figure C-1.

> **NOTE:** If you make any changes to AUTOEXEC.BAT or CONFIG.SYS, you must reboot your computer for the changes to take effect.

Adding NET Commands to Batch Files

One of the benefits of NET commands you can issue at the DOS prompt (instead of using the NET menu system) is that you can place NET commands into batch files. If you tend to use the same mapped drives and captured ports with each work session, you can place the appropriate NET commands in a batch file and then execute the batch file after you run STARTNET.BAT.

Suppose, for example, that you create a batch file named LANSETUP.BAT, which looks like this:

```
NET LOGIN SUPERVISOR
NET CAPTURE LPT2 LASER JUANITA
NET MAP F: CDRIVE MAXWELL
NET MAP G: TEXT_DOCUMENT JUANITA
```

This file logs you in to the network as SUPERVISOR. It then captures the LPT2 port to the network printer named LASER on the server JUANITA. Finally, it captures drives F and G into two different network directories. You should place this file in the \NWLITE directory.

You can run this file after you run STARTNET.BAT. Just type **lansetup** at the DOS prompt and press Enter.

NOTE: If you omit the NET LOGIN command from the batch file, NetWare Lite will prompt you to log in and supply your user name.

Starting NetWare Lite When You Turn On Your Computer

As explained in Chapter 5, when you install NetWare Lite, one of the default options is to automatically start the NetWare Lite software whenever you turn on (or reboot) your computer. NetWare Lite accomplishes this by invoking STARTNET.BAT directly from the AUTOEXEC.BAT file. To invoke STARTNET.BAT from another batch file, add the line STARTNET as the last line of the other batch file.

CAUTION: If one batch file invokes another, DOS control passes completely to the second batch file. When the second batch file terminates, control does not return to the original batch file. Therefore, if you place STARTNET at the end of your AUTOEXEC.BAT file, you should not place any commands after STARTNET because those additional commands will not execute.

If you did not select the installation option to start NetWare Lite automatically, you can modify your AUTOEXEC.BAT file in either of the following ways:

1. Add STARTNET to the end of AUTOEXEC.BAT.

   Your modified AUTOEXEC.BAT file might look like the following example:

Sample Batch Files

```
PROMPT $P$G
PATH C:\;C:\DOS;C:\NWLITE
STARTNET
```

Remember, if you use this technique, you cannot add additional commands after STARTNET.

2. Add all the commands from STARTNET.BAT directly into AUTOEXEC.BAT.

Your modified AUTOEXEC.BAT file might look like following example:

```
PROMPT $P$G
PATH C:\;C:\DOS;C:\NWLITE
SHARE
LSL
NE2000.COM
IPXODI A
SERVER
CLIENT
```

The advantage of this technique is that you can add additional commands, such as NET commands, to the end of the file.

Files for a "Typical" Configuration

The files presented in this section configure DOS and NetWare Lite for a small LAN (two to five nodes). The NetWare Lite 1.1 INSTALL program creates files very similar to these sample files. The installation option of adding STARTNET to the AUTOEXEC.BAT file is not exercised in these files.

These files make no attempt to optimize NetWare Lite for high performance or to reduce the use of conventional RAM (see subsequent configurations to achieve those goals). The files assume that Windows is not running. Also, some application programs (such as word processors or databases) and utility programs (such as memory managers) may require additional parameters or changes to some of the parameters shown in these files. Think of these files as a starting point for future changes that fit the needs of your LAN and your workgroup.

AUTOEXEC.BAT

The following listing shows an AUTOEXEC.BAT file for a node configured as both a server and a client:

```
PROMPT $P$G
PATH C:\;C:\DOS;C:\NWLITE
```

CONFIG.SYS

The following listing shows a CONFIG.SYS file for a node configured as both a server and a client:

```
SHELL=C:\DOS\COMMAND.COM C:\DOS /P
FILES=30
BUFFERS=30
LASTDRIVE=M
```

STARTNET.BAT for a Node Configured as a Server and a Client

The following listing shows a STARTNET.BAT file for a node configured as both a server and a client:

```
SHARE
LSL
NE2000.COM
IPXODI A
SERVER
CLIENT
```

STARTNET.BAT for a Node Configured as a Client Only

The following listing shows a STARTNET.BAT file for a node configured exclusively as a client:

```
LSL
NE2000.COM
IPXODI A
CLIENT
```

Sample Batch Files

Troubleshooting Configuration

The files in this section provide a minimum ("stripped-down") configuration to aid in troubleshooting problems with NetWare Lite. Note that the sample STARTNET.BAT file in this section has a PAUSE statement after the statement to load each NetWare Lite TSR. Each PAUSE gives you a chance, before you press a key to continue, to examine the messages displayed by the preceding NetWare Lite TSR program. You can read any error messages or review the displayed default parameters. Also, you can interrupt the STARTNET.BAT file if you want to run any diagnostic tests when only some NetWare Lite programs are active, to help pin down a specific incompatibility.

CONFIG.SYS

The following listing shows a CONFIG.SYS file for a node configured as both a server and a client:

```
FILES=30
BUFFERS=30
LASTDRIVE=M
```

STARTNET.BAT

The following listing shows a STARTNET.BAT file for a node configured as both a server and a client:

```
SHARE
PAUSE
LSL
PAUSE
NE2000.COM
PAUSE
IPXODI A
PAUSE
SERVER
PAUSE
CLIENT
```

High-Performance LAN Server Configuration

The files in this section configure a NetWare Lite server to provide better-than-default performance at the cost of using more than minimal RAM. The server, which has extended memory, runs the NetWare Lite disk cache program in extended memory. If your server does not have extended memory, change NLCACHEX to NLCACHEC (for conventional memory) or NLCACHEM (for expanded memory). DOS 5 is assumed.

These files are a working starting point. Depending on your LAN environment, you may want to specify additional parameters for NLCACHEX, as discussed in Chapter 14.

STARTNET.BAT

The following listing shows a STARTNET.BAT file for a server that runs the NetWare Lite cache:

```
SHARE /F:4096 /L:200
LSL
NE2000.COM
IPXODI A
SERVER
NLCACHEX 1024
NETBIOS
```

CONFIG.SYS

The following listing shows a CONFIG.SYS file for a server that runs the NetWare Lite cache:

```
DEVICE=C:\DOS\SETVER.EXE
DEVICE=C:\DOS\HIMEM.SYS
DEVICE=C:\DOS\ANSI.SYS
SHELL=C:\DOS\COMMAND.COM C:\DOS\  /p
STACKS=9,256
FILES=70
BUFFERS=20
LASTDRIVE=X
```

Sample Batch Files

Minimum RAM Configuration

The following configuration does not use the absolute minimum of conventional RAM possible with NetWare Lite and DOS. Rather, this configuration uses a slightly smaller amount of RAM than other configurations, without totally sacrificing performance. (Most of NetWare Lite's default parameters are about as low as you dare go.) This configuration is designed for a computer that needs to free up as much as possible of its 640K or 512K of RAM.

If your computer has more than 640K of RAM, use DOS 5 (as in the next sample configuration) or another memory manager to load DOS and/or NetWare Lite into the extra RAM. These parameters should be adequate, however, if your LAN has no more than three users, uses a single server with a small workload, and you don't put a high priority on the best possible response time. If you run even a small shared database application, however, these parameters probably will be insufficient.

CONFIG.SYS

The following listing shows a CONFIG.SYS file for a node configured as both a server and a client:

```
STACKS=0,0
FILES=20
BUFFERS=20
LASTDRIVE=G
```

STARTNET.BAT

The following listing shows a STARTNET.BAT file for a node configured as both a server and a client:

```
SHARE
LSL
NE2000.COM
IPXODI A
CLIENT
```

DOS 5 Extended Memory Configuration

If your computer is a 386 (or 486) with some extended RAM, and is running DOS 5, you can have the best of both worlds: high performance and a large amount of available conventional RAM. You can configure such a system in many ways. The sample files in this section show a starting point. This starting point is basically the high-performance configuration listed earlier, combined with DOS and some of the NetWare Lite TSRs loaded into high memory. The NetWare Lite cache operates in extended memory. The sample configuration does not load a mouse driver nor does it run Windows.

The configuration shown here leaves available approximately 563K of conventional RAM for a node configured as a server and a client, with the NetWare Lite cache running without the minimum buffer sizes. Depending on how much UMB (*upper memory block*) memory your computer leaves available, you may be able to use LOADHIGH on other NetWare Lite TSR programs than those shown here, further increasing the available RAM.

Two notes about changes you may need to make, depending on your computer configuration:

- ◆ You may need to add the X= parameter on the CONFIG.SYS EMM386 line to exclude a RAMBASE address for your LAN card or other peripheral device (example: X=D800-DFFF). You do not need to do so for the Novell/Eagle Ethernet cards, such as the NE2000. Check your LAN card manual and jumper settings to see specifically which address range you may need to exclude.

- ◆ You will need to adjust the numerical value on the NLCACHEX line of the STARTNET.BAT file to fit your available XMS memory size. Try a number slightly more than 1MB less than your total RAM. If you have 4MB (4096K) of RAM, for example, try 3000 or 2900. Clearly, if you run an application that needs to use some of the extra memory, give correspondingly less to the NetWare Lite cache.

CONFIG.SYS

The following listing shows a CONFIG.SYS file for a node configured as a both a server and a client:

Sample Batch Files

```
DEVICE=C:\DOS\HIMEM.SYS
DEVICE=C:\DOS\EMM386.EXE NOEMS
DOS=HIGH, UMB
SHELL=C:\DOS\COMMAND.COM C:\DOS\  /p
FILES=30
BUFFERS=30
LASTDRIVE=M
```

STARTNET.BAT

The following listing shows a STARTNET.BAT file for a node configured as a both a server and a client:

```
SHARE
LSL
NE2000.COM
IPXODI A
LOADHIGH SERVER
LOADHIGH CLIENT
NLCACHEX.EXE  2048
```

APPENDIX

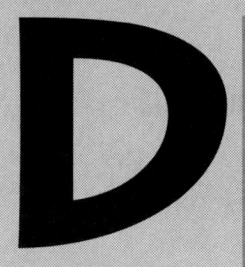

SUPPORT FROM THE AUTHORS

The authors invite your comments. When the time comes for a revised edition of this book, your feedback is invaluable. If you have any new tips and traps, or find anything in the book unclear, please let the authors know. All correspondence is welcome and will be read.

Although no reply is guaranteed, the authors will try to respond to questions and problems concerning NetWare Lite. Be as specific as possible. To receive an answer, you must include a self-addressed stamped envelope. Please understand if your question cannot be answered or if the reply takes several weeks.

You can reach the authors through the publisher or at the following address:

Phil Feldman & Tom Rugg
NetWare Lite Made Easy
P.O. Box 24815
Los Angeles, CA 90024

NetWare Lite Software from the Authors

The authors have created a series of programs that should benefit any NetWare Lite administrator or user. One of the programs is the BENCH program mentioned in Chapter 14, which allows you to run your own benchmarks and optimize your NetWare Lite LAN. Other programs include a variety of utilities to do such things as check the status and error statistics for any LAN card, monitor a group of LAN cards, cancel the mappings of all your server connections at once, and so on. The list continues to grow.

If you would like a disk with these programs, send $19.00 (U.S.) to the authors at the address just provided. If you send a formatted floppy disk and a return disk mailer with return postage, the cost is $16.00. California residents, please add sales tax. If you send a check, make it payable to Tom Rugg. You'll get a 5 1/4-inch, 360K floppy disk unless you request another format.

INDEX

10BASE2 LANs. See Thin Ethernet LANs
10BASE5 LANs. See Thick Ethernet LANs
10BASE-T LANs, 60-61
    cable length and, 64, 68
    installing, 88
    versus thin Ethernet LANs, 67
    troubleshooting, 338, 339
    See also Ethernet LAN products;
        Hub-based LANs; Twisted-pair cables
\ (backslash), 155

A

Access rights, 297-298, 311-316
    network directories and, 311-315
    network printers and, 315-316
    restricting, 312-315
    troubleshooting, 343-344
    See also Passwords; Security
Account names. See User accounts
Adapter cards. See LAN cards
Administrator. See LAN administrator
[Alt] key, 140, 150, 333, 341
Application software, 247-269
    accounting, 267
    compatibility levels of, 248-249
    compatible with LAN support, 255-257
    compatible without LAN support, 31-33, 251-255
    database, 261-262
    e-mail, 264-265, 266-267
    graphics, 263-264
    incompatible, 249-251
    installing shared, 253
    LAN dependent, 257-258
    LAN planning and, 70-71
    licensing and, 32-33, 254
    listed, 268-269
    message system and, 216
    overview of, 12
    running outside NetWare Lite, 133
    setup configuration of, 254
    sharing violations and, 255
    simultaneous access and, 251-252
    spreadsheet, 259-261
    troubleshooting, 121-122, 333, 340, 343
    word processing, 258-259
    See also Compatibility; Groupware;
        Microsoft Windows; Software
ARCnet, 9, 62

See also IEEE standards
Arrow keys. See Cursor keys
ArtiCom, 231-239
　　installing, 232
　　modem server installation and, 233-234
　　running, 235-239
　　two-way serial devices and, 231-232
　　workstation software installation and, 235
　　See also Modems
Audit command, NET, 319-320
Audit logs, 317-320
　　See also Error logs; Security
AUTOEXEC.BAT
　　editing, 427-429
　　example of, 432
　　explained, 425
　　installation and, 108-112
　　SHARE program and, 396
　　starting NetWare Lite from, 132, 430-431
　　troubleshooting and, 331-333
　　See also CONFIG.SYS; STARTNET.BAT

B

Backslash character (\), 155
Backspace key, 140
Backups
　　incremental, 280
　　LAN administrator and, 275-276
　　off-site, 279-280
　　overview of, 276-278
　　rotation method for, 279
　　of server system files, 320-322
　　strategies for, 278-281
　　See also Tape backup drives
Banner setting, printer, 191-192
Baseband signalling, 60
Batch files
　　editing, 427-429
　　explained, 423-425
　　installation and, 110-111
　　NET commands in, 148, 173, 429-430
　　starting NetWare Lite with, 430-431
　　See also AUTOEXEC.BAT; CONFIG.SYS; STARTNET.BAT
BENCH program, 364-365, 373-375

Benchmark tests
　　DEDICATE program and, 366
　　disk caches and, 364-365
　　guidelines for, 352-353
　　LAN administrator and, 292
　　large versus small block, 350-351
　　overview of, 349-350
　　server buffers and, 373-375
　　See also Optimization
BIOS. See NetBIOS program; ROM BIOS
BNC T-connectors
　　bus topology and, 53-54
　　coaxial cables and, 11, 60
　　installation of, 86-87, 88
　　terminators and, 90
　　See also Connectors
Boards. See LAN cards
Borland International
　　dBASE III Plus, 261
　　Paradox, 261-262
　　Quattro Pro, 260-261
Broadband signalling, 60
Budgeting, 71, 291
Buffers. See Disk buffers; Print buffers; Server buffers
BUFFERS statement (DOS)
　　installation and, 114-115
　　NLCACHE programs and, 363
　　optimization and, 367-368, 381-382
Bus LANs, 42, 66-67
Bus topology, 53-340
Buses
　　LAN versus data, 53
　　starter kits and, 43
　　See also EISA buses; ISA buses; MCA buses
Bytes, defined, 154

C

Cables
　　floor plans and, 65-66
　　illustrated, 10, 22
　　installation of, 87-89
　　null modem, 15, 48
　　optimization and, 378-379
　　overview of, 10

Index

purchasing tips for, 88
routing, 62-65, 89
troubleshooting, 330, 337-338
See also 10BASE-T LANs; Coaxial cables; Ethernet LAN products; RG58 cables; Thick Ethernet LANs; Thin Ethernet LANs; Twisted-pair cables
Capture command, NET, 197, 198
Card slots. See Expansion slots
Cards. See LAN cards
cc:Mail, 266-267
CDRIVE directory, 123-124
CD-ROM disk drives, 217-229
    accessing, 227-229
    costs of, 220-221
    data capacity of, 218-219
    databases available on, 34-35
    external, 222
    installing, 222-227
    interface cards for, 222-224
    internal, 222
    LAN planning and, 52
    limitations of, 221-222
    searches on, 219-220
    sharing, 24, 33-35
    sources for products for, 229
    See also Disk drives; Hard disk drives
CHDIR (or CD) command, DOS, 156
Checklists, planning, 417-420
CHKDSK command, DOS, 134
CLIENT.EXE, 121, 126-127, 131
Client nodes
    batch files for configuring, 432
    installation for, 98, 104-105, 107-108
    logging out and, 172
    message system and, 210
    overview of, 6-7, 20
    synchronizing times on, 400, 401-402
    See also Server nodes; Workstations
Client-server LANs, 5-7, 20
    See also LANs; Peer-to-peer LANs
Coaxial cables
    BNC connectors and, 11
    installing, 88
    overview of, 10
    versus twisted-pair cables, 56, 57

    See also Ethernet LAN products; RG58 cables; Thick Ethernet LANs; Thin Ethernet LANs; Twisted-pair cables
Collisions, defined, 59
Communications (COM) ports. See Serial ports
Communications software, 232
Compatibility
    of CD-ROM disk drives, 221
    incompatible programs, 249-250
    LAN dependent programs, 257-258
    with LAN support, 255-257
    without LAN support, 251-255
    of modem software, 231, 240
    NetWare Lite and software, 44
    of NetWare Lite versus NetWare, 256, 398-399
    simultaneous access and, 251-252
    of TSR programs, 249
    types of, 248-249
    See also Application software
Computer lockups, 333-337, 341
Computer Select database, 35
Computer viruses. See Viruses
Computers. See PCs
Concentrators, 61
    See also Hub-based LANs
CONFIG.SYS
    CD-ROM installation and, 225-226
    editing, 427-429
    examples of, 432-437
    explained, 426
    NetWare Lite installation and, 108-110, 113-115
    NLCACHE programs and, 363
    RAM optimization and, 381-382
    SHARE program and, 396
    troubleshooting and, 331-333, 433
    See also AUTOEXEC.BAT; STARTNET.BAT
Connectivity
    alternatives to LANs, 14-17
    defined, 1-2
    Frisbeenets and, 16-17
    multiuser operating systems and, 16
    parallel ports and, 15-16
    print buffers and, 14-15
    serial ports and, 15-16

Sneakernets and, 16
    See also LANs
Connectors, 11, 338
    See also BNC T-connectors
Contention, 59
COPY CON command, DOS, 427
Covers, installation and, 83-84, 87
CSMA/CD access method, 59
Ctrl key, + Alt + Del, 150, 333, 341
Cursor keys, 137, 140

D

Daisy-chain topology. See Bus topology
Daisy-chaining, 11, 60, 224-225
Data integrity, 274-275
Database applications
    CD-ROMs and, 34-35
    sharing, 25, 28-31
    software for, 261-262
dBASE III Plus, 261
DEDICATE program, 365-366
Dedicated servers, 6, 210, 365-366
    See also Server nodes
Default settings, 79, 80
Defragmentation, disk, 376
Del key, 140, 150, 333, 341
Designs, LAN, 3, 5-8
    See also Client-server LANs; Peer-to-peer LANs
Despooling, 194
Device drivers. See Drivers
Directories
    default, 155-156
    defined, 154-155
    installation and, 107-108
    LANs and, 27-28
    See also Network directories; NWLITE directory
Disk buffers, 367-368, 379-382
    See also Print buffers; Server buffers
Disk caches, 354-365
    benchmark tests and, 364-365
    installation of, 112-113
    memory types and, 355-358
    overview of, 354-355
    versus processor caches, 364
    third-party, 362-363
    tips on using, 363-364
    troubleshooting and, 333, 339-340
    See also NLCACHE programs; Optimization
Disk drives, 27, 154
    See also CD-ROM disk drives; Hard disk drives; Mapped drives; Mapping drive letters
Disk fragmentation, 376
Disk partitions, 369-370
Disk sharing, 156-157
DOS
    batch files and installation, 110-111
    changing passwords from, 304
    CHDIR (or CD) command, 156
    CHKDSK command, 134
    COPY CON command, 427
    FASTOPEN program, 340, 368
    FILES statement, 114-115, 381-382
    getting help from, 149
    issuing NET commands from, 146-148, 172-175
    issuing printer commands from, 196-198
    LAN planning and, 48
    LASTDRIVE statement, 114, 381-382
    NetWare Lite and, 27, 44
    optimization and, 367-370, 381-382
    sending messages via, 214-215
    system files and installation, 108-115
    See also BUFFERS statement; Error messages; Menu system; SHARE program
Drive mapping. See Mapped drives; Mapping drive letters
Drivers
    CD-ROM, 225-227
    installation of, 91-92, 115-116, 119
    LAN installation and, 96-97
Dual-twisted pair (DTP) cables, 10
    See also Twisted-pair cables

E

Eagle Technology LAN cards, 74-76
    See also Novell, Inc.

Index

EISA buses, LAN cards for, 75-76
    See also Buses; ISA buses; MCA buses
Electromagnetic interference, 64, 68, 338
Electronic messages. *See* Message system
E-mail software, 264-265, 266-267
    LANs and, 30
    versus message system, 211, 265
End users. *See* Users
[Enter] key, 137, 140
Error logs, 317, 320
    See also Audit logs; Security
Error messages
    "Bad command or file name," 132
    "Insufficient memory," 337
    network printers and, 196
    "Share violation," 340
    See also Status Report messages;
        Troubleshooting
[Esc] key, 137, 140
Ethernet LAN products
    cables, 59-61
    LAN cards, 74-76
    LAN protocols, 9
    See also 10BASE-T LANs; Coaxial cables;
        LAN cards; Thick Ethernet LANs; Thin
        Ethernet LANs
Expansion slots, 49, 84-86

F

[F] keys, 140
FASTOPEN program, DOS, 340, 368
File allocation tables (FAT), 370
File servers, 6, 21
    See also Server nodes
Filenames. See Naming conventions
Files
    corruption of, 339-341
    defined, 154-155
    loading and saving, 27
    SHARE program and, 251-252
    See also Batch files
FILES statement, DOS, 114-115, 381-382
Floppy disk drives, 154
    See also Disk drives; Hard disk drives
Floppy disks, 125-126, 277

Font cartridges, 201-202
Form feed setting, printer, 192
Fragmentation, disk, 376
Freelance, 263
Frisbeenets, 16-17
Function keys, 140

G

Gateways, defined, 49
Getting Started with Microsoft Windows,
    390, 396
Graphics software, 263-264
Groupware
    defined, 12, 257-258
    examples of, 264-266
    LANs and, 29-30
    See also Application software

H

Hard disk drives
    defined, 154
    LAN planning and, 46-47
    optimizing, 382-383
    partitioning, 369-370
    sharing, 25, 26-28
    See also CD-ROM disk drives; Disk drives;
        Mapped drives; Mapping drive letters
Hardware
    LAN layout and, 62-70
    LAN planning and, 52-57
    LAN signalling methods and, 58-62
    maintenance of, 288
    NetWare Lite requirements for, 21-22, 23
    overview of, 8-12
    purchasing tips for, 77-78
    troubleshooting, 330-331
    See also Cables; Ethernet LAN products;
        Installation, of hardware; LAN cards;
        Starter kits
Harvard Graphics, 263
Help, from authors, 439-440
Help system, NetWare Lite, 148-149
Hewlett-Packard laser printers, 199-201

Hub-based LANs
    10BASE-T LANs and, 60-61
    cable length and, 64, 68
    defined, 42
    laying out, 67-68
    troubleshooting, 339
    See also 10BASE-T LANs; LANs; Star topology; Topologies

I

I/O Base Address settings
    hardware and, 82-83
    software and, 97-98, 116-118
    troubleshooting, 334-335
    See also IRQ settings
IBM PS/2 computers, 76
IEEE standards, 59-62
    See also ARCnet
Indexes, of CD-ROMs, 219-220
[Ins] key, 140
INSTALL program
    optimization and, 378
    SHARE program and, 396
    troubleshooting and, 329, 332
Installation disks, 100-103, 119-120
Installation, of hardware, 73-92
    of BNC T-connectors, 86-87, 88
    of cables, 87-89
    for CD-ROMs, 222-225
    covers and, 83-84, 87
    of drivers, 91-92
    I/O Base Address settings and, 82-83
    of independent hardware, 90-92
    IRQ settings and, 81-82
    LAN card settings and, 79-83
    LAN card types and, 75-76
    of LAN cards, 84-86
    of Novell hardware, 78-79
    overview of, 78
    starter kits and, 76-77
    of terminators, 89-90
Installation, of software, 95-127
    AUTOEXEC.BAT and, 108-112
    Base Memory Address and, 97
    CLIENT.EXE and, 121, 126-127
    for clients, 98, 104-105, 107-108
    CONFIG.SYS and, 108-110, 113-115
    disk cache feature and, 112-113
    DOS batch files and, 110-111
    DOS system files and, 108-115
    drivers and, 96-97, 115-116, 119
    to floppy disks, 125-126
    I/O Base Address settings and, 97-98, 116-118
    initializing NetWare Lite, 120-121, 131-132
    installation disks and, 100-103, 119-120
    into upper memory, 126-127
    IRQ settings and, 97-98, 116-118
    LAN cards and, 96-98, 115-116
    of NetWare Lite files, 118
    overview of, 98-99, 104-105
    prerequisites for, 96-98
    README.TXT and, 101-102
    reconfiguring nodes and, 125
    SERVER.EXE and, 121, 126-127
    for servers, 98, 104-107
    STARTNET.BAT and, 112, 120-121
    testing NetWare Lite, 122-123
    troubleshooting, 121-122
    verifying network connections, 123-124
Institute of Electrical Electronics Engineers. See IEEE
Interface cards, CD-ROM, 222-224
Interference. See Electromagnetic interference
Interleave factor, 375-376
IRQ settings
    hardware and, 81-82
    software and, 97-98, 116-118
    troubleshooting, 334-335
    See also I/O Base Address settings
ISA buses, 43, 74, 75-76, 77
    See also Buses; EISA buses; MCA buses

J

Job hold setting, printer, 192
Jumpers, on LAN cards, 79-83
    See also IRQ settings

Index

K

Keys, in menu system, 140

L

LAN administrator, 271-292
    budgeting and, 291
    communication with users and, 287
    configuration management and, 290-291
    data integrity and, 274-275
    duties of, 273-274
    hardware maintenance and, 288
    optimization and, 291-292
    overview of, 13-14
    primary, 272-273
    secondary, 273
    security and, 286
    selecting, 272-273
    server maintenance and, 289
    user support and, 286-287
    See also Access rights; Backups; Passwords; Security; Viruses
LAN cables. See Cables; Coaxial cables; Ethernet LAN products; Thick Ethernet LANs; Thin Ethernet LANs; Twisted-pair cables
LAN cards
    creating LANs with, 21-22
    I/O Base Address settings on, 82-83
    installing, 78, 79-83, 84-86
    IRQ settings on, 81-82
    listed, 74-76
    optimization and, 378-379
    overview of, 8-10
    purchasing tips for, 69-70
    settings on, 79-83
    software installation and, 96-98, 115-116
    troubleshooting, 330-331, 339
    types of, 75-76
LAN operating system. *See* Network operating system (NOS)
LAN-compatible software. *See* Application software; Compatibility
LANs
    alternatives to, 14-17
    defined, 1-2, 8
    design philosophy of, 5-8
    hardware components of, 8-12
    history of, 2-4
    software components of, 12-13
    uses of, 36-37
    See also Bus LANs; Client-server LANs; Connectivity; Hub-based LANs; NetWare Lite; Peer-to-peer LANs; Wireless LANs; Zero-slot LANs
Laptops. See Portable computers
Laser printers
    font cartridges for, 201-202
    Hewlett-Packard, 199-201
    network printers and, 199-202
    PostScript, 199
    See also Network printers; Printer ports; other Print entries
LASTDRIVE statement, DOS, 114, 381-382
Licensing restrictions, 32-33, 100, 254
Linear bus topology. See Bus topology
Locked-up computers, 333-337, 341
Logging on, 135-136
    with an account name, 208-209
    with passwords, 302-303
    See also Access rights; Passwords; Security
Logging out, 172
Login command, NET, 430
Lotus Development Corp.
    cc:Mail, 266-267
    Freelance, 263-264
    Lotus 1-2-3, 260
LPT ports. See Printer ports

M

Macintosh computers, 44, 49-50
    See also PCs
MACLAN Connect, 49
Main menu, 137-139
Map command, NET, 145, 173-175
Mapped drives
    canceling, 169-171, 174
    displaying list of, 173
    logging out and, 172
    saving record of, 174-175

terminating, 145-146
testing, 142-145
verifying, 145
Mapping drive letters
    defined, 27
    disk sharing and, 156-157
    from DOS, 174
    to network directories, 165-169
    steps for, 141-142
MCA buses
    installing LAN cards on, 81
    LAN cards for, 74, 76
    starter kits and, 43, 77
    See also Buses; EISA buses; ISA buses
Memory, 355-358
    conventional, 355-356, 357
    expanded (EMS), 356, 358
    extended (XMS), 357-358
    NetWare Lite and, 23, 126-127
    NLCACHE programs and, 358
    optimizing, 435-437
    troubleshooting, 336, 337
    upper, 126-127, 356, 357, 382
    See also RAM
Memory managers, 333, 357
Menu system, 136-141
    changing passwords from, 303-304
    exiting, 140-141
    function keys and, 137, 140
    getting help from, 148
    Main menu, 137-139
    sending messages via, 211-214
    status screen of, 378-379
    viewing print queue from, 194-195
    See also DOS
Message system, 210-217
    versus e-mail, 211, 265
    Microsoft Windows and, 395
    overview of, 210-211
    receiving messages, 210, 215-216
    selecting recipients in, 213-214
    sending via DOS, 214-215
    sending via menu system, 211-214
    turning on/off, 216-217
    See also Error messages; Status Report messages
Microsoft CD Extensions, 225

Microsoft Windows, 388-396
    optimization and, 379
    overview of, 388-389
    shared use of, 395-396
    single-user configuration of, 389-395
    See also Application software
Microsoft Windows User's Guide, 389, 396
Microsoft Word, 259
Modem servers, 232
    See also Server nodes
Modems, 230-240
    LAN planning and, 51
    overview of, 230-231
    products for sharing, 240
    sharing, 24-25, 35-36
    See also ArtiCom
Mouse, menu system and, 137
MSCDEX (Microsoft CD Extensions), 225
Multiport serial adapters, 231

N

Naming conventions
    for directories, files, paths, 155
    for servers, 105-107
Ndlist command, NET, 173
NE2000 LAN card
    installing, 78, 79
    overview of, 75-76
    See also LAN cards
NET commands
    Audit command, 319-320
    Capture command, 197, 198
    command reference, 147-148
    issuing from DOS, 146-148, 172-175, 196-198
    Login command, 430
    Map command, 145, 173-175
    menu system and, 136
    Ndlist command, 173
    overview of, 133-134
    Print command, 196-198
    Save command, 174-175
    Send command, 214
    Setpass command, 304
    shutting down and, 150

Index

Time command, 401-402
Ulist command, 214
NET Help system. *See* Help system
NET menu system. *See* Menu system
NetBIOS program
    groupware and, 257-258
    modem software and, 231, 232
    use of, 397-398
NetWare
    versus NetWare Lite, 256, 398-399
    upgrading to, 399-400
NetWare Lite
    CD-ROM sharing and, 24, 33-35
    database sharing and, 25, 28-31
    disk cache feature, 112-113
    disk sharing and, 25, 26-28
    hardware requirements for, 21-22, 23
    history of LANs and, 4-5
    inappropriate situations for, 44
    initializing, 120-121, 131-132
    Installation of software, 95-127
    LAN cards for, 74-76
    LAN size and, 44
    licensing restrictions on, 100
    memory requirements for, 23
    modem sharing and, 24-25, 35-36
    versus NetWare, 256, 398-399
    peer-to-peer LANs and, 20-21
    physical layout of, 21-22
    printer sharing and, 24, 26
    ring topologies and, 57
    running applications outside of, 133
    SHARE program and, 251-252
    software compatibility with, 44
    software copyrights and, 32-33, 254
    software requirements for, 23
    software sharing and, 25, 31-33
    starting from AUTOEXEC.BAT, 430-431
    testing, 122-123
    thin Ethernet LANs and, 60
    token ring LANs and, 62
    as a TSR program, 23
    upgrading, 103, 399-400
    uses of, 23-26, 36-37, 44
    See also Installation, of hardware; Installation, of software; LANs; Starter kits

Network Basic Input/Output System. *See* NetBIOS program
Network directories
    access rights and, 311-315
    canceling, 169-171
    CDRIVE directory and, 316-317
    creating, 156-157, 160-165
    deleting, 171
    disk sharing and, 157
    displaying list of, 173
    mapped, 166-169
    mapping drive letters to, 165-169
    scope of, 159-160, 316-317
    See also Directories; NWLITE directory
Network interface cards (NICs). *See* LAN cards
Network operating system (NOS)
    overview of, 12
    as TSR program, 7, 12
    See also Operating systems
Network printers, 24, 26, 177-202
    access rights and, 315-316
    accessing, 189-190
    canceling redirection of, 190
    controlling from DOS, 196-198
    creating, 178-184
    deleting, 184-185
    error messages and, 196
    font cartridges and, 201-202
    LAN configurations for, 180
    LAN planning and, 50-51, 65-66
    laser printers and, 199-202
    print queues and, 193-196
    printer port capture settings and, 190-193
    printer ports and, 178, 179, 182-183, 185-188
    renaming, 184-185
    Status Report messages and, 196
    testing, 188-189
    See also Print entries; Printer ports
Network productivity software, 29-30
NLCACHE programs, 358-364
    how they work, 361-362
    installing, 359-360
    memory configuration and, 358
    overview of, 354-355
    preparing to run, 358-359
    RAM optimization and, 381

using, 360-361
  See also Disk caches
Nodes
  defined, 5, 20
  logging into, 135
  reconfiguring, 125
  See also Client nodes; Server nodes
Notify upon completion setting, printer, 192
Novell, Inc., 4, 74-76
  See also NetWare; NetWare Lite;
    Starter kits
Null modem cables, 15, 48
NWLITE directory, 130-131
  See also Directories; Network directories

O

Operating systems, 16
  See also Network operating system (NOS)
Optimization, 347-384
  batch files for, 434-437
  cable problems and, 378-379
  DEDICATE program and, 365-366
  disk buffers and, 367-368, 379-380, 381-382
  disk fragmentation and, 376
  disk partitions and, 369-370
  of disk space, 382-383
  DOS parameters and, 367-370, 381-382
  FASTOPEN program and, 368
  interleave factor and, 375-376
  LAN administrator and, 291-292
  LAN card problems and, 378-379
  overview of, 347-348, 383-384
  print buffers and, 372-373
  of RAM, 379-382
  RAM disks and, 368-369
  server disk space and, 377
  server parameters and, 370-375, 379-380, 381
  SHARE program and, 369
  for speed, 353-379
  troubleshooting and, 344
  upgrades and, 377
  upper memory and, 382

Windows and, 379
  See also Benchmark tests; Disk caches

P

Paper type setting, printer, 192
Paradox, 261-262
Parallel ports, 15-16, 179
  See also Printer ports; Serial ports
Parallel printers, 179
Parameters
  NET commands and, 146-148
  SUPERVISOR, 135-136
Partitions, hard disk, 369-370
Passwords, 298-307
  changing from DOS, 304
  changing from menu system, 303-304
  changing other's, 305
  choosing, 298-299
  creating, 299-302
  logging in with, 302-303
  removing, 304
  setting attributes of, 306-307
  SUPERVISOR account and, 305-306
  See also Access rights; Security; User accounts
PATH command, DOS, 111-112, 132
Paths, defined, 155
PCs, LAN planning and, 46
  See also Macintosh computers; Portable computers
Peer-to-peer LANs
  NetWare Lite and, 20-21
  network operating system and, 12
  overview of, 7-8
  See also Client-server LANs; LANs
Performance. See Optimization
Peripherals, LAN planning and, 50-52
  See also CD-ROM disk drives; Modems; Network printers; Plotters
Planning, 39-71
  analyzing needs, 41-42
  application software and, 70-71
  budgets and, 71
  cable planning, 66-68

Index

checklists for, 417-420
floor plan and, 65-66
hardware location, 52-57, 62-65
LAN standards and, 58-62
Macintosh computers and, 49-50
NetWare Lite and, 42-44
peripherals and, 50-52
reasons for, 40-41
sources of equipment, 69-70
surge suppressors, UPSs and, 68-69
workgroup characteristics and,
  41-42, 46-50
Plotters, LAN planning and, 51-52
Pocket Ethernet Adapters, 244-245
Portable computers, 47-48, 244-245
  See also PCs
Ports, *See also* I/O Base Address settings; IRQ
  settings; Parallel ports; Printer ports;
  Serial ports
PostScript printers, 199
  See also Network printers
Power sources, troubleshooting, 341
Print buffers, 14-15, 372-373
  See also Disk buffers; Server buffers
Print command, NET, 196-198
Print files, 194
Print queues, 193-196
  deleting print jobs, 195-196
  overview of, 193-194
  viewing status of, 194-195
  See also Network printers
Print servers, 6, 21
  See also Network printers; Server nodes
Print spool, 194
Printer commands, 196-198
Printer ports
  capture settings of, 190-193
  capturing, 185-188
  network printers and, 178
  overview of, 179
  selecting, 182-183
  See also Network printers; Parallel ports
Printer wait setting, printer, 192
Printers. See Network printers
Problems. See Troubleshooting
Processor caches, 364

Protocols, network, 9-10
Punchdown blocks, 56

Q

Q&A, 262
Quattro Pro, 260-261
Queues. See Print queues

R

RAM
  defined, 355
  LAN planning and, 46-47
  NetWare Lite and, 134
  optimizing, 379-382, 435
  troubleshooting and, 336
  See also Memory
RAM base address conflicts, 336
RAM disks, 368-369
README.TXT, 101-102
Rebooting, 149-150, 333, 341, 429
Redirection, defined, 156
Repeaters, defined, 60
Resource sharing, 141-146
RG58 cables, 10, 60, 88
  See also Coaxial cables
Ring topology, 57
RJ45 modular plugs, 11
ROM BIOS, 48-49

S

Save command, NET, 174-175
SCSI controllers, 223, 224-225
Security, 295-321
  audit logs and, 317-320
  error logs and, 320
  LAN administrator and, 286
  network directories and, 160, 316-317
  overview of, 295-297
  physical, 296
  server system files and, 320-321
  See also Access rights; Passwords

Segments, defined, 60
Send command, NET, 214
Serial adapters, multiport, 231
Serial ports, 15-16, 179
    See also Parallel ports; Printer ports
Server buffers, 370-375, 379-380, 381
    See also Disk buffers; Print buffers
SERVER.EXE
    installation of, 121, 126-127
    NWLITE directory and, 131
Server nodes
    accessing network printers from, 189-190
    batch files for configuring, 432, 434-437
    benchmark tests on, 373-375
    changing parameters of, 370-371
    installation for, 98, 104-107
    logging out and, 172
    maintenance of, 289, 377
    message system and, 210
    optimizing disk space on, 377
    overview of, 5-6, 20
    RAM optimization and, 379-380, 381
    shutting down, 149-150, 172
    speed optimization and, 370-375
    synchronizing times on, 400-402
    system files on, 320-321
    See also Client nodes; Client-server LANs;
        Dedicated servers; File servers;
        Modem servers; Print servers
Setpass command, NET, 304
Setup string setting, printer, 192
SHARE program, 251-252
    optimization and, 369
    troubleshooting and, 340
    use of, 396-397
Shared directories. *See* Network directories
Shared printers. *See* Network printers
Sharing violations, 255, 340, 344
Shutting down, 149-150, 341
Slots. *See* Expansion slots
Sneakernets, 16
Software
    compatibility with NetWare Lite, 44
    installing CD-ROM, 225-227
    LAN planning and, 70-71
    LAN versions of, 31-33, 257
    legal use of on LANs, 32-33
    sharing, 25, 31-33
    troubleshooting, 121-122, 333, 340, 343
    utilities from authors, 440
    See also Application software
Software drivers. *See* Drivers
Speed. *See* Optimization
Spool, print, 194
Spreadsheet software, 259-261
Stacker, 383
Star topology, 54-57, 60-61
    See also Hub-based LANs; Token ring LANs
Starter kits
    LAN planning and, 41-43
    makes of, 76-77
    purchasing tips for, 69-70, 77-78
    thin Ethernet LANs and, 60
    See also NetWare Lite
STARTNET.BAT
    contents of, 131
    editing, 427-429
    examples of, 432-437
    explained, 425
    installation of, 112, 120-121
    running, 132-133
    SHARE program and, 396
    troubleshooting and, 331-333, 433-434
    See also AUTOEXEC.BAT; CONFIG.SYS
Status Report messages
    listed, 405-415
    network printers and, 196
    troubleshooting and, 341
    See also Error messages; Troubleshooting
SUPERVISOR account, 135-136
    denying privileges of, 309
    messages and, 214
    passwords and, 305-306
    privileges of, 309-310
    user accounts and, 209
    See also User accounts
Surge suppressors, 68

T

[Tab] expansion setting, printer, 192
[Tab] key, 140
Tape backup drives, 240-244

LANs and, 50
location of, 280-281
NetWare Lite and, 241-242
optimization and, 382-383
overview of, 240-241, 278
purchasing tips for, 243-244
suppliers of, 242-243
See also Backups
T-connectors. See BNC T-connectors
Technical support, authors', 439-440
Telephone cables, 61
Terminate-and-stay-resident programs.
　　See TSR programs
Terminators
installation of, 89-90
LAN topologies and, 54, 57
overview of, 11-12
troubleshooting and, 331, 339
Text messages. See Message system
Thick Ethernet LANs, 59-60
　　See also 10BASE-T LANs; Coaxial cables;
　　　Ethernet LAN products
Thin Ethernet LANs
versus 10BASE-T LANs, 67
cable length and, 64, 66-67
IEEE standards for, 59-60, 64
laying out, 66-67
troubleshooting, 338, 339
　　See also 10BASE-T LANs; Coaxial cables;
　　　Ethernet LAN products
Time command, NET, 401-402
Token ring LANs, 9, 61-62
Topologies, LAN, 53-57
Troubleshooting, 323-344
access problems, 343-344
AUTOEXEC.BAT and, 331-333
cable problems, 330, 337-338
communication problems, 337-339
computer lockups, 333-337, 341
CONFIG.SYS and, 331-333, 433
connector problems, 338
disk caches and, 333, 339-340
electromagnetic interference and, 338
error messages and, 328-329, 341
FASTOPEN program and, 340
file corruption, 339-341
hardware problems, 330-331

hub/concentrators and, 339
I/O address conflicts, 334-335
INSTALL program and, 329, 332
installation problems, 121-122
insufficient memory, 337
IRQ conflicts, 334-335
LAN cards, 330-331, 339
memory managers and, 333
overview of, 323-328
performance problems, 344
power problems and, 341
RAM address conflicts, 336
rebooting and, 333, 341
SHARE program and, 340
sharing violations, 340, 344
shutting down and, 341
software problems, 333, 340, 343
STARTNET.BAT and, 331-333, 433
Status Report messages and, 328-329, 341
terminator problems, 331, 339
TSR programs and, 332-333, 336
user errors and, 325, 339
viruses, 337
　　See also Error messages; Status Report
　　　messages
TSR programs
compatibility of, 249
NetBIOS and, 397-398
NetWare Lite as, 23
network software as, 7
STARTNET.BAT and, 134
troubleshooting and, 332-333, 336
Tuning. See Optimization
Twisted-pair cables
10BASE-T LANs and, 60-61
electromagnetic interference and, 68
overview of, 10
purchasing tips for, 88
RJ45 modular plugs and, 11
versus thin coaxial cables, 56, 57
　　See also Coaxial cables

U

Ulist command, NET, 214
Uninterruptible power supplies. *See* UPSs

Unshielded twisted pair cables.
    See Twisted-pair cables
Upgrading, 103, 377
Upper memory
    defined, 356, 357
    installation and, 126-127
    optimization and, 382
    See also Memory
UPSs, 68-69, 341, 342
User accounts, 206-209
    creating, 206-208
    determining status of, 311
    disabling, 307-308
    logging into, 208-209
    SUPERVISOR parameter and, 209, 309-310
    See also Access rights; Passwords;
        SUPERVISOR account
Users
    LAN administrator and, 286-287
    LAN planning and, 45-46
    troubleshooting and, 325, 339
Utility software, 13, 440
UTP (unshielded twisted pair) cables.
    See Twisted-pair cables

V

Virtual disk drives, 27, 144, 368
Viruses, 281-286
    how they spread, 282-283
    how they work, 283
    overview of, 281-282
    software for, 285-286
    treatment of, 284-285
    troubleshooting and, 337
    See also Security

W

Warnings. See Error messages; Status Report
    messages
Windows. See Microsoft Windows
Wireless LANs, 10, 65
Word, Microsoft, 259
Word processing software, 258-261, 427
WordPerfect, 258-259
WordPerfect Office LAN, 265-266
Workgroups, 24, 45-50
Workstations
    defined, 20
    LAN versus engineering, 22
    synchronizing times on, 401-402
    See also Client nodes

Z

Zero-slot LANs, 16

LAN Times Buyers Directory

How many network products are there to choose from?

THOUSANDS!

How do you find and compare them?

There is only ONE SOURCE—The LAN Times Buyers Directory. IT'S NEW!

The LAN Times Buyers Directory contains descriptions of thousands network hardware and software products and network services. Each listing contains product specifications, pricing, and company contact information. If you only want to have one resource for network products and services, the LAN Times Buyers Directory is it!

And now its available in two formats: PRINTED and ELECTRONIC.

The printed version includes all descriptions of products and services plus indexes by product type, company, and region. It is printed annually.

The electronic version comes as a runtime hypertext diskette (DOS / Folio). You can instantly search on product names, specifications, or compatibility standards as well as company names or locations. It's simple and intuitive to use. The electronic version is available on a subscription basis with monthly updates.

ORDER TODAY! Call (801) 565-5812 or mail the attatched form.

BUYERS DIRECTORY

A Comprehensive Guide to Products and Services

THE LAN TIMES BUYERS DIRECTORY
Thousands of network products and services

Printed version: complete guide to products, vendors, and services.

Electronic version: instantly find products, addresses, and product specs, and check compatibility.

Name_____
Company_____
Address_____
City/State/Zip_____
VISA or MC#_____
Expiration Date_____
Signature_____

Please Send Me:
- ❏ Printed Version — **$14.95**
- ❏ Electronic Version, current mo. (DOS/Folio) **$14.95**
- ❏ Electronic Version; 1-year subscription — **$79.95**
  (with monthly updates)
- ❏ 5.25" Disk   ❏ 3.5" Disk

- ❏ I subscribe to LAN Times
- ❏ I DO NOT subscribe to LAN Times

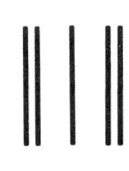

PLEASE
AFFIX
CORRECT
POSTAGE

LAN TIMES BUYERS DIRECTORY
7050 Union Park Center
Suite 240
Midvale, UT 84047